RED CARD

RED CARD

FIFA AND THE FALL OF THE MOST POWERFUL MEN IN SPORTS

KEN BENSINGER

PROFILE BOOKS

First published in Great Britain in 2018 by
Profile Books Ltd
3 Holford Yard
Bevin Way
London
WC1X 9HD

www.profilebooks.com

First published in the United States of America by
Simon & Schuster, Inc.

1 3 5 7 9 10 8 6 4 2

Printed and bound in Great Britain by Clays, St Ives plc

A CIP catalogue record for this book is available from the British Library.

ISBN 978 1 78125 671 8
Export ISBN 978 1 78816 062 9
eISBN 978 1 78283 266 9

For my wife, Patricia,
and for my children, Mateo & Sofia

For among My people are found wicked men; They lie in wait as one who sets snares; They set a trap; They catch men. As a cage is full of birds, so their houses are full of deceit. Therefore they have become great and grown rich.

They have grown fat, they are sleek; Yes, they surpass the deeds of the wicked; They do not plead the cause, The cause of the fatherless; Yet they prosper, And the right of the needy they do not defend.

"Shall I not punish them for these things?" says the LORD. "Shall I not avenge Myself on such a nation as this?"

—JEREMIAH 5:26–29

CONTENTS

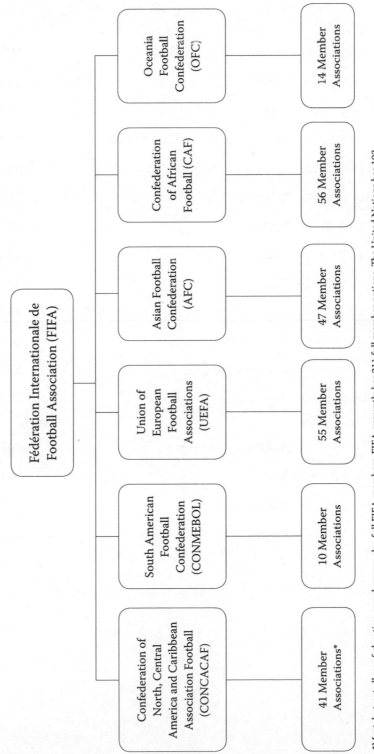

Fédération Internationale de Football Association (FIFA)

Confederation of North, Central America and Caribbean Association Football (CONCACAF) — 41 Member Associations*

South American Football Confederation (CONMEBOL) — 10 Member Associations

Union of European Football Associations (UEFA) — 55 Member Associations

Asian Football Confederation (AFC) — 47 Member Associations

Confederation of African Football (CAF) — 56 Member Associations

Oceania Football Confederation (OFC) — 14 Member Associations

*Most, but not all, confederation members are also full FIFA members. FIFA currently has 211 full member nations. The United Nations has 193.

CAST OF CHARACTERS

Fédération Internationale de Football Association (FIFA), Zurich

Jean-Marie Faustin Godefroid "João" Havelange, *president (1974–1998)*
Joseph "Sepp" Blatter, *president (1998–2015); general secretary (1981–1998)*
Jérôme Valcke, *general secretary (2007–2015)*

Confederation of North, Central America and Caribbean Association Football (CONCACAF), New York & Miami

Austin "Jack" Warner, *president (1990–2011); FIFA vice president & ExCo (1983–2011)*
Charles Gordon "Chuck" Blazer, *general secretary (1990–2011); FIFA ExCo (1997–2013)*
Jeffrey Webb, *president (2012–2015); FIFA vice president & ExCo (2012–2015)*
Enrique Sanz, *general secretary (2012–2015)*
Alfredo Hawit, *president (2015); FIFA vice president & ExCo (2015)*

Confederación Sudamericana de Futbol (CONMEBOL), Asunción, Paraguay

Nicolás Leoz, *president (1986–2013); FIFA ExCo (1998–2013)*
Eugenio Figueredo, *president (2013–2014), vice president (1993–2013); FIFA vice president and FIFA ExCo (2014–2015)*
Juan Ángel Napout, *president (2014–15); FIFA vice president & ExCo (2015)*

Asian Football Confederation
(AFC), Kuala Lumpur

Mohamed bin Hammam, *president (2002–2011); FIFA ExCo (1996–2011)*

National Soccer Associations

Julio Humberto Grondona, *president, Asociación del Fútbol Argentino (1979–2014); FIFA vice president & ExCo (1998–2014)*

Ricardo Terra Teixeira, *president, Confederação Brasileira de Futebol (1989–2012); FIFA ExCo (1994–2012)*

José Maria Marin, president, *Confederação Brasileira de Futebol (2012–2015)*

Marco Polo Del Nero, *president, Confederação Brasileira de Futebol (2015–); FIFA ExCo (2012–2015)*

Sunil Gulati, *president, United States Soccer Federation (2006–2018); FIFA ExCo (2013–)*

Eduardo Li, *president, Federación Costarricense de Futbol (2007–2015); FIFA ExCo (2015)*

Vitaly Mutko, *president, Russian Football Union (2005–2009; 2015–2017); FIFA ExCo (2009–2017)*

Rafael Esquivel, *president, Federación Venezolana de Futbol (1988–2015)*

Manuel Burga, *president, Federación Peruana de Futbol (2002–2014)*

Grupo Traffic, São Paulo & Miami

José Hawilla, *owner and founder*
Aaron Davidson, *president, Traffic Sports USA*

Torneos y Competencias, Buenos Aires

Alejandro Burzaco, *chief executive officer*

Full Play Group, Buenos Aires

Hugo Jinkis, *cofounder & co-owner*
Mariano Jinkis, *cofounder & co-owner*

International Soccer Marketing, Jersey City

Zorana Danis, *owner*

Federal Bureau of Investigation, New York Field Office

Mike Gaeta, *supervisory special agent*
Jared Randall, *special agent*
John Penza, *supervisory special agent*

Internal Revenue Service Criminal Investigation Division, Los Angeles Field Office

Steven Berryman, *special agent*
J. J. Kacic, *special agent*

United States Attorney's Office for the Eastern District of New York, Brooklyn

Loretta Lynch, *United States attorney (2010–2015); U.S. attorney general (2015–2017)*
Evan M. Norris, *assistant United States attorney*
Amanda Hector, *assistant United States attorney*
Darren LaVerne, *assistant United States attorney*
Samuel P. Nitze, *assistant United States attorney*
Keith Edelman, *assistant United States attorney*
M. Kristin Mace, *assistant United States attorney*

RED CARD

ONE

BERRYMAN

SHORTLY AFTER TEN ON THE MORNING OF AUGUST 16, 2011, Steve Berryman, a forty-seven-year-old special agent for the Internal Revenue Service, was in his cubicle on the third floor of a huge federal office building known as the Ziggurat in Laguna Niguel, California, when his mobile phone vibrated. There was a new Google Alert email in his inbox.

Berryman, six feet tall and slender, with brown eyes so dark they looked almost black, thick eyebrows, pale skin, and a neatly trimmed white mustache that matched his slicked-back hair, had set up a number of such alerts. His choice of keywords betrayed a sensibility that, after twenty-five years at the IRS, had become highly refined when it came to financial crimes. Berryman had alerts for "money laundering"; "corruption"; "Bank Secrecy Act"; and "Foreign Corrupt Practices Act," among many others. The messages arrived in batches throughout the day, delivering dozens of news articles from around the world about various cases of financial misbehavior that Berryman would quickly scan before returning to whatever case he happened to be working.

But this particular notification stopped him in his tracks. The alert was under the search term "bribery," and contained a link to an article by the Reuters news service. The headline was "FBI Examines U.S. Soccer Boss's Financial Records."

The story described a set of documents, allegedly being scrutinized by the FBI, that outlined more than $500,000 in suspicious payments received over a fifteen-year period by an American soccer official named Chuck Blazer.

Blazer was a high-ranking official of FIFA, the governing body of world soccer. Berryman thought he might have heard his name some-where, but he didn't recognize the photo of a scowling, tousle-haired man with bushy eyebrows and an unruly gray beard. An intoxicating surge of excitement swept over him as he reread the article several times, taking special note of the fact that Blazer had several offshore bank ac-counts, including one in the Cayman Islands.

He forwarded the article to his supervisor, Aimee Schabilion, then dashed into her office to make sure she'd read it.

"This could be huge," he said.

————

Berryman loved soccer ever since he was a kid.

He grew up in England, because his father was in the Air Force, and spent most of his first eleven years living outside military bases there, playing soccer most afternoons. When his family moved back to the States, settling in Southern California's hot, dusty Inland Empire, he couldn't find anyone to play with, so he transferred his soccer skills to the gridiron, becoming a star placekicker.

His strong left foot earned him an athletic scholarship to Eastern Illinois University. Berryman could launch the ball sixty-five yards through the uprights about three-quarters of the time, but was not good enough to cut it in the professional ranks. Berryman loathed the Mid-west's bitter winters. As soon as he realized that his future wasn't going to be in the NFL, he abandoned his scholarship, transferred to Cal State San Bernardino, completed his degree in accounting, and signed up to become an IRS agent.

His first case was against the owner of a luxury hair salon who hadn't reported all of his income. Berryman spent his early years at the IRS investigating petty tax evaders and crooked accountants. But he was drawn to bigger, more complicated types of financial crime. He soon moved into narcotics, teaming up with other agencies on long, involved international investigations.

Berryman's big revelation, working those cases, was that drugs, guns, and violence were only half the story. A full accounting of the crimes could only be told once all the money had been traced. While DEA agents dreamed up dramatic stings aimed at turning up troves of drugs, Berryman spent his time meticulously chasing the dealers' money around the world, adding additional charges—and, often, defendants—to the indictments. People were fallible, he realized. They played games, forgot facts, succumbed to temptation, exaggerated, and contradicted themselves. Documents never lied.

After having kids, Berryman and his wife bought a house close to the ocean. He transferred to the Laguna Niguel office of the IRS, deep in Orange County, where he began working on public corruption cases, including a massive investigation that landed the county's well-known sheriff, Mike Carona, in prison. He traveled to other field offices, teaching agents about the Foreign Corrupt Practices Act, spearheaded a public and foreign corrupt officials project in the IRS's main Los Angeles field office, and volunteered as a witness for federal prosecutors who needed experts on money laundering on the stand.

"I'm an accountant with a gun," Berryman liked to say. "What could be more fun?"

Berryman was not motivated, as some cops are, by a sense of moral indignity. Indeed, he often found himself admiring the men and women he pursued, wondering if, in other circumstances, they could have been friends. What made him tick, instead, was the thrill of the hunt.

He wasn't a lawyer, but he gained a reputation as a prosecutor's agent whose relentless focus on the mechanics of cases was matched only by his passionate attention to detail. Some higher-ups in the agency privately considered Berryman one of the best IRS agents in the entire country: ambitious and willing to travel and work as many hours as it took to make a case stick.

When he wasn't working, however, he was more likely than not thinking about soccer, which he called football, the word most of the planet uses for the game.

Berryman would wake up early on weekends, sometimes before five a.m., to watch his favorite team, Liverpool, play English Premier League matches on cable. In 2006, he and two friends traveled to the World Cup in Germany and attended all three games played by the U.S. national team, as well as a match between Brazil and Ghana. He played in an adult soccer league, coached his kids' teams, and frequently attended MLS matches. And like a lot of soccer fans, he'd become increasingly dismayed by constant rumors of corruption and mismanagement at the sport's highest levels.

For years, Berryman had been hearing about greedy soccer officials stealing from the game, depriving teams, players, and especially fans of money that could improve and better develop the sport. But the problem had always seemed so distant. The reports were certainly troubling to someone who cared about soccer, but these things were happening in faraway places like Switzerland, Italy, or Africa, and at any rate certainly not in America, where soccer was still a second-rate sport, too minor for big-time corruption. Soccer might be dirty, but Berryman had never thought of the sport's problems as potentially criminal.

The Reuters article changed that. Blazer was an American, living in New York. That meant potential jurisdiction, the chance to apply one of Berryman's great passions, investigating financial crimes, to his other: the world's most popular sport.

If this homegrown soccer official had been involved in anything criminal, then Berryman believed he'd been born to figure out what that might be.

————

Taxes are so fundamental to the experience of being an American that they are seen as almost sacred: dull, number-laden documents that act as Rosetta stones to the secret financial lives of every person. The United States is one of only two countries in the world—the other being tiny, war-torn Eritrea—that requires citizens to file even when living abroad, and every year the Internal Revenue Service processes more than 150 million individual income tax returns.

There is in fact a special section of federal law dedicated to enshrining the private status of filings, prohibiting almost everyone, under pain of punishment, from viewing or disclosing income tax returns. That restriction includes law enforcement, up to and including the FBI itself, whose agents must jump through a series of legal hoops before they can so much as glance at a tax return.

There is one group entrusted by the government to review tax returns, a caste whose unique powers have perversely earned them society's fear and disgust: employees of the IRS. As an IRS agent, Steve

Berryman had the unique power to look at anyone's taxes, provided he had good cause to believe a crime might have been committed. Thanks to the Reuters piece, he could move forward.

Standing in his supervisor's office on that August Tuesday, he asked permission to pull Chuck Blazer's tax returns. Within minutes, he got his first glimpse of that crucial information.

Berryman was expecting some obvious omissions or telltale signs of hidden income. The result was far better than hoped. "No record found."

His eyes went wide. The system was telling him that Chuck Blazer hadn't filed his taxes in at least seventeen years.

It can be a misdemeanor to fail to file. But if Blazer had received any income anywhere, and intentionally hid it, that could elevate the omission to a felony. And if he had foreign bank accounts that he didn't report to the government, that was a felony as well.

Chuck Blazer, the only American on the Executive Committee of FIFA, the Fédération Internationale de Football Association, the supreme body overseeing all of global soccer, looked awfully like a tax criminal.

Heart pounding, Berryman dashed back into Schabilion's office. He explained who Blazer was, what FIFA did, and how this slam-dunk tax case he'd unearthed could be a foot in the door to something far bigger.

"Can I get involved?" he pleaded.

Berryman wasn't one to buck authority. But for the most part, his superiors trusted his ability to select cases that were worth his time, and they stayed out of the way. Schabilion had no problem with him looking into this, but what about the FBI? The article suggested it was already an open case. If he wanted to pursue it, he'd need to clear it with the Bureau first.

Berryman had no way of checking the FBI's computer systems to see if there was indeed an open case involving Blazer. So he called an FBI agent he'd worked with in Santa Ana and asked her to check for him.

The agent called back soon thereafter.

"Yes," she said. "There's an agent on it in New York."

There are dozens of federal law enforcement agencies in the United States, each with their own responsibilities and powers, down to the gun-toting agents of the National Zoological Park Police and the inspector general of the Small Business Administration.

But the largest, best funded, and most powerful of all is the Federal Bureau of Investigation. It has tens of thousands of agents, vast resources, and offices around the world. It is the star of America's legal show, basking in the attention lavished by journalists, Hollywood, and, particularly, members of Congress with budget authority. Although it's common for multiple law enforcement authorities to team up on cases, investigators from other agencies quickly learn to tiptoe when dealing with the FBI. It had an uncanny knack for always coming out on top.

Berryman asked his friend at the Bureau if she'd reach out to the agent in New York to see if he would consider discussing the case. You bet, she said. She'd get back to him when she heard something.

As he anxiously waited, Berryman learned everything he could about Blazer, FIFA, and international soccer. He stayed up late researching Jack Warner, a soccer official from Trinidad and Tobago who had cut $512,750 in checks to Blazer that were now under scrutiny, according to the Reuters article, and the Confederation of North, Central America and Caribbean Association Football, which the two men had run together for more than two decades. He also read about a fabulously wealthy Qatari named Mohamed bin Hammam, who had helped the tiny Middle Eastern nation win the right to host the World Cup in 2022.

He soon began to imagine a possible case, the ways it could be investigated and prosecuted, and the reach it could have. With each passing day, Berryman's enthusiasm grew until he felt more excited about this lead than any in his career. He desperately wanted in.

He had no idea where the FBI's investigation had gone, but was certain its agents couldn't look at Blazer's tax returns without a court order. Berryman half-hoped that they were stuck. They needed an IRS agent on the case. That was the way to muscle his way in to the case, he thought, and Blazer could be just the beginning.

After nearly a week, the FBI agent in Santa Ana called again.

"The case agent's name is Jared Randall," she said, passing along his contact information. "He's open to it."

———

Berryman had been prescient.

Investigating Chuck Blazer's tax problem was like pulling someone over for a bum taillight only to discover a trunk stuffed with dead bodies.

Over the next four years, Berryman would work in secret with the FBI and federal prosecutors in Brooklyn to build one of the largest and most ambitious investigations of international corruption and money laundering in American history.

After almost a year, the FBI investigation was indeed stuck, mired in the challenges of taking on an institution as vast, complex, and powerful as FIFA. But thanks in great part to Berryman, the tiny case was about to explode, with the U.S. government confronting the fundamental business underpinning the world's most popular game. Dozens of people from more than fifteen different countries would eventually be charged with violating the United States' stiff racketeering, money laundering, fraud, and tax laws, exposed for their part in what prosecutors described as a decades-long, highly orchestrated criminal conspiracy calculated to twist the beloved sport to their selfish designs.

Many of those caught up in the investigation would throw themselves at the mercy of the Department of Justice, forfeiting hundreds of millions of dollars and quietly agreeing to cooperate. This allowed prosecutors to secretly cast the net ever wider as the sport's officials betrayed their friends and colleagues. The case finally became public with the dramatic arrest of seven soccer officials in an early morning raid in Switzerland in May 2015, shaking the foundations of the sport. Soon, nearly every significant official at FIFA was ousted, including its genial yet ruthless president, the Swiss Sepp Blatter. Prosecutors in countries around the world would be inspired to open their own separate criminal investigations, helping further reveal the ugly inner workings of the sport known as the beautiful game.

After decades of unchecked impunity in the face of scandals, the global soccer cartel was finally brought to its knees by one of the few countries in the entire world that didn't seem to care much about the sport at all. That irony wasn't lost on the game's hundreds of millions of fans around the globe, who found themselves in the unfamiliar position of rooting for the United States to actually stick its nose in other countries' business: Uncle Sam, implausibly, had become soccer's biggest superstar.

When the clandestine case finally became public, critics accused the prosecution, led by a cerebral Harvard Law graduate named Evan Norris, of arrogance and overreach, arguing that America shouldn't try to police the entire planet or impose its laws on foreign countries. Others claimed the case represented its own kind of conspiracy, a plot by the world's wealthiest and most powerful nation to bring down a foreign sport it detested and feared. Perhaps the most popular theory was that the case was high-level retribution for passing over the U.S.'s bid to host the World Cup in 2022.

Prosecutors anticipated such concerns and went to great lengths to charge only crimes that allegedly took place—at least in part—on American soil or with the use of the American financial system. Awake to the emotional and political power of soccer in the rest of the world, the feds went to considerable lengths to protect the sensitivities of other nations and drive home the point that they weren't indicting the sport, only the men who had sullied its reputation. Indeed, they took pains to argue that soccer was itself the victim of the crimes being charged and had a right to eventually recover the money that had been stolen from it.

As for the notion that some insidious, vindictive, or downright xenophobic agenda was driving the case, the truth is the FIFA probe commenced months *before* the voting members of FIFA's powerful Executive Committee chose Qatar over the U.S. to host the sport's most important tournament.

America's case against soccer corruption didn't start at the top, some dictum from on high. It was the product of careful, patient police work by dedicated investigators; something that began small and grew into a far vaster endeavor than anyone involved could have imagined. And it is still very much ongoing.

The saga of corruption within FIFA and worldwide soccer as a whole is immeasurably complicated—far too sprawling to capture or make sense of in any comprehensive fashion in these pages. It encompasses decades of deceit, bribery, self-dealing, and impunity, all taking place as soccer expanded geometrically to become the planet's great sporting juggernaut, a multibillion-dollar pastime driven by the ardent passions of its devoted fans.

This book traces the broadest outlines of a single criminal case notable for its numbing complexity and scope, one that pushed the boundaries of what anyone—especially disillusioned fans of the world's game—ever thought possible. It is also the tale of some of the people, brilliant and corruptible, dedicated and careless, humble and arrogant, loyal and treacherous, who made this the world's greatest sports scandal.

TWO

TICKLING THE WIRE

UNIMAGINABLY FAR REMOVED FROM ITS HUMBLE NINETEENTH-century roots as a simple pastime for the working classes amid the grind of the industrial revolution, soccer has become, in many countries, as powerful a social and cultural institution as government or the church. Fueled by the passions of hundreds of millions of devoted fans around the globe, soccer also has matured into a churning economic dynamo, pumping out vast sums of money that line the pockets of the elite who organize the sport, broadcast its matches, and plaster their corporate logos around its stadiums and across the chests of the gifted young athletes who chase after the ball.

Played in every nation on earth, endless combinations of amateur and professional soccer matches, tournaments, and championships run almost continuously throughout the year. But the single event around which all global soccer is organized, the anchor to the sport's calendar and its throbbing emotional heart, is the World Cup. Created by a more modest FIFA in a more modest time, the quadrennial tournament has over the decades come to represent the apogee of the power and influence of sport: a uniquely modern, transnational mass public spectacle for a televised era, blending rampant consumerism, corporate interests, political ambition, and unchecked financial opportunism.

The month-long event, pitting the top national soccer teams against one another in an orgy of patriotic fervor, is the greatest sporting event mankind has ever conceived.

On June 9, 2010, three days before the kickoff of the World Cup in South Africa, envoys from Russia and England stood outside a meeting room in Johannesburg's Sandton Convention Centre, nervously waiting to make their pitch to host the 2018 tournament.

Their audience: elected representatives of the Confederation of North, Central America and Caribbean Association Football, or CONCACAF. FIFA's 207 member associations, each governing soccer in their countries, were split between six confederations, which oversaw the sport on a regional basis. CONCACAF, with thirty-five member associations under its umbrella, was one of them, and it, in turn, reported up to FIFA. Its territory stretched from Panama in the south to Canada in the north, and included the United States, as well as all of the Caribbean and the sparsely populated South American countries Suriname and Guyana.

With the possible exception of Mexico, the confederation's members were not considered particularly formidable on the soccer pitch, but in the cutthroat field of international soccer politics, CONCACAF was a powerhouse.

That influence was largely due to Jack Warner, its Trinidadian president. Wiry, with glasses over a deeply lined face, he made a point of reminding people that he was a black man who had risen from abject poverty. He was also a born politician, able to whip all of his confederation's member nations into a reliably unified voting bloc at FIFA's annual congresses. That unrivaled discipline gave CONCACAF an outsized influence compared to other, larger soccer confederations, which constantly struggled with internal strife and factionalism, splitting their votes, sometimes several ways.

It also made Warner, sixty-seven years old at the time, one of the most powerful and feared men in all of soccer. Over the previous three decades, he had deployed guile, persistence, and ruthless discipline to bring the Caribbean—and, with it, the whole confederation—to heel. His position was rarely, if ever, challenged. In exchange for the generous disbursement of money that spilled down through him from the highest reaches of the sport, he expected his member associations to vote exactly as he instructed.

Born into grinding poverty in the Trinidadian countryside, the slender, combative Warner had risen to become the third-ranking vice president of FIFA and the longest-serving member of its Executive Committee, or ExCo, the twenty-four-man body tasked with making FIFA's most important decisions, including determining where World Cups are held. Warner was also powerful in other circles: less than two weeks before flying to South Africa to attend the tournament, he had been sworn in as Trinidad and Tobago's Minister of Works and Transport.

Warner's power within FIFA was enhanced by his closest ally, Chuck Blazer, a morbidly obese Jewish New Yorker with a head for business and a shaggy white beard that made him a dead ringer for Santa Claus. A compulsive gambler guided by seemingly insatiable appetites and inextinguishable opportunism, Blazer had been the brains behind Warner's political fortunes and, in great measure, the spectacular growth of soccer in North America. He'd been CONCACAF's general secretary—a second-in-command charged with manning day-to-day operations—since 1990, and had sat with Warner on FIFA's ExCo since 1997. A third CONCACAF official, Guatemalan Rafael Salguero, also sat on the FIFA's twenty-four-member governing committee, and he was expected to cast his votes in lockstep with his confederation colleagues.

Anyone bidding for the tournament knew that courting Warner and Blazer was critical, and that both men were willing to put a price on anything, including soccer's highest prize. The ExCo vote on where to host both the 2018 and 2022 World Cups was to be held in Zurich on December 2, and with just under six months to go, the CONCACAF meeting in Johannesburg was viewed as a critical sales opportunity.

England hadn't hosted the tournament since 1966. Its soccer-crazed population was desperate to do so again. London was slated to host the 2012 Olympics, and the British government calculated that a World Cup would boost its economy by nearly $5 billion. It would also have incalculable social and psychological value for the country, which, as its fans were quick to note, invented the sport in the first place.

England was up against a number of competitors. Belgium and the Netherlands had joined together to make up one rival bid; and Spain and Portugal another. A host of other countries were battling separately for the rights to the 2022 World Cup, among them the United States, Australia, and Qatar. But England's most formidable adversary for 2018 was without a doubt Russia.

Russia had been awarded the 2014 Winter Olympics just eighteen months earlier, and had been riding nearly a decade of spectacular economic growth, thanks largely to record prices for oil and other natural resources.

The country, and particularly its leader, Vladimir Putin, had been eager to take advantage of that boom to reassert its long-relinquished role as a world power. Winning the right to host the World Cup, watched by hundreds of millions around the world, would undoubtedly be an effective way to help plant that idea, projecting strength and stability. Most critically, it would boost Putin's image among the Russian people. Losing the vote, for Putin, was unthinkable.

———

In a nod to fairness and, perhaps, the short attention span of many of its delegates, CONCACAF had allotted twelve minutes for each bid team to make its best case.

Russia's delegation, led by Alexey Sorokin, the Russian Football Union's general secretary, presented first. It did not go well.

For starters, Russia's national soccer team had failed to qualify for the 2010 World Cup thanks to a humiliating loss the prior November to lowly Slovenia, a country with a total population only slightly larger than the Siberian city of Novosibirsk. And Blazer, viewed as a likely vote for England, was not even in the room. A diabetic with nagging respiratory problems, he had decided to avoid Johannesburg because the city's high altitude affected his health.

Russia's presentation, meanwhile, was embarrassingly marred by a glitchy PowerPoint deck that failed three times as Sorokin spoke. Sorokin, handsome and polished, with excellent American-accented English and a toothy smile, exuded confidence. But his pitch, spotlighting drab, distant cities like Yekaterinburg, lacked any sparkle or charm. The audience of mostly Caribbean and Central American officials seemed unmoved if not downright bored.

By comparison, England's bid team turned in a dazzling performance. David Dein, a debonair, impeccably tailored former vice chairman of London's Arsenal soccer club, looked and sounded like the kindly rich uncle everyone wished they had, with regal features and the poshest of accents. He warmed up the room with a joke—"The last time I did it in 12 minutes, I was 18 years old"—that brought forth peals of laughter. Then he cued up a video starring superstar midfielder David Beckham. It highlighted the fact that England already possessed enough state-of-the-art stadiums, not to mention airports, hotels, and highways, to host the World Cup more or less immediately, no construction needed.

The English press, in a fit of uncharacteristic optimism, hailed the presentation as a sign that England's chances looked good and that technical prowess, existing infrastructure, and general competency— merit—would win the day.

The Russians, however, were playing a different game.

———

South Africa is not a wealthy country. More than half its population, some 30 million people, lives below the poverty line, and unemployment perennially hovers around 25 percent. Soccer is its most popular sport, followed avidly by the nation's black African population, which makes up an overwhelming majority of the citizenry.

To prepare for the 2010 World Cup, which it had desperately sought to host for years, South Africa spent more than $3 billion in public money, largely on stadiums and transportation infrastructure. Original projections had been as little as a tenth of that amount, but the stringent requirements imposed by FIFA, motivated almost entirely by a desire to maximize revenue during the short-lived tournament, drove the figure up massively.

Rather than improving or expanding many existing sports venues, South Africa was compelled by FIFA to construct half of the World Cup stadiums from the ground up, mostly in affluent, tourist-friendly, white neighborhoods where soccer is far less popular than rugby and cricket. So, many of the country's top professional clubs continued to play in decaying old arenas while some stadiums built for the World Cup would not regularly be used for soccer after the tournament concluded. A new high-speed rail system that opened just prior to the tournament ended up serving largely as a shuttle between wealthy areas and the stadiums, with no service anywhere close to the vast shantytowns where many of the nation's poor live. The message: poor people were apparently not welcome.

FIFA's profound influence over the sovereign nation was hardly limited to infrastructure boondoggles. In order to host the tournament, South Africa had to agree to comply with scores of strict requirements imposed by the Swiss nonprofit, including amending or suspending many of its tax and immigration laws, sometimes at great financial cost to the country. South Africa was even made to employ its police and judicial system to rigorously enforce FIFA's trademarks and copyrights in order to protect profits from sales of merchandise that the country had, ironically, promised not to tax.

In exchange for all the generosity, FIFA had pledged to pour huge sums into development of the sport in South Africa. But in the end it paid for little more than a handful of artificial turf soccer fields it had promised, along with a number of buses and vans it donated to South Africa's soccer federation for clubs to transport players to matches. By some estimates, FIFA donated less than one-tenth of one percent of its profits from the tournament.

So it was nearly everywhere FIFA held sway. While the ruling football body reported ever-growing profits, those who most passionately followed the sport saw little benefit or were shut out of it altogether.

South Africa has never been a formidable soccer power; its national team has never progressed beyond the group stage at the World Cup. But even in countries such as Brazil and Argentina, the spiritual Meccas of the sport and homelands to legendary talents including Pelé, Diego Maradona, and Lionel Messi, glaring examples of the sport's inequities abounded. Professional clubs in those nations played in dank and outdated stadiums, often lacking even the most rudimentary bathroom facilities for fans. Many children in South America learned the sport without the benefit of proper pitches, coaching, balls, or even shoes. Young girls were given little, if any, opportunity to play at all.

The men who controlled soccer in each country, meanwhile, enjoyed a life of rare privilege, jetting from tournament to tournament to be lavished with the finest luxuries, praised, revered, and wooed as overlords of the people's sport. These officials of their national associations, FIFA's six regional confederations, and FIFA itself, lived in a rarefied bubble, one that often seemed strangely removed from the sport itself but was never more frothy than when another World Cup—or in this case two of them—was up for grabs.

Two days after the CONCACAF meeting in Johannesburg, FIFA held what it dubbed a "bidding expo." A sort of commercial trade show for the World Cup itself, the event provided all nine countries competing for the right to host the 2018 and 2022 tournaments the chance to meet delegates from around the world. In particular, it was an opportunity to mingle with nearly every Executive Committee member.

Several hours beforehand, Russian billionaire Roman Abramovich walked into Johannesburg's Gallagher Convention Centre. Abramovich, who owned England's Chelsea Football Club, had arrived that day on his private jet, accompanied by Igor Shuvalov, Russia's first deputy prime minister.

A high school dropout and former auto mechanic and commodities trader whose fortune was made thanks to his staunch support of Boris Yeltsin, Abramovich came to control Sibneft, one of Russia's largest oil producers. Subsequently, he supported Vladimir Putin as a candidate to succeed Yeltsin and was richly rewarded for his loyalty.

A devoted soccer fan, Abramovich bought Chelsea, one of England's most storied clubs, in 2003 and moved to London five years later after selling off much of his Russian holdings. Unlike many oligarchs who left Russia, Abramovich maintained a close relationship with Putin. A frequent Kremlin visitor, he regarded the former KGB officer as a kind of father figure, speaking to him in the most formal, reverent tones. Among those who followed such things, it was well known that Putin occasionally called on Abramovich for special favors.

As a rule, billionaires hate to wait for anything. But once the bidding expo began, the normally shy and retiring Abramovich, wearing a tailored charcoal suit rather than his usual jeans, made an unusually enthusiastic show of good cheer.

A smile plastered over his unshaven jaw, he joined a contingent of countrymen, including Andrey Arshavin, a star forward for English club Arsenal, in the Russian booth, greeting soccer officials from around the world, and mugging for photographs with David Beckham.

And finally, when the expo was drawing to a close, Abramovich walked out of the hall alongside Sepp Blatter, the Swiss president of FIFA. With so much attention cast in Beckham's direction, scarcely anyone even noticed them quietly departing together.

Earlier in the day, Blatter had bragged to FIFA's entire membership about the organization's record profits in the four years leading up to 2010. He boasted of FIFA having $1 billion in the bank, and grandly pledged to distribute $250,000 to each member association as a bonus, plus $2.5 million to each confederation. It was the kind of naked patronage that had earned him the adoration of many of FIFA's 207 members—a larger assembly than that of the United Nations.

As he announced in a press conference after the congress concluded, Blatter was planning to run for a fourth consecutive term as FIFA president. "We shall work for the next generation," he said, intentionally paraphrasing Winston Churchill.

After a dozen years in office, and seventeen years before that as general secretary, Blatter had grown acutely aware of the cost of maintaining power in an organization as wealthy, diverse, and cutthroat as FIFA. More than anyone, he had mastered the darker arts of administering the world's most popular sport, and had a hand in many of its most Machiavellian deals and accommodations over the years.

Engrossed in hushed conversation, the unusually jocular Russian billionaire and the balding, diminutive FIFA president rode an escalator together up to the convention center's second floor. Then the two powerful men slipped into a private meeting room and quietly closed the door.

———

While most of the world was caught up in the drama and passion of the South African World Cup, retired spy Christopher Steele, sitting in a sparsely decorated office suite on the second floor of a nineteenth-century building in the posh Belgravia district of West London, found himself occupied by other matters.

A Cambridge graduate, Steele had spent several years undercover in Moscow in the early 1990s, and in the mid-2000s held a senior post on the Russia desk at MI6 headquarters in London. In that job, he played a key role in determining that the mysterious death of former Russian spy Alexander Litvinenko, who was killed by ingesting radioactive polonium in 2006, was likely a hit approved by Vladimir Putin.

Steele, with a shock of graying brown hair, remarkably even features, and clear blue eyes, was urbane, well mannered, and self-assured. Serious, precise, and careful, he was known, among those who cared about such things, as someone who could procure the most sensitive information concerning Russia's clandestine activities. Since the prior year, Steele had also become a capitalist, opening a research firm called Orbis Business Intelligence and looking for opportunities to convert his deep knowledge of Russian affairs—based in great part on his web of well-placed contacts still in the country—into profits.

He did some government work, providing information for intelligence and police agencies, but Steele's bread-and-butter was private companies and law firms that wanted to dig up dirt on business rivals in Russia or gather gossip about the commercial activities of the country's fantastically wealthy oligarchs.

Most recently, Steele had been retained by a group of individuals and companies supporting England's World Cup bid and willing to pay to gain an edge in the competition to host soccer's greatest prize.

For those running England 2018, as the bid was officially called, it was evident that winning the right to host was going to depend on more than just the quality of each country's stadiums, airports, and soccer. Steele was brought in to gather intelligence on the competing bids and help England 2018, he would later note, "better understand what they were up against, and what they were up against was a completely alien way of doing business."

Vladimir Putin was a passionate ice hockey fan with no interest in soccer, but he nonetheless recognized the propaganda value of hosting such an event. A Russia World Cup would build off the 2014 Sochi Olympics, creating a nationalistic furor that could help the strongman maintain power for years to come.

At first, he had entrusted his sports minister and trusted advisor, Vitaly Mutko, who also was a member of the FIFA ExCo, to run the bid. But it had become clear that Mother Russia was not a front-runner. She was losing the public relations battle. The World Cup could easily slip out of her grasp.

Then in the spring of 2010, not long after sources began saying that Putin had suddenly taken a strong personal interest in the bid, Steele began hearing a string of curious and troubling rumors, the detailed evidence for which would eventually be placed before a Select Parliamentary Committee inquiry into the bidding process.

In April, deputy prime minister Igor Sechin went to Qatar to discuss a massive natural gas extraction project at almost the exact same time that Russia's World Cup bid team also traveled to Doha. One of Steele's best sources said the timing was no coincidence and that on top of massive gas deals, the emissaries were colluding to swap World Cup votes. Russia, the theory went, would pledge its ExCo member's vote for 2022 to Qatar, and Qatar would promise that, in exchange, its ExCo member would pick Russia for 2018.

Other sources, meanwhile, began whispering that Russian bid officials had taken valuable paintings from the Hermitage Museum and offered them to ExCo members in exchange for votes.

Then in mid-May, Lord David Triesman, the chairman of England's 147-year-old Football Association, was caught on tape discussing what he described as a Russian plot to bribe referees at the 2010 World Cup to favor Spain in exchange for a promise from the Iberian country to drop its bid for 2018.

Triesman had been secretly recorded by a young woman he was with in a London café. Speaking unguardedly, he commented that such a plan wouldn't hurt Russia, since it wasn't even competing in the 2010 tournament.

"My assumption is that the Latin Americans, although they've not said so, will vote for Spain," Triesman confided to his companion. "And if Spain drop out, because Spain are looking for help from the Russians to help bribe the referees in the World Cup, their votes may then switch to Russia."

Incredulous, his date asked, "Would Russia help them with that?"

"Oh," Triesman replied, "I think Russia will cut deals."

Unhappily for Triesman, and for the panicked English bid, his café companion gave the tape recording to a London tabloid. Its publication generated a burst of outrage in Britain as well as sharp protestations of innocence from both the Russians and the Spanish. Triesman, who had headed the FA since early 2008, resigned within days, citing concern his comments could hurt the English bid.

For Steele, Triesman's loose lips weren't the issue. As far as the ex-spy was concerned, the headline, bolstered by the fresh reports of Abramovich's private meeting with Blatter in Johannesburg, was clearly Russia.

He reported his findings to his client, and members of the bid team were predictably alarmed. England was doomed, Steele felt certain; it was never going to beat out a country like Russia, which was clearly prepared to do anything to avoid a humiliating defeat on the world stage.

But the former spy then had a second thought. The information he had been developing on Russia and FIFA was highly specific, but also unique and potentially valuable—perhaps extremely so. It would be a shame to see it go to waste. And it just so happened that Steele could think of another potential client for that info, an American in law enforcement whom he'd only recently met.

———

Special Agent Mike Gaeta took command of the FBI's Eurasian Organized Crime Squad in New York at the tail end of 2009.

Every squad in the New York field office is assigned a number. C-1, for example, is a white-collar crime team and C-13 is one of several narcotics groups. When C-24, the Eurasian Organized Crime Squad, was established in 1994, it was the first of its kind in the nation, created to focus on the illicit activities of organized groups of Russians, Ukrainians, Chechens, Georgians, Armenians, and even ethnic Koreans hailing from eastern stretches of Russia, Uzbekistan, and Kazakhstan.

After the fall of the Soviet Union, crime syndicates from these regions flooded into the United States. Although they dipped their hands into old-fashioned protection rackets and narcotics, they also had a flair for complex tax, bankruptcy, insurance, and health care frauds, and displayed an unusual propensity for violence.

C-24 flourished in the 1990s, with big busts of godfathers such as

Vyacheslav Ivankov, a former wrestler who terrorized Brighton Beach with vast extortion scams. But after September 11, things changed. FBI director Robert Mueller shifted more than two thousand agents into counterterrorism and counterintelligence, and C-24, like a lot of squads, took a hit.

By the time Gaeta took over C-24 in late 2009, fully half of the FBI's resources were allocated to national security and counterterrorism. What FBI brass often called "traditional organized crime," meanwhile was starved of resources. Far more important, Mueller made clear, was a vaguely defined category he called "transnational organized crime."

Gaeta's new squad was understaffed, but he figured if he made the case that the Russian mob was in fact committing transnational organized crime, and if he could bring some cases that stretched beyond the border, C-24 could get more support.

The son of an NYPD detective, Gaeta, with smooth Mediterranean skin and a muscular build, made a point of wearing expensive suits and shirts with eye-catching cuff links. He went to law school at Fordham, and after two miserable years doing insurance work in a Manhattan law firm, signed on with the FBI.

Gaeta had spent most of his career working Italian mafia cases, including a dozen years on the Genovese Crime Squad, a special task force focused on just one of New York's five ruling mafia families.

The job taught Gaeta about old-school police work, about getting out of the office and talking to people, and, whenever possible, recording suspects. His favorite trick was to knock, unannounced, on the front door of a suspect's house and identify himself as an FBI agent, all smiles, pretending to know nothing before handing over his business card and leaving. Little did the guy know, but the Bureau had already secretly tapped the guy's phone, and tapes were rolling to capture the panicked call the suspect would invariably place soon afterward: "Boss, I just got a visit from the feds. What are we gonna do?"

Gaeta called that "tickling the wire."

Over the years, his speech grew thick with mafia jargon; at times it sounded as if he saw everything through the same lens he used when busting people named "Hot Dogs" Battaglia and Vincent "Chin" Gigante. La Cosa Nostra was Gaeta's world. It was one populated by capos, soldiers, made men, and wiseguys who could do ten years in the joint standing on their head.

He didn't speak a word of Russian. Other than a brief trip to Moscow as an undergrad, he knew little about the country, and even less about its network of criminals. But Gaeta figured it couldn't be all that different than running after Genovese bosses. Criminals fascinated him and he loved the thrill of chasing them down. So he started off by reviewing C-24's open cases. One, involving an illegal gambling ring, seemed to hold particular promise.

Tips from informants and a series of wiretaps suggested that a small cadre of Russians had been running high-stakes poker games in New York and Los Angeles as well as a sophisticated online sports book. The case involved a who's-who of wealthy and powerful suspects, including celebrities and professional poker players, but the most intriguing figure was Alimzhan Tokhtakhounov.

Born in Uzbekistan in an Uighur family, Tokhtakhounov's nickname was Taiwanchik. As a young man, he had been an amateur soccer player. In 2002, he was indicted by a federal grand jury for allegedly bribing a figure skating judge at the Salt Lake City Olympics to give the gold medal to a pair of Russian skaters.

Taiwanchik had been arrested in Italy soon thereafter, but when prosecutors failed in their bid to extradite him to the U.S., he returned to Russia for good. Now one of Gaeta's agents was building evidence that Taiwanchik had helped finance the gambling operation, laundering tens of millions of dollars from Russia and Ukraine through the U.S. in the process.

Making a case against a man the Justice Department already considered an international fugitive, and one who allegedly had deep ties to organized crime in multiple countries—that certainly seemed to qualify as transnational.

———

Outside of Moscow and St. Petersburg, London was the world's hub for Russians. Since the Soviet Union collapsed, the United Kingdom had been awash in cash from Russians looking to buy property abroad.

London was also thick with academics, diplomats, consultants, and other experts in Russian affairs. Because of the city's role as one of the world's principal banking centers, British law enforcement kept close watch on money laundering activity, particularly by Russians.

In April 2010, Gaeta traveled to London to gather leads. Given the FBI agent's interest in suspects within Russia's borders, he was soon directed to Christopher Steele, who was always on the lookout for new business. The Bureau, the retired spy knew, was known to be a gold-plated client.

Sitting in his cozy offices during their first meeting, Steele had assured Gaeta that he could certainly look into Taiwanchik and sports corruption, and the two had pledged to stay in touch.

Only two months had passed, but now Steele had something that felt quite a bit hotter on his hands: the intelligence he was getting on the World Cup, Russia, and FIFA in general. Never mind online sports betting and poker rooms. There was high-level bribery, money laundering, and other cross-border crimes at play—exactly what Gaeta had expressed so much interest in when they first met.

So Steele reached out to the FBI agent to ask if by any chance he'd be visiting London again soon. There was someone he wanted him to meet.

THREE

"HAVE YOU EVER TAKEN A BRIBE?"

IN THE SOCCER WORLD, INVESTIGATIVE JOURNALIST Andrew Jennings occupied a unique place. He was far from the only reporter to have ever dug into the sordid business of the beautiful game; legions of scribes from all over Europe and South America have been picking apart the sport's management at the local level since the 1970s.

But few, if any, journalists could match Jennings's obsessive drive to root out corruption or his manic flair for the dramatic. Whether standing among the crowd at a press conference or chasing an ExCo member down the street, Jennings always found a way to draw attention to himself as well as the men he excoriated.

After years of covering corruption in the Olympics, and writing several books on the subject, Jennings turned to FIFA, which had received scant if any critical attention from a press corps more interested in access and boosterism.

Jennings, bored by the sport of soccer itself, wasted little time in making it known he would be taking a different approach. At a press conference recorded on video soon after Blatter was elected for his second term as FIFA president in 2002, Jennings—whose typical work uniform of T-shirt, photographer vest, and hiking boots contrasted sharply with the rigorously formal attire of the FIFA elite—grabbed the microphone. "Herr Blatter," the snowy-haired Jennings inquired in his high, nasally voice. "Have you ever taken a bribe?"

That kind of TV-friendly, in-the-face interaction, along with a long string of scandalous scoops, became a Jennings trademark, and over the years he found a thousand creative ways to be screamed at, insulted, and sued for libel by many of the biggest names in the sport. He wrote another book, overflowing with revelations about soccer eminences but in particular Sepp Blatter and Jack Warner, and he gloated to anyone who would listen that FIFA, tired of his antics, finally banned him from all its events.

Over time, the irascible Jennings became the go-to source for leaks in the close-knit soccer community. Although he relentlessly dug up more dirt, Jennings also grew frustrated at how little, other than out-rage, ever came of all his exposés. As far as he was concerned, the men controlling the sport belonged behind bars, but nobody seemed to be listening.

Then in late 2009, he got a call from Christopher Steele, wondering if the two could have a little chat about soccer. Jennings agreed, on the condition that Steele come to him in Penrith, the sleepy town in the far northern reaches of England where he lived, and that he give him £250 for his time.

Not long thereafter, Steele paid for Jennings to make a trip to Zu-rich, where he met with some of his soccer sources, whom he had been wanting to meet with anyway, then dutifully filed a report on what they told him.

The two followed up with a few phone calls, and the former spy struck Jennings as friendly and intelligent, even if the information Steele was seeking seemed rather basic. It was clear he had a client, but he would never tell Jennings who it was, and communications dropped off until the summer of 2010, when Steele called again to ask if he'd make the trip to London to meet some very important people.

————

The train from Penrith to central London takes just under four hours, and during the journey, the wily reporter didn't know what to expect. But what greeted him when he walked into the second-floor Belgravia offices of Orbis Business Intelligence on a warm July day in 2010 was in fact exactly what he had been waiting so many years to see.

The main room, behind an unmarked door with a quirky porthole window, was spare and quiet, with white walls and a scattering of desks staffed by young researchers. Behind a second door was the smaller office Steele shared with his business partner. Inside waited the FBI.

Mike Gaeta, impeccably dressed as always, radiated experience and self-confidence, and his New York accent, straight out of a prime-time police procedural, only added to the package. Another FBI agent, younger, with short-cropped hair and wide eyes, looked to Jennings like he must have come to the Bureau directly from the Marine Corps. A third man introduced himself as chief of the Justice Department's Organized Crime and Racketeering Section in Washington, D.C.

The men told Jennings they specialized in organized crime, particularly focusing on Russian and Ukrainian matters. They had lately become interested in FIFA, they said, and wondered if maybe he'd help them get up to speed on the topic and tell them about the ways it might be corrupt. Jennings's building excitement was now rounding the corner to flat-out giddiness.

At last, he thought.

———

Action movies aside, FBI agents spend very little time smashing down doors, conducting high-speed car chases, and getting into bloody shootouts with steely-eyed crime lords. Much of what they do involves calmly and patiently talking to people.

Agents search out and recruit people who can help build cases. It might be a perpetrator or witness to a crime, someone in a position where they could attain useful information, or a person with significant knowledge on a relevant topic.

The FBI's formal term for such informants is "confidential human sources," and they are the lifeblood of most investigations. Agents learn that the core of their job is to build and nurture relationships with them, sometimes over the space of years.

Gaeta, in particular, preached this kind of police work, based on his belief that real live human beings testifying before a jury, rather than colorless and boring documents, win convictions.

Convincing people to talk, Gaeta felt, was his specialty, what made him an effective agent. He prided himself on being able to detect the vulnerabilities and motivations of sources on the insides of conspiracies, and then get them to agree to wear a wire and make clandestine recordings of criminal confessions.

As a supervisor, Gaeta constantly pushed young agents to "get out in the field" in search of sources, but he also reminded them to be cautious. The goal was to get information, not to share it: Agents listen. Sources talk. Including eccentric British journalists.

Sitting in Steele's office, the two agents and the Justice Department lawyer looked on expectantly as Jennings took a deep breath and gathered his thoughts.

The story of modern soccer was really about the emergence of a new kind of business, one that turned out to have corruption baked into it nearly from the moment it was born. That business was built around the buying and selling of the rights to sponsor and broadcast events. This marketplace is so fundamental to the way all sporting activities are administered today that it almost escapes notice, but the idea of a brand like Adidas acquiring the exclusive right to plaster its logo at all FIFA events worldwide, for years at a time and with one single contract, was revolutionary a generation ago.

The rapid growth of that new industry unlocked vast stores of value in events like the World Cup and Olympics, showering both those who ran the sports, and those who marketed them, with enormous sums of money. But it also proved susceptible, almost from the outset, to bribery and greed, leading directly to some of the most profound and intractable problems in sports.

For FIFA, that story began some thirty-five years earlier, when the world soccer authority was a far smaller and simpler organization. That was where the story had to start, and there was a lot of ground to cover.

———

By the time the Brazilian João Havelange was elected as FIFA's first non-European president on July 11, 1974, FIFA still had fewer than ten full-time employees, and, he later recalled, "the General Secretary, his wife, and their cat and dog lived in the same building. Meetings always had to be held somewhere else."

Soccer, more than a century old by then, was still an unsophisticated enterprise; the tiny sums of money that it did generate came almost entirely from fans willing to buy tickets to sit in bare concrete bleachers and root for their teams. Player salaries were small, sponsorship nonexistent, and the men who administered the sport were driven largely by a sense of public service and a love of the game.

Havelange's predecessor, Sir Stanley Rous, was a near perfect embodiment of that romantic spirit. A tweedy Englishman who seemed allergic to the sport's commercial possibilities, he largely occupied himself with preserving increasingly rusty notions of amateurism that seemed Victorian—if not downright colonialist—to FIFA's fast-growing international membership.

Havelange, a lawyer and a businessman, was a distinctly different animal. He liked to tell the story of how FIFA had little more than $30 in its bank account when he took over.

"FIFA," he would say, "had no money. Not a cent."

He exaggerated. The nonprofit organization in fact had revenue of about $25 million in 1974, mostly from the World Cup. But it was clear that the sport's supreme body came up far short in terms of maximizing its revenue potential.

Havelange had built his campaign platform around an eight-point pledge to change the game, focused largely on assistance to the developing nations that voted him into office, as well as a promise to expand the number of teams playing in the World Cup so that more countries would have a chance to reap its substantial financial benefits.

But accomplishing all that would cost considerable sums of money that FIFA simply did not have. Help came in the person of Horst Dassler, the scion of the family that founded Adidas, and young British advertising man Patrick Nally. Their vision was to bring in large corporate brands that would pump cash into soccer in exchange for a complete and exclusive sponsorship deal that would last for years and would include the World Cup and all other FIFA events.

Until then, advertisers simply paid money to stadium owners to rent space where they could plaster their logos on a game-by-game or seasonal basis. Little if any of that money went to teams, leagues, or FIFA itself. What Dassler and Nally recognized was that FIFA and all the soccer organizations beneath it were the entities with the valuable asset, not the stadium owners, and that asset was soccer. Soccer was why people went to the stadium; soccer was the golden goose. As a result, Dassler and Nally figured, soccer organizations could assert—for the first time—the right to control all advertising and sponsorship related to matches. Once that was done, the rights could be bundled into huge, all-inclusive rights packages worth millions of dollars that guaranteed brands exclusivity and uniformity.

Dassler and Nally would place themselves in the middle of those transactions, creating a new kind of business that came to be called a sports marketing firm, which would buy the commercial rights to FIFA events wholesale, and then resell them piecemeal, with a rich margin built into the price.

The model they invented would soon become ubiquitous in sports, but in the mid-1970s it seemed revolutionary if not downright crazy, and it took the two men more than eighteen months of aggressive sales-manship to convince Coca-Cola to commit at least $8 million to become FIFA's first brand partner and the first exclusive worldwide sponsor in the history of sports.

It was a watershed moment. The FIFA/Coca-Cola World Football Development Programme that Dassler and Nally created marked the be-ginning of a new kind of symbiotic relationship directly between inter-national brands and sports organizations, which started providing most of their revenue.

Coca-Cola's cash allowed Havelange to deliver on his pledges, in-creasing the size of the World Cup, allotting more guaranteed berths to teams from Africa, Asia, and Oceania, the region incorporating New Zealand and the South Pacific, and continually nurturing relationships with politically influential officials through direct patronage. First he gave away equipment, coaching, and medical training, mostly through the Coca-Cola program, to impoverished federations.

Later, when FIFA's revenue began soaring, the support took the form of either development grants or loans that came with few strings attached and vanishingly little oversight. Havelange would provide for all of FIFA's member associations and they, dutifully, would reelect him every four years. It was, simply put, cash for votes.

The growing dependence on multinational sponsors meant that the fundamental mission, image, and activities of FIFA, the IOC, and similar organizations would be increasingly determined by the profit-seeking motives of huge multinational corporations. And the explosion in value of television rights, starting a few years later as global transmission technology improved, would only push things further in that direction.

Dassler and Nally, meanwhile, saw in the Coca-Cola deal the foundation of a new commercial era, with giant companies paying ever-increasing sums for rights, and specialized sports marketing at the center of everything, controlling all aspects of deals, speaking for both sides, and, of course, taking their considerable cut of everything. The key to success in the emerging industry was gaining control of the rights—at any cost.

Over the decades, Coca-Cola would pump hundreds of millions of dollars into FIFA in one of the longest-lasting branding partnerships in all of sports. But when it first signed the deal, marketing executives at the Atlanta soft drink giant saw it as a significant risk, and insisted that Dassler and Nally find someone who could protect its interests within FIFA.

The ideal candidate, everyone agreed, would be someone Swiss, with experience in public relations and administration. A loyal person who understood sports as primarily a commercial activity. Someone who would travel the world promoting soccer and fizzy, caramel-colored beverages, while handing out free uniforms, balls, and cleats to Havelange's electoral base, starting with a trip to Ethiopia on November 17, 1976.

That someone was Sepp Blatter, FIFA's first development officer and future president.

———

Joseph Blatter, son of a bicycle mechanic and factory worker, was born in March 1936, two months premature, too young to even have nails on his fingertips.

Without a neonatal ward in the local hospital, his mother, Bertha, was forced to care for him in the family home in the Swiss town of Visp. Bertha doted on him, calling her son "chéri." Everyone else just used the common diminutive for Joseph: Sepp.

Visp is in the canton of Valais, in the south of Switzerland, home to the jagged, imposing Matterhorn, and the area's verdant green hills are dotted with small dairy farms and vineyards. It is not a wealthy region, and locals pride themselves on their toughness, independence, simplicity, and deep sense of loyalty. Other Swiss view natives with suspicion, as insular, guarded, and even downright unfriendly.

"If you have a friend visiting you from faraway, that is what hotels are for," Blatter's father was fond of saying. "If he needs a ride, that is what taxis are for. And if he is hungry, that is what restaurants are for."

As a child, Blatter was drawn to athletic endeavors, and he particularly loved ice hockey, hugely popular in the German-speaking regions of Switzerland. But his small stature made a sporting future highly unlikely. Instead he turned to the business behind the games.

By the time he took the development job at FIFA, Blatter, age thirty-nine, had spent four years in the Swiss army, earned degrees in economics and public relations, worked for the Valais Tourism Board, the Swiss Ice Hockey Federation, and finally for watchmaker Longines, where he ran its Olympic timing division.

Havelange promoted Blatter to general secretary of FIFA in 1981, in significant part because he had developed an excellent working relationship with Dassler. The Adidas man had rapidly expanded his budding business into other sports organizations, including the Olympics, but FIFA and the World Cup were its bread and butter.

As general secretary, Blatter played an integral role in a period of significant economic growth for FIFA, overseeing World Cups in Spain, Mexico, Italy, and the U.S. in 1994. By the time soccer's premier event reached the shores of America, Blatter had been in the position for thirteen years and his ambitions were now fixated on FIFA's highest throne.

After an aborted attempt to campaign against Havelange in 1994, Blatter was finally given the Brazilian's blessings when the older man decided to retire after twenty-four years as FIFA president; he was elected in Paris, on the eve of the 1998 World Cup in France, defeating the head of the European soccer confederation, known as UEFA. The election was marred with accusations of foul play, as Blatter had been the underdog, and was expected to lose by at least twenty votes.

Among Blatter's most enthusiastic supporters had been Jack Warner, who wrangled CONCACAF's votes in his favor, and a fabulously wealthy Qatari construction magnate named Mohamed bin Hammam, who also sat on the ExCo. Four years later, the president of the Somali Football Federation would claim he had been offered $100,000, half of it in cash, to vote for Blatter, and that "18 African voters accepted bribes to vote for Blatter"—enough to swing the election.

The financial inducements, the Somali alleged, were handed out the night before the election in the toney Le Méridien hotel, where Blatter was staying. People "were lining up," he said, "to receive money."

Blatter and Bin Hammam sued the Somali for libel, then dragged him before the FIFA disciplinary committee, where he was banned from the sport for two years for failing to provide enough evidence to support his accusations.

The allegations, FIFA said in a terse statement, "undermined the interests of football as a whole," and were soon forgotten.

The biggest blow to Blatter's young presidency, one that would haunt the entire organization for years and foreshadow later crises, came on May 21, 2001, when FIFA's main commercial partner, International Sport and Leisure, or ISL, declared bankruptcy in the Swiss canton of Zug.

ISL had been founded by Horst Dassler in the early 1980s after breaking with Nally. It continued with the same business model, adding television rights to the advertising packages it bought up en masse from FIFA, and soon expanding to buy rights to the Olympics as well.

Although Dassler died of cancer in 1987, ISL still maintained control of most of FIFA's commercial activities, and in 1996 pledged to pay the soccer body $1.6 billion for the television and marketing rights to the 2002 and 2006 World Cups.

But ISL had run out of cash after overextending itself on numerous other sports rights deals and, after futile attempts to sell itself, was pushed into liquidation. Without its longtime marketing partner, FIFA faced the prospect of crippling losses, and was forced to negotiate a cascading series of economic and logistical headaches in order to ensure that broadcast and advertising rights to the 2002 World Cup, in South Korea and Japan, were properly sold and managed.

Scarcely a week after the bankruptcy filing, FIFA filed a criminal complaint against ISL's executives, charging them with "suspicion of fraud," "embezzlement," and "disloyal business management," and arguing that the defunct firm had purposely withheld a $60 million payment it owed FIFA for sale of World Cup television rights.

Despite mounting criticism and accusations of bribery, fraud, and corruption, Blatter was reelected the following year, and in 2004 FIFA quietly withdrew its criminal complaint against ISL, apparently consigning the marketing firm to oblivion.

But a prosecutor in the obscure Swiss canton of Zug named Thomas Hildbrand continued digging into the matter. Tirelessly poring over bank records from around the world, as well as documents seized in a raid of FIFA headquarters in 2005, Hildbrand began to assemble a mammoth case alleging that ISL had paid millions of dollars in bribes and kickbacks to sports officials in exchange for the television and marketing rights contracts that were its lifeblood.

Eventually, Hildbrand's probe uncovered evidence that between 1989 and 2001, at least $22 million in illicit payments were wired through a complicated series of offshore companies to accounts controlled by João Havelange and his son-in-law, Ricardo Teixeira, who was president of Brazil's soccer association. Considerable sums were also paid to Nicolás Leoz, president of the South American confederation, known as CONMEBOL.

Yet commercial bribery, at the time, was not a crime in Switzerland. Not one of those FIFA officials was ever charged, and their identities were kept a secret from the public. Hildbrand did eventually bring charges against six ISL executives, but in 2008, judges hearing the case acquitted most of them, with three forced to pay only modest fines. None ever went to prison.

Far from denying the corruption allegations against them, the ISL executives freely admitted during trial that bribes had been paid. One of them, who had been chief executive of the firm when it collapsed, explained in court that ISL and rival marketing companies had been paying sports officials bribes—he called them "commissions"—for *decades* to ensure they'd maintain control over lucrative marketing and television rights contracts.

Indeed, Dassler had confided to Nally as far back as 1978 that he intended to bribe Havelange. Once Havelange started taking money under the table, he belonged to Dassler. The FIFA president would not cede rights to anyone else. It was the birth of modern sports bribery. From there, Dassler began paying off more and more officials, until it became the defining feature of ISL's business.

The appeal of such payments was that they guaranteed there wouldn't ever be any competition for rights, keeping the price low. In exchange for under-the-table cash, sports officials would sign over their rights for prices far below market value, often for years or even decades at a time, and would reject any outside offers.

That created the opportunity for huge profits for the bribe-paying sports marketing firms, and secret fortunes for the bribe-receiving sports officials, but it also effectively robbed the sport of money it would have received had the rights been sold in a truly open and competitive market.

Sports officials, meanwhile, who had once sought leadership positions out of an abiding love for the game, came to view them as viable financial opportunities. They began to insist on bribes and refused to sign rights contracts without them.

"The company would not have existed if it had not made such payments," the disgraced ISL executive said. All of international sports, he was trying to explain to the black-robed judges, was propped up by corruption.

As it turned out, very few people were listening at the time.

———

With all his breathless talk of corruption and secret payoffs behind closed doors, Jennings certainly had Gaeta's attention. The two men had the same instincts when it came to crime, as well as a shared gut feeling that everyone, on some level, was on the take. Jennings's tale of FIFA corruption was complicated and dense, but also packed with what seemed like significant leads to chase. And what Jennings had outlined in that first meeting was just the beginning. Gaeta could see that FIFA's tendrils reached across a vast of territory and a huge cast of characters.

There were, for example, the photographs Jennings had published of Blatter, in 2005, enjoying a cocktail at a Moscow nightclub with Tai-wanchik, the Russian Gaeta's squad already believed was a major crime boss. If the FBI could somehow tie corruption within FIFA to the Russian mob, well, that would tick off just about every box.

Gaeta knew he could learn a lot from a man like Jennings, who seemed to have an answer—and a rollicking anecdote—to every question.

He and the others quizzed him on every soccer figure they could think of, and when they'd finally had enough for the day, they gave the journalist their business cards, which bore the FBI seal embossed in gold leaf, along with their titles, email addresses, and cell phone numbers.

They would take all this information back to New York and try to figure out if there was a case that could be made. Soon enough, they'd be talking to him again.

FOUR

A GUY FROM QUEENS

ON AUGUST 5, 2010, CONCACAF GENERAL SECRETARY Chuck Blazer, in a dark blue suit, white shirt, suspenders, and a gaudy pink, black, and gray floral tie, was escorted into the Russian White House on the banks of the Moskva River for what he called a "very special occasion." The Soviet-era building, with its white marble facade and polished marble floors, is the seat of government for the Russian Federation and serves as the office of its prime minister.

Accompanied by a translator, Blazer was escorted by a raft of cabinet ministers into the office of Vladimir Putin. Grinning, Blazer clasped Putin's hand, then took a seat beside fellow ExCo member Vitaly Mutko.

"You know," Putin said. "You look just like Karl Marx!"

Blazer, sixty-five years old and with a massive belly pressed against the coffee table, winked and said, "I know."

Putin raised his hand and gave the American a high five.

As prime minister of a country of 150 million people, Putin was a busy man. That very morning he had been frantically attempting to manage a disastrous string of forest fires that had broken out across the country. But with the competition to win the World Cup bid in full swing, Putin seemed to have nothing but time on his hands for the ExCo member. He had ensured that Blazer had been treated solicitously during his stay in Moscow, and now, in his office, he made sure to ask about Blazer's pet project, a travel blog he'd started during the 2006 World Cup in Germany.

The blog, which had started as "Inside the World Cup" and then became "Travels with Chuck Blazer," was stuffed with pictures of Blazer in the company of friends, soccer officials, sports marketers, and the more than occasional beauty pageant contestant. Bright and cheerful, it provided a glimpse into the profoundly luxurious life Blazer and other ExCo members led. The blog was largely populated with snapshots of soccer events around the world and had little in the way of commentary or analysis, because, Blazer noted, "recreational writing at times can be very demanding in the face of other obligations."

Many of the posts showed Blazer out to dinner with friends from the world of sports, visiting museums, or commemorating holidays. Fond of wearing costumes for special occasions, one post showed him dressed up as a pirate, while another had him elaborately frocked as Obi-Wan Kenobi from *Star Wars*, taking his grandchildren out for Halloween trick-or-treating.

Putin listened intently as Blazer told him in great detail about the blog and its origins. The Russian leader peered fixedly into his eyes, then casually mentioned that he'd be taking a long trip into the Russian countryside at the end of summer.

"If I sent you pictures from my trip," he asked, "will you post them in your blog?"

Blazer, flattered, quickly agreed, pledging not only to post the photos, but also that he'd rename his blog "Travels with Chuck Blazer and His Friends" to commemorate his newly struck friendship with Vladimir Putin, one of the world's most feared and powerful men.

———

The Youth Soccer Association of New Rochelle, New York, where Charles Gordon Blazer got his start in the game in the mid-1970s, was run by volunteers, mostly business executives and lawyers who saw the sport as a wholesome pastime for their children and who promoted it with almost religious fervor.

The mission of the league, founded in 1973, was to ensure "the growth of children through what we believe to be a healthy and challenging sport."

Long ignored to the point of irrelevance in America, soccer had in less than a decade found significant purchase among middle-class suburban families eager to embrace an outdoor sport other than baseball and tackle football for their children to play. That spurt coincided with the birth of the North American Soccer League, or NASL, a glitzy professional association, which thanks to an influx of marketable stars like Pelé, brought the sport mainstream U.S. attention for the first time.

Around the country, parents of little children were suddenly willing to fork over $50, $100, or more every year for their children to play this odd game where you can't use your hands and nobody ever seemed to score.

Most of the men and women involved in the New Rochelle league were working parents who didn't have the time to take on the complexities of managing a fast-growing soccer organization. The league's founder ran a textile mill and its first president was an insurance executive who worked long hours in Manhattan.

They viewed the league as a simple way to do something for their kids. Blazer, on the other hand, developed a very different, and in some ways visionary, perspective on the game. He recognized tremendous untapped financial opportunity for himself in soccer—a sport with almost zero commercial viability in the U.S. at the time.

Born in 1945 and raised in Flushing, Queens, Blazer had never played the sport. A strong student, he got a degree in accounting from NYU, started coursework for an MBA, but then dropped out to get into sales, eventually hawking promotional items like T-shirts and Frisbees.

His daughter, Marci, was born in 1968, and his son, Jason, came two years later, and by the time they were old enough to join the New Rochelle league, Blazer had plenty of free time on his hands.

Within a few years of seeing his first-ever soccer match, Blazer became a director of the New Rochelle league, cofounded the Westchester Youth Soccer League, and in 1980 was elected first vice president of the Southern New York Youth Soccer Association, which oversaw the sport across a large swath of the state.

In 1984, he took a big leap, winning the vote for executive vice president of the United States Soccer Federation, which oversaw all soccer in the country. The federation, housed on the fortieth floor of the Empire State Building, was flat broke, having run a $600,000 deficit in the prior year, and Blazer's position was unpaid. For Blazer, however, it was a turning point, the moment his ideas about a career in global soccer—an almost preposterous idea for an American at the time—began to seem possible.

Traveling extensively, Blazer oversaw the struggling national team, which hadn't qualified for a World Cup since 1950, as well as the committee that sanctioned international matches playing in the U.S., a key source of revenue for the federation. In those roles, Blazer began to see the workings of the sport's financial side, still rudimentary and underdeveloped, and recognized the potential lurking beyond the field of play.

"There's no magic," Blazer, assuming the tone of a business executive, told a reporter shortly after taking the job. "To erase the deficit, we have to have a viable, saleable product that attracts sponsors."

But the product did not prove saleable.

The glitzy North American Soccer League, wilting after its late 1970s heyday, played its final match in October 1984. FIFA had rejected America's bid to host the 1986 World Cup in favor of Mexico, and the U.S. national team was eliminated from qualifying for that tournament in May 1985 before a "home" crowd in Torrance, California, that seemed far more interested in rooting for its opponent, Costa Rica.

In July 1986, just days after he returned from the Mexico World Cup, Blazer lost his bid for a second term to a Louisiana lawyer who campaigned on the promise to focus on youth soccer rather than the international side of the game.

But Blazer, by then fully committed to a career in soccer, quickly bounced back, and in early 1987 he and a British expat cofounded the American Soccer League, a low-budget alternative to the NASL, which folded after the 1984 season. As commissioner of the upstart new league, Blazer paid himself a $48,000 salary and ran operations out of his house in Scarsdale. "We intend to appeal to the suburban soccer family," he said.

The league played its first match in April 1988, but by year's end Blazer had been run out of the commissioner's job by owners furious that he refused to share information about finances with them, was unwilling to delegate, and appeared to be abusing his expense account. Undeterred, he immediately landed a job as president of one of the league's franchises, the Miami Sharks, where Blazer set his own salary at $72,000, despite the fact that the team drew fewer than 1,000 spectators per game. In May 1989, Blazer was fired by the team's Brazilian owner.

Less than a year later, however, he pulled off his greatest coup, masterminding the campaign of Trinidad's Jack Warner for the CONCACAF presidency, and serving as his campaign manager. In April 1990, Warner upset a longtime incumbent from Mexico, and soon after rewarded Blazer by making him the confederation's general secretary.

While Warner occupied himself with the game's political side, Blazer went about figuring out how to make CONCACAF money. When he and Warner took over, the organization, founded in the early 1960s, had a budget of $140,000, just $57,000 in the bank, and its main office in Guatemala City.

Blazer moved CONCACAF's headquarters to New York, and within a few months Donald Trump personally offered him offices taking up the seventeenth floor of Trump Tower. With the economy in recession and occupancy rates low, the real estate magnate proposed giving Blazer a year's rent for free and eleven additional years at half the market rate. Blazer, who came to consider Trump a close friend, called the deal evidence of "some spiritual force looking after us."

He soon created the Gold Cup, a tournament that pitted the confederation's national teams against one another in a format similar to the World Cup. Launched as a showpiece focusing on the U.S. and Mexican national teams, the Gold Cup soon would bring in tens of millions of dollars in television and sponsorship money every time it was played.

In early 1997, a seat on the FIFA ExCo opened when one of CONCACAF's three representatives died of a sudden heart attack. Although others had expressed interest in the open seat, none was given a real chance. Warner, in a typically dictatorial move, allowed no campaigning, insisted on a vote via fax, and announced that Blazer had been elected to soccer's most powerful board three days later.

Over time, Blazer would come to sit on five FIFA committees, including the ExCo. On his watch, soccer in North America went from obscurity to a viable enterprise, with income cascading in from sponsorships, advertising, and television deals.

Blazer not only helped FIFA through the catastrophic collapse of its outside marketing and television partner, ISL, but he was instrumental in steering it to far greater revenue down the road. CONCACAF, meanwhile, saw its receipts grow from nearly zero in 1990 to $35 million in 2009, while its prestige and influence within FIFA skyrocketed.

The United States' professional soccer league, Major League Soccer, which did not even exist when Blazer joined CONCACAF, won a long-term contract with ESPN, thanks largely to Blazer's direct influence. Women's soccer, which he championed while at the U.S. Soccer Federation, played its first World Cup on Blazer's watch and the tournament had twice been held in the U.S. since then.

Divorced, Blazer lived with his girlfriend, an attractive former soap opera actress, in a roomy luxury apartment on the forty-ninth floor of Trump Tower; he had a $900,000 beachside condo in the Bahamas; and arranged for the purchase of adjacent apartments with views of Biscayne Bay, high above Miami's South Beach, for his exclusive use.

As it did for all two dozen ExCo members, FIFA paid for Blazer to travel first-class to its numerous events and meetings around the world, showering him with five-star luxury accommodations, chauffeured limousines, gourmet meals, fine wine, gifts, and a seemingly endless supply of match tickets. It paid him an annual stipend of $100,000, not including additional travel expenses, a yearly bonus of at least $75,000, and a generous per diem, in cash, whenever he was on the road.

He socialized with presidents, royalty, and billionaires, counted celebrities and successful television producers as friends, spent nights carousing at legendary New York hotspot Elaine's, and even won the occasional personal favor from his good pal Donald Trump, who, for example, once allowed Blazer to host his high school reunion in Trump Tower's glittering lobby.

Famous among soccer fans outside the U.S. for his massive size and bushy white beard, he enjoyed almost total anonymity at home, and could freely make trips around Central Park on his mobility scooter, his pet parrot perched on his shoulder, without fear of being bothered by soccer fans or members of the sporting press.

It was, in sum, a rather impressive and altogether unexpected lifestyle for an overweight guy from Queens who never so much as kicked a soccer ball until he was more than thirty years old.

On August 23, 2010, soon after returning from Moscow, Blazer received an email from his old friend Jack Warner.

The two men were different in seemingly every way. Where Blazer, the stereotypical New Yorker, was loud and gregarious, Warner, from the Trinidadian countryside, was quiet and reserved. Boisterous and sociable, Blazer loved a big spectacle and, particularly, drawing attention to himself. Warner, who suffered from a mild speech impediment that made his already thick Caribbean accent nearly impenetrable, tended to prefer intimate dinners. He insisted on elaborate, formal shows of respect, and his anger over perceived slights could simmer for years.

Blazer's domain was Manhattan, while Warner lived in the suburbs of Trinidad's capital, Port of Spain. Still, they often made international trips together, attended official events in each other's company, and presided in tandem over an endless series of CONCACAF meetings. And despite their differences, the unlikely pair complemented each other, and grew close, even taking family vacations together on occasion.

Thanks to his position as a FIFA vice president and president of CONCACAF, Warner was far better known in the soccer world than Blazer, the focus of constant attention in the sporting press. But those who followed soccer closely viewed the pair as inseparable.

Jack and Chuck, everyone called them.

The August email from Warner was brief, advising the general secretary that he would soon receive a payment he had been inquiring about, with increasing urgency, for some time.

The money was part of a $10 million sum South Africa had secretly pledged to Warner more than six years earlier. At the time, South Africa was bidding to host the 2010 World Cup, and had been competing against Morocco and Egypt for the honor.

Ostensibly, the money was sent to "support the African Diaspora in Caribbean countries as part of the World Cup legacy," but nobody had illusions about what it was: a bribe for favorable votes.

And indeed, when the ExCo met in Zurich in May 2004 to decide who would host the tournament, Warner and Blazer dutifully cast their ballots in South Africa's favor. Their votes proved decisive: by a 14–10 margin, South Africa had won the right to host the 2010 World Cup.

Warner promised Blazer that when the money arrived, $1 million of it would be his.

"I'm proud of my vote for South Africa and proud of FIFA," Blazer told a reporter a few days later from his apartment high above Manhattan.

But as time passed, Blazer realized he had never seen a dime. He occasionally asked Warner about it, but never managed to get a straight answer. It seemed, he slowly gathered, that the South Africans had run into difficulties in finding a way to make the payment, and Warner had eventually turned to FIFA's general secretary to intercede on his behalf.

After a long and heated negotiation, a total of $10 million, in three payments, was wired by FIFA in early 2008 to accounts that were registered under the names of CONCACAF and the Caribbean Football Union, but were in fact controlled solely by Jack Warner. That December, Warner finally gave Blazer part of what he was owed, wiring $298,500 to an account he held in a Cayman Islands bank.

It was aggravating, and yet typical of how things had evolved between the two old friends.

Blazer's vote on the FIFA ExCo counted exactly as much as Warner's, yet he was forced to beg for full payment of his meager slice of the big pot. The email Warner sent to Blazer, then, came as a relief. Hopefully this unpleasant remnant of old business could at last be put to rest.

On September 23, a check for $205,000, drawing from the Caribbean Football Union account at a Republic Bank branch in Port of Spain, was drafted and then sent to Blazer. It was made out to a company he controlled, Sportvertising Inc., which was registered in the Cayman Islands. It wasn't the full $701,500 Warner still owed him for his purchased vote, but at least it was a start.

Four days later, Blazer deposited the check into an account he used for day trading stocks at Merrill Lynch. The brokerage had an office on Fifth Avenue less than a block away from Trump Tower, and taking the check there was certainly much less hassle than mailing it to his bank in the Caymans.

"For deposit only," Blazer wrote on the reverse.

The minor convenience would come at a very high price.

FIVE

THE VOTE

A THIN CRUST OF ICY SNOW COATED THE GROUNDS OF FIFA's Zurich headquarters early on December 2, 2010, as members of the Executive Committee arrived to cast perhaps the most important votes in soccer history. Without stopping, they glided past security in black chauffeur-driven Mercedes S-Class sedans, then down a long ramp leading directly into the bowels of the building.

There they alighted on the third subfloor without ever having to step outside or be observed by the crowds of journalists who had been gathering since before dawn at the building's entrance. The building, known in soccer circles as FIFA House, was an imposing symbol of what the once humble sports governing body had become.

Designed by a noted Swiss architect and built for $200 million, the building, opened in 2007, presented a cold, inscrutable facade of shiny glass covered by steel mesh, set so far back from perimeter fences and guard posts that it could not be seen from the street.

It stood in remarkable contrast to FIFA's first Zurich home, a shabby two-room suite that it rented above the city's busiest avenue for more than twenty years. The new headquarters stood on a secluded, eleven-acre lot high above the city. The expansive property boasted a full-sized soccer pitch, several smaller playing fields, and a fitness center, as well as six carefully maintained gardens stocked with exotic plants imported from around the globe at great expense. Each represented one of the different regional confederations governing world soccer; a lush rain forest made of Pacific Northwest pines, ferns, and mosses stood in for CONCACAF, for example.

Sometimes called an "underground skyscraper," five of FIFA House's eight floors were subterranean, and the building's grand lobby, redolent in contrasting polished and rough-hewn stone, was quietly decorated with expensively discreet flowers. Access was tightly controlled, and doors throughout the building could be opened only with high-tech fingerprint sensors, giving visitors the distinct impression of being in a clandestine military installation. Or a bank vault.

The aesthetic was rigorously Swiss, with almost no adornment anywhere, but it was clear that no expense had been spared. Even the elevators, with see-through glass doors, were fitted with strangely entrancing glowing lights on the outside of their carriages. The lights served no obvious purpose, but seemed to whisper, softly yet confidently, that money had been spent here.

The beating heart of both building and institution was found on the third sublevel. There sat the executive boardroom, where FIFA's ExCo made soccer's most critical decisions. It was a room within a room—a dark impenetrable war chamber ripped from some Cold War political drama, with tall curved walls sheathed in hammered aluminum and floors of polished lapis lazuli. Black-stained oak desks were arrayed in a large square beneath a massive crystal chandelier in the oval form of a stadium bowl.

No sunlight was allowed to penetrate the enclosure, Blatter explained on occasion of the building's opening, because "places where people make decisions should contain only indirect light."

Nearby was a suite of immaculate, spacious bathrooms reserved for FIFA executives, and beyond them an achingly beautiful, and staggeringly expensive, glowing meditation chamber made entirely of onyx slabs illuminated from within. The room, created in deference to Muslim members of FIFA's Executive Committee, contained two simple benches and a prayer rug, with a green arrow in the doorjamb pointing in the direction of Mecca.

Finally, at the far end of the floor, there was a lounge furnished with modern upholstered sofas and armchairs, where, between meetings, ExCo members were served refreshments beneath a crepe chandelier.

Hanging on the wall at one end of the lounge was one of the only works of art visible anywhere within FIFA headquarters: a neon installation in curving script by the Italian artist Mario Merz. It posed an intriguing question: *Noi giriamo intorno alle case o le case girano intorno a noi?*

"Do we revolve around the house, or does the house revolve around us?"

———

At the turn of the twentieth century, the soaring popularity of the relatively new sport of soccer led to demand for organizing matches between clubs hailing from different nations. But the way the sport was played varied enormously from place to place, and the need for a single organizing body that could ensure fair matches between countries grew increasingly apparent.

Britain's four soccer associations, which viewed themselves as the sport's inventors and greatest practitioners, were uninterested in submitting to a higher authority. England's Football Association, already forty years old, was particularly skeptical, writing dourly that it "cannot see the advantages of such a federation," and refusing to have anything further to do with it.

Undaunted, seven continental groups—representing France, Belgium, Denmark, the Netherlands, Spain, Sweden, and Switzerland—met in the back room of a Parisian sports club on May 21, 1904, and decided to organize without the Brits.

They called their nonprofit organization the Fédération Internationale de Football Association, and by joining, the pioneering officials pledged to adhere exclusively to its statutes, giving it supreme authority over the sport. Everyone was to play the game by the same set of rules on the pitch. Perhaps most importantly, FIFA would demand absolute allegiance from its members, and the complete exclusion of any soccer associations that did not prove to be faithful members of the club.

Within a few months, Germany agreed to pay the annual membership fee of 50 French francs, and eventually England, Scotland, Wales, and Northern Ireland joined as well. South Africa became the first non-European member, affiliating in 1909; Argentina and Chile joined in 1912; and the United States entered the fold the following year.

In 1928, under pressure from its members to create a tournament that would rival the popularity of soccer at the Olympics, while also admitting professional players—which the International Olympic Committee did not—FIFA announced plans for the first World Cup.

Five countries submitted bids to host. But Uruguay's soccer association, which had won gold medals in the 1924 and 1928 Olympics, offered to cover the travel costs of visiting teams, to build a huge new stadium at its own expense, and to share any profits with FIFA, while absorbing all the risk of a financial loss by itself.

"These arguments," FIFA later noted, "were decisive." Unwilling or unable to make such financial commitments, the other countries dropped their bids and thirteen nations ultimately competed in the first World Cup, which was an instant hit. On July 30, 1930, seventy thousand fans filled Montevideo's brand-new Estadio Centenario to watch Uruguay defeat Argentina, 4–2, in the final.

The event's surging popularity did not, however, net substantial financial gains for many years. For its first several decades, FIFA largely persisted thanks to annual fees paid by its members, plus small commissions it charged on ticket sales at international matches. It gave away, free of charge, the broadcast rights to its first televised World Cup, held in Switzerland in 1954, and even at the 1974 World Cup in West Germany, the majority of tournament revenue still came from ticket sales.

That rapidly changed with the advent of modern communications and advertising, and soon television and sponsorship deals far outstripped gate income. Because such a large share of FIFA's revenue began to derive from the World Cup, the nonprofit opted to measure its finances in four-year cycles concluding with the championship tournament.

The cycle ending with the 1974 World Cup netted a tidy profit of just under $20 million. For the 2007–2010 period culminating in South Africa, FIFA booked a record profit of $631 million and FIFA's cash reserves reached $1.3 billion. The World Cup had become the largest and most lucrative sporting event in human history.

———

When in Zurich, FIFA ExCo members stayed at the Baur au Lac, a 165-year-old monument to the very Swiss aesthetic of expensive understatement. The hotel, close on the banks of Lake Zurich, prides itself on absolute discretion, but does admit to having put up, among others, Haile Selassie, Austrian Empress Elisabeth, and Kaiser Wilhelm II.

During FIFA meetings, the men controlling world soccer could often be found sprawled on overstuffed couches in the Baur au Lac's lounge, in suits, thawbs, and robes, gossiping about the sport's recondite politics over pricey cocktails and elaborate tea services on silver trays.

Just weeks before the December 2010 World Cup vote, two ExCo members, Nigerian Amos Adamu and Tahitian Reynald Temarii, had been suspended by FIFA's Ethics Committee following an undercover sting operation by *The Times* of London that caught them on tape offering to sell their votes in exchange for six- and seven-figure bribes. Blatter called it "a sad day for football."

The committee's remaining twenty-two constituents were a colorful, if motley group that included a number of former professional soccer players, a medical doctor, a hardware store owner, executives of airlines and oil companies, a champion middle-distance runner, several professional politicians, a handful of lawyers, and at least two billionaires.

On the eve of the vote, December 1, the nine nations making World Cup bids had staked out the Baur au Lac to make one last lobbying push, bringing in as much firepower as they could muster to sway the ExCo members their way.

Australia, vying for 2022, had dispatched supermodel Elle Macpherson to Zurich, along with the billionaire chairman of its soccer federation, mall developer Frank Lowy. The rival American delegation included national team star Landon Donovan, actor Morgan Freeman, sitting attorney general Eric Holder, and former president Bill Clinton.

England, the odds-on-favorite for 2018, meanwhile, had been humiliated several days earlier by the airing of a BBC documentary accusing three ExCo members of taking millions of dollars in bribes from the sports marketing firm International Sport and Leisure. The report also claimed that Jack Warner, a fourth ExCo member, had attempted to scalp more than $80,000 worth of tickets at the 2010 World Cup.

Terrified of the thin-skinned FIFA officials' wrath, England's bid team had tried to get the BBC to delay broadcast of the report, produced by investigative journalist Andrew Jennings. Unsuccessful, the English bid resorted to insults, calling the report "unpatriotic" and "an embarrassment."

Despite growing signs that the odds were stacked against it, England had rented two suites at the Baur au Lac and flown in its "Three Lions"— Prime Minister David Cameron, Prince William, and David Beckham— to make a final appeal. Then, in a bit of encouraging news for the English, word came that Vladimir Putin would not be coming to Zurich for the vote. The Russian leader noted he was staying away because, he told the press, ExCo members should "make their decision in peace and without any outside pressure."

For their part, members of England's bid had lurked in the Baur au Lac until well after midnight, buying ExCo members glasses of aged single-malt whisky and desperately attempting to cut last-minute deals to push their effort across the victory line. Before turning in, Jack Warner had effusively embraced Prince William, a sure sign, it seemed, he'd send his vote England's way.

Shortly before going to bed in his immaculate residence tucked away on a secluded street in a posh Zurich neighborhood, Blatter received a phone call from President Barack Obama.

He had met the president in the Oval Office during a four-day visit the previous year, and couldn't help but feel a surge of excitement when he heard his voice on the line. The call, short and formal, lasted only a few minutes.

Blatter had publicly expressed support for the U.S. bid on numerous occasions, pointing to the vast commercial opportunities that such an event would provide. Speaking in heavily accented but precise English, he reiterated that posture on the phone, deliberately noting that he had only one vote and could not tell other ExCo members what to do.

"How are our chances?" Obama asked.

Blatter paused and softly sighed. "Mr. President, it will be difficult."

"I understand. Well, good luck," Obama replied before hanging up.

They never spoke again.

———

"I am a happy president," said Blatter, looking not particularly happy as he announced that Russia and Qatar had won and would be hosting the World Cup in 2018 and 2022.

He stood at the podium before a huge crowd and grimaced. The hundreds of journalists on hand to witness the result of that morning's vote rushed to file accounts of the Russian delegation, including Roman Abramovich, high-fiving and whooping as Blatter handed deputy prime minister Igor Shuvalov the World Cup trophy onstage. Minutes later, Qatar's royal family followed suit, embracing one another, close to tears.

Chuck Blazer, in a dark suit and one of his trademark colorful ties, was sitting in the auditorium's front row, which had been reserved for the ExCo. Squeezed between Mohamed bin Hammam of Qatar and Nicolás Leoz of Paraguay, he did not join in the cheering, and rose only to briefly embrace the suddenly exultant Qatari beside him, before slumping back into the chair.

Directly behind him, Bill Clinton whispered with Sunil Gulati, president of the U.S. Soccer Federation, then rose to shake hands with the politicians and royals in the room. Blazer, America's highest-ranking soccer official, remained motionless, staring stonily ahead. He had voted for Russia rather than England to host the 2018 World Cup, but later admitted he had been shocked when the U.S. did not win the 2022 World Cup.

Just a few hours later, Vladimir Putin touched down in Zurich, exultant.

At a hastily assembled press conference, he thanked Blatter and insisted that Russia would be ready by 2018, and that he hoped Abramovich, who he said was "wallowing in money," would chip in for some of the stadium construction.

"Would it be fair to say," one excited journalist fawned, "that you are the cleverest prime minister in the world by staying away and winning the contest from so many thousands of miles away?"

"Thank you," Putin said, replying in Russian and smiling. "I'm glad I insisted on giving you the floor. Thank you, it's very nice to hear this."

Soccer fans in Australia, Korea, Japan, Spain, Portugal, Belgium, and Holland, all of whom had come up empty-handed, bemoaned the vote and questioned its fairness.

Commentators in the press questioned how it could be possible that the two countries least suited to host the World Cup had won, pointing to the inhospitable climatic conditions of Qatar, where daytime temperatures in June and July, when the World Cup was always held, routinely surpassed 115 degrees.

Nobody took it harder than England, where the vote dominated headlines for weeks on end, and all conversation on the topic was reduced to agonized soul-searching, finger-pointing, and anguished gnashing of teeth. Despite all its efforts, the country had humiliatingly garnered only two votes—from its own representative on the ExCo and from Cameroon's Issa Hayatou—to host the tournament.

British Prime Minister David Cameron, who had flown back to London on pressing business earlier that day, first heard the news from an advisor sharing the back seat of his bulletproof Jaguar on the way to Downing Street from Heathrow. The two men slumped in their seats.

"We did our best," Cameron finally said before lapsing into stunned silence.

One member of England's bid team cornered Jack Warner and asked him why he had promised his vote and then voted otherwise. The Trinidadian hissed his reply: "Who is going to stop us?"

Another member of that team, riding in a shuttle back to central Zurich from the auditorium where the results had been announced, noticed FIFA's general secretary, the tall and handsome French lawyer Jérôme Valcke, burying his face in his hands, and muttering to himself.

"This," Valcke kept saying, "is the end of FIFA."

————

The FBI's New York field office occupies seven floors of 26 Federal Plaza, a heavily guarded federal office tower in downtown Manhattan sandwiched between Chinatown and City Hall. It is the FBI's largest field office; with roughly 1,200 agents, it's about twice the size of the Los Angeles office, and that's not counting the roughly five hundred New York Police Department officers assigned to FBI task forces in the building.

Sitting in his cubicle on the twenty-third floor the morning after the vote, December 3, special agent Jared Randall lazily flipped through a copy of *The New York Times*, scanning the day's news.

The paper of record had not bothered to dispatch a reporter to Zurich to cover FIFA's vote. The three articles it did carry on FIFA were buried deep inside, starting on page B11 under the headline "Russia and Qatar Expand Soccer's Global Footprint."

The *Times's* muted reaction fell in line with that of the American

public as a whole, which—save for dedicated soccer fans—seemed profoundly uninterested. Even President Obama appeared to take the news
in stride, calling the vote "the wrong decision," but confidently predicting
that the U.S. national team would play well no matter where the World
Cup was held.

Randall, however, found the articles riveting. He got up and rushed
into Mike Gaeta's office, just a few yards from his desk. Lean and athletic
with intense dark eyes, Randall was one of the youngest agents in the
New York field office.

Like a lot of FBI agents, his father was a cop—in Narragansett, Rhode
Island, where Randall grew up—but he'd shown little interest in law enforcement as a kid. In high school, he'd started a web design business,
and he'd majored in computer information systems in college.

He considered the FBI only after a recruiter visited campus during
his senior year, noting that the Bureau was looking for agents to fight
cyber crime. That seemed exciting, and Randall applied at twenty-five,
the minimum age allowed.

He was assigned to the New York field office straight out of the
academy, but never spent a day on cyber crime. After a few training
rotations and a short stint in asset forfeiture, a complex and technical area, Randall was transferred in early 2010 to the Eurasian crime
squad, C-24.

Gaeta was happy to take him. His new squad was pretty thin, and besides, he loved working with young agents. They didn't have any bad habits that needed breaking, soaked up his advice like sponges, and didn't
challenge his theories about cases.

With as many as twenty investigations going at once, there was
no way Gaeta could do everything. But by relying on motivated young
agents to sit in surveillance, listen to wires, keep track of cooperators,
and take care of a million other details, he figured he could operate as
what he called a "senior case agent," running everything at once.

One of those things was the soccer investigation.

Gaeta had returned from multiple meetings with Christopher Steele
convinced there was a case to be made involving FIFA, but he wasn't
sure what. It seemed a bit amorphous and hazy, but lots of great cases
started that way. Gaeta called Evan Norris, a prosecutor he knew in the

Eastern District of New York, the federal district covering Brooklyn, Queens, and Long Island. He'd worked with Norris before and believed he was the right man for what seemed a juicy case. Norris didn't hesitate. The FIFA Case was now officially open.

The only thing missing was someone to run the investigation on a daily basis, and looking over his roster of agents, Jared Randall jumped to mind. He'd had only one or two cases before, and they hadn't gone anywhere. But with Gaeta's more experienced agents tied up on other matters, there just weren't too many other bodies available.

Besides, Randall had been a scholarship soccer player at Manhattan College and actively played on the NYPD soccer team. That alone, Gaeta figured, made Randall the most qualified guy on the squad.

Now, sitting in his cramped interior office, Gaeta took the newspaper out of Randall's hand and scanned the news story.

"Russia got the World Cup," Randall said.

"Yeah," Gaeta shrugged, unsurprised.

The veteran agent paused to look out of his office across the dozens of dingy cubicles that constituted the field office's various organized crime squads. Trophies of successful takedowns were scattered here and there, mixed in with reams of paper, boxes of evidence, bulletproof vests, riot gear, and FBI windbreakers hanging over backs of chairs. Clean-cut agents, nursing cups of coffee, chatted quietly, bullshitting before getting down to the day's work.

The disheveled tableau seemed appropriate for busting two-bit thugs controlling petty crime in the city's outer boroughs, yet far removed from the opulent, pristine meeting rooms in FIFA's aerie high above Zurich. Still, Gaeta was an ambitious agent and loved the idea of bringing down the seemingly untouchable mandarins who controlled all of soccer as they ate canapés and quaffed fine champagne.

"Imagine," he said to Randall, "if we could get all the way up to that level."

SIX

JACK VS. CHUCK

"JACK," CHUCK BLAZER BEGAN TO TYPE ON HIS COM-
puter. "I hope this is an April Fool's Joke."

Over the more than twenty-five years he'd known the man, Chuck
Blazer had seen Jack Warner pull more than his share of outrageous
stunts, such as the time in 2003 when he sabotaged a gala dinner for
1,200 celebrating the opening of a new soccer stadium in Carson, California, by launching into a racially charged tirade because he wasn't
picked up from the airport in a limo.

Or when Warner insisted Trinidad host the U-17 World Championships, awarded himself, friends, and family nearly every concession
and contract, and then almost failed to pull it off. Or the moment, in
2010, after the Russian World Cup bid team made a presentation to
CONCACAF's leadership, and Warner turned to them and archly said,
to the shock of everyone in the room, "What's in it for us?"

Now, sitting in his apartment high in Trump Tower, early on April 1,
2011, it seemed to Blazer that his irascible old friend was on the verge of
another bizarre performance. Warner had been, as was his habit, up before dawn, and his email had popped into Blazer's inbox before six a.m.,
long before he woke up.

Fellow ExCo member Mohamed bin Hammam had emailed Warner
a few minutes earlier, expressing his desire to address the confederation's
membership directly at a "special congress" sometime around April 18,
less than two weeks before CONCACAF's already scheduled annual
congress in Miami at the beginning of May. The billionaire, after more
than a dozen years of loyal service to Blatter, had recently announced
his intentions to run against him for the FIFA presidency. Beyond his

wealth, he was the president of the Asian Football Confederation, and had played a key role in Qatar's winning bid to host the tournament in 2022, making him a national hero and emboldening him, perhaps, to challenge the most powerful man in soccer.

After so many years at Blatter's side, he was familiar with the many tactics the Swiss employed to maintain his position. Bin Hammam wanted the opportunity to solicit all thirty-five CONCACAF votes alone and in person ahead of the presidential election in Zurich on June 1.

Warner immediately responded by saying he would "do my utmost to assist you by hosting such a meeting" in Trinidad, then forwarded the message to his general secretary, instructing him to "make this happen."

Blazer could scarcely contain his fury upon reading the email. He drafted a strongly worded reply, but before sending it first ran the email by a trusted colleague. Finally, at 9:43 a.m. New York time, he responded.

"I regret the need to address this issue after the fact and that you didn't see fit to talk with me prior to your response to Mohamed," he wrote. "Mohamed's request, while convenient for him, is really quite impossible for us."

For starters, CONCACAF's staff in New York and Miami were racing to prepare the Gold Cup competition starting in June even as they were organizing the congress in Miami. A youth World Cup qualifying tournament was being played in Guatemala at that very moment, tying up additional confederation resources, and the marketing team had an event planned for Mexico City on the same days Bin Hammam had proposed.

But even more troubling than the migraine-inducing logistics of fulfilling such a request at such a late hour were Warner's motives for asking in the first place.

The office of the president of FIFA enjoyed a status closer to that of a monarch or autocrat than a democratically elected figurehead, and the exalted man's every whim was taken as a command to put into action. Leaders of nations, public intellectuals, and celebrities wanted to be around the president, took his ideas seriously, and showered him with praise. The Swiss authorities, meanwhile, tended to take a hands-off approach to regulating the organization he controlled, charging it a fraction of the taxes paid by for-profit ventures and giving it freedom to do as it pleased.

Forfeiting all that would be devastating. After overcoming the ISL crisis to win in 2002, Blatter had run unopposed in 2007, and made it clear he had every intention to hold on to the vaunted position for many years to come.

Blazer and Warner had built their careers at FIFA around allegiance to Blatter, vehemently and tirelessly defending him amid numerous public crises, and routinely delivering all thirty-five of their confederation's votes as tribute.

In exchange, Blatter had offered magnanimity, lavishing FIFA funds earmarked for soccer development on pet projects of theirs, such as a $3 million television studio in CONCACAF's Trump Tower offices that Blazer had coveted, or the vast majority of the $26 million spent to pay for a sprawling sports, entertainment, and hotel complex Warner built in Trinidad. Blazer's daughter, a lawyer, had for several years been given a seat on FIFA's Legal Committee, while Warner's younger son, Daryll, currently worked as a FIFA development officer in the Caribbean, helping dole out more of the organization's largesse.

When Cameroon soccer official Issa Hayatou had run against Blatter for FIFA president in 2002, he, too, had asked to address CONCACAF's membership. But Warner, in a bold and cunning display of loyalty, made the unprecedented ruling that only a sitting FIFA president could address the formal CONCACAF congress, effectively shutting out Blatter's rival.

Allowing Bin Hammam to speak in Miami would not only fly in the face of that decision, but also risk alienating Warner and Blazer from their Swiss benefactor, who was known for eliminating those who did not support him.

Then again, thought Blazer, this wasn't entirely out of character for Warner. In the cutthroat world of FIFA politics, he had never been an easy man to get along with. After more than a quarter century on the ExCo, Warner was prideful, vindictive, and easily provoked, coiled like a cobra ready to strike. Though he worked constantly, his administrative skills left much to be desired, and Blazer and his staff pulled most of the weight when it came to the actual work of running the confederation.

Worse still was Warner's insatiable greed. Even Blazer, who was certainly adept at using his office for personal gain, was startled at how nakedly his friend pursued money, and how many times he'd escaped seeming disaster unscathed.

"Jack Warner thinks that he can go through anything," Blazer once wrote.

The cagey old Warner had survived so long because of his innate feel for politics. He instinctively understood the rough business of securing votes, shoring up alliances, and punishing dissent. For decades, the key to his power had been the way he lorded over the Caribbean, his little fiefdom, and now Blazer feared his sly old comrade was losing his edge.

Bin Hammam was well liked in the FIFA crowd, sure, and deeply generous in his own right. With Qatar's fortunes on the rise, he was a good friend to have. But aiding Bin Hammam's campaign was tantamount to a betrayal. Atop the FIFA pyramid, one was either with Blatter or against him.

"Please," Blazer begged of Warner in his email, "do not destroy the work that needs to be done by rushing into decisions which cause problems for us."

———

If it hadn't been for Blazer, Warner would have never been in such a lofty position in the first place.

The two had met at a CONCACAF congress in Tobago barely a month after the New Yorker was elected vice president of the U.S. Soccer Federation, and they had immediately hit it off, despite never working directly together.

Then, on November 20, 1989, the bell rang at Warner's house in Arouca, a suburb east of Port of Spain, just as he was taking his morning tea. At the door was a rather hopeful-looking Chuck Blazer. His unscheduled visit was particularly surprising considering the result of the previous day's contest between the U.S. and Trinidad and Tobago at the National Stadium twenty-five miles away.

During the 31st minute of the tightly contested match, American midfielder Paul Caligiuri had broken free, finding enough space to drill a long, arcing left-footed shot into the back of the net, breaking a scoreless tie. It was the day's only goal, and became known in soccer circles as "the shot heard round the world" because it sent the United States national team to the World Cup for the first time in forty years. In the same stroke, Trinidad's side, which had never qualified, was eliminated from contention.

Now, sitting with Warner and his wife at their kitchen table, Blazer took a breath and made his big pitch. Warner, he said excitedly, should resign from Trinidad and Tobago's soccer association and run for the CONCACAF presidency.

The confederation's sitting president, Mexican Joaquín Soria Terrazas, was gravely ill with diabetes and couldn't possibly live out another four-year term, Blazer said. Under confederation statutes, the most senior CONCACAF vice president would take over should the president die or or be removed from office; that meant Gene Edwards, former president of the U.S. Soccer Federation, would get the job. And since the U.S. was scheduled to host the 1994 World Cup, Edwards would be a lock to keep the job when elections were held again on the eve of the world's biggest sporting event.

If Warner didn't move now, Blazer explained, the presidency would be out of reach for years, if not forever. Blazer offered to work, for free, as campaign manager, but victory would depend on Warner's ability to whip his colleagues in the Caribbean into line. Once they won, Blazer added, he would be more than glad to handle the daily operations of the confederation as general secretary, leaving Warner free to maintain unity among the membership.

Blazer had been out of work since the previous May, when he'd been fired as president of the Miami Sharks. He had a pile of unpaid bills waiting for him in Scarsdale, including multiple mortgages and car notes, not to mention a pending lawsuit from a neighbor he'd stiffed on a personal loan, and had discovered there were extremely few paying jobs of any sort in American soccer. This admittedly wild idea felt like the last best hope.

"If you are to be the president of CONCACAF," Blazer implored, "you would have to make yourself available for the next elections in a few months time or wait until 1998, which is far too long."

Warner, born in January 1943 to a poor family in Trinidad's southeast, was the third child of an alcoholic and frequently absent father and a stern, devoutly Catholic mother, who scraped together a living cleaning houses. His childhood home had no running water, like many in the rural area where virtually every family, including his own, was black.

An above-average student and passionate, but poor soccer player, he'd gone on to get a teaching degree while also channeling his love of the sport into climbing the administrative ladder of Trinidad's chaotic amateur leagues. For most of his life, his only salaried "job" was as a secondary school teacher in Port of Spain, and as he slowly lifted himself into the ranks of the nation's middle classes, he managed to gain and hold power in soccer as well.

Warner was elected secretary of Trinidad and Tobago's soccer association in 1974, but his big break came on December 8, 1982, when soldiers came to the house of André Kamperveen in Paramaribo, the capital of Suriname, shot his dogs, smashed his phones, and dragged the fifty-eight-year-old away.

Kamperveen, a former professional soccer player and successful businessman, had publicly criticized the tiny South American nation's government, a repressive dictatorship. That night he was savagely beaten and then shot to death, along with fourteen other dissidents.

Kamperveen had also been president of the Caribbean Football Union, an organization he had helped found five years earlier, which automatically entitled him to a seat on FIFA's ExCo. In the wake of his death, Warner, who had been the CFU's second-ranking official, took both vacant positions, instantly becoming one of the most powerful men in soccer.

The Caribbean was by no means a hotbed for soccer talent. Only one team from the region had ever qualified for the World Cup and interest in the sport in most of the countries was so tepid as to be virtually nonexistent. Many national associations were penniless and their officials rarely traveled abroad, serving as little more than organizers of occasional amateur competitions. Some association presidents seemed completely oblivious to what CONCACAF or FIFA even did.

But FIFA and its six regional confederations operated as a simple democracy, allocating one vote to each country, regardless of size or soccer prowess. Thus tiny Curaçao had the same voting power in CONCACAF as the United States. British territory Bermuda, with a national team that has never ranked higher than 58th worldwide, had exactly the same vote as Brazil, hundreds of times larger and winner of multiple World Cups.

The CFU had been formed in 1978 as a way to give Caribbean nations a seat at the table in a confederation long dominated by Mexican and Central American interests. But what Blazer recognized in the Union was an unbeatable voting bloc that could dictate the direction of CONCACAF as a whole and, by extension, be a formidable force in FIFA as well.

By the time he arrived at Warner's door in 1989, the CFU had eighteen members, compared to just nine for all of North and Central America. If Warner could bring the entire Caribbean into line, Blazer explained, then there would be no obstacle to attaining and holding power for decades to come.

On April 6, 1990, Warner was elected president of CONCACAF, just as Blazer had predicted. He promptly made his American friend the confederation's general secretary.

———

In the more than forty years since Warner had first become a soccer official, helping run Trinidad's Central Football Association when he was still a schoolboy, he had been subject to a string of accusations of financial mismanagement, self-dealing, bribery, vote-selling, and, especially, ticket-scalping.

When Trinidad hosted the U.S. for that momentous November 19, 1989, World Cup qualifier, for example, Trinidad's soccer association had somehow managed to print twenty thousand more tickets for the match than there were seats in Port of Spain's National Stadium.

The facility was designed to hold only 25,000 people, but almost 40,000 crammed in nonetheless, leaving thousands of bewildered ticketholders stuck outside. Furious, the fans swarmed the team buses for both countries, and the subsequent outcry prompted a federal inquiry.

Warner, the soccer association's secretary since 1974, initially said only 28,500 tickets had been sold. He claimed that the remaining stubs, which had been painstakingly counted by investigators, were counterfeit and refused to issue refunds to people denied entry.

But several months later, Warner admitted that the total number of tickets had in fact been 43,000. He denied profiting and was never held to account, but the ticket sale money was never accounted for and no refunds were issued.

In 2006, Trinidad finally qualified for its first World Cup, triggering a large allocation of tickets by FIFA to Trinidad. Under FIFA rules, its officials could not resell tickets for more than face value, but late that year two secret investigations by auditors Ernst & Young were leaked, showing that Warner had made more than $900,000 from scalping the World Cup passes.

The scheme involved a company that was owned by Warner and had exclusive rights to sell Trinidad's block of tickets, which it did, along with travel packages, to brokers in a variety of countries—at huge mark-ups. After rumors of the scheme reached Zurich, Warner told FIFA he had severed connections with the company when in fact he had simply transferred control to his elder son, Daryan.

Faced with significant evidence of misdeeds by one of its most powerful officials, FIFA expressed "disapproval" of Warner's conduct, but said it would not discipline him and closed the case.

"It cannot be proven that Jack Warner knew about the resale of tickets at higher prices," said the head of FIFA's Disciplinary Committee at the time. FIFA couldn't punish Daryan Warner, either, because he had no official position in soccer and thus was out if its jurisdiction. It did ask the company to repay $1 million, which would be sent to charity, but only $250,000 of that was ever sent to Zurich.

It was hardly just tickets. All the way back to his days at the Trinidad & Tobago Football Association, Warner had figured out that the nation's Ministry of Sport would cover two-thirds of the costs of staging international competitions or hosting sports congresses, and such things were notoriously hard to audit.

At the first ever Caribbean Football Union meeting back in 1978, Warner proposed a pan-Caribbean tournament, and offered to host. Prior to then, Trinidad had rarely held any sort of international soccer event, but by 2009 Trinidad had hosted the regional championship nine times, and had also been the site of three Caribbean youth cups, three CONCACAF under-seventeen youth championships, and five CONCACAF under-twenty championships. No other country in CONCACAF—including huge and wealthy countries like the United States or Mexico—came anywhere near that record of hospitality.

Each was an opportunity to rake in cash. Warner's CFU staff learned to routinely double or even triple the actual costs of events when submitting budgets, and Warner's travel agency handled all the travel arrangements.

Warner was always working an angle. Blazer knew he kept secret bank accounts in Trinidad and elsewhere in the Caribbean, some of them in the name of the CFU but separate from the actual CFU accounts and administered only by him. Everything revolved around Warner's unquenchable thirst for money. He had even been accused of pocketing hundreds of thousands of dollars meant to rebuild Haiti after its devastating earthquake, and he still owed Blazer a quarter of the long-overdue South Africa World Cup bribe money.

For years, Warner and Blazer had been inseparable. In their early days at CONCACAF, Warner would sleep in the guest room at Blazer's house in Scarsdale when in town. When he moved to a big apartment high in Trump Tower, Warner would stay with there, too. Blazer often called Warner his "best friend."

But over time, their relationship soured. When Warner came to New York, he'd stay in a hotel, and Blazer didn't even bother inviting him out to dinner. Instead, he would head to Elaine's for a lively evening on the Upper East Side, while Warner would opt for a quiet meal at Sevilla, a Spanish restaurant he loved in the West Village.

Their relationship had become almost purely transactional, with each man focused on his own side projects. That chilly distance increased when Warner was elected to Trinidad's parliament in 2007. Money, unsurprisingly, was at the root of most of their escalating conflicts.

———

The April 1 email seemed of a piece with Warner's increasingly erratic behavior. From where Blazer sat, the whole Bin Hammam affair reeked of lucre. The Qatari could have arranged to meet the CONCACAF membership anywhere, and indeed they were already all going to be in Miami during the first two days of May. But Warner kept insisting on a special conference in Trinidad, which was a logistical nightmare to get to. It wasn't hard for Blazer to guess why: Warner had surely figured out some way to make a bundle of cash by handling the travel arrangements, which he insisted be paid for by Bin Hammam.

Blazer rarely appeared in CONCACAF's seventeenth-floor offices before the stock market closed at four, instead spending his days in his upstairs apartment in shorts and a T-shirt. Most Fridays, he didn't bother coming down at all.

On this particular Friday, he beat his employees to work, though most had no idea he was even there until they heard him yelling on his phone from behind his closed office door. Since receiving Warner's email that morning, he'd spent hours desperately trying to talk some sense into the man. His clumsy plot to abet a rival to Sepp Blatter, the king of all soccer, seemed beyond reckless. It seemed like mutiny and career suicide.

But Warner was a stubborn man, and the more his general secretary pushed, the more he dug in. Blazer proposed that Bin Hammam come to Miami and make a presentation to the membership either before or after the formal congress, but Warner demurred. He now claimed Bin Hammam had been denied a U.S. visa and couldn't enter the country.

That seemed patently ridiculous. Bin Hammam was a wealthy construction magnate with his own private jet and a clean record. America might make it hard for impoverished Mexicans to cross the border, but who ever heard of a billionaire being denied entry into the United States?

Two days later, Warner wrote Blazer again.

"It will not be feasible to have Bin Hammam make his presentation at the Congress for all kinds of reasons, some articulated and some not," he wrote. "If it is that your staff will not be able to assist due to the various events and meetings, then I will have no problem with using the CFU Secretariat and local support staff to facilitate or even finding another date in May."

Blazer responded an hour later. The delegates for North and Central America wanted to support Blatter, he explained, and calling a special congress just for Bin Hammam's sake at such short notice was a bad idea.

"There is also an ethical issue of his paying for a meeting and bringing in delegates," Blazer added.

At 3:16 Monday morning, Warner wrote back.

"Chuck, Bin Hammam does not wish to speak to our members at our May 3 Congress and, in some ways, neither do I wish for him to do so," his email read. "I will let him talk to the members of the Caribbean Football Union instead and invite such other members who are willing to attend to do so. This is really my final advice on this matter."

Warner, hard to control when he was merely a soccer administrator, had become nearly impossible now that he was a lofty government minister, sending these imperious diktats as if everyone was his servant.

If Warner was going to try to burn all they'd achieved to the ground just to make a buck off Mohamed bin Hammam, Blazer would be damned if he'd throw any kindling on the fire.

SEVEN

PORT OF SPAIN

ANGENIE KANHAI SETTLED INTO A CHAIR IN THE BALL-
room of the Hyatt Regency in Port of Spain on the morning of May 10,
2011, and took a long, slow breath. After several exhausting weeks, the
frenzied work of organizing the CFU conference was finally finished.

A neatly dressed, slim twenty-nine-year-old Trinidadian, with long,
meticulously straightened hair and fashionable glasses, Kanhai surveyed
the room.

As general secretary of the Caribbean Football Union, it was her
business to know almost everyone in attendance, and she recognized the
faces of soccer dignitaries who had been flown to Trinidad, all expenses
paid, from Aruba, Puerto Rico, St. Thomas, and nearly two dozen other
tropical islands. The seating charts were finalized. The simultaneous
French and Spanish translators were in the room and ready. The hotel's
kitchen staff was busily preparing lunch. Everything appeared in place.

On the low stage at the front of the room, the day's guest of honor,
Mohamed bin Hammam, was attempting to give a speech that few
seemed to be listening to. Slight and reserved, with light curly black hair
and a neatly trimmed beard, he spoke in heavily accented English, promising "more say, more support, and more pay" if elected FIFA president.
As he droned on, Kanhai's boss, Jack Warner, sitting two seats away,
passed her a note.

"Remind me about the gifts," it read.

Kanhai furrowed her brow, quickly scribbling a reply.

"Gifts?"

Despite being responsible for signing off on every detail of the event,
Kanhai had heard nothing about gifts. She tried to push down a sudden

wave of anxiety, worried she had somehow forgotten some critical element and would face Warner's wrath.

Kanhai had started working for Warner three and a half years earlier, after answering a help-wanted ad for an administrative position at the CFU. She had imagined herself faxing, filing, and photocopying, but instead found herself jetting around organizing soccer tournaments and putting together meetings like this one, just a week after the CONCACAF congress in Miami.

As Bin Hammam spoke, she and Warner passed a flurry of notes, establishing that she should pick up what her boss called "token gifts" after lunch, and that they should be distributed that afternoon in the impromptu office set up in the hotel's executive boardroom.

After the speeches ended, Kanhai chatted with some of the delegates for a few minutes and then departed.

She made the short drive to the Ministry of Works & Transport, just a few blocks away, parking in the building's underground garage. Upstairs, she met Warner's personal assistant, who led her into the minister's office and handed her a locked suitcase from behind the desk, noting that the key was in the outside pocket.

With the temperature creeping past 90 degrees on a typically hot and sticky May afternoon, Kanhai rushed back to the Hyatt, eager to finish up so she would have time to go home, shower, and change before returning to the hotel for dinner.

A few minutes before three, Kanhai hustled through the Hyatt's sliding front doors, heels clicking on the polished floor as she swept past the illuminated fountain bubbling in the main lobby and up the escalator.

Kanhai took the suitcase to the makeshift office, where two of her CFU co-workers, Debbie Minguell and Jason Sylvester, were waiting. Together, the three fished out the key and unlocked the suitcase, which was filled with two dozen manila envelopes, one for each delegation. They pulled out one envelope: it was unmarked, sealed, and tightly packed with what appeared to Kanhai like a rectangular box. Satisfied, she went home.

On the drive, Kanhai scarcely gave the envelopes a second thought; she figured they were stuffed with more of the same kind of tacky souvenirs handed out at any one of the innumerable conferences international soccer officials seemed to love—perhaps a pen, commemorative coin, or lapel pin. If anything, Kanhai was more intrigued by the bag itself, which, with its flamboyant orange piping, wasn't the kind of luggage Warner ordinarily used.

The matter soon slipped out of her mind, and Kanhai thought little more of it until the next morning at the Hyatt's breakfast buffet, when Minguell raced up to her, eyes wide.

"Angenie," she gasped. "It was cash!"

———

Chuck Blazer's cell phone rang soon after 4:30 that same afternoon.

He'd remained in Miami after the CONCACAF congress concluded, enjoying his South Beach apartment, which he'd only had use of for about a year, and spending a little time with a few friends in town.

The unexpected call came from Anton Sealey, president of the Bahamas Football Association, who was in Zurich for a FIFA event and had been unable to attend the CFU gathering. Sealey wanted to know: Did the CFU have enough money to be handing out cash gifts of $40,000 to each soccer federation?

What?

Sealey explained that his vice president, Fred Lunn, was in Port of Spain for the CFU meeting and he reached out just over an hour earlier with news that two of Jack Warner's employees had given him an envelope marked "Bahamas" containing 400 crisp, new, one-hundred-dollar bills, divided into four neat stacks.

The staffers told Lunn it was a gift from the CFU, and that he was free to count the money right then and there. Lunn, incredulous, asked how he was supposed to get that much cash through U.S. customs on his connecting flight back home.

"You could mail it," Minguell had suggested.

"Are you kidding?" replied Lunn, in shock.

It was no joke, Minguell had said. The money was a gift and Lunn shouldn't tell anyone about it, or let anybody see the money.

Lunn hurried back to his hotel room and texted Sealey, "Pls call URGENT." Something smelled very wrong, and Sealey and Lunn agreed that the money couldn't be kept. Before returning it, Lunn took a photo of the cash, neatly laid out beside the manila envelope, and when he returned to the boardroom, he noticed a number of other Caribbean soccer officials nearby, some with manila envelopes in their hands and smiles on their faces.

"A lot of the boys taking the cash," Lunn texted Sealey. "I'm truly surprised it's happening at this conference."

Blazer had seen the CFU's financial statements, and knew that it didn't have enough money on hand to pay for a hastily planned meeting, let alone what must have been somewhere around $1 million in cash handouts. CONCACAF was constantly covering the cost of things that the CFU could not, down to paying referees at Caribbean tournaments.

So where was all this money coming from? The dots weren't hard to connect.

With the FIFA presidential election only three weeks away, Bin Hammam was scratching for every vote he could muster. The whole purpose of the Trinidad meeting was to put the Qatari before the CFU voters and now, just hours after he met them, stacks of cash were being tossed around.

There was no polite word for it. These were bribes.

Floored, Blazer thanked Sealey for letting him know, hung up, and fired off an email to Warner demanding an explanation.

———

Soon after Blatter was first elected in 1998, he created several new programs that helped him win loyalty from soccer federations through financial patronage in the name of soccer development.

One, the Financial Assistance Program, was created in 1999 "to motivate and empower the associations and confederations" and "strengthen football and its administration in the long term." In practice, that meant $250,000 wired from Zurich to every single FIFA member federation each and every year.

For big federations, that was a trivial amount of money; but for small ones, often operated with almost no oversight in countries with little public interest in the sport, it was by far the largest source of revenue. How much of that money actually went to soccer programs, rather than to lining the pockets of the men lucky enough to be elected to office, was anyone's guess.

Another Blatter innovation, the Goal Program, allowed federations to apply for grants to pay for specific projects, such as soccer pitches or training facilities.

Tiny Montserrat, a volcanic atoll in the Caribbean with only 5,200 inhabitants, is the smallest federation in all of FIFA and its national team has never been ranked higher than 165th in the world. Nevertheless, it has received some $1.51 million over the life of the Goal Program, largely to fund construction of a set of bleachers and a bathroom overlooking a soccer pitch. Mexico, with a population of 125 million, has received a total of $1.3 million.

Over the years, Goal Program money has gone to nearly every country in the world, and nearly every time a pitch is laid, or a headquarters is completed, there is invariably a plaque installed nearby noting that it was Sepp Blatter who paid for it: a not so subtle reminder to the federation presidents of Asia, Africa, Oceania, and the Caribbean of who buttered their bread.

The huge financial success of the 2010 World Cup left FIFA with an enormous cash reserve, and Blatter wasn't afraid to deploy some of that to his advantage. Addressing CONCACAF's congress in Miami during the first days of May, Blatter pledged an additional $1 million to distribute to members, calling it a "birthday present" in honor of the confederation's fiftieth anniversary.

———

After a buffet breakfast at the Hyatt on the morning of May 11, the CFU delegates in Port of Spain gathered for what was supposed to be a brainstorming session about the future of soccer in the Caribbean. Instead, the delegates heard a venomous tirade from Warner, who was furious that Blazer had found out about the gifts.

When "Bin Hammam asked to come to the Caribbean, he wanted to bring some silver plaques and wooden trophies and buntings and so on," Warner began in his thick patois. "I told him he need not bring anything; he said yes, he wants to bring something for the countries that will be equivalent to the value of the gift that he would have brought.

"I said to him, 'If you bring cash, I don't want you to give cash to anybody, but what you do, you can give it to the CFU and the CFU will give it to its members,'" Warner continued. "'Because I don't want to even remotely appear that anyone has any obligation to vote for you because of what gifts you have given them.'"

The delegates, in shirts and sport coats, sat in stunned silence as the speech went on. Warner said he'd be happy to take back the money from anyone who didn't want it; that Blatter himself had been aware of the gifts; that he felt Bin Hammam could protect the Caribbean's interests in Zurich; and that it was critical the CFU maintain its control of CONCACAF by voting as a unified bloc.

"I know there are people here who believe they are more pious than thou," Warner fulminated. "If you are pious, go to a church, friends, but the fact is that our business is our business. We come in the room here, we cuss and disagree, and rave and rant, but when we leave here, our business is our business, and that is what solidarity is all about."

––––––

It wasn't until two that afternoon that Warner finally called his increasingly agitated general secretary.

Warner's explanation only made Blazer more incredulous. The cash, he said, had come from Bin Hammam, who originally wanted to give it out personally to all the delegates. Instead, Warner had told the Qatari it should be distributed as a gift from the CFU. That way, Warner figured, he would get the credit, and it wouldn't appear that Bin Hammam was directly buying votes.

Blazer was beside himself.

"In twenty-one years we have never bought a vote," he said. "We have had elections and been in office all that time and never bought a vote. Now you have allowed this to happen here, it completely changes the entire dynamic of the confederation."

This reckless behavior was putting them both at risk. But Warner was defiant. If anyone had a problem, he said, they should contact him directly.

After hanging up, Blazer's mind raced. Sure, he'd seen far bigger payments in his years in soccer, but they were always behind closed doors, veiled in secrecy and neatly covered up with anonymous shell companies using bank accounts in remote countries.

This was a different story. Too many people knew. It couldn't possibly be contained, and if word got back to Blatter before Blazer had a chance to tell him personally, the repercussions could be dire. Desperate, he called his lawyer in Chicago, a former prosecutor named John Collins, for guidance.

"I just can't live with this," Blazer said, adding that he was considering telling FIFA.

Collins had carved out a niche as a soccer lawyer. He'd first worked for the Chicago-based U.S. Soccer Federation starting in the late 1990s, had advised a women's pro soccer league and the American Youth Soccer Organization, and starting in 2002 was outside counsel for CONCACAF.

He took care of a thousand odd jobs for the confederation and had been awarded a seat on FIFA's Legal Committee. Collins paid close attention to the complicated politics of the sport, and had a gimlet-eyed, unsentimental view on the potential ramifications of sitting on something as explosive as this. Collins saw little alternative, and told Blazer as much.

"Sometimes," Collins said, "you gotta do what you gotta do."

Two days later, Blazer called Jérôme Valcke, FIFA's general secretary, with the news about Warner and Bin Hammam. Valcke thanked Blazer and asked him to prepare a formal report on the matter.

After hanging up, Valcke summoned FIFA's top attorney, Marco Villiger, as well as its new head of security, a rangy Australian named Chris Eaton, to his office deep inside FIFA headquarters.

The two men arrived to find Valcke in an unusually cheerful mood. Restraining a smile, the tall Frenchman told the two men what Blazer had said about the bribes in Port of Spain, and how the wealthy Qatari seemed to have been the source of the cash.

Finally, Valcke told them, we can be rid of Bin Hammam.

On May 24, Collins submitted his findings, citing "clear evidence of violations of the FIFA code of ethics," to Valcke.

Working the phone in his Chicago office, he had managed to interview Lunn, Sealey, several officials from the Bermuda and Turks and Caicos soccer associations, and Jeffrey Webb, president of the Cayman Islands Football Association. After hearing three independent accounts, Collins felt satisfied that bribes had been handed out.

FIFA made the matter public the day after receiving his report, mentioning "bribery allegations," that were "linked to the upcoming FIFA presidential election," and announcing Ethics Committee hearings on the matter the following Sunday, May 29, just two days before the presidential election.

By that weekend, the vast community of global soccer dignitaries had descended on Zurich in anticipation of the congress, and the city's hotels, restaurants, and bars overflowed with gossip and speculation about what had happened in Port of Spain.

Then, on the eve of the hearing, Bin Hammam abruptly withdrew from the presidential race. "I cannot allow the game that I loved to be dragged more and more in the mud because of competition between two individuals," he said in a statement. "The game itself and the people who love it around the world must come first."

Early on May 29, FIFA's Ethics Committee met to hear about the events in Trinidad from Warner, Bin Hammam, Debbie Minguell, and Jason Sylvester. It would also hear from Blatter himself, because Warner had filed his own ethics complaint against the FIFA president, alleging he had told him about the plan to distribute cash a month earlier and had met no objection.

Under questioning, Warner admitted that Bin Hammam had covered the costs of the Caribbean meeting. Bank statements later showed that on April 28, Bin Hammam had wired $363,557.98 to Warner's account at Republic Bank in Trinidad, while Bin Hammam himself testified that his staffers had handed CFU staff an additional $50,000 in cash to cover "expenses."

But Warner claimed no money had ever changed hands, submitting statements from thirteen Caribbean soccer officials flatly denying the payments to delegates were made.

"I remain firm and intransigent in my view," the CFU president told the committee during a long and combative session. "I received nothing from Mr. Bin Hammam to give delegates. I know nothing of any money. I never spoke about any cash gifts to collect and I am therefore saying today that I don't even know why I'm here."

For his part, Blatter admitted that Warner, in a meeting on April 10 in Guatemala, had brought up his idea to hold a special CFU meeting, but that he, Blatter, had told him it was a bad idea. "I was asked for advice or an opinion, and I informed Jack Warner that it should not happen," the FIFA president told the panel.

At six in the evening, the Ethics Committee's chairman, flanked by Valcke, took a seat at the front of the spacious auditorium deep inside FIFA's headquarters to inform the press of the day's decision.

Citing the possibility that "possible acts of corruption appear to have been committed," the chairman said Bin Hammam and Warner were provisionally suspended from all soccer activities. Blatter, meanwhile, was cleared of all charges.

"I agree, the timing is the worst, but what's happened, happened," Valcke told the astonished press corps, adding that the presidential elections would continue as planned. "There is no reason for them not taking place."

Blatter had survived once again. Without an opponent standing against him, he was elected three days later by FIFA's congress for a fourth consecutive term, with 186 out of 203 votes in his favor.

———

Before departing for Zurich, Warner had spent all day on the floor of the Red House, Trinidad's century-old Beaux Arts parliament building. Once parliament adjourned, he stepped outside and spoke to local reporters gathered there. He was characteristically ready for a fight, and he spoke for an extended time in his florid, pugilistic language, laying particularly into Blazer and John Collins, who he felt had betrayed him.

"I am in FIFA for 29 consecutive years. I was the first black man to have ever been in FIFA at this level. I have come from the smallest country ever to be on the FIFA Executive Committee," he said. "I am wielding more power in FIFA now than sometimes even the president. I must be the envy of others.

"I have lived three score and almost ten and my Jack hasn't been hanged as yet. Why should it be now? By whom? The American Chuck Blazer? His American lawyer John Collins? Give me a break," Warner, in a froth, continued.

"I tell you something, in the next couple days you will see a football tsunami that will hit FIFA and the world."

EIGHT

A MADE MAN

JARED RANDALL PINNED THE RESTAURANT RECEIPT TO the wall of his cubicle as soon as he got back to the FBI field office. It wasn't every day that a young agent got to eat lunch with someone like Chuck Blazer, and he wanted a memento.

The meeting had fallen into his lap after Blazer had spontaneously reached out to the Bureau to complain about allegations of match fixing during CONCACAF's Gold Cup, which kicked off June 5, 2011, in Dallas. Blazer had been tipped off to the issue a few weeks earlier by Chris Eaton, FIFA's head of security, and he had been deeply troubled by the rumor.

He'd reached out to a friend who worked at the Bureau, and his complaint eventually wound its way to Randall, who eagerly set up a meeting.

The Gold Cup was Blazer's baby—and his golden goose. He'd first proposed the tournament only weeks after signing his first contract as CONCACAF's general secretary, on July 31, 1990.

The eight-page contract—which only he and Warner had copies of—entitled Blazer to a number of fees in lieu of an actual salary, including 10 percent of "all sponsorships and TV rights fees from all sources received by CONCACAF." It was a salesman's idea of an employment agreement, one based on commissions, which made sense since Blazer was at heart a salesman. Television and sponsorships were the biggest ticket items in soccer, and for every $100 worth of CONCACAF rights Blazer managed to sell, he'd take home $10.

Since its first edition, held in Los Angeles in the summer of 1991, the Gold Cup had grown to become CONCACAF's cash cow, driven primarily by massive commercial interest in the U.S. and Mexican national teams. By 2009, the Gold Cup had driven CONCACAF's revenue to a record $35 million. Blazer's commissions on marketing and television sales that year reached $2.3 million, his largest take ever.

The idea, then, that some bookies—*common criminals, for God's sake*—could undermine all that by paying off a few lousy referees was incredibly unnerving.

Blazer had suggested meeting at a Midtown restaurant, and Randall was more than happy to accommodate him. It was, after all, a chance to meet a member of FIFA's Executive Committee in the flesh on what seemed like a perfect pretext, allowing the young agent to size the man up without letting him know what he was working on.

Blazer was what Randall's boss, Mike Gaeta, liked to call "a made man," fully initiated into the FIFA family. But he wasn't some piddling soldier, following orders and keeping his head down; no, Blazer was clearly a *caporegime*, one of the top men in the organization. He'd been in the soccer game for years, decades even, and surely knew where a lot of bodies were buried.

Not only that, but unlike every other FIFA capo, Blazer was American. He wasn't living in some far-off corner of the world, far from reach. He was right up the street, just a subway ride away from the FBI offices in lower Manhattan. And he spoke English.

Until he had been assigned to the case, international soccer, for Randall, was all about the superstars on the field. Eye-popping scoring machines like Leo Messi, impenetrable goalies like Gianluigi Buffon, rugged, relentless fullbacks—Randall's own position—like Philipp Lahm, brilliant managers like Alex Ferguson, and powerhouse clubs like Real Madrid.

Randall had thought he knew a lot about the sport, but a simple Internet search of soccer corruption brought up a mind-boggling universe of strange and unfamiliar names, places, and events stretching back for decades and spanning the planet.

There were entire blogs dedicated to the topic, not to mention innumerable books and documentaries. And that was just in English. Searches of particular names often brought up articles in French, German, Spanish, and who knows what other languages. There were stories of vote rigging, ticket scalping, match fixing, and player transfer scams, each with its own array of obscure soccer officials at the center of the schemes.

It was overwhelming. The FBI had no history investigating international soccer corruption. There were no old cases to build off, or grizzled agents who had worked the soccer beat for years to teach Randall the ropes.

He had started by trying to put together a link chart, a kind of diagram of the hierarchy of a criminal organization that was often used in big complex cases with lots of potential targets, with neat little lines drawn between each person. The charts were helpful in mob cases. The godfather was placed at the top, the lieutenants below him, and the lowly soldiers down at the bottom. The idea was to create a who's who of the soccer world, laying out how one person involved in FIFA was linked to another, and that one to a third, and so on.

Randall put Blatter at the top; that much was easy. Filling in the rest was tougher. There were so many names and their various roles seemed unclear: Was a FIFA vice president more or less powerful than its general secretary? What about confederation presidents? One thing that was clear, though, was that Chuck Blazer deserved a place near the top.

If Randall could get him talking, he could explain how the whole thing worked. That was how big cases were done. You flip one guy and he helps you gather evidence to flip another and that one helps you get two more and it's off to the grand jury. An investigation might have a half-dozen or more cooperators at any one time as it built toward an indictment. The goal was to get as high up the pyramid as possible, and when it comes to big, complex organizations like FIFA, insiders were the best way to get to the top in a hurry.

Blazer had been interesting to both Randall and Gaeta for some time, but in the weeks since the suspicious events of Port of Spain had become public, he'd become something of a celebrity. Photos of Blazer's big, furry face were constantly on CNN, and he was quoted in newspapers around the world.

One story, a glowing profile by the Associated Press that got picked up in dailies around the country, painted him as an idealistic whistle-blower out to clean up the sport, a "witty, gregarious" man who is a "tireless advocate" for soccer.

Randall suspected otherwise, but unlike the wiseguys the FBI agents were accustomed to chasing, Blazer was no hardened criminal. His record was spotless; he didn't have any priors, not so much as a speeding ticket.

Over lunch Randall had quietly listened as the bearded New Yorker talked at length about the Gold Cup and the menace of rigged games. He was a surprisingly compelling, engaging person to listen to, and Randall, who was by nature quiet to the point of being taciturn, liked to listen.

Match fixing, it turned out, was a fascinating topic.

International syndicates of gamblers conspired to pay off athletes and referees to change the outcome of games so that bets made in advance could be counted on to come in favorably. Since it was next to impossible to bribe someone to score a goal or make a brilliant save, match fixers generally arranged for teams to lose, or at least underperform. For superstars like Messi or Ronaldo, stratospheric salaries and an unblinking press made them unlikely targets for such impropriety.

Underpaid players on second-rate teams, as well as low-rent referees, were the way to go, especially since a bettor could make as much money on the outcome of an obscure match as a World Cup final. All that was required was enough interest for bookies to take action. And teams didn't even have to lose for a match to be fixed; sometimes gamblers would simply bet on the score at halftime, for example, or on which team would give up a goal first.

In a big confederation like CONCACAF, there were plenty of weaker teams with rosters full of players who might be willing to make some cash on the side. Nobody expected a team like Nicaragua, which had never qualified for the World Cup, to win too many matches. Those national teams were often run by easily corrupted administrators as well, giving rise to concerns that nobody was even watching to ensure clean play.

Particularly interesting were the connections between the match rigging and organized crime. Guys in Randall's own squad were still neck-deep in the illegal gambling investigation, involving the Russian gangster Taiwanchik. Randall had personally spent many long hours helping out that case in the field office's wire room, listening on a series of telephone wiretaps for evidence of criminal activity. In what seemed like a strange coincidence, several suspects in that case happened to live in Trump Tower, just like Blazer.

It was true that match fixing didn't seem to have much to do with the World Cup vote buying and high-level administrative skulduggery that had gotten Gaeta interested in opening a soccer case, but it certainly seemed to have some potential for crossover, especially since it involved shadowy Russians. It looked to Randall like yet another example of the way that global soccer was profoundly dirty.

The topic was, in fact, interesting enough to prompt Randall to reach out to FIFA's head of security, Chris Eaton, directly and request the first of a series of meetings on the topic. But that angle went nowhere and, in any case, it didn't get the special agent any closer to reeling in the investigation's first cooperating witness.

It was frustrating. People didn't generally cooperate willingly with an investigation. They had to be encouraged, sometimes strongly encouraged, and the best way to do that was by digging up some incriminating piece of information against the person and giving him a choice: either help or go straight to jail. But Randall didn't have a thing on Blazer.

The lunch had been memorable, but ultimately unproductive. After nearly a year, the soccer case had barely moved. If only Randall could find some kind of hook.

———

Soon after temporarily suspending Warner and Bin Hammam, FIFA opened a full investigation into the events of Port of Spain. It hired an outside firm headed by former FBI director Louis Freeh to conduct the probe, and as its investigators dug into the case, it became increasingly apparent that they were turning up substantial evidence to support the bribery allegations.

Although some Caribbean delegates remained loyal to Warner and refused to cooperate with the probe, others, perhaps fearing rebuke from FIFA, began to talk. In a series of interviews in Zurich and the Bahamas, officials from seven different Caribbean nations admitted that they had entered the boardroom at the Hyatt and been offered an envelope full of cash, and some provided photographs and other evidence of the payments.

Warner, back in Port of Spain, had been quietly negotiating another huge payment from Bin Hammam. Warner had contacted him not long after his initial suspension and the two, using intermediaries, agreed upon a roughly $1.2 million payment, to be wired to three different accounts in Trinidad: one held by his personal assistant, one by his son Daryll, and a third account controlled by his other son, Daryan.

Although Bin Hammam wired the money, in installments of $412,000, $368,000, and $432,000, the payments were held up by compliance officers at the Trinidadian banks, who demanded an explanation for the motives behind the payments. It proved a thorny problem, as the stories concocted by Warner—something about unspecified work conducted between 2005 and 2010—failed to convince the banks the wires were for legitimate services. There was simply no proof of any such work having been done.

Even as he quietly struggled behind the scenes to convince the banks to let Bin Hammam's money through, Warner made one of the biggest decisions of his life.

In a letter sent to FIFA dated June 17, 2011, Warner resigned from all positions in international soccer. Three days later, FIFA made the news public with a brief statement noting that it had accepted Warner's offer of resignation and thanking the Trinidadian for his service to the game.

"As a consequence of Mr. Warner's self-determined resignation, all Ethics Committee procedures against him have been closed," FIFA wrote in the statement. "The presumption of innocence is maintained."

In his resignation letter, Warner had reaffirmed what he called his "offer of cooperation with the FIFA Ethics Committee" in its ongoing probe of Bin Hammam. But Freeh's investigators found that proved very far from the truth. The only stick FIFA had to compel cooperation from its officials was the threat of sanction; with Warner not only out of soccer but completely exonerated, the organization's investigation couldn't touch him.

Warner said as much in public, telling a reporter he would "die first" before helping with an investigation that was initiated by Chuck Blazer, his oldest and closest partner, who in the space of a few weeks had become his greatest nemesis.

"I'm not going to back a complaint made by an American and

investigated by Americans and an attempt to put it on American soil," Warner defiantly added. A few days later, he wrote an email to Freeh's lead investigator on the case stating that he would not help the probe, and adding that he had proof that there was a "trans-Atlantic cabal" within FIFA bent on destroying him.

————

Following Warner's resignation from CONCACAF, Lisle Austin, a Barbadian who had been on the confederation's Executive Committee since the late 1970s, was the most senior vice president and, by statute, next in line for the presidency. But when he tried to assume the post, he met resistance, particularly from Blazer, who instead arranged to name another CONCACAF vice president, Honduran Alfredo Hawit, to the position. Austin responded by attempting to fire Blazer, but the general secretary refused to go.

Austin quickly hired American lawyers, who in turn retained a corporate investigations firm called FTI Consulting to conduct a forensic review of the confederation's finances. But after FTI employees were repeatedly denied entry to Trump Tower and CONCACAF's Miami offices, the lead on the case, a Miami-based investigator named Simon Strong, was handed a different assignment: dig up dirt on Chuck Blazer.

So Strong, a tall, slender Englishman with blue eyes and a cool, unassuming manner that made some people think he might be a spy, began what people in his line of work called "developing information," which translated to calling around, working contacts, and asking favors. He spoke to Jack Warner, asked Lisle Austin for contacts, and flew around the Caribbean to meet with current and former CFU officials and employees, some of whom had left the organization as soon as Warner was suspended.

Although Austin hadn't been at the infamous meeting in Port of Spain, most CFU officials had, and many quite happily pocketed the $40,000. From where they stood, FIFA's ruling wasn't just an attack on Jack Warner, who had led and empowered them for so many years; it also felt like a direct and very personal threat to their own lifestyles. Blazer's subsequent attempt to override CONCACAF bylaws and prevent Austin from becoming interim president only underscored those feelings. To them, it felt like a coup d'état. It was perhaps no surprise then that Strong was able in relatively short order to root out a considerable trove of documents shining a light on Blazer.

The meaning of some of the documents had been explained to Strong by the sources who had handed them over, while others had less obvious connotations, but collectively they painted the picture of a man who had been taking in great sums of money that nobody knew anything about. Strong had the distinct feeling there was a lot more to be had as well.

In the weeks since Warner's ouster, Blazer had worked hard to portray himself as a pillar of rectitude and transparency, telling one journalist "we don't tolerate the type of behavior that was manifested by senior members" of the confederation.

But in fact, nobody had anything close to a clear picture of what Blazer, who served as CONCACAF's treasurer as well as its general secretary, was up to. For one thing, he never showed the confederation's books to anyone, guarding them more closely than a private diary. There was no sense, no matter how vague, of how well he had had been managing CONCACAF for all these years, and nobody seemed to have the foggiest notion of how much money he was making.

Indeed, the topic of his income had only been so much as mentioned within the organization three times over the previous twenty years. The last time it was brought up was in 2002, when Blazer brushed off a query about nearly $1.2 million in "commissions" that were being booked as a marketing expense. The question had been asked by a delegate before the entire CONCACAF congress and Blazer had been forced to acknowledge that the payments were in fact part of his compensation, but his public comments somehow failed to appear in the official minutes of the meeting and were soon forgotten.

What Strong had dug up, however, suggested that Blazer had been raking in millions of dollars, over many years, and most of it had never been declared. That much was clear from his original 1990 contract, with its clause entitling Blazer to 10 percent commissions on all "sponsorship and TV rights fees," which amounted to nearly all of CONCACAF's revenue.

But that was hardly everything. Among the documents Strong had procured was a letter Jack Warner sent to Republic Bank in Trinidad on

March 31, just a few months earlier, instructing it to draft a check for $250,000 to Blazer. Strong also had a copy of the canceled check for that amount, which had been deposited in a bank account in the Bahamas on May 3, immediately following the CONCACAF congress in Miami.

That quarter-of-a-million-dollar payment clearly wasn't sponsorship or television rights fees. It also wasn't at all clear why Blazer had accounts in tax havens like the Bahamas, and why he used shell companies, rather than his own name, on the vast majority of his financial documents.

The 10 percent contract was between CONCACAF and some entity called Sportvertising, and other documents in Strong's possession showed that the company, originally incorporated in New York State, had since been registered in the Cayman Islands, where companies are not subject to corporate tax, and ownership disclosures are extremely minimal.

At the very least, Strong thought, the documents suggested an aggressive tax avoidance strategy, though it was far from clear where all the money was coming from.

Before moving to Miami, Strong had been a reporter, working for newspapers on London's Fleet Street and then in Australia. Eventually he moved to South America, where he was a foreign correspondent for a few British dailies. He wrote a book on communist guerrillas in Peru, and a few years later a second book that was one of the first serious examinations of the career of Colombian drug lord Pablo Escobar. The book focused especially on money laundering, and Strong was familiar with the many ways crooks use offshore accounts to clean up dirty cash.

Although he had given up journalism, Strong maintained extensive contacts with journalists throughout Latin America and the U.K. He was also a soccer fan, having grown up supporting Burnley Football Club.

Like the millions of other people around the planet who followed the sport, he felt a sense of outrage when he thought about the way the people's game had been exploited by unscrupulous officials who milked it for every penny they could. Chuck Blazer, it was plain to see, was one of those officials, and fans ought to be able to read about what he had been up to in black-and-white.

Strong could think of at least one British journalist who felt the same way.

————

The first of Andrew Jennings's articles about Chuck Blazer's finances was buried on page 13 of the July 17, 2011, edition of the *Sunday Herald*, a Scottish daily with a circulation around 25,000. At the same time, Jennings posted the article on his own website, "Transparency in Sport," adding links to some of the documents and the cheeky headline "Lucky Chuckie! Blazer takes secret 10% on sponsor deals."

The story, barely five hundred words long, was classic Jennings, jammed full with explosive facts and liberally salted with arch comments and sarcasm. It contained the first public mention of Sportvertising, and Blazer's unusual contract with CONCACAF, which allowed him to be "paid millions in 'commissions.' " It also described Warner's $250,000 request for a check to be sent to Blazer the previous March, but offered no theories about what the payment could have been for.

Two days prior to publication, Blazer responded to a series of emailed questions from Jennings, acknowledging the 10 percent commission, but arguing that the payments were "consistent with industry standards." As for the $250,000 check, Blazer explained, it was "repayment of a personal loan advanced by me to Jack Warner over 5 years ago."

Hours after publication, Blazer wrote Jennings again, taking issue with the reporter's descriptions of his physical size, which he said was irrelevant to his job, as well his characterization of the commissions as "secret."

"Find another villain," Blazer angrily wrote. "I am not your guy."

Part of Jennings's revelation was mentioned in a *New York Times* story on the exorbitant lifestyles of FIFA officials, but otherwise it landed with little notice. The sporting press seemed more interested in the continued fallout from Port of Spain. FIFA's investigation into the event had been completed in early July, and a series of leaks out of Zurich about the findings dominated the headlines.

On July 23, 2011, FIFA banned Bin Hammam from soccer for life, while Jason Sylvester and Debbie Minguell, who had handed out the cash in the Hyatt Regency boardroom, were given year-long bans from the sport. Bin Hammam had honored his deal with Warner, finally finding a small bank in Trinidad that would accept the rationale that his transfer of $1.2 million was for "professional services provided over the period 2005–2010," and Warner, in turn, had dutifully kept his mouth closed.

Then on August 9, the FIFA Ethics Committee turned to Lisle Austin, banning him from the sport for a year because he had filed suit to resolve his ongoing dispute with CONCACAF. Officials in Zurich had been aghast at his move, which threatened FIFA's deep-seated belief that it was a higher power above any meddling from sovereign nations.

That same day, Jennings wrote Blazer again, telling him that "more information has come to hand" and laying out twenty detailed questions about his financial affairs, assets, and compensation. The reporter's sources in Miami and the Caribbean had sent him another pile of documents. He demanded to learn the story behind a $205,000 check from late the previous summer, as well as wire instructions for a $57,500 payment to Sportvertising from 1996. He also asked whether it was true that Blazer's son, an athletic trainer, received a $7,000 a month salary from CONCACAF, and if Blazer was the owner of several luxury condominiums in the Bahamas.

Although in prior communications Jennings had been silent on the issue, this time he inquired—repeatedly—about Blazer's tax situation.

"Are you confident," Jennings wondered, "that all offshore payments and benefits to you have been reported to the IRS?"

Throughout his lengthy career, Jennings had rarely held down a staff job at any publication. He wrote in bursts, was known to be prickly when it came to editing, and his monomaniacal focus on a single topic for years at a time seemed best suited to the freelance life. Although he was held up as an icon by some journalists, he had suffered more than a few falling-outs with others. He was, in other words, always on the lookout for a steady paycheck. This time around, the article found a home in the Sunday edition of *The Independent*, published in London.

Before it went to press, Jennings called Jared Randall at the FBI to let him know that he had in his possession what he believed were important papers. The two talked frequently, and Randall said he'd be happy to take a look. Jennings emailed over his whole cache. There was no way for him to know what the FBI thought of the documents, but Jennings used the mere fact that Randall had received them as evidence that the agency was in fact looking into their contents.

"FBI Investigates Secret Payments to FIFA Whistleblower," read the headline, on page 10 of *The Independent*'s August 13 edition.

"The man credited with blowing the whistle on bribery and corruption in Fifa, the body that runs world football, is now himself the subject of an FBI inquiry," the article began. "US investigators are examining documents appearing to show confidential payments to offshore accounts operated by an American Fifa official, Chuck Blazer."

Once again, Jennings posted the story to his website, adding photos of Blazer, his son, his girlfriend, and links to several of the underlying documents. This time, however, the online story ran more than twice as long as the version in *The Independent*, and included multiple denials of impropriety by Blazer, who claimed the transactions "were not income items nor subject to tax."

Three days later, August 16, 2011, the story was picked up by a reporter at the newswire Reuters, which places stories in thousands of newspapers and websites around the world every day. The journalist, a seasoned investigative hand in Reuters's Washington, D.C., office named Mark Hosenball, repeated much of Jennings's story, and added a few additional details.

"A New York–based FBI squad assigned to investigate 'Eurasian organized crime' is examining evidence related to payments made to Chuck Blazer," Hosenball reported, noting that he had personally reviewed all the documents.

The two reporters were old friends, and in an unusual show of generosity in the competitive news business, Hosenball credited both *The Independent* and Jennings, helpfully providing the web address where the British journalist's full article could be found.

Google's news alerts picked up the Reuters story as soon as it was published, dropping it automatically into inboxes around the globe, including one belonging to a particularly avid soccer fan with a keen interest in criminal tax law in faraway Orange County, California.

NINE

RICO

THE STORY OF ELIOT NESS'S PURSUIT OF AL CAPONE, THE most powerful and feared gangster in America during Prohibition, is a classic of the true crime genre. Ness, a dashing young G-man, along with his incorruptible team of "Untouchables," did what nobody else could, fearlessly raiding Capone's bootlegging operation until Scarface was brought to his knees.

This version is, however, largely a fiction.

The true hero behind Capone's fall was a stout, cigar-puffing, near-sighted business school dropout from Buffalo named Frank J. Wilson, who was an agent for the Treasury Department's Intelligence Unit.

Assigned to the Capone case in 1927, Wilson moved from Baltimore to Chicago, and spent most of the next four years holed up on the fourth floor of an old post office building, complaining of "questionable persons hanging around the halls," as he tirelessly reviewed reams of documents. Eventually he unearthed several ledgers showing Capone had unreported income, used handwriting analysis to identify their author, then went undercover in Miami to track that man down and convince him to testify against the mobster in court.

From there, Wilson and his team of special agents methodically built the most famous tax evasion case in history, leading to Capone's conviction in 1931, which sent the gangster to prison for eleven years. Wilson went on to play a key role in solving the Lindbergh kidnapping, and later headed the Secret Service, where he vastly reduced counterfeiting in America. In 1978, the Treasury's Intelligence Unit was rechristened: IRS Criminal Investigation.

Within IRS-CI, as agents called the division, Wilson was a source of institutional pride, embodying the virtues of an agency that never seemed to get the attention or credit that other law enforcement agencies, chiefly the FBI, did. Wilson, the Intelligence Unit's chief once admiringly remarked, "is a genius for details. Wilson fears nothing that walks. He will sit quietly looking at books eighteen hours a day, seven days a week, forever, if he wants to find something in those books."

Steve Berryman joined the IRS when he was twenty-three years old and, other than a few summer jobs in bookstores during high school, had never worked anywhere else.

He believed that IRS agents had unique tools and training at their disposal that nobody else did. Like other federal law enforcement, IRS agents carry a badge and gun, can make arrests, and serve warrants, but their greatest power, Berryman felt, was the ability to digest complicated financial records, converting endless rows of numbers into powerful narratives of lawlessness.

"We do," Berryman was fond of saying to anyone who would listen, "the financial shit nobody else wants to touch."

After more than twenty years on the job, Berryman had become focused almost entirely on complex international cases. In recent years, he'd helped win convictions in cases involving a pair of Hollywood producers who had been paying kickbacks to officials in Thailand so that they could manage an annual film festival in the country, and a Riverside County, California, company whose executives had bribed officials at the U.K. Ministry of Defence to win equipment contracts. More recently, he'd been looking into several Israeli banks that hadn't complied with reporting laws and seemed to be covering up international tax evasion.

The cases were interesting. Berryman got to travel abroad and experiment with different ways to apply little-known aspects of the law. But they were also relatively contained, focusing on one or two defendants, and he ached to try something really big, with many defendants, that would truly put his sleuthing skills to the test.

What he longed for was a very specific type of investigation, one that the IRS wasn't particularly known for working and that he himself had never had a chance to try.

———

It was still morning when Berryman stepped out of his SoHo hotel, but already it was uncomfortably warm, the beginning of one of those sticky days in New York when it feels like summer's oppressive heat will never end.

It was mid-September 2011, and the IRS agent hadn't set foot in New York in sixteen years. His government-issued cell phone didn't have a map function, so he had stopped at a drugstore the previous day to buy a folding laminated map of the city. Feeling stuffy in a suit and tie, Berryman peered down at the map from time to time as he crossed Canal Street, cut through Chinatown, and passed the city's various courthouses to 26 Federal Plaza, where he rode up to the twenty-third floor.

Jared Randall greeted him at the elevator bank, escorting him to briefly meet Mike Gaeta before leading him into a small conference room. Berryman was surprised at how young the FBI agent was, and as he laid out his theory for a soccer case, Randall sat quietly eyeing him.

"You don't know me from Adam," Berryman said, "but I've been doing this kind of thing for a very long time."

"I know who you are," Randall replied.

It was awkward for Berryman, a veteran used to picking and choosing cases as he pleased. He was the guy FBI agents and prosecutors called asking for help on tough cases, yet now he was trying to sell himself to someone who looked like he'd just left the academy.

In the weeks since he'd gotten the Google Alert containing the Reuters article about Blazer, Berryman had gathered enough material to talk for hours. Sepp Blatter, Mohamed bin Hammam, Jack Warner. He could recite the names of most of FIFA's Executive Committee members from memory. Referring to a bullet-point outline he'd typed up, Berryman reeled off names of soccer officials he thought could be targets, of others he'd like to interview as witnesses, and of specific criminal statutes he thought might have been violated. As he talked, he could see a faint smile flicker across the FBI agent's face.

Berryman suspected he was on the right track, and shifted gears, telling Randall about some of the cases he'd done in the past. But just as he got going, Randall interrupted him, leaning back in his chair with a quick laugh.

"Yeah," he said. "You seem like the right guy for this."

Berryman felt a wave of relief. "Great," he replied, then said something he'd carefully rehearsed ahead of time. "Can you please contact your prosecutor and let him know I'd like to meet him?"

"Oh, I already talked to him about you," Randall said, adding that they could head over to Brooklyn after lunch.

————

As far as Berryman could tell, the people who controlled soccer weren't murderers, kidnappers, or drug dealers.

They were sports bureaucrats; aging men in fancy suits tippling champagne in the VIP box at the World Cup. But without a doubt they were all bound together by a single organization, FIFA, which felt to him like the very definition of an "enterprise" as defined by the federal RICO statute.

Under the Racketeer Influenced and Corrupt Organizations Act, large numbers of people can be charged en masse for crimes stretching back years or even decades provided it can be shown they took place as part of a "pattern of racketeering activity," that at least two people were involved in the scheme, and that the most recent crime took place within ten years of the prior crime. Under RICO, one needn't have directly committed the criminal act to be convicted for it, so long as he was part of the same criminal enterprise as the one who did perpetrate it.

RICO prosecution could not only put people behind bars, it could dismantle an entire organization, brick by brick, until there was nothing left. And though the law, enacted in 1970, was originally created to target traditional mafia, it soon expanded into other realms, becoming a favorite tool of prosecutors gunning for white-collar criminals such as the network of junk bond traders led by Michael Milken in the 1980s, as well as Ponzi scheme operators, bribe-paying government contractors, and even corrupt police departments.

Sitting at a conference table in the United States Attorney's Office for the Eastern District of New York, overlooking downtown Brooklyn's Cadman Plaza that September afternoon, Berryman rattled off the same list of potential targets that he'd shared with Randall earlier. Then he worked through eight different criminal statutes he thought could apply to a case involving global soccer. They encompassed a range of potential charges and legal strategies, some fairly novel, but he was particularly excited about one of them, and finally laid it out.

"I've done the research," Berryman said. "And I think FIFA is perfect for RICO."

The two assistant U.S. attorneys sitting across the table from Berryman, Evan Norris and Amanda Hector, were much younger than he was, and they had sat impassively during his presentation, asking few questions. But now Hector, intense and serious, with long chestnut brown hair, frowned and shot Norris a look.

RICO was one of the most powerful cudgels the Department of Justice had at its disposal. It had generated some of the most sensational, headline-grabbing prosecutions on record. But the cases weren't easy. Successful racketeering investigations frequently required massive manpower and coordination across multiple agencies. Even the best lawyers had trouble, at times, wrapping their heads around RICO's bewildering complexity. And explaining to a jury the abstract subtleties of a law that made one man responsible for another's crimes was daunting to say the least. Berryman was clearly taking a leap.

"You're kind of getting ahead of yourself, aren't you?" Hector coolly said to Berryman.

The agent tried to push down a suddenly swelling feeling of panic. The FBI may have been investigating the case, but it was the U.S. Attorney's Office that ran the show. The prosecutors oversaw the case and they could decide to invite Berryman to join in, take his ideas and hand them off to the FBI or a local IRS agent to pursue, or simply ignore them altogether.

Scrambling, Berryman looked down at his typed notes and launched into what he hoped would be the most winning portion of his pitch.

The challenge with a case like this, he said, was that the vast majority of FIFA officials weren't American. But, he said, eyes growing wide, he knew of at least a half-dozen ways to hang fraud, money laundering, and tax charges on foreigners.

The key, he explained, is the fact that whenever there's an international wire transfer between banks, even ones in far-flung countries, the money usually flows through American financial institutions.

Wire transfers can be made only between banks that have a relationship with one another, and since most of the thousands of banks around the world do not have such relationships, they must rely on so-called "correspondent banks" to complete the transfers on their behalf. And because the United States is home to so many of the world's largest banks, which have huge networks with other financial institutions around the world, they often act as middlemen correspondent banks.

If a soccer official in Qatar wanted to wire a several-hundred-thousand-dollar bribe to an official in Trinidad, it's unlikely that their banks transact often enough to make it worth establishing a permanent commercial relationship.

On the other hand, it's quite likely that a huge American bank, such as JPMorgan Chase, regularly does business with both the Qatari's bank and the Trinidadian's bank and thus, for a fee, could process the transfer. If not, it's a near certainty that Chase has a relationship with another huge U.S. bank, like Wells Fargo, that in turn works with the Trinidadian bank. The money in that wire, then, flows from the Qatari official's bank account, through Chase, then on to Wells Fargo, and finally to the bank account of the corrupt official in Trinidad.

It was complicated, Berryman knew, and to help keep the prosecutors' eyes from glazing over, he pulled a blank sheet of paper out of his portfolio, placed it on the table in front of him, and drew a curved line between two boxes, representing banks. He then added additional boxes along the span of the arc, representing correspondent banks. He called the whole thing a money transfer "rainbow."

What the rainbow showed, Berryman said, was that the money passed through the United States. That was critical. It meant criminal jurisdiction could be established for, say, a bribe paid to a member of the FIFA ExCo to vote a certain way, even if neither party to the conspiracy was American and their meeting took place in some other country.

But that wasn't all. The entire system functioned, Berryman said, adding several more lines to the rainbow, thanks to a handful of electronic wire transfer systems that automate the whole correspondent bank process. Happily, it just so happened that two of the largest wire transfer systems in the world, Fedwire and the Clearing House Interbank Payments System, or CHIPS, were based in the U.S., and Berryman had great relationships with both.

Instead of blindly hunting down sources they hoped would tell them about bribes, Berryman could easily subpoena Fedwire and CHIPS for a list of international wires involving a possible suspect, such as Julio Grondona, a powerful FIFA vice president from Argentina. Within days he'd get back a spreadsheet listing every transfer Grondona made or received, as well as the names and account numbers of who sent or received them.

Best of all, the tracing could be done in secret, without having to contact foreign banks and running the risk of them informing their clients. The takeaway, Berryman said, was that he could unearth bribe payments he knew absolutely nothing about beforehand, essentially reverse-engineering the entire investigative process. That information could be used to indict people, or to force them to flip and cooperate with the investigation.

He paused, and there was a moment of stunned silence in the conference room. It was, from the prosecutors' perspective, a strange and wonderful kind of alchemy being described, something akin perhaps to being handed a pneumatic jackhammer after a lifetime of digging with bare hands.

But before either prosecutor could respond, Berryman was at full speed again, reeling off some of his other favorite tricks, including ways to use subpoenas to force individuals to reveal the existence of foreign bank accounts, and one obscure loophole in the federal code that vastly expanded the definition of money laundering.

The point, Berryman said, was that he could use all this to help clean up soccer. It didn't matter that he was based in California; he had the knowledge and drive to push this case all the way to the top.

"If we can get Blazer and Warner," he concluded, "we can get Bin Hammam. And if we can get Bin Hammam, we can get Blatter."

Berryman looked entreatingly at Norris, the lead prosecutor on the case. He was tall and slender with long, sensitive fingers and a thick mane of black hair so impeccably combed it looked as if it were made of molded plastic. He had said almost nothing during the meeting, but Berryman thought he caught something in his eye.

Norris seemed to get it.

Evan Mahran Norris was only thirty-five, but he'd already proven himself to be one of the most talented young prosecutors in the Eastern District of New York.

The son of an immigrant from Iran and a high school administrator, he grew up in an intellectual family, moving from city to city as his father got new jobs at private schools in cities like Minneapolis. Along the way, he developed a strong moral sense of right and wrong, and an unwavering confidence in his own opinion.

As an undergraduate studying political science at Columbia University, he once wrote a letter to the editor of the student newspaper just to "say how concerned I am by the lack of selflessness and compassion" shown by the author of an op-ed he found offensive.

While at Harvard Law, Norris eschewed the famed and prestigious *Law Review*, instead volunteering at the school's Legal Aid Bureau, where he spent as many as thirty hours a week helping needy families deal with legal problems free of charge. He called the clinic "hands down, far and away the best thing I've done at the law school."

By the time he graduated, he knew he wanted to be a prosecutor, and after a few years at a big Manhattan law firm, he took a job as an assistant U.S. attorney for the Eastern District of New York. He was soon assigned to organized crime, and revealed himself to be a remarkably careful, measured litigator. Norris played a critical role in convicting a number of Gambino Family members, and shone brilliantly in the trial of one of them, a particularly nasty assassin with a predilection for dissolving his victims in vats of acid to hide the evidence.

But he wasn't just good in court. His supervisors recognized in Norris a knack for leadership, and soon put him on long-running and highly sensitive investigations involving complicated and often arcane criminal schemes. It was while running one such case—which never produced an indictment—that Norris first worked with Mike Gaeta of the FBI.

Gaeta, too, saw in the young prosecutor the ability to run complicated investigations, and thought they had similar philosophies of building a case. Which is why he took his rough-hewn idea of going after FIFA to Norris in Brooklyn, rather than someone in the Southern District of New York, based in Manhattan. The SDNY was the highest-profile office in the country, and landed most of the biggest cases, but Gaeta trusted his gut, and thought Norris was the man for the job.

Norris was intensely private, almost never letting his feelings outwardly show, but he cared deeply about his work and developed a degree of personal umbrage at the misdeeds of those he targeted. He believed the people being prosecuted ultimately deserved it, and were personally responsible for their own legal woes.

Special agents might be the guys with the guns in their pockets, but a successful criminal investigation goes nowhere without a lead prosecutor who can maintain discipline, see the big picture, think strategically, and, above all else, keep calm. A good prosecutor has to write well, have an instinctual feel for the law, think on his feet, and be passionate about winning. But most of all, the job requires judgment.

Investigations get blown up by moving too fast, for lack of preparation, or because of reckless mistakes. Convictions—the ultimate goal—depended on making smart decisions about how to run a case and who to bring into it.

A few hours after their meeting, Norris called Berryman's cell phone.

The IRS agent was standing on the corner of Canal and West Broadway, not far from his hotel. He had been too nervous to sit still since leaving the office in Brooklyn, worried that the prosecutors might just take his ideas and shut him out of the most exciting case he'd ever come across. He had never wanted to be on an investigation as badly as this one, and had been almost unable to sleep in the days leading up to his big presentation.

"I'd like to welcome you aboard," Norris said.

Berryman's face broke into a wide grin. After hanging up, he walked around SoHo beaming, oblivious to the heat and his uncomfortable suit.

TEN

BLAZER'S MONEY

ON JULY 20, 2000, A FEDERAL GRAND JURY IN SALT LAKE City handed down a fifteen-count indictment against Thomas K. Welch and David R. Johnson, the former president and vice president of the Salt Lake City bid committee for the 2002 Winter Olympic Games.

Prosecutors had brought the charges following a lengthy investigation of alleged bribery by the bid committee as part of a successful effort to convince International Olympic Committee members to choose Salt Lake City over competing cities in Sweden, Switzerland, and Canada. They presented evidence that more than $1 million in cash, scholarships, gifts, travel, and even medical care to IOC members had been paid to voters, as well as documentation of efforts to cover up the payments with sham contracts and altered financial reports.

Despite what prosecutors believed was a strong case, neither Welch nor Johnson was ever convicted. A year after the indictment, the judge overseeing the case dismissed the bribery counts, and when the case finally went to trial, the judge granted a motion for acquittal by the defense. Afterward he said the case offended his "sense of justice."

The IOC case, Berryman thought, with its international bribery and vote buying, had obvious parallels to the soccer investigation, and it had been an unmitigated disaster.

If he and his new colleagues in New York were going to take on FIFA, it wouldn't be enough to show that money had changed hands, that officials had been bribed, or that payments had been covered up. They needed to be absolutely solid on every level, and to make sure there were no holes a keen defense lawyer could use to undermine the entire case. No matter how much dirt they dug up, it would mean nothing unless it stuck in court.

An indictment involving world soccer, if it ever became public, was clearly going to be high-profile, and there would be enormous public attention, and pressure, on the prosecution. If they picked the wrong law to build their case on, or had a problem with a witness, it could be fatal. Everything had to be by the book, Berryman thought. No mistakes could be made.

He'd taken that attitude into his initial meeting in Brooklyn.

"Has Chuck Blazer not filed his taxes? Is that why you are here?" the prosecutor, Amanda Hector, had asked. "What are you seeing?"

Berryman had said nothing because he knew that by law he couldn't discuss the status of a tax return, even with federal prosecutors, until the investigation had been formally expanded to become a tax case by the Justice Department. If he told them, and some clever white-collar attorney ever figured out that he'd done things in the wrong order, it could blow up the whole investigation.

Taxes, Berryman well knew, were special. In the wake of Watergate, when it was revealed that the Nixon administration had used tax information about perceived enemies to further its ends, the IRS code was rewritten to enhance privacy protections. One of the principal changes was an amendment to a provision called Section 6103, making tax information strictly confidential unless very rigid restrictions are met. It's the same section that makes it extremely cumbersome, if not impossible, for any law enforcement official other than IRS agents to pull tax returns, even those belonging to targets of a grand jury investigation.

Before Berryman could breathe a word about Blazer's tax issues to anyone on the soccer case, he had to get approval from his supervisor in Laguna Niguel, then from criminal tax attorneys in the IRS chief counsel's office in Washington, and finally from the Tax Division of the Department of Justice. Only then could Berryman call up Norris and say what he had longed to tell him from the moment they met: "Chuck Blazer hasn't filed in years, since at least 1994."

As he anxiously awaited that moment, Berryman began taking the steps that were necessary to build evidence against Blazer. To charge tax evasion, it wasn't enough to show someone hadn't filed returns. He needed to prove Blazer had willfully hidden income.

To start with, Berryman spent hour after hour on the website of journalist Andrew Jennings, which had been credited and linked to in the Reuters article that had drawn him into the case. Berryman had never heard of Jennings, but he was impressed at his deep focus on corruption in soccer. The site had scores of articles about FIFA, tales of skulduggery, chicanery, and outright criminality stretching back to the Havelange era of the 1970s.

It was all fascinating, but Berryman focused on one document Jennings had posted. It was a grainy, low-quality photocopy of both sides of a canceled, year-old check for $205,000 made out to a company called Sportvertising.

Berryman enlarged the check on his computer and looked it over. The scan was so bad that some parts, such as the signature, were illegible. But on the back side, he thought he could just make out the handwritten endorsement. He squinted at it, moved his face close to the screen, and even held up a magnifying glass to get a closer look. Finally he was able to make out the handwriting. It said:

For Deposit Only
Sportvertising Inc.
Merrill Lynch

It felt like a huge break. Berryman had been worried that Blazer might have done all of his banking overseas, which would make getting information about his accounts both difficult and risky. If, as the articles about Blazer suggested, he had accounts in the Cayman Islands or the Bahamas, there were significant legal and diplomatic obstacles to requesting any associated records. And even then, banks in Caribbean tax havens weren't known for their generous disclosure policies.

There was also the significant risk that bankers in Cayman or the Bahamas, after reviewing such requests, might decide to reach out to Blazer to tell him the feds were poking around, which could have disastrous results on the case. Alerted to an investigation, Blazer could destroy records, tell other soccer officials, or even flee the country.

But Merrill Lynch, the brokerage house and money manager famous for its bull logo, was based in the United States, and subject to its laws. That meant Berryman could subpoena Merrill, demanding any and all information about accounts in the name of Sportvertising or Chuck Blazer, monthly statements, lists of transactions, or info on any associated accounts or beneficial owners, and the firm would be legally bound not only to hand it all over, but to keep the request absolutely secret, even from the account holder.

So that's exactly what Berryman did. It took him all of twenty minutes.

———

Sunil Gulati considered Chuck Blazer one of his closest friends and mentors; he'd known the man nearly his entire adult life. They'd seen countless soccer matches in each other's company, spent endless hours together on airplanes, and sat through too many meetings to count. And now Gulati had to tell him he was fired.

He'd first met Blazer on the sidelines when he was fresh out of college, helping run the all-star teams of the Connecticut Junior Soccer Association while studying for his master's in economics at Columbia. Blazer, sixteen years older, was at the time in charge of the all-star select teams in neighboring New York State, and the two collaborated to schedule tournaments and other events.

Gulati, passionate about the sport and determined to rise in its ranks, crossed paths with him again when Blazer was elected vice president of the U.S. Soccer Federation, where Gulati sat with him on a committee. They worked together on the 1994 World Cup, for which Gulati served as a vice president, and for several years, while the younger man was a Major League Soccer executive, Blazer loaned him office space, free of charge, inside CONCACAF's Trump Tower offices.

In 2007, when a slot opened on the confederation's Executive Committee, Blazer helped Gulati win an appointment without having to be elected by the confederation's full congress. Gulati, who had been voted in as president of the U.S. Soccer Federation the previous year, had remained on the CONCACAF board ever since.

Amid the tumult following Blazer's decision to report Jack Warner and Mohamed bin Hammam to FIFA, Gulati had stood by his old friend. As one of the staunchest supporters of the American bid for a World Cup, Gulati was infuriated by rumors that Warner may have voted for Qatar instead and, like many in CONCACAF, seemed happy to see him go.

But the political winds had shifted since the spring of 2011. CONCACAF's Executive Committee had never questioned Blazer's financial management, signing off on the confederation's audited financial statements year after year without comment. After Jennings's articles revealed Blazer's unusually lucrative 10 percent contract, that tolerant attitude abruptly changed. The CONCACAF Executive Committee, meeting in Panama in August, asked the general secretary to turn over information about his compensation.

Cornered, Blazer said he expected to earn $2 million in 2011, and provided copies of his contracts. The first was the original agreement from 1990, when he was appointed by Warner; the second, from 1994, had essentially the same terms and expired on July 17, 1998. There were no others. In other words, Blazer had been working without a valid contract for more than thirteen years, but continued taking his generous commission on nearly everything, regardless.

Then on August 31, Jack Warner responded to Blazer's claim that the $250,000 check he'd received from the Caribbean Football Union was repayment of a loan.

In fact, Warner said, Blazer had received a total of $750,000 from the CFU account, and that it was not a loan because he had "never had occasion to borrow money from Blazer," and that the money had originally come from FIFA. Warner added that despite repeated entreaties over many years, Blazer had steadfastly refused to share information about his compensation.

Whatever private opinions Gulati and the other officials might have had, the matter was now in the public eye, a glaring embarrassment. CONCACAF's leadership realized it could no longer sit idly by.

For months, the confederation had been trying to elect someone to take Warner's vacant seat on the FIFA Executive Committee, but with large portions of its membership still under investigation for allegedly taking bribes in Port of Spain, that was proving impossible.

Meanwhile, the dispute over who would serve as CONCACAF's acting president hadn't been resolved. Although the confederation's Executive Committee had installed Alfredo Hawit, its Caribbean membership refused to recognize the Honduran and was outraged about Lisle Austin's year-long ban from FIFA. It was becoming obvious that CONCACAF would have no legitimate president until its elections scheduled for the following May.

As for the Caribbean, the CFU was planning its own elections in a few weeks, but there was every indication those would either be called off or end in disaster.

CONCACAF, in other words, was in chaos.

On October 3, Gulati met with the three other members of the CONCACAF Executive Committee in New York. In the face of the building evidence of serious financial impropriety, they saw little alternative but to jettison Blazer. Gulati knew the man best. It would fall on his shoulders to deliver the bad news, which he did in a visit to Blazer's apartment upstairs from the confederation's offices. His time at CONCACAF was over. Blazer could save face, and resign immediately, or be publicly pushed out.

It had been a great run, twenty-one years atop CONCACAF, turning it from a nothing organization into a financial powerhouse, and besides, Blazer would still be sitting on FIFA's Executive Committee, which was of course the best gig in all of soccer.

Without Warner to protect him and the confederation's leadership turning against him, Blazer knew he had little choice, and agreed to go quietly. But he did ask one concession: that he be allowed to stay on as general secretary until year's end.

Gulati and the rest of CONCACAF's Executive Committee were happy to concede that small favor. They asked only that Blazer refrain from making any more payments to himself from CONCACAF accounts until the committee could figure out what, if anything, he was actually owed.

Three days later, Blazer publicly announced his resignation as CONCACAF's general secretary, citing a desire to "pursue other career opportunities in the burgeoning industry of international football" and a strong preference for leaving the country to do so.

The 2011 Gold Cup had been the most successful ever. More than a million people attended the tournament, held in June and July, and the fact that the final was between Mexico and the U.S. guaranteed that its sponsors, such as Miller Lite, went away happy. The tournament contributed to CONCACAF's best financial year ever. For all of 2011, the confederation had $60 million in revenue, a huge increase from the $37 million it collected in 2009, the prior Gold Cup year.

By Blazer's reckoning, his commission was not limited to sponsorship and TV rights fees. Instead, he took his slice of tournament ticket sales, luxury suite income, parking fees, and even the beers and hot dogs sold at stadium concession stands. On almost every dollar that came in, Blazer took 10 percent, accruing it in an internal account called "commissions payable." He even took 10 percent of development money sent to the confederation by FIFA, in one instance paying himself $300,000 of a $3 million FIFA grant used to build the television production studio within CONCACAF's Trump Tower offices.

At the same time, Blazer had for years charged almost anything he could think of to his corporate American Express card, using it for travel, meals at Elaine's, clothing, gifts, pretty much everything. CONCACAF would pay the Amex bills in full, and then Blazer, once a year, would review his statements and deduct anything he judged to be a personal expense from the "commissions payable" account. In that way, Blazer never had to pay a dime out of pocket to cover his personal expenses, and at the same time he'd accumulate all the Amex membership points for his personal use. Over a seven-year period, CONCACAF paid $26 million to Amex—which earned Blazer enough points to swap for two hundred round-trip, first-class tickets from the U.S. to Europe.

Blazer did the same thing with his rent. Over the years, he lived in several different apartments in Trump Tower, and since 2001 had occupied two adjoining units on the forty-ninth floor that together cost $18,000 a month. Because Blazer frequently worked out of the apartment and didn't even come down to CONCACAF's seventeenth-floor offices on many days, he justified a third of the apartment rental as a home office payable by CONCACAF. The remaining $12,000 he simply deducted from the amounts he had calculated CONCACAF owed him in commissions. Again, not a dime out of pocket.

Blazer was an accountant by training. Making the confederation pay for everything not only saved him money, but also meant there was virtually no paper trail of his income and expenses. Indeed, Blazer made a point of putting as little in his own name as possible.

Rather than buy a car, he had CONCACAF purchase a Hummer that only he used. Rather than acquire condos in Miami and the Bahamas, he put them in CONCACAF's name even though only he had the keys. Dating back to his days selling gewgaws and throwaway promotional items, Blazer had found ways to hide money, setting up a string of shell companies with names like Windmill Promotions and Sand Castle Distributors.

Once he got to CONCACAF, he became more sophisticated, registering his companies in Caribbean tax havens where the ownership was almost impossible to determine. His commissions from CONCACAF went directly to his anonymous shell companies, and he insisted that other, less legitimate payments be sent to them as well.

As a result, there was little if any suggestion that Blazer received any income at all. He had no W-2s, no property tax to pay, not even utility bills. Like Al Capone in the 1920s, Blazer was, from a financial perspective, almost a ghost—which was exactly how a man who hadn't filed income taxes in well over a decade, despite collecting millions of dollars in income during that time, would want it. Blazer was so fixated on leaving no traces that he even refused to use a loyalty card during his frequent visits to the card tables in Las Vegas casinos, out of concern that the IRS would be alerted to his gambling winnings and audit him.

Years of successfully operating under that clandestine system had emboldened Blazer and given him a sense of impunity, as he awarded himself ever-expanding sums of money without paying a dime of tax on any of it. If 2011 was CONCACAF's best year ever, then it followed that it would be Blazer's best year as well.

By the time Gulati confronted Blazer in early October, the general secretary had already allocated himself $4.2 million in 2011 commissions.

He divided the sum, nearly twice as much as he'd ever paid himself, between two shell companies he'd established years earlier: Multisport Games Development and En Passant Ltd.

Blazer had promised to leave CONCACAF for good on December 31. Now, with time atop the institution he had built up from almost nothing dwindling, the general secretary had one last commission to collect.

On November 10, Blazer contacted the confederation's bank in Miami, BAC Florida Bank, instructing it to wire $1.4 million to his Sportvertising account in the Cayman Islands. It was, he wrote in the wire instructions, "in payment of Gold Cup commissions."

Shortly thereafter, he got an email from his Cayman Islands bank, confirming the money had arrived safely.

"Yippee," Blazer replied.

ELEVEN

THE FLIP

THE SUBPOENAS STARTED ROLLING BACK IN BEFORE THE end of September, at first just a trickle, and then a torrent, one after the next.

For Berryman, it was like Christmas. He'd check his email and, boom, there was another one, with its precise boilerplate legal language and attachments containing row after row of beautiful numbers. From Fedwire and CHIPS, both based in New York, he'd get spreadsheets of every wire involving a particular account, and peering into the records he could see the originating banks, the correspondent banks, the amount being transferred, and the accounts on the other end of the transfer.

Then, if any of the correspondent banks were in the U.S., he'd send out another set of subpoenas, asking each one to cough up information about the transfer, and any other wires it might have handled from that same account. Berryman had a knack for visualizing the flow of money, as if it were a tangible thing, something he could see bouncing from place to place.

Sometimes, when he was particularly lucky, he'd come across a wire that started or ended in a domestic bank, and then he could ask for everything, what he called "the kitchen sink" down to the names of each signatory to the account, of the beneficial owner, of any other accounts those people had at the same bank, and copies of every monthly statement stretching back years. Then he'd sit and contentedly go through it all, line, by line, by line.

He sent out hundreds of subpoenas in a constant blast. It got to the point where he talked to the employees in the legal departments of the big banks so frequently they seemed like close personal friends. One in particular, a kind lady who worked for Merrill Lynch in Chicago, had first called him when he was back in New York a second time, for a meeting with the prosecutors in late September. He was just walking down the street, and she serenely started reading off the bank account information over the phone. Berryman felt like he wanted to reach through the phone and hug her.

He subpoenaed every FIFA-related name he could think of: Sepp Blatter, Jack Warner, Mohamed bin Hammam, Jérôme Valcke, on and on. Some would come up dry, but many would turn up something, and when something promising came in, Berryman would upload the document to a folder in a secure server entitled "All Transactions," which was accessible to the other agents and prosecutors on the case. As the files piled up, dozens becoming hundreds, Norris taught Berryman a little organizational trick: put the date of the questionable wire first in the title, being careful to list the year first, then the month, then the day. The result would look something like this:

2008-12-19 Wire from CFU Republic Bank Trinidad to Sportvertising

FirstCaribbean International Bank for $298,500

That way, as the contents of the shared server grew, each new addition slotted into the larger whole in chronological order, and over time they had created a painstakingly constructed shareable timeline of apparent financial misdeeds.

Then in early October, the final bureaucratic approvals from Washington had gone through clearing the way for Berryman to tell the rest of the team about Blazer's tax troubles. It gave the whole investigation an immediate and razor-sharp focus.

Every week, Norris would initiate a conference call with Randall in Manhattan and Berryman in Southern California to discuss what they were digging up, where it might lead, and what the next steps might be. Soccer may not have been a big deal in the U.S., but all three were aware of how closely it was scrutinized in the rest of the world; with so many potential targets living overseas, the slightest peep about what they were doing could severely damage the case. They had to be absolutely confident about their plan for Blazer.

Norris wasn't a diehard fan like Berryman, and in fact didn't even own a television, to the amusement of his peers. But he did follow Tottenham Hotspur, a team that seemed perennially doomed to fall just below the top ranks of English soccer. Early on Saturday and Sunday mornings, when English Premier League games were shown in the U.S., he'd call Berryman to chat about the case, knowing the agent would be up before sunrise, glued to his television.

In short order, the two had grown close, recognizing in each other a deep appreciation for the craft of building a case. They bounced ideas off one another and delighted in sharing new discoveries in the increasingly byzantine investigation. In his career, Berryman could think of only one or two other prosecutors who understood him as well as Norris. And Norris, eager to keep chatting with Berryman late into the night, would sometimes call him from inside the bathroom of his cramped Brooklyn apartment to avoid waking his sleeping wife and young children.

In one of their calls, Berryman suggested a code name that they could use as shorthand to refer to the investigation. Something like "Abscam," the FBI's name for a public corruption sting in the late 1970s, or "Operation Silver Shovel," which brought down a ton of politicians in Chicago in the 1990s. Berryman's idea, which he said came to him in a flash, was "Operation Own Goal." He liked the idea that crooked soccer officials had brought defeat on themselves due to their corrupt ways. Just as a soccer player might accidentally put the ball into his own net.

Norris rejected the notion out of hand, leaving no opening for debate. The soccer case would have no name.

The 58-story Trump Tower, with its jagged steel and black glass exterior, shares its Midtown Manhattan block with the only slightly less imposing IBM Building. The two skyscrapers were completed within months of each other in the early 1980s, and are connected at ground level by an enclosed glass atrium built under an incentive system that allows developers to exceed zoning restrictions in exchange for incorporating public spaces into their projects.

In contrast to the chaotic and profoundly glitzy lobby of the Trump Tower, swathed entirely in garish pink Breccia Pernice marble that a *New York Times* critic once said "gives off a glow of happy, if self-satisfied, affluence," the adjoining atrium presents an oasis of peace and tranquility. With light gray granite floors and tall stands of bamboo, the 8,000-square-foot space is uncluttered and calm, devoid of the constant noise and commercial bravado that permeate its next-door neighbor. Businessmen come to find a few moments of respite from the bustle of the city, tourists rest and eat sandwiches, and schoolchildren frequently cluster beneath its tall glass roof to hear afternoon concerts. The plants and airy open space baffle the sounds of the city and, at the right angle, can even block out the tall buildings all around, creating a small island for quiet reflection.

On the evening of November 30, 2011, Randall and Berryman walked into the atrium together, took a seat at a small round table near the entrance, and waited. The day was winding down, and only a few other people, scattered around the tables, remained. An hour earlier, Randall had called Chuck Blazer to say he'd like to talk again. Blazer had been at dinner, but said he'd be glad to meet later if he didn't mind the trip uptown. The two agents, dressed in suits, arrived together and peered through the atrium's glass walls, watching intently for their target.

Finally, a van pulled over near the atrium's entrance on Fifty-Sixth Street, and the driver unloaded a scooter, which Blazer then mounted and navigated through the doorway. Berryman tried not to stare. Somehow, the many photos of the soccer executive on the Internet had failed to do justice to the physical scale of the man. He seemed larger and hairier in real life, and he smiled amiably through his shaggy beard as he wheeled over to the agents.

Randall greeted Blazer familiarly, though not warmly, shaking his hand.

"As you may know, we're investigating corruption in soccer," Randall said. "This is Steve, and he'll tell you what we're doing."

Berryman reached out and gave Blazer his business card, which clearly identified him as an agent of the Internal Revenue Service. He paused to let Blazer look it over before he delivered a speech he had rehearsed several times in his mind.

"My name is Steve Berryman and I want you to know that I'm doing this case for the right reasons," he began. "I love football; it's in my blood. And I want to do something to clean up all this corruption. I have been working on foreign corruption and money laundering cases and I am going to be successful at this."

He paused for a moment, looked at Blazer seriously, and said: "You haven't filed taxes for years."

Berryman explained to Blazer that he had traced his accounts and had found evidence of more than a half-dozen sources of income, totaling millions of dollars that had never been reported to the IRS. In addition, Berryman said, he knew that Blazer had foreign bank accounts, which he had never disclosed. That was illegal under the Bank Secrecy Act, which required taxpayers to report the existence of such accounts to the federal government.

All together, Berryman said, the evidence they'd found painted a clear picture of tax evasion, a felony punishable by up to five years in prison for each year that a return was not willfully filed. The statute of limitations was six years, which meant Blazer faced a maximum of thirty years behind bars for his tax crimes alone.

Then, to punctuate his speech, Berryman handed Blazer a subpoena.

It was an unusual move, pulled straight from Berryman's bag of investigative tricks, compelling the recipient to turn over information about all foreign bank accounts he or she held. Normally under the Fifth Amendment, individuals are protected from providing potentially self-incriminating information. But such Title 31 subpoenas, Berryman knew, wiggle right through a useful loophole to put the person targeted by the subpoena in a rather awkward spot: either hand over documents that could be used to build a criminal case against them, or face being held in contempt of court.

Berryman gave Blazer a moment to look over the subpoena, then concluded. "We want your help," he said, and then both agents stared intently at Blazer. It was a critical moment, and they had discussed it endlessly with Norris and Hector in recent weeks.

Busting Chuck Blazer for tax evasion was fine, but that wasn't really the goal. They could have just arrested him on the spot and dragged him away in handcuffs, but a stand-alone tax case would get them nowhere.

They wanted Blazer to cooperate, to trade his knowledge and access for a chance at a reduced sentence. This Trump Tower confrontation was their big play, and Blazer had a clear choice.

If he went for it, then there were a million ways the case might go. He could open up the entire soccer world to them. But if Blazer refused, then they would have little choice but to prosecute him right away and potentially never get his help. They'd have to charge him and arraign him in open court and the whole world would know what they had been up to. The stakes were incredibly high.

At first Blazer said nothing, sitting in stunned silence.

Then he let out a long, slow sigh, and Berryman could feel a warm tingling sensation in his gut.

"I want to help," Blazer said.

His girlfriend, former soap opera actress Mary Lynn Blanks, had been begging him to come clean for some time, he explained. She'd told him over and over he had to deal with it. "This has been weighing on me, my tax situation. I want to fix it and set it right," Blazer said, a pained look on his face.

Corruption in soccer, he added, "has gone on for far too long and it needs to stop."

Berryman and Randall glanced at each other, restraining smiles, and told Blazer he was making the right choice. He'd need a lawyer, they said, who should get in touch with the prosecution as soon as possible. Berryman took back his business card and wrote Evan Norris's phone number on the back. Returning it, he told Blazer he couldn't tell anyone other than his lawyers about this. Then he and Randall said good night and departed, leaving Blazer alone amid all the bamboo.

It was a cool early winter night, but not cold. When the two agents had arrived at Trump Tower several hours earlier, Fifth Avenue had been crowded with cheerful families on their way to the annual Christmas tree lighting ceremony held just a few blocks away at Rockefeller Center that same evening. Now the Midtown streets were deserted.

It was pretty late, but Berryman couldn't wait to share the good news. He called Norris on his cell phone, a grin on his lips; Blazer he said, had flipped. Big things were sure to come soon.

———

Three days later, Blazer wheeled into the offices of Friedman Kaplan Seiler & Adelman, a boutique litigation firm located on the twenty-eighth floor of an office tower just off Times Square.

After his encounter with the agents, Blazer had first reached out to his personal attorney, Stuart Friedman, a subdued, bookish man who advised him on commercial matters and had some experience in commercial sports law. Friedman wanted to help, but he was not a criminal lawyer, so he had made the referral and accompanied Blazer to the meeting.

To reduce the risk that somebody might spot Blazer—who, after all, cut a rather noticeable figure—walking into a law firm, the attorneys agreed to meet early that Saturday morning, when there was little traffic in Times Square and he could pop out of a car and through the building's revolving doors without drawing attention.

Friedman introduced him to his new white-collar defense attorneys, Mary Mulligan and Eric Corngold. Mulligan had been a federal prosecutor in New York's Southern District, and taught classes on criminal law. Corngold had also been a federal prosecutor, but in the Eastern District, where the FIFA Case was being run, and was later a deputy attorney general for New York State.

Gathered around a conference table, the lawyers carefully explained what it meant to cooperate with a federal investigation. The prosecution's goal was simple: to expand the case, gathering enough evidence to charge additional people with crimes. Norris and Hector believed Blazer could help them do that.

If he decided to go through with it, Blazer would have to tell the prosecutors everything he knew. He'd have to share documents, emails, text messages, financial records, photographs—anything they asked for. Blazer would also most likely be asked to do things to help the case. He'd have to make calls and secretly record the conversations, send and receive emails, and meet people while wearing a wire. Eventually, he would probably have to testify against friends and colleagues in open court, talking about their deeds while they glared at him.

He would, in other words, become a snitch. But in the jargon of law enforcement, it all fell under the umbrella of providing "substantial assistance." And the reward for substantial assistance, for doing exactly as asked, for spilling his guts, for leading a secret life, for betraying his friends, and for helping secure their convictions, was leniency.

First Blazer would participate in a long series of meetings with the prosecutors, called proffers, and they'd hear his story. After he had given everything he could, and convinced the feds he'd been honest, Blazer would have to plead guilty to one or more crimes. There was no avoiding that. He'd almost certainly be forced to pay a large fine. In exchange, he'd be rewarded with a cooperation agreement, which promised Blazer that, when it was time for his sentencing, the prosecutors would write a letter asking the judge for a "downward departure from sentencing guidelines." That translated to: Please go easy on this guy because he was helpful.

With any luck, it might be possible for Blazer to avoid prison entirely. It wouldn't be cheap, but he'd be able to live in his own home, and since his cooperation would be a secret, nobody in his social circle would have to know he had been busted—at least until the case become public. In fact, they absolutely should not ever learn about what he was up to, because talking about cooperating was forbidden. If Blazer blabbed, or lied, or did anything to interfere with the case, all deals were off. He could be arrested, locked up, or forced to plea to additional crimes, including obstruction of justice.

Cooperation, in other words, would be like a really terrible, unpaid second job that Blazer couldn't tell anyone about. He would spend untold hours with prosecutors and special agents, and he'd be at their beck and call. He'd need permission to travel. And since a crucial part of cooperation was being available as a witness at trial, his sentencing wouldn't come until every other potential defendant had either been convicted or acquitted. The whole process could take years, during which time the feds more or less would own Blazer.

The alternatives were simple, but far more perilous: plead not guilty and fight the charges in court, which could lead to a long prison term if Blazer was convicted, or agree to plead guilty but refuse to cooperate, abandoning any hope of calls for moderation from the prosecutors.

Blazer stood firm. He wanted to cooperate. His lawyers would reach out to Norris and set up an initial meeting. But first they needed to understand how their new client had come to this place. So Blazer started to tell the story of his life in soccer. By the time he had finished, it was dark and cold outside and nine hours had passed.

TWELVE

THE CROWN JEWEL

CHUCK BLAZER LIKED TO TAKE CREDIT FOR CREATING the Gold Cup, CONCACAF's marquee tournament, which pitted the region's national teams against one another. Dreaming it up and getting it off the ground were, in fact, his first major accomplishments as the confederation's general secretary.

But the part of the story he tended not to dwell on was how the event was initially a commercial disaster and was saved only thanks to the efforts of a little-known but ingenious Brazilian soccer marketer. That man was named José Hawilla, and he had a special talent for taking struggling, third-rate tournaments and turning them into huge money-makers.

The first Gold Cup was held in 1991, and initial commercial interest in the event was almost nonexistent. Chuck Blazer had envisioned the tournament as a profit center for both CONCACAF and himself thanks to his unusual contract, but he struggled to attract sponsors and was barely able to command any money at all trying to sell the TV rights to broadcasters, cable channels, or pay-per-view.

Selling commercial rights to soccer matches, particularly in a country where the sport ranked fifth in popularity behind football, basketball, baseball, and hockey, was significantly harder than it looked. Still, Blazer had seen how lucrative events like the World Cup and the European Championship could be, and realized he could use some advice.

He had first met Hawilla in 1987, when Blazer, then commissioner of the American Soccer League, was looking for investors to buy additional franchises. Retired Brazilian star player Carlos Alberto Torres introduced him to Hawilla, who flew up to New York from São Paulo and spent two days in Blazer's home office in Scarsdale, assessing the league's prospects.

In the end, the Brazilian opted against buying a team. But in anticipation of the 1994 World Cup in the U.S., he moved to Boca Raton for two years starting in 1992 to get a feel for the American market, which he believed held tremendous commercial potential thanks to the country's large and growing Hispanic population.

Blazer bumped into Hawilla at the second Gold Cup, in 1993, which he'd decided to split between the U.S. and Mexico in what ultimately proved to be an unsuccessful attempt at ginning up more interest from potential sponsors. Spotting the Brazilian in a VIP box during a match, Blazer seized upon the opportunity to ask his advice.

Three years earlier, Hawilla had cofounded the sports marketing firm Inter/Forever Sports in Miami, and he'd started scooping up inexpensive rights to club team matches in Central America and the Caribbean, as well as the occasional one-off friendly exhibition match featuring national teams flown into South Florida. Most of the revenue from such events came from ticket sales, and from pay-per-view contracts from restaurants and bars that catered to a Hispanic clientele.

Hawilla told Blazer to forget about Mexico, which might be soccer mad but presented numerous logistical challenges. Instead, he said, the Gold Cup should be hosted only in the U.S., the world's richest country, where maximum revenue and minimal organizational challenges presented themselves. Handled correctly, the tournament could be a big success, but, Hawilla said, the best course of action would be for CONCACAF to sell the Gold Cup's broadcasting and commercial rights to a marketing firm with expertise and contacts in the business, rather than Blazer trying to do everything himself.

In fact, Hawilla added, he might be interested in buying the rights, and he ultimately did just that, signing a contract in October 1994 to pay the confederation $9.75 million for the next three editions. When that deal expired, Hawilla signed on for two more tournaments, and the tournament steadily grew in both prestige and revenue.

When Blazer, eager to boost his 10 percent commissions, decided to take the sale of CONCACAF's rights in-house in 2003, refusing to renew with Hawilla, the Brazilian felt slightly betrayed. He had taken an essentially lifeless tournament that couldn't even be seen on cable television and turned it into a reliable moneymaker drawing multinational sponsors. And now that it was self-sustaining, Blazer was taking it away.

But Hawilla took the news in stride. For the most part, he busied himself with his much larger business in South America, where his primary company, Traffic, was based, and where he had been a pioneer in the field, building a sports marketing empire and making him a very wealthy man.

He had helped the Gold Cup grow in value and prominence, but the quality of play was still fairly low, and soccer fans in North America seemed far more interested in watching tournaments from other parts of the world, featuring the planet's best players. And it just so happened that Hawilla had for more than fifteen years controlled the rights to one of those tournaments: the Copa América, which was packed with stars from Brazil and Argentina, two of the greatest soccer nations in the world.

Losing the Gold Cup was disappointing, but Hawilla wasn't overly concerned. So long as he had the Copa América, his crown jewel, he would continue to be, as Brazilian soccer legend Tostão once called him, the "owner of the entire soccer world."

————

When José Hawilla was an eager young sports reporter, clutching a hulking microphone and transmitter and racing up and down the sidelines of second division Brazilian soccer matches in the late 1950s and early 1960s, the business of soccer was a simple affair.

Teams sold tickets and stadium owners rented space on a few billboards to local businesses, as well as charging radio stations to use a soundproof press booth and bring in equipment. There was no concept of an exclusive broadcaster, and for important contests, a half-dozen or more radio stations might compete for listeners.

Enterprising journalists like Hawilla not only had to rattle off ninety minutes of play-by-play during matches, provide analysis at halftime, and interview players after the match, they also were responsible for selling advertising. There was no sales staff and no producers: in those days the reporters did everything.

The energetic Hawilla was good at all of that, and to draw a larger audience, and thus more advertising, he developed a distinctive persona.

He decided to go by only his first initial—J—and by the time he was twenty, he had moved to São Paulo from the remote agricultural town where he grew up. Soon J—which was pronounced Jota—had made a name for himself, and by the late 1970s was running the sports department at TV Globo, Brazil's most important broadcaster.

But after being fired for supporting a strike by sports journalists, Hawilla decided he wanted more financial security, and in 1980 he bought Traffic Assessoria e Comunicações, a small São Paulo company that sold bus stop advertising.

By then, Hawilla had spent more than twenty years in soccer, and had become consumed with the idea that the sport, from a business perspective, was a poorly run farce. Brazil was the greatest force the sport had ever known, winner of three World Cups, and its fans were monomaniacal, thinking of little else but their teams.

Yet the country's professional clubs were perpetually saddled with huge debts, the leagues were crippled by poor organization and infighting, and the vaunted national team barely had enough money to pay for its own uniforms. Improving technology meant that it was increasingly easy for people around the world to watch the Brazilian national team, known as the *Seleção*, at home, yet little was done to exploit that demand.

When selling bus ads didn't turn out to be very profitable, Hawilla decided to test his theories about sports marketing. In 1982, Traffic signed its first deal with the Brazilian Football Confederation, known by its Portuguese acronym CBF, giving him exclusive rights to sell advertising space inside stadiums where the national team played.

Soon, Traffic was branching into various aspects of Brazilian sports, buying the rights to promote Brazil's professional volleyball league, for example, or signing a deal to overhaul the sports department at broadcaster Sistema Brasileiro de Televisão.

Traffic's big breakthrough, however, came in 1986, when Hawilla met Nicolás Leoz, the newly elected president of the FIFA-based confederation that oversaw South American soccer, known as CONMEBOL. The two men got along and, sensing an opportunity, Hawilla asked about buying the rights to the Copa América.

One of soccer's oldest tournaments, predating even the World Cup, the Copa América was created in 1916, when Argentina's foreign ministry invited Chile, Uruguay, and Brazil to meet in a competition in honor of the 100th anniversary of Argentina's independence. The event proved so popular that a Uruguayan journalist in attendance proposed forming an institution to regularly organize the tournament, and the world's first regional soccer confederation was born.

The tournament eventually fell into neglect. The most recent three editions prior to 1986 had been organized as round-robin tournaments with no fixed host, were largely ignored by soccer fans, and generated less than $25,000 for CONMEBOL. As far as Leoz was concerned, the Copa América was a dog.

But Hawilla had a vision: the tournament would be held in a single host country on a rotating basis and he would oversee almost every aspect of running it for a lump sum paid to the confederation in advance. Traffic would offer a cash prize to the winner to motivate national federations to field their best players, and the sports marketing company would keep 100 percent of the proceeds from sponsorship, licensing, advertising, television, and radio.

CONMEBOL, like most soccer confederations at the time, didn't have much cash. Leoz, a lawyer and former president of Paraguay's soccer federation, was delighted to let a third party pay to manage the thing and on October 3, 1986, sold Traffic the rights to the 1987 edition, to be held in Argentina, for $1.7 million.

That first tournament was poorly organized and badly attended, and lost Traffic money. Nonetheless, Hawilla snapped up the rights to the 1989 and 1991 Copa América tournaments for a total of $3.9 million, and over time the event turned into a huge commercial success. Hawilla had correctly anticipated an explosion in television money for the tournament and had pushed hard to ensure the biggest stars from each country played in every edition.

With interest in South American superstars booming and cable television becoming ubiquitous, networks and sponsors around the world began clamoring for a piece of the Copa América. By the late 1990s, Traffic was fending off entreaties from sponsors willing to pay millions of dollars for each edition, and in the run-up to the 2011 edition, it was selling television rights to the tournament in 199 different countries.

The huge profits helped Hawilla expand into a wide range of other soccer rights deals, including youth competitions, World Cup qualifiers, and the popular Copa Libertadores tournament, which pitted Latin America's best pro teams against one another every year. Closer to home, Hawilla bought rights to the Brasileirão, Brazil's top professional soccer league, brokered sponsorship deals for the Brazilian national team with Pepsi, Coca-Cola, Umbro, and Nike, and bought his own professional clubs in Brazil and Portugal, while creating an entire second-division professional league in the United States, the North American Soccer League, named after the long-defunct league that shuttered in 1985.

Hawilla, the grandchild of impoverished Lebanese immigrants, grew enormously wealthy and bought several television stations, a pair of newspapers, and a production company in Brazil; he opened a soccer academy for promising youth, and managed the contractual and publicity rights to dozens of professional soccer players around the world. He owned farms near his hometown, had numerous houses in Brazil and one in South Florida, and of course, owned fleets of luxury cars, including, briefly, a $400,000 Bentley.

Bald and bespectacled, Hawilla played lots of golf, had a share in a company that gave him use of a private jet, and appeared on Brazil's society pages along with his wife and three children, the eldest of whom married a *Vogue* cover model. Glossy business magazines called on him at his opulent São Paulo offices to write glowing profiles, and he proudly told reporters his life story.

"I'm daring," he boasted to one journalist. "You have to know how to take risks."

But what Hawilla never mentioned in those interviews was the true price he had to pay for all of his success, the ugly reality of the modern soccer business that he played a fundamental role in creating.

All of it was based on bribes.

At least as far back as 1991 every Copa América deal included side payments. At first, the president of CONMEBOL, Leoz, began demanding money before he would sign the rights contracts. Then the presidents of the Argentine and Brazilian soccer associations threatened to keep their best and most popular players out of the tournament unless they got cash as well. And the bribes didn't stop there. What started relatively small, as a few hundred thousand dollars paid once every few years, had become enormous, with millions of dollars going to soccer officials every year to ensure Traffic continued to receive the commercial rights it needed, as well as the superstar players required to make the tournament a commercial success.

After a few years, Blazer and Warner, too, began demanding money on the side in exchange for Gold Cup rights. One payment, for example, of $200,000, was wired—through an intermediary with a shell company that had a bank account in Uruguay—in March 1999 to one of Blazer's accounts in the Caymans; Blazer then sent along half of that to Warner's accounts in Trinidad.

Over time, these soccer politicians grew increasingly insistent, demanding more and more money with each new contract. It got to the point that Hawilla had to hire full-time intermediaries using phony consulting contracts so that he could make the payments while keeping them off Traffic's books.

It didn't matter that Hawilla was the innovator, the one whose vision had turned the penniless, parochial world of Latin American soccer into a viable commercial enterprise followed by fans around the world, or that his sales staff were the ones doing all the hard work of brokering all those sponsorship and television deals, while these petty sports dictators did nothing but enjoy a gold-plated lifestyle. Without the payments, the soccer officials simply wouldn't sign, and then everything would collapse.

But as the commercial value of soccer skyrocketed, it became apparent that Hawilla wasn't the only one willing to go to great lengths to acquire those rights.

———

Perhaps the first sign that Hawilla's empire was under attack had come in the spring of 2005, when the Honduras soccer federation informed Traffic it no longer wished to do business with the company.

Over the years, Traffic had locked up the broadcast rights to World

Cup qualifiers for every soccer federation in Central America, as well as Canada and the entire Caribbean Football Union.

The contracts weren't by any means gigantic—a million or two dollars at most—but thanks to the large numbers of Central American expatriates living in the U.S., those rights could pay off handsomely when one of the national teams went far in World Cup qualifying. And they were particularly valuable when those teams played against Mexico or the U.S., matches with very large prospective audiences.

Traffic had inked its first deal with the Federación Nacional Autónoma de Fútbol de Honduras back in 1997, and had renewed or extended the agreements several times since then. The federation's refusal to sign again in 2005 mystified Hawilla's Miami employees who believed they had a contractual right of first refusal, and the dispute ended up in court.

The lawsuit revealed that a rival sports marketing company, Media World, had been trying to break into the World Cup qualifiers niche and, advised by a former Traffic employee who knew exactly how Hawilla kept soccer officials happy, had been secretly meeting with the Honduras federation for months. The litigation proved unsuccessful, and Media World retained the rights.

Still, to Hawilla and his staff, losing a pipsqueak like Honduras didn't feel tragic, and nobody got too exercised when competitors soon snatched away qualifier rights for El Salvador and Guatemala as well.

It wasn't until the 2010 World Cup in South Africa that Hawilla realized he had a full-fledged crisis on his hands.

Most of FIFA's top officials were lodged at the five-star Michelangelo Hotel in Johannesburg during the tournament. In a series of meetings, first with Nicolás Leoz, and then with a number of other South American soccer officials, Hawilla was informed that he was losing his contract for the Copa América and that instead the rights were going to be assigned to an Argentine sports marketing firm called Full Play.

The news was shocking.

As far as Hawilla was concerned, he had a valid contract, signed nine years earlier, giving him rights to the 2011 and 2015 editions of the tournament, as well as the first option to purchase the 2019, 2023, and 2027 editions as well. He had agreed to pay CONMEBOL $46 million for the deal, and had generously bribed several officials—including Leoz, who alone got $1 million—to ensure they signed the deal.

Yet apparently it hadn't been enough. In one meeting at the Michelangelo, the head of Ecuador's soccer federation told Hawilla that he was losing the Copa América because he had bribed only the top three CONMEBOL officials, and not every single president of every single South American federation.

The previous year, the Ecuadorian explained, six of the ten members of the confederation, none of whom had received Copa América bribes from Hawilla, had formed a unified bloc they called the *Grupo de los Seis*—the Group of Six. They then used the threat of their majority vote within the confederation to push Leoz for a piece of the action on a number of CONMEBOL deals. One of them was the Copa América.

"The contract is ours," Hawilla had protested. "You cannot come in and just tear up a valid contract and sign another contract with another company for the same product."

"I can," the Ecuadorian replied. "And I've already done that."

Hawilla's crown jewel was being stolen.

———

For decades, the presidents of the soccer associations from South America's two economic and athletic powerhouses, Argentina and Brazil, along with Nicolás Leoz, the CONMEBOL president, had exercised total control of the sport in the region. Traffic negotiated its Copa América deals exclusively with those three officials, and paid bribes only to them.

The rest of the continent—Ecuador, Paraguay, Peru, Chile, Colombia, Uruguay, Bolivia, and Venezuela—were mere afterthoughts. With little, if any, political power, the officials of those federations received none of the special benefits that were whispered about at congresses and in stadium luxury boxes.

Full Play's owners, a father-and-son team named Hugo and Mariano Jinkis, offered to change that system. They had been slowly breaking into the South American rights business over a period of years, snapping up World Cup qualifiers from a few of the continent's smaller countries, and now were angling for bigger prizes. Starting with Ecuador, the Jinkises built close relationships with the presidents of nearly every one of the marginalized South American soccer associations.

They hosted the officials at their vacation houses in Uruguay, plied them with pricey concert tickets, gourmet food and wine, and other gifts, and one by one convinced them they had been getting a raw deal and could do much better working with Full Play. The message clearly resonated; only the presidents from Uruguay and Chile seemed uninterested.

Why, the Jinkises asked, was it fair for Julio Grondona, president of the Argentine Football Association, and Ricardo Teixeira, president of the Brazilian Football Confederation, to get what must be huge bribes from Traffic in exchange for the Copa América rights, while the confederation's other top officials got nothing? Didn't Paraguay play in that tournament as well? Or Colombia? Those countries may not have won the World Cup, but could the Copa América be played without them?

On the other hand, the Jinkises said, if they signed with Full Play, each president would get $1 million under the table. That message spoke very clearly to the officials, and emboldened them. They pledged to ensure Full Play would get the tournament.

But not quite yet. Since sponsorships and television rights for the 2011 edition of the Copa América had already been sold off, it would have been almost impossible for another firm to come in and take control of the tournament on such short notice, so Traffic still organized that year's edition.

Following the World Cup, both CONMEBOL and Full Play had made multiple public denials that they had a formal deal, and Hawilla used the 2011 tournament, held in Argentina, as an opportunity to make a last-ditch, in-person effort to salvage his rights to the 2015 and 2019 editions.

He'd heard rumors about the bribes that Full Play was offering, as well as the above-the-board price the firm would pay CONMEBOL for the rights themselves, and he met with one federation president after another, desperately offering to match any competing payments.

The president of the Venezuelan federation, Rafael Esquivel, used his encounter with Hawilla to complain that he hadn't made enough from the prior edition of the Copa América, which was held in his home country. According to Esquivel, Traffic had promised him a $1.5 million kickback from the sale of domestic television rights, yet he'd received only $500,000.

Venezuela was consistently one of the weakest teams in South America, the only country in the confederation to have never qualified for a World Cup. The oil-rich nation was far more enthusiastic about baseball than soccer, and Hawilla normally would have laughed off Esquivel's demand for more money.

But given his current plight, the Brazilian felt he couldn't afford to say no. He grudgingly obliged, using a series of intermediaries to wire Esquivel $1 million in late July.

It was in vain. Despite the public denials, CONMEBOL and Full Play had in fact secretly signed a contract for the Copa América more than a year earlier at the World Cup. And even as he was cheekily demanding a kickback from Hawilla in Argentina, Esquivel had joined the presidents of every other South American soccer federation, as well as Leoz, in signing a letter formally confirming that deal.

Attorneys hired by Hawilla eventually sent cease-and-desist letters to Full Play and CONMEBOL, and when those accomplished nothing, Traffic sued. The civil complaint, filed in Miami-Dade county court on November 21, 2011, alleged "willful, flagrant, and deliberate breach of contract."

Full Play, the Brazilian firm said, had conspired to "take over the activities of CONMEBOL."

———

On December 1, 2011, Mariano Jinkis wired $450,000 from one of Full Play's accounts, number 7063420, at a Zurich branch of Bank Hapoalim, through a correspondent account held at Citibank in New York, and finally into Banco Citibank S.A. account number 000-045-01-020017-7, in the name of Lexani Advisors Inc., in Panama City.

The owner of Lexani Advisors, a soccer marketing consultant named Miguel Trujillo, subsequently used the Panama account, as well as Banco Citibank account number 000-045-01-020008-2, in the name of Sponsports S.A., which he also controlled, to wire a $250,000 bribe to Honduran Alfredo Hawit, as well as $100,000 apiece to two other Central American soccer officials.

The payments had been agreed upon several weeks earlier in the Uruguayan resort town of Punta del Este, where Full Play's owners, Hugo and Mariano Jinkis, had entertained Hawit and the other Central Americans for several days, all expenses paid.

The Jinkises had flown the officials to Punta del Este on a private jet, to talk to them about the possibility of Full Play acquiring the commercial rights to the Gold Cup from CONCACAF, as well as World Cup qualifying matches for several Central American countries, and eventually handling all of the confederation's properties.

Since Jack Warner's departure, Hawit had served as the interim president of CONCACAF and in theory was well placed to decide how to allocate rights to its most valuable properties. Amid all the tumult at the confederation, Hugo Jinkis and his son perceived a great opportunity to acquire rights to a major CONCACAF event. The U.S. and Mexico were highly valuable commercial marketplaces, and the Gold Cup, the Jinkises believed, could be hugely profitable if handled properly.

Over lunch in Punta del Este, Mariano Jinkis made a proposal not unlike the one Full Play made to the Group of Six roughly two years earlier. For too long, Central America had been marginalized in CON-CACAF by Chuck Blazer, Jack Warner, and their impenetrable Caribbean bloc. Those two men had controlled everything, and reaped all the spoils. But Honduras had played in two World Cups and looked to have a good shot at playing again in 2014. The Central Americans had more than paid their dues, and with Hawit now atop the federation, it was their turn. Wasn't it well past time they got a piece of the action, too?

Yes, Hawit agreed, in exchange for a few well-placed dollars here or there, passed through a convenient intermediary in order to avoid any suspicions, he and his friends would be delighted to help out their new friends. In fact, he said, there was a CONCACAF Executive Committee meeting coming up in Miami in mid-January. That would be a perfect time to propose that the confederation start doing business with Full Play.

But first, of course, Hawit and his two associates needed to see the money.

THIRTEEN

QUEEN FOR A DAY

**FBI LAUNCHES INVESTIGATION INTO WORLD
CUP "DIRTY TRICKS" CAMPAIGN**
Investigators from the FBI have interviewed members of England's failed 2018 World Cup bid as part of an investigation by
the American law-enforcement agency into alleged corruption,
Telegraph Sport can reveal.

THE ARTICLE, PUBLISHED DECEMBER 7, 2011, WAS FULL
of details about the soccer investigation that were supposed to be secret,
certainly not splashed across the pages of a London broadsheet.

It noted that American law enforcement had met with members
of the English bid in November, that they were investigating possible
foul play associated with World Cup voting as well as the events that
had occurred in Port of Spain, and that one of the potential crimes was
CFU delegates taking the cash they had been given into the U.S. without
properly declaring it. It said the authorities were examining payments to
Chuck Blazer, and that FBI agents had been meeting with FIFA's head of
security, Chris Eaton, to discuss progress.

Then, a week later, the *Telegraph* published a second article, confirming that Blazer had "been questioned by FBI officials" and that "the
investigation is being handled by financial specialists based in New York,
who have powers to access bank accounts and track financial transactions."

For Evan Norris and Amanda Hector, the prosecutors working the
case, the two articles were highly aggravating.

They were investigating an international organization; possible targets were spread all over the world. Leaks could jeopardize the whole thing. Warned of a probe, corrupt FIFA officials could hide or destroy evidence, move assets, threaten possible witnesses, or even retreat to countries that don't have extradition treaties with the U.S.

The case was now formally before a federal grand jury, which gave the prosecutors the power to issue subpoenas, but also tightly bound them not to disclose anything nonpublic about it. If either of them violated grand jury secrecy, they could be prosecuted for criminal contempt, and they had formally notified the agents on the case that they, too, had to keep things absolutely quiet.

They'd already had a problem with details of the case appearing in the media back in August, when Andrew Jennings and the Reuters reporter published stories revealing that the FBI, and specifically the Eurasian crime unit, was in possession of documents pertaining to Chuck Blazer.

If the investigation was going to go any further—and now that they had Blazer in hand, it certainly was—this kind of thing had to immediately stop. Norris got the whole team together, looping in the IRS's Steve Berryman on a conference line.

Norris was, by nature, a reasoned and careful man. He liked to listen, but volunteered little when he spoke and valued the benefits of patience and restraint. On first impression, he could seem flat and devoid of emotion, but those who knew him learned that he could express very powerful feelings with just a slight narrowing of his brown eyes. Addressing the team, he tried to balance the seriousness of the leak with a measure of rationality, calmly citing "concerns" about information getting out, and trying to figure out who on the small team to hold responsible.

But nobody was willing to cop to such an impropriety. Perhaps there was another explanation. Perhaps nobody on the team had leaked. In order to conduct formal interviews with the English bid officials, American investigators had been obliged to get permission from British law enforcement, and several members of a Metropolitan Police unit dedicated to organized crime had tagged along to the meetings.

The U.K. was both obsessed with soccer and possessed a highly aggressive press that was deeply sourced in law enforcement. The *Telegraph* reporters had been covering the World Cup bidding story for some time and had broken numerous big stories on the topic. Barring any other evidence, the most likely explanation, Norris decided, was that someone from Scotland Yard had been the source of the leak.

There was no way to be sure, and it would be pointless to try to get the Brits to confess. But the newspaper story made clear that despite soccer's low profile in the U.S., it was a gigantic deal in the rest of the world, and it would be hard to keep a lid on any operations they undertook abroad.

So Norris delivered a new mandate. They would stop working with foreign law enforcement entirely. No conducting interviews abroad. No requesting records from foreign governments or overseas banks. And absolutely no more talking to the press. Andrew Jennings, helpful though he might be, was out.

There was no question that all those restrictions were, in some ways, going to make the case trickier to develop. Considering how many meetings, tournaments, and other soccer events took place outside the borders of the United States, and how many of the potential targets weren't American, it was as if they were intentionally tying their hands behind their backs. But they would just have to get creative and figure out different ways to gather evidence. Secrecy was paramount.

The case was going dark.

———

Chuck Blazer was Queen for a Day.

It was December 29, a Thursday, and cold, with temperatures in Brooklyn hovering right around freezing. Blazer settled into a conference room in the United States Attorney's Office overlooking Cadman Plaza.

Blazer had been caught in a crime, a serious and easy-to-prove felony, and his goal was to trade useful information for a better deal down the road.

First, however, Norris spoke. Although he was nearly as tall as Blazer, the prosecutor seemed almost comically slender beside the hulking man, occupying just a fraction of the space at the table, swimming in his dark suit while the soccer official threatened to burst out of his. Norris's face betrayed no emotion, other than a slight furrowing of his thick eyebrows, as he stared at Blazer and calmly explained exactly what was about to happen. If there had been any confusion about who was in charge, it immediately dissipated.

This was a proffer session. Blazer was not being offered a plea deal or immunity of any kind. Instead, Norris assured Blazer that any information he provided, including indications of any crimes he himself had committed, would not be held against him in court. The prosecution would simply use whatever he told them as "leads" to hunt down evidence of other crimes by others. Although that protection did not extend beyond what was said that day, in that room, it meant that for the moment Blazer could freely share without fearing it would leave him in worse shape.

Criminal attorneys snidely called proffer sessions "Queen for a Day" meetings, after the 1950s and 1960s game show by the same name, in which four down-on-their-luck women would be interviewed by host Jack Bailey about their hardships. After they were all done, the studio audience would vote with applause on whose sob story was most heart-wrenching, and the winner would be wrapped in velvet robes, crowned, seated on a throne, given four dozen roses, and showered with gifts, inevitably breaking into tears.

This, then, was Blazer's big chance to be Queen Chuck.

Unless, of course, he lied. Or told anyone else he was cooperating. Or got caught holding back. Or came up with some other creative way to hold up the investigation. If Blazer misbehaved, then the prosecutors were free to dredge up every crime he mentioned and use them directly against him.

The prosecutors would ask the questions, and Blazer would answer. They wouldn't reveal who else they might be talking to, or where the investigation was going, and, Norris suggested, Blazer should refrain from even trying to guess. They wouldn't even tell him what crimes they felt they could charge him for. They would test him. They would see if they could catch him in lies. They would compare what he said to what they already knew. No promises, whatsoever, would be made; a proffer was a one-way street.

Of course, everything would be very professional. This was a federal case, not some good cop, bad cop routine in a two-bit precinct house.

There was no yelling, no two-way mirror mounted on a grimy cinder block wall opposite a steel table. The conversation was not being secretly recorded. The stone-faced FBI agents in the room weren't there to interrogate, threaten, or cajole. They were there to quietly take handwritten notes—prosecutors sometimes jokingly referred to the agents as "scribes"—and after it was over, to type them up into an official memorandum for the case file.

That was the deal. If it didn't seem fair, that's because it most certainly was not. But for Blazer, it represented the first step toward earning the cooperation agreement he coveted, his chance at avoiding a long prison term, and it started with him signing the document Norris slid across the table.

Proffer letters vary widely among the country's ninety-four judicial districts. Some are a little softer, offer a tiny bit of wiggle room for the defendant, or give them a bit more protection should things go south. But the Eastern District of New York has one of the toughest, least generous letters anywhere, with terms that very much favor the prosecution.

"This is not a cooperation agreement," it read. "The Office makes no representation about the likelihood that any such agreement will be reached in connection with this proffer."

Blazer signed. He would sign a similar agreement at each additional proffer session he attended, nineteen in all, spread over the next two years.

––––––––

The main offices of Fedwire and CHIPS were just a few minutes' walk from each other in lower Manhattan, and after sending so many subpoenas to them over the past several months, Berryman thought it was well past time to go visit in person.

The IRS agent found himself in New York constantly as the case progressed, staying in a government-rate hotel downtown and working out of either the FBI field office, which he found stuffy and noisy, or his hotel room. Given the distance from home, Berryman often stayed for several weeks at a time, far from his wife back in California.

In January 2012, he was in New York again to attend Blazer's initial proffers, and took time one day to visit CHIPS, which was a private company owned and operated by a consortium of banks. Berryman hit it off with the general counsel, and as they chatted, it occurred to him that the rest of the team would benefit from gaining a better understanding of how tracing worked. So he asked the lawyer if he wouldn't mind getting together with a few other agents and a prosecutor or two to explain to them the kind of information they could get through subpoenaing the system.

Within a few days, Berryman had set up meetings at both CHIPS and Fedwire, and convinced Norris, Hector, and the FBI's Jared Randall to come along. The first meeting was at government-owned Fedwire, housed within the Federal Reserve Bank of New York building on Liberty Street. The building, opened in 1924 and modeled after a Medici palace, is a kind of fortress, occupying an entire city block, and its basement vault contains the world's largest deposits of gold bullion, some 17.7 million pounds of the shiny stuff at the time of the meeting.

High above all that wealth, the team working the soccer case watched a presentation about how money moved in an electronic and almost instantaneous era. More expensive for banks to use than CHIPS because of the way it accounted for transactions and the speed with which it conducts them, Fedwire was the smaller domestic service. Nonetheless, it had originated 127 million wire transfers in 2011, moving $664 billion among the more than nine thousand banks around the world with which it worked. That meant that the names, addresses, and account numbers associated with hundreds of millions of wire transfers were just a subpoena away.

Money laundering was a very modern crime, apt for a globalized age of international commerce. Anyone could commit murder, but only the wealthy and powerful had the resources required to move ill-gotten capital through complicated webs of companies created at their behest by expensive lawyers. Almost by definition, money laundering deprived governments of taxes that could be used to the benefit of law-abiding citizens, and it helped obscure the frequently serious crimes that generated the money in the first place. Yet despite the gravity of the offense, money launderers typically operated with the impunity that comes with great privilege, unable to believe that they could ever be touched.

To Berryman, it was fascinating. Hunting down money launderers was, to his mind, the most exciting thing happening in law enforcement. The U.S. government had busted huge money laundering operations in recent years, ranging from narcos in Mexico washing drug profits through money exchanges and New York banks, to Russian oligarchs using remote South Pacific islands to clean up their plunder. Those cases barely scratched the surface of a giant global industry dedicated to hiding dirty money.

The soccer investigation was an excellent case in point. FIFA officials taking bribes needed to hide that income since it couldn't be justified, and they frequently used shell companies in tax havens and phony service contracts in order to make the fruit of their crimes disappear. Fans of the sport, meanwhile, were left helplessly bemoaning what had become an open secret: the sport was dirty from top to bottom. The people's game had become the property of selfish men pretending to be some species of public servant, while hiding countless millions of dollars in far-flung corners of the world.

It had been that way for years, if not decades, and nobody had been able to do a thing about it, despite widespread accusations of corruption. But that, Berryman thought to himself, was because nobody had ever had the combination of desire, knowledge, and opportunity to take it on.

After the meeting, Berryman chatted excitedly with the rest of the team, happy to see they were beginning to understand the incredible power Fedwire and CHIPS represented for a big international investigation like this one. But not everyone seemed so impressed.

"Good job, Steve," was all Randall said, before heading back to the FBI field office a dozen blocks uptown and skipping out on the second presentation at CHIPS.

The cool response came as a surprise to Berryman, who assumed that his voracious appetite for information that could help the case would be shared by everyone else on the team. As soon as he had joined, Randall had passed Berryman a folder of documents related to corruption in soccer, and he had responded by regularly sharing articles on the topic on the assumption the FBI agent was as captivated by the topic as he was.

Berryman knew that Randall had talked numerous times with

Andrew Jennings, a formidable repository of information about the sport in his own right; he'd even listened in on one of Randall's calls with Jennings. And after reading Jennings's 2006 exposé *Foul!*, documenting corruption within FIFA and focusing in particular on Blatter and Warner, Berryman had bought copies of the book for Norris and Randall.

The truth was that few people could match Berryman's enthusiasm for the tortuously slow grind of money laundering investigations and, at the same time, his degree of righteous indignation at the idea of people corrupting soccer. On a case with as much potential as this one, it went without saying that everyone would work long hours and make sacrifices. But not everyone seemed to care as much as Berryman that foul play could have played a role in determining where the World Cup would be held.

For most of the people on the case, it all seemed rather straightforward: run it like any other investigation and when the well went dry, pack up and move on. But Berryman didn't see it that way at all. He had no intention of stopping until he had brought down every corrupt FIFA boss, all of the men who sat in that underground bunker in Zurich and stole from the game.

When he wasn't filing subpoenas or combing through the results of them, he spent every spare moment reading up on soccer corruption. He forwarded the articles, one after the next, to the rest of the team, excited for them to learn the latest developments on the subject. But all too often, the articles he enthusiastically passed along to the rest of the team sat in their inboxes, unopened and unread.

———

Norris and Hector had gone into the Blazer proffers hoping to confirm suspicions that FIFA elections were rigged and that high officials routinely accepted bribes in exchange for their votes. They were not disappointed.

Blazer's tale was complicated but fascinating, and often downright funny, peppered with off-color anecdotes and dirty jokes. The man's charisma, difficult to spot in the photos of him dressed in silly Halloween costumes on the Internet, was obvious to everyone in the room. He had a certain magnetic presence and it was becoming easier to see how a soccer outsider from a country with little interest in the sport could have risen so far.

Right off the bat, Blazer confessed he had agreed to take money in exchange for his vote for South Africa to host the 2010 World Cup, and that other countries had tried to bribe him at the same time as well. He had also, he said, helped coordinate a bribe for Warner to vote for Morocco to host the 1998 World Cup, although he personally received no money because he wasn't a member of FIFA's ExCo at the time.

This kind of activity wasn't rare, Blazer said—it was the rule, and everybody on the FIFA ExCo knew it was happening. But if the prosecutors wanted to know where the real filth was in soccer, the truly big money and pervasive corruption, then they needed to look beyond the periodic big votes in Zurich, beyond the selection of World Cup sites or FIFA presidents and all the other events that garnered the headlines.

The financial heart of the sport, Blazer explained, was in the marketplace for commercial rights, the contracts that allowed broadcasters to put soccer matches on the air and advertisers to plaster their logos on uniforms, stadiums, and halftime shows. It was those deals, thousands of them around the world, that made up nearly all of FIFA's billions of dollars in revenue.

And it was hardly just FIFA. Each of the six regional confederations had its own set of rights to sell, and in turn each of the more than two hundred national associations around the world had a variety of rights to offer as well. There were massive tournaments such as the ultra-popular annual Champions League of Europe's top professional clubs, run by UEFA, the European confederation, or CONMEBOL's Copa América, held every four years and showcasing superstars like Argentina's Lionel Messi; there were hotly contested World Cup qualifying matches in each region; and there were sponsorship opportunities for every national team. Nobody wore a Nike or Adidas uniform for free, after all.

The counterparty to nearly every one of those right deals, Blazer explained, was a sports marketing company, the middlemen of the international sports world. It was a vast and robust, though little-known, industry dedicated to scooping up sponsorship and television rights to sporting events wholesale, then turning around and reselling them a la carte to networks, brands, and advertisers. Operating on the principle that organizations such as FIFA, the Oceania Football Confederation, or the Federación Panameña de Fútbol don't have the staff or expertise to sell their rights directly, sports marketing companies offered a fixed price ahead of time to take the rights off the soccer officials' hands.

As with any business, profits depended on paying as little as possible for the goods they turned around and resold, and the best way to ensure that the cost for soccer rights stayed below market value was to shut out the competition. That, Blazer emphasized, was where corruption came in: sports marketing companies systematically bribed soccer officials to keep prices low and not sell their rights to anyone else.

The bribes came each time a contract was negotiated, or extended, and occasionally even in advance of a negotiation just to ensure things ran as expected. Sometimes officials demanded the payments; other times the sports marketing firms offered them. Either way, the understanding was the same: we pay you under the table, and in return you give us an exclusive sweetheart deal for the rights. While the sporting press agonized over each political development that emerged from FIFA's Zurich headquarters, hundreds if not thousands of soccer officials around the world were getting bribes and kickbacks for television and marketing rights with little, if any, scrutiny.

Without doubt, there were legitimate rights deals out there, and soccer officials that were either too clean or too closely watched to take bribes. But it was a safe bet that the vast majority of soccer marketing deals, from the most prominent international tournaments to meaningless regional friendlies, involved no-bid contracts that undercut the actual value of the rights. That, by definition, deprived the sport of money that could be spent on development—literally giving balls and cleats to impoverished children—while the officials running soccer secretly pocketed huge sums and sports marketing executives got filthy rich in the process.

The sums of money were huge. FIFA, for example, booked $2.4 billion in television rights sales from the 2010 World Cup, and an additional $1.1 billion in sponsorship and other advertising rights. There was also more money in the U.S. than might be apparent. Thanks to the country's roughly fifty million Hispanics, it was in fact one of the most valuable markets in the world.

In 2005, for example, Blazer had helped negotiate a deal for the U.S. television rights to the 2010 and 2014 World Cups, a package that also included two Women's World Cups and two Confederations Cups, a smaller tournament played in World Cup host countries one year before the big event.

ABC and ESPN had paid a respectable $100 million for the English language rights to that package. But Univision, which perennially ranked far behind the traditional broadcast heavyweights, paid more than three times that, a whopping $325 million, to transmit the same slate of matches to the country's Spanish-speaking audience. By comparison, TV Globo of Brazil paid $340 million for the same rights in the most soccer-crazy nation on earth.

The fast-growing value of the sport helped to underscore the scale of the corruption. Since 2003, CONCACAF had sold rights to the Gold Cup directly to networks and sponsors, using its own dedicated in-house sales team in order to cut out the middleman. As a result, in 2011, CONCACAF took in $31.1 million in television revenue alone, the vast majority from the Gold Cup.

By contrast, the Copa América, a far more popular and competitive tournament starring some of the biggest stars in global soccer, brought in surprisingly little to CONMEBOL. The deal the South American confederation had years earlier signed with Traffic for the tournament paid a measly $18 million for the complete package of television and sponsorship rights to the 2011 edition.

Clearly the Copa América should have been worth vastly more than the Gold Cup. But by agreeing to sell the tournament for far below market value in exchange for bribes from José Hawilla, the men who controlled CONMEBOL had vastly limited the amount the confederation could bring in for its most valuable asset.

It was hardly a coincidence, Blazer continued, that Traffic had for years paid bribes to him and Warner for rights to the Gold Cup as well, and that Hawilla had years earlier opened on office in Miami just to handle CONCACAF-related rights.

Soccer, Blazer made clear, was populated by two kinds of people: those who took bribes, and those who paid them. If the Justice Department really wanted to clean up the sport, it needed to take a hard look at men like Hawilla, who sat, perched like fat spiders, at the very center of the vast web of corruption.

Nobody in the room had ever heard of Traffic or Hawilla. Even Berryman, despite all his late night reading on the soccer business, drew a blank when Blazer mentioned his name.

———

It took a long time for Blazer to explain the complicated world of sports marketing and the equally complex structure of FIFA and its many satellite entities.

As Blazer spoke, an idea slowly started to form in Norris's head, and he felt a growing current of excitement. Midway through the third proffer, on January 18, 2012, he called a break and walked out into the hallway outside the conference room to huddle with the rest of the team.

Norris seemed unusually animated, and his eyes lit up as he made a triangle shape with his hands, joining his fingers together in front of his face. International soccer—FIFA, CONCACAF, CONMEBOL, and the Trinidad & Tobago Football Association—were all part of a single whole. They clearly fit the definition of a top-down enterprise, the classic organized crime "triangle chart."

There was a boss: Sepp Blatter. There were underbosses: the FIFA Executive Committee and the executives of the six regional confederations. And there were soldiers: the officers of each national federation. There were even consiglieri, the advisors and lawyers who helped the bosses run the show.

A $10 million bribe to Warner and Blazer for their 2010 World Cup votes; an envelope stuffed with $40,000 in cash for the president of some obscure Caribbean soccer federation; a kickback for the TV rights to a handful of Central American World Cup qualifiers. These weren't unconnected events. They weren't discrete and unrelated scams. It was *all* connected, Norris said, eyes shining.

FIFA sanctioned the confederations; the confederations sanctioned the national associations. And the sports marketing firms greased everyone's palms. Men like Blazer, or Blatter, or Nicolás Leoz in South America, or Mohamed bin Hammam atop the Asian confederation, might not have a hand in every crooked deal, but they were all part of the same cohesive enterprise. They had taken over soccer and corrupted it and now this was how the sport operated all the time.

Norris, Hector, and the FBI agents all had organized crime backgrounds. They recognized these kinds of structures and perhaps were overly primed to see them everywhere they looked. But they had tried to go into Blazer's proffers with open minds, unsure of what they were really dealing with in a still developing case. Now it was abundantly clear: global soccer was a kind of organized crime. In fact, they increasingly felt, it looked just like the mafia.

It was a crucial intellectual leap for the case. It meant that everything was fair game and everyone could, at least in theory, be prosecuted together under a single statute that would allow the prosecutors to leap across oceans and back through decades of corruption to build one unified, sweeping argument.

Berryman had been right. This did look like a RICO case.

FOURTEEN

THE KING IS DEAD, LONG LIVE THE KING

ENRIQUE SANZ, A TRAFFIC VICE PRESIDENT IN MIAMI, spent the early months of 2012 trying to handicap who the next president of CONCACAF would be.

Sanz, a serious young Colombian, had been the Brazilian sports marketing firm's man in the Caribbean for more than a decade, and had deep contacts in the region. He understood that the Caribbean's three-to-one majority in the confederation all but guaranteed that the winning candidate would come from one of the islands.

Full Play, Traffic's increasingly bitter rival, had failed to grasp that rather critical fact, and the $450,000 in bribes it had paid at the end of the previous year to try to secure rights to the Gold Cup had been in vain.

The Port of Spain bribery scandal was still reverberating, and numerous Caribbean officials were either under FIFA investigation or had been suspended, making it tough to predict which Caribbean would get the job. As far as Traffic was concerned, however, it was critical that Sanz answer the burning question as soon as possible.

With the Copa América lost, Traffic simply could not cede any more ground in soccer rights. The firm still controlled all of the CFU's 2014 World Cup qualifiers, and most of Central America's as well, but Media World, a rival in Miami, was steadily stripping those away. Since the greatest value, when it came to reselling rights to sponsors and broadcasters, was to bundle them by region, Traffic in early 2012 finally elected to join forces with Media World. The two firms signed an accord to split all costs and revenue, including bribes.

The question of exactly whom to bribe became much clearer toward the end of February when Sanz, conferring with contacts in the Caribbean, learned that the confederation's next president was almost certainly going to be Jeffrey Webb.

An affable forty-seven-year-old from the Cayman Islands, Webb was not a well-known figure in world soccer. He had never played the game, but seemed to enjoy it, helping run an amateur club in George Town, Strikers FC, when he was still in college. In 1991, he was elected president of the Cayman Islands Football Association, known as CIFA, and eventually worked his way onto FIFA's Internal Audit Committee and its transparency and compliance committee.

He also had the distinct advantage, unlike many of his Caribbean colleagues, of remaining untainted by the Port of Spain scandal. Although Webb had been in Trinidad for the meeting, he had never been accused of taking money and, indeed, had helped Blazer and Collins with their initial investigation in the days following the conference.

Good-looking, sharply dressed, almost debonair, he seemed the antithesis of Jack Warner: approachable where the Trinidadian was threatening; compromising where Warner was rigid; clean and respectable where the longtime CFU president radiated gangsterism and self-interest. But despite his low profile, Webb had built an influential network of friends in the Caribbean thanks, in great part, to his day job.

Since 1990, Webb had worked at Fidelity Bank Cayman Limited, rising to become manager of business development and a director at the bank. In that role, he oversaw a variety of financial services divisions, including investment banking, corporate finance, risk management, and, especially, money transfer operations at the Western Union branches Fidelity operated in the Caymans.

Over the years, Webb helped numerous Caribbean soccer officials set up anonymous offshore companies and bank accounts where they could receive payments without drawing unwanted attention. In 1995, for example, he incorporated one such company, J&D International, that was used by Jack Warner to receive income from sales of television rights he'd been awarded—sometimes for as little as $1—in sweetheart patronage deals from FIFA.

Enrique Sanz knew Webb well, and had chatted with him at a hundred different CONCACAF events over the years. But because Warner had always exclusively negotiated rights deals for the entire CFU, keeping the bribes for himself, Sanz had never had occasion to talk to Webb about how the business really worked. Now he had little choice.

Working fast, Sanz approached Webb even before the man had officially announced his political intentions, offering Traffic's full financial support for his campaign. Sanz also delicately made it clear that, should Webb be elected, he could expect to receive "side payments" in exchange for awarding Traffic the rights to the CFU's qualifying matches for both the 2018 and 2022 World Cup cycles.

Webb, it turned out, didn't require much explanation. In fact, the banker immediately understood what Sanz was hinting at, seemed to be expecting the offer, and was clearly of the opinion that such payments were a standard perk of the job, ones he'd been looking forward to receiving. But he also made a special request: Sanz should never negotiate bribes directly with Webb, but instead with a close friend, a British-born Greek-Cypriot named Costas Takkas, who had briefly served as CIFA's general secretary a decade earlier.

Takkas controlled several holding companies in the Caymans and the British Virgin Islands that had bank accounts at Webb's bank, Fidelity. Soon after talking with Webb, Sanz wired $50,000 to one of Takkas's companies, CPL Ltd., calling it "candidacy" money.

No rival candidates ever declared, and by late March, Webb had won the support not only of most of the Caribbean, but several Central American officials as well. On March 26, Webb accepted the formal nomination to be CONCACAF's next president, resigning his position at Fidelity Bank.

"I am humbled by the tremendous outpouring of support and encouragement received from so many of the member countries," Webb said. "If elected, it is my intention to build on that unity through collaboration, transparency, integrity, engagement and accountability."

The Boscolo New York Palace hotel in Budapest is not, by any measure, understated. Built at the end of the nineteenth century to house the local offices of New York Life Insurance Company, it blends Greek, Roman,

Renaissance, Rococo, and Baroque styles into a kaleidoscope of orna-
mentation and curlicue that the building's current owners describe as
"eclectic."

It was, in other words, precisely the kind of forum that proves ir-
resistible to international soccer officials. With its abundant gold leaf,
towering frescoes, and generously apportioned marble, the Boscolo was
a perfect venue for a sporting coronation.

Early on May 23, 2012, CONCACAF's delegates crowded into the
hotel's brightly lit Roma conference room, along with Sepp Blatter, numerous other soccer officials, and a raft of consultants, attorneys, and
sports marketing executives. The confederation had organized the one-
day meeting around FIFA's annual congress, scheduled to start the following day at the Congress and World Trade Center in Budapest.

But before Jeffrey Webb, impeccably turned out in a navy suit and
burgundy tie, could celebrate the start of his new, three-year mandate,
the American lawyer John Collins addressed the room to announce the
results of a preliminary audit of the confederation's finances. They were,
to put it mildly, worrisome.

The review had turned up numerous irregularities, among them
Blazer's 10 percent contracts, which had cost the confederation tens
of millions of dollars over the years. It had also discovered that the
$22.5 million Dr. João Havelange Centre of Excellence, a sports training
center in Trinidad, supposedly the property of CONCACAF and largely
paid for with grants from FIFA, was in fact the sole property of Jack
Warner. The former president had even taken out a $1.7 million mort-
gage against the property for his own benefit without the knowledge of
the confederation's Executive Committee.

Finally, Collins noted, it appeared that Blazer had for years failed to
file tax returns on behalf of CONCACAF, which as a registered United
States nonprofit was bound by law to do so. As a result, the confederation had, two years earlier, lost its tax-exempt status and was in serious
jeopardy of owing huge sums to the Internal Revenue Service.

"It is difficult to predict what CONCACAF's exposure will be," Collins grimly declared.

The confederation's delegates, including those who sat on its Executive Committee and had blithely signed off on its financial statements for so many years, now responded with horror and outrage, decrying the "obscene irregularities" of these "robbers with white collars."

Newly elected president Webb, for his part, said he felt "shock, dismay, upset" at the news, adding that "we must move the clouds and allow the sunshine in" before taking up the gavel and concluding the day's agenda. He had, indeed, many activities lined up, including a splendid private dinner in his honor at the even more elaborately decorated Karpatia Restaurant in a nearby part of Budapest.

That evening, over traditional Hungarian plates of goulash and strudel, Webb worked the room, which overflowed with the cream of the sporting scene as far as North America, Central America, and the Caribbean were concerned. Sunil Gulati, the president of the U.S. Soccer Federation, was there, and introduced Webb to Samir Gandhi, an attorney from law firm Sidley Austin's New York office.

Gandhi, a commercial litigator and soccer fan who grew up playing the game on some of the same Westchester County fields Blazer once roamed, suggested that Webb retain Sidley to conduct a full investigation of CONCACAF's finances under the prior administration. Considering the unpaid taxes and unauthorized loans, Gandhi thought the confederation might even be facing potential criminal exposure.

Since Webb had made transparency and reform his campaign platform, the lawyer also proposed creating a working group to signal that his new administration was making a clean break from the past. Gandhi suggested calling it the "Integrity Committee."

This all seemed like a great idea to Webb, who eventually did hire Sidley, but for the moment the new president had more urgent priorities, and soon moved on to other conversations, taking care to greet his friends from Traffic, especially Enrique Sanz.

Before traveling to Hungary, Sanz had been in touch with Costas Takkas, working out specifics of the first rights deal Traffic hoped to strike with CONCACAF's new president.

Traffic had controlled commercial rights to the World Cup qualifying matches to all the Caribbean Football Union member associations for a decade, and Jack Warner had demanded side payments on each successive deal. But with Warner gone, the rights for the 2018 and 2022 rounds of qualifiers had not yet been claimed. What would it take for Webb to cede those rights to Traffic, Sanz asked.

The price, Takkas responded, would be $23 million for the CFU, and $3 million for Webb. Take it or leave it.

A $3 million bribe was a huge ask for a relatively minor rights package. Including Warner's share, the rights to the 2006 qualifiers had cost Traffic a total of just $1.7 million. But Traffic was in no position to alienate the brand-new president of CONCACAF. Sanz agreed, then reached out to Media World to inform its executives that its 50 percent share of the bribe to Webb would be $1.5 million.

Now, standing amid the hubbub in the Karpatia restaurant, watching the new soccer president work the room, it was hard for a man like Sanz not to detect the irony that hung, almost palpably, in the air. Blazer was gone. Warner was gone. Not a thing had changed.

Sanz could also perceive something else in the moment. Opportunity.

———

On July 14, Jeff Webb announced he had appointed Enrique Sanz CONCACAF's new general secretary.

If anyone paused to wonder why a thirty-eight-year-old sports marketing executive with no history of political leadership in soccer but a potentially giant conflict of interest was a good fit for the job, there is no record of such dissent. According to a CONCACAF press release, Sanz had been "unanimously approved" by the Executive Committee.

"I am certain," Webb said, "that we have found a professional with competence and integrity to implement our road map to reform."

Sanz, a championship-caliber squash player from a wealthy Colombian family, said the appointment was an honor, and that he hoped to move the confederation's headquarters to Miami, where he and all his dear friends at Traffic lived.

Sanz had never previously shown interest in getting personally involved in soccer governance. He'd always been on the business side and though it was not unprecedented for a sports marketing executive to jump to the other side of the equation, it was exceedingly rare. Who could afford the cut in pay?

Yet somehow Sanz's colleagues at Traffic seemed unsurprised by his sudden move. Aaron Davidson, the president of Traffic Sports USA and Sanz's closest friend at work, seemed downright jubilant in fact. The firm had been in a panic for two years as it watched its empire slowly crumble. Now Traffic had managed to place an inside man in the number two job at one of FIFA's most valuable confederations.

"They could have conducted a worldwide search and not found a better qualified guy for the job," Davidson crowed to a sports columnist from *The Miami Herald*. "It's going to be fun to see his impact. He knows about selling TV, radio and internet rights. He knows about getting sponsors. He is a very professional guy with new ideas, which is what CONCACAF needs."

One idea that Sanz had been struggling with since returning from Budapest was how exactly to pay Traffic's share of the $3 million bribe to Webb. He and Hawilla had spent many hours figuring out the mechanics of doing it without anyone finding out.

Finally, they settled a plan: Once Webb signed off on the rights contract, Traffic would use its account at Delta National Bank & Trust Co. in Miami to wire money to a company called Time Winner Investments, with an account at an HSBC branch in Hong Kong. From there, the payment would be wired a second time, to an account in the name of Kosson Ventures, a company owned by Takkas, at Fidelity Bank in the Cayman Islands. From there the money could be wired to whichever accounts Webb desired.

Webb had been a banker for more than twenty years, and had extensive experience with international money transfers. So though perhaps the others could be forgiven for overlooking the fact that each of those wires would pass through easily traceable correspondent banks inside the United States of America before reaching their final destination, CONCACAF's newly elected president, who had campaigned on the promise of a new, corruption-free future for soccer, could not.

FIFTEEN

FASTER, HIGHER, STRONGER

ONE EVENING IN THE SPRING OF 2012, CHUCK BLAZER wheeled on his scooter into CUT, a trendy steakhouse in the Beverly Wilshire Hotel in Beverly Hills. He was meeting Alan Rothenberg, a politically connected lawyer who had over his career been the president of the U.S. Soccer Federation, helped create Major League Soccer, and been chief executive of the 1994 World Cup.

The two men had known each other for decades. Over steaks and wine they swapped gossip about soccer, Blazer regaling Rothenberg with stories of his exploits, some of them sexual. Blazer had called to propose the meal, but Rothenberg had thought little of it since they often got together when he was in town.

Unlike prior encounters, however, this time Blazer hadn't come alone.

Sitting on the other side of the busy restaurant were Steve Berryman and Jared Randall, doing their best to look inconspicuous as they observed the conversation from a distance, a job complicated by the appearance of numerous celebrities in the restaurant.

The goal of the meeting, which the agents had rehearsed with Blazer beforehand, was to talk about Morocco's failed bid for the 2010 World Cup. Rothenberg had been a consultant for the North African country's bid team, which, according to Blazer, had attempted to bribe him and Warner for their votes.

But when Randall and Berryman reviewed the recording their co-operator had secretly made during the dinner, they were disappointed. Rothenberg had said nothing of particular interest, and the investigators soon moved on.

Blazer began making secret recordings soon after agreeing to co-operate. He had close relationships with an astounding number of soc-cer officials, and, according to what he was proffering in Brooklyn, he'd conspired with many of them to commit illegal acts. The trick was to get those people to confess on tape and, thanks to the powerful FIFA ExCo seat Blazer still held, there weren't too many people in the soccer world who wouldn't meet with him, or pick up the phone when he called, un-aware that he was recording every word.

Thanks to modern technology, the days of heavy, bulky reel-to-reel tape recorders strapped across the chest were long gone. Blazer could walk into meetings carrying devices smaller than a nickel that could be discreetly hidden in a lapel, on the strap of a bag, inside a cell phone or key chain, or even a disposable water bottle with no worries of being discovered, or getting drenched in nervous sweat, or losing half his chest hair when it was removed.

The device wasn't the problem. The problem was that most of the people of interest to the case weren't in the United States.

In their weekly phone calls, Norris, Berryman, and Randall would strategize about whom Blazer should reach out to, on what pretext, and what he could say to convince them to incriminate themselves.

But because they were so terrified of leaks, the prosecutor resisted sending Blazer on covert operations abroad. He'd skipped the FIFA congress in Budapest for that very reason; his new federal taskmasters didn't trust Hungarian police, with whom they'd have to work, to keep their mouths shut, and so instead they'd concocted a story about Blazer's health that he could use to explain his absence.

But the 2012 Summer Olympics in London were coming up and they were just too tempting to the prosecutors. Not only would the en-tire FIFA ExCo and all its hangers-on be there, but the full galaxy of bid committee members, intermediaries, sports marketing executives, consultants, and IOC officials would be packed into town. The opportu-nities for interactions where potentially incriminating recordings could be made were tremendous. FIFA had a large contingent due at the games and so nobody would be at all surprised to see Blazer there; besides, the football official's time on the ExCo wouldn't last forever, at which point his value for covert operations would dramatically diminish.

And yet they did not trust the Metropolitan Police, not after the leaks to *The Telegraph.* They also couldn't operate in London without local law enforcement, so Randall and his supervisor, Mike Gaeta, got creative.

Reaching out to FBI agents stationed in the U.S. embassy in London, they came up with a clever plan. The Metropolitan Police Service, known as Scotland Yard, was gigantic. With 32,000 sworn officers, it ranked among the world's largest police forces, only slightly smaller than the New York Police Department. But tucked inside the sprawling metropolis was a little known, much smaller law enforcement agency: the City of London Police. Officially that force patrolled the one square mile area at the very center of London, and had only about seven hundred officers. Yet because the City of London contained Britain's financial center, the tiny police department had developed a highly regarded Economic Crime Directorate, which included a specialized overseas anticorruption unit.

It was staffed with a small number of elite investigators who said they would be happy to aid an American investigation. Assured by Gaeta and Randall that there would be no leaks, the team could move ahead with setting up meetings for Blazer in London.

Once the secret cooperator started getting replies to the first tentative emails he sent out, it was clear the investigators were going to have plenty of opportunities, as they called it, to make tape.

————

Less than two weeks into the Olympics, Berryman found himself flat on his back in his London hotel room bed, trying to listen to his own heart.

It felt funny. Laboring and out of rhythm, as if it were skipping a beat. Berryman had never felt it this way, and he suddenly grew very frightened.

"Did I make the right decision?" he asked himself.

Since arriving in London, Berryman had been engaged in what felt like the most exciting work of his career. London's enthusiasm over the Olympics had reached fever levels and the city was overrun with movie stars, tycoons, and politicians eager to be at the center of the world for a few days.

Like the World Cup, the Games are an opportunity for the elite of the sports governance world to mingle with the barons and billionaires who rule over the planet's nonsporting activities. FIFA's brass, including Sepp Blatter, were all camped at the five-star May Fair hotel in the heart of the action.

For days on end, Berryman and Randall, accompanied by a City of London policeman, had crouched in an unmarked van parked unobtrusively on the streets of central London, where FIFA's top officials were all lodged, as Blazer, wheeling around on his scooter, chatted with some of the most powerful men in sports.

He had, for example, secretly recorded a handful of Russians, including Vitaly Mutko, who had been a member of the FIFA ExCo since 2009, was Russia's minister of sport, and had been president of the Russian Football Union, and Alexey Sorokin, the dashing, smooth-talking former head of Russia's World Cup bid, who had since been named chief executive of the local organizing committee for the 2018 tournament.

Digging further, Blazer crossed Mayfair to the second story offices of Peter Hargitay, a Hungarian public relations man who had been paid roughly $1.3 million by the Australian bid in 2009 to provide "targeted lobbying within the body of the FIFA Executive Committee."

Hargitay, a chain-smoker with long stringy hair and a pencil-thin mustache, also had offices in Zurich, and seemed either to be friends with, or have worked for, every power broker in soccer. He had for many years been a consultant to Sepp Blatter, and had also lived in Jamaica for a decade, so he intimately knew Jack Warner and many other Caribbean soccer officials well. Before joining the Australian bid, he had worked for England's World Cup effort, and had also worked as an advisor to Mohamed bin Hammam.

Yet when Blazer huffed and puffed his way up the stairs to his office in early August, the only substantive topic the men discussed was the rumor that Hargitay's computers had been hacked during the World Cup bidding process. The meeting ended in just twenty minutes.

Then, as he did after every such meeting, Blazer rode over to the unmarked van and handed over his recording devices, one of which was hidden inside a fob on a keychain Randall had supplied him. Inside the van, Berryman and Randall would plug the devices into a laptop to ensure the recording had been made, and would listen to a few snippets before reviewing the conversation in detail from their hotel rooms. Some tapes, including those with the Russians, revealed little that seemed actionable, while others were much more promising.

Berryman loved being in London, his favorite city, and being there while making tapes of the criminals who had perverted the sport he loved made the experience unforgettable.

But now, flat on the hotel bed, Berryman questioned his desire to come at all.

In preparation for the trip, he'd visited his doctor to check out a nagging sinus infection. It was a routine thing, but when the physician listened to the special agent's heart, she made a face. Soon, Berryman was going through a battery of tests and consulting with concerned-looking cardiologists and surgeons. The left atrium of his heart was enlarged, they said, likely the result of a minor valve problem he'd had for his entire adult life, and now he'd developed a dangerous arrhythmia.

He needed surgery, soon, and the timing couldn't be worse.

Berryman wasn't about to miss out on London. He and the others had been planning this trip for months. He couldn't tell the doctors why he was so desperate to travel, so he simply begged: they had to let him go.

Berryman's cardiac surgeon told him not to worry, and said he could travel without problems. But when Berryman came back, he'd have to go under the knife, and if anything happened while abroad, he should drop everything and come home.

Struggling to stabilize his straining heart, Berryman thought about the past dozen days. He'd had a dark premonition one afternoon while eating a sandwich on a park bench in central London. A fortune-teller had approached, asked him a series of questions, then stared him in the face.

"You are having something done to you that will change your life forever," the old man had said before walking off without saying another word.

Another time, while sitting alone in the surveillance van on St. James's Street, Berryman had spotted Blazer scooting in his direction in the sideview mirror and got the distinct impression he was being followed. Blazer, who had just finished a recording, would stop to look into a store window and a strange man trailing behind would stop as well.

Panicked, Berryman called Randall, and when Blazer approached, he waved him off. Were they being watched? Was their cover blown?

The pressure Berryman put on himself as the case developed was immense and steadily growing larger. He was forty-nine years old and had been an IRS agent for more than a quarter-century. Because he started at the agency right out of college, he was eligible for retirement at year's end, but Berryman had put that off to work this case.

He could have been at home, puttering in his yard and spending time with his wife, or working on a crime novel he was writing about an IRS agent who teams up with an FBI agent to solve a series of anti-immigrant hate crimes. Instead Berryman could think of little else but the case. Normally he avoided surveillance operations, leaving the technical, time-consuming, and, frankly, boring task of overseeing consensual recording to the FBI. He preferred to sift through bank subpoenas. But now he wanted to be in on everything, flying across the country to attend nearly every proffer with Blazer, sitting in on each strategy session, planning every step in meticulous detail.

Berryman had completely dismissed the idea of retirement. He took every case seriously, but this one was special, and he knew that no matter how it ended, it would be his last.

And then, suddenly, he was on an airplane back to California, where on August 15, 2012, a cardiac surgeon cracked open his chest and saved Berryman's life.

———

Blazer's final recording in London was with José Hawilla.

He had emailed the executive's personal secretary prior to the Olympics to propose a meeting, and the men finally met for breakfast in the final days of the Games.

Since Blazer had told the prosecutors about Hawilla, the Brazilian had become a subject of great interest, and the hope was to catch him admitting to paying a bribe. The plan was to focus on a peculiar payment Hawilla had made to the former general secretary back in 2003.

The story behind the payment, according to Blazer, was that he had been short on cash and called to ask Hawilla to loan him $600,000.

It was of course no loan at all, and both men knew that Blazer never intended to repay a cent. Hawilla, using a trusted intermediary, arranged to send the money to Blazer's Sportvertising account at FirstCaribbean International Bank in the Cayman Islands. But the large payment raised a red flag with FirstCaribbean's compliance department, which wrote asking for "the source of these funds, along with supporting documentary evidence."

Blazer, of course, had no such thing, and dashed off an email to Hawilla's secretary. "We will need to construct a contract regarding this and other transfers," he wrote.

To justify the payment, the two men conspired to create a phony consulting services contract between Sportvertising and Valente, a Panamanian company owned by Hawilla's most trusted bagman, who made the payment. The hastily prepared, four-page document was riddled with errors, saying Sportvertising would "render consulting services to CLIENT in connection with the events sports, which aim is to assist CLIENT in the development of sponsors and publicities business."

These vaguely defined services would allegedly cost Valente a total of $1.3 million, split into a first, $600,000 installment and a second, $700,000 payment due later that year. The contract was deliberately backdated to October 1, 2002, in order to convince the FirstCaribbean bankers the document was legitimate so they would release the funds to Blazer.

From a prosecutor's perspective, the phony agreement, along with the bank's correspondence and Blazer's emails to Traffic, neatly traced the full narrative arc of a criminal act, all tied up in a beautiful silver bow. The key was to get Hawilla talking about it on tape.

But bringing up a nine-year-old secret payment over a meal in London was just not done. Soccer officials didn't talk about that sort of thing after the fact, especially not in public. And so Norris and the others concocted a cover story, relying on recent news out of FIFA. Michael Garcia, a former United States attorney from New York, had just weeks earlier been appointed as the new head investigator for FIFA's Ethics

Committee. He had been charged with reviewing the incident in Port of Spain and, by extension, CONCACAF as a whole. So, it was decided, Blazer would tell Hawilla he was under pressure from Garcia to review old contracts from the confederation.

Of course, Garcia hadn't so much as talked to Blazer, but it seemed a believable enough pretext. Blazer, hidden recording devices on his person, trotted the fiction out when he and Hawilla met in London.

After the usual greetings, Blazer, speaking in Spanish, asked Hawilla about the $600,000 payment, making sure to state for the tape that he'd gotten the money in two batches, one from a bank in Uruguay and another from a company in Panama. Did Hawilla recall those? Did he happen to have the documents? Blazer felt bad asking, he said, but he was being investigated by this FIFA prosecutor, Garcia, and needed to show the man the documents to get him off his back.

Hawilla and Blazer had known each other for years, and they got along well. Even after Blazer had cut Traffic out of CONCACAF's rights deals, they'd stayed in touch, and Hawilla had invited Blazer to the wedding of his eldest son in Brazil several years earlier. But something seemed off to the South American, and he denied ever making any payment, insisting the two men had no business together. But Blazer was insistent, and so Hawilla, eager to end the conversation, finally said he'd look into it when he got back to Brazil.

It was Blazer's final recording at the Olympics, the only one Berryman hadn't been able to help coordinate. Hawilla, who had been paying bribes to soccer officials for nearly a quarter century, had avoided implicating himself.

SIXTEEN

MY WAY

WHEN JEFFREY WEBB TOOK OVER CONCACAF, HE DOU-
bled down with his message of reform, never missing an opportunity
to condemn his predecessors, Warner and Blazer, and promise a new,
clean era of soccer governance. For starters, the new president made a
public show of not accepting a salary, despite warnings from advisors
that doing so might actually look bad, especially since Webb had quit his
banking job and had no obvious means of financial support.

Then, on September 14, 2012, Webb called the first meeting of the
Integrity Committee, empaneling an ex-PricewaterhouseCoopers partner, the former chief justice of Barbados, and a retired U.S. federal judge
to chair the three-person group, which was charged with "ensuring accountability, transparency, and good governance" in CONCACAF and,
in particular, overseeing "all investigations pertaining to past practices
from the previous leadership."

The investigations themselves would be handled by attorneys at Sidley Austin, led by a personable and detail-oriented former federal prosecutor in New York named Tim Treanor.

His mandate was to unpack twenty years of financial misdeeds, and
it was no easy task. For months, Treanor and his colleagues sat with
CONCACAF employees in marathon interview sessions, drilling them
with questions about the confederation's finances, operations, and the
many complicated arrangements dreamed up by Blazer and Warner.
Staffers were asked to hand over documents, dig through endless spreadsheets, and return multiple times for interviews. Those who complained
that the sessions felt more like interrogations were given a simple choice:
cooperate or be fired.

Not everyone was willing to help, of course. Sanz, the new general secretary, told the Sidley lawyers that during a September visit to Warner's former offices in Trinidad, he noticed documents being shredded and Warner himself refusing requests for interviews.

And when the Integrity Committee wrote to Blazer asking for documents, it went nowhere. "We decline to comply with your request for documents, interviews or other information," Blazer's attorney, Stuart Friedman, wrote. The former general secretary had kept visiting the confederation's seventeenth-floor offices for four months after his last day on the job, and by the time Sidley showed up to collect documents and copy hard drives, all of Blazer's records were long gone.

Even without the documents, Treanor and his colleagues began to suspect that there was indeed quite a bit of criminal exposure, particularly due to Blazer's failure to file CONCACAF's federal taxes for so many years. And in exchange for their diligent work, the firm charged handsomely, billing the confederation roughly $1 million a month.

There was one area where Treanor and his colleagues didn't poke around, however; anything that took place after December 31, 2011, when Blazer and Warner were both gone from the confederation. Sidley's was strictly a backward-looking mandate, and while the lawyers hailed "the reform efforts initiated by Webb," as well as the "additional measures intended to safeguard the integrity of the sport" by Sanz, they paid scant, if any, attention to what those two men were actually up to now that they controlled the purse strings of the confederation.

———

"Out with Frank Sinatra," Webb grandly declared to wide-eyed CONCACAF employees in New York on occasion of his first post-election visit. "In with Jay-Z."

The new president immediately declared that Chuck Blazer's and Jack Warner's adjacent offices in Trump Tower needed updating, so he brought in Sanz's Brazilian wife, Roberta, to redecorate. She soon had redone the entire space, ripping out sheets of heavy marble in favor of clean lines and high-design furniture, then handed in a huge, six-figure bill for the job.

Then just as quickly, Webb abandoned the place, claiming he

preferred to work at home in Cayman, while Sanz, who couldn't stand the frigid New York winters, set up shop in Miami. Webb went to a tailor, on CONCACAF's dime, and got new suits fitting his state position. He hired a public relations specialist to teach him how to look good on camera and, with any luck, attain higher standing within FIFA.

Webb loved flash and glitter. He adored big watches, and eye-catching cars that made a lot of noise; expensive hotels, private jets, and luxurious accommodations. A divorced father of two, he was at the time of his election already engaged to be married a second time, but that didn't stop him from going out, night after night, paying all the bills with CONCACAF's corporate card, of course.

In Sanz, Webb had found a perfect general secretary, willing to approve his extravagant expenses if he'd do the same in return. Webb hired his fiancée's cousin, a lawyer in Miami, to be his in-house advisor, while Sanz brought in his best friend's wife to handle human resources, despite her total lack of experience in the field. The two officials traveled where they liked, hired whom they wanted to hire, and did what they wanted to do. A soccer confederation, truly, was a wonderful toy to have.

In mid-July, Webb invited CONCACAF's Executive Committee, at the confederation's expense, to a several-day retreat at the luxurious Ritz-Carlton on Grand Cayman, where a gala dinner was held in his own honor. Before a room of 250 people, Webb was showered with praise before being awarded the Queen's Diamond Jubilee Medal of Honour by McKeeva Bush, the island nation's highest elected official.

Then he traveled to London for the Olympics and was introduced by Sanz to José Hawilla. The two men had never met, and though the Brazilian spoke excellent Spanish as well as his native Portuguese, his English was quite poor. As a result, they spoke for only a few minutes; little more than a handshake and a few smiled formalities. But Webb dispatched Sanz right afterward to convey an important message to his former boss.

Webb wanted Traffic "to become the official company of CONCACAF," Sanz told Hawilla, sitting in the lobby bar of the May Fair hotel. Webb would agree to sell all of the confederation's television and sponsorship rights exclusively to the firm. But, Sanz added, Webb also demanded bribes worth 25 percent above every deal, a figure that left Hawilla's jaw on the floor.

After more than two decades of negotiating payoffs to soccer officials, Hawilla had thought he had seen everything. Leoz, the South American confederation president, had once taken a rights contract, unsigned, into his hotel room and refused to endorse it until Hawilla promised him $1 million on the spot. Heads of national associations routinely demanded free uniforms, balls, and other equipment on top of money, not to mention free airfare, accommodations, and VIP tickets to events. Some officials wouldn't even send their national team's best players to compete in tournaments if they didn't get a little extra money on the side first.

These men weren't blind; they saw how profitable Traffic was, and how wealthy buying up soccer rights had made Hawilla. If there was so much money to be made from the game, the officials figured, they wanted their piece.

But Webb's expectations were truly astronomical. He'd already extracted $3 million to sign the piddling CFU World Cup Qualifiers contract, which amounted to almost 15 percent of the face value of the accord. That deal had been in conjunction with Media World, as part of Traffic's arrangement to split CONCACAF qualifier contracts between the two firms. As a result, Hawilla's own share of the bribe was only $1.5 million, but then again, $1.5 million was still quite a lot of money.

At first, Hawilla flatly dismissed the notion of agreeing to pay even larger bribes to Webb. Considering how rapidly the value of rights contracts had been escalating, he could soon be on the hook for tens of millions of dollars if he didn't push back.

"You shouldn't get involved in this kind of thing," Hawilla told Sanz in London. "You're just starting your career."

"It's not me," Sanz protested. "It's Jeff."

"You're just an intermediary, Enrique," Hawilla replied. "This isn't going to happen."

But Sanz kept insisting as the weeks and months went by, saying Traffic had to keep Webb happy if it wanted to lock down the region and keep out competitors like Full Play. Besides, he pleaded, it would help him prove to Webb that he, as general secretary, could deliver.

Hawilla had known Sanz for a dozen years, had attended his wedding, and felt protective of him. On the one hand, it troubled him that his protégé was getting so deeply involved in the filthiest side of the business, the part that he personally hated the most. But on the other hand, Hawilla desperately wanted Sanz to succeed—for both of their sakes.

On November 13, Traffic wired $1 million of the bribe it owed Webb for the CFU qualifiers. It used the complicated series of transfers Sanz and Hawilla had settled upon months earlier and included a $200,000 fee to pay the middlemen who helped obscure the payment. Two weeks later, CONCACAF officially announced its latest rights agreement, ceding exclusively to Traffic the sponsorship, marketing, advertising, and hospitality rights for the 2013 Gold Cup, the next two editions of the CONCACAF Champions League, and several smaller tournaments.

Hawilla hadn't been terribly excited about the new deal. It was true that it brought the confederation's premier tournament back to Traffic for the first time in more than a decade. But the 2013 Gold Cup was scarcely six months away, leaving no time to properly market the event or line up new sponsors. In the end, all Traffic was able to do was renew Miller Lite as the exclusive beer of the tournament. Seen in that light, the $15.5 million price tag for the package didn't seem so terrific.

But Sanz had somehow managed to talk Webb down to a mere $1.1 million bribe in order to sign the new contract. Compared to the CONCACAF president's demands from the previous summer, that suddenly seemed like a downright bargain.

SEVENTEEN

THE PACT

WITH WELL OVER 100 MILLION FOLLOWERS OF THE faith, Brazil is the world's largest Roman Catholic country. While still a Portuguese colony, all Brazilians were forced to pay taxes to the Church, and well into the nineteenth century priests were paid government salaries. Divorce wasn't legal in Brazil until 1977, when nearly 90 percent of the population still described itself as Catholic.

On August 6, 1978, Pope Paul VI suffered a massive heart attack just after communion while staying at the papal summer residence in Castel Gandolfo and died three hours later. But the pope's death also happened to fall on the same day as the semifinals of Brazil's professional soccer championship. And as it happened, the news reached Porto Alegre in the middle of a crucial match there between Internacional and Palmeiras, with José Hawilla of TV Globo calling the action from the broadcast booth in Beira-Rio stadium.

Hawilla, one of the nation's top commentators, paused from his patter for a report from one of his men on the sidelines. "Internacional's fans are devastated to have just heard news over the loudspeaker of the Pope's death," the reporter said. But the man's handheld microphone betrayed him. Far from weeping and gnashing of teeth, television audiences instead heard the booming chants of more than fifty thousand euphoric fans packed in the stands, desperately urging Internacional to victory and oblivious to the news.

Hawilla, too, was Catholic, but he didn't utter a single word in response. Without mentioning the pope, he simply returned to his play-by-play without comment, and let the match come to its conclusion: a 1–1 tie that gave Palmeiras a pass to the finals.

In Brazil the one true religion is soccer and the sport had been at the center of Hawilla's life for more than fifty years. It had shown him the world, helped him become friends with legends like Pelé, and provided his family with a lifestyle he could never have imagined as the son of a dairy farmer.

He had fallen in love with the sport early, and it had consumed him with passion and excitement. But now he wanted out.

Hawilla was proud of what he'd built, but at the age of sixty-nine, the fun was long gone. Competition had grown much fiercer, margins had shrunk, and every year soccer officials grew bolder with their endless demands for bribes.

On top of losing rights to most of the South American World Cup qualifiers and being forced to sign a cost and revenue sharing agreement with the little upstart Media World to keep its hand in CONCACAF's World Cup qualifiers, Traffic had also lost ground at home. In August 2012, Hawilla had been obliged to sign another collaboration agreement, this time with a former associate who had left Traffic and promptly stolen away rights to the Copa do Brasil, the country's top-level professional league, by offering millions of dollars in bribes to three of the country's top soccer officials.

Traffic had held those rights since 1990, and Hawilla saw little choice but to join up with his former friend. Gritting his teeth, he agreed to help pay the bribes for the next decade in exchange for half the profits from the deal.

The headaches hardly stopped there. Traffic's investment in a second-tier American professional soccer league, the NASL, was hemorrhaging more cash every year as franchises faced low attendance and teetered on the edge of insolvency. The clubs Hawilla owned in Portugal and Brazil didn't make any money either; a huge training ground he had built two hours outside of São Paulo wasn't working out; and a youth soccer academy that was supposed to turn out star players Traffic could represent was mismanaged and a money-loser.

Then there were the newspapers. Harking to his journalistic past, Hawilla bought his hometown paper, *Folha de Rio Preto*, for roughly $2.5 million in 2005 and four years later bought the metropolitan daily

Diário de S. Paulo, for 100 million reals, or about $50 million. By late 2012, he owned six Brazilian dailies and, like traditional papers all around the world in the Internet age, they were in a death spiral. Hawilla had cut costs, consolidated offices, and, in a painful last resort, laid off reporters, but all to no avail. As far as he could reckon, the newspapers had a value of approximately nothing.

The only saving grace was the TV stations. Hawilla owned four, plus a production studio, and they were highly profitable: He figured they were worth north of $160 million, making them by some stretch his most attractive asset. As for the rest of it—all of Traffic—he would happily sell and walk away from *futebol* once and for all.

He had tried to get out before. In 1999, Hawilla unloaded 49 percent of Traffic to Dallas investment fund Hicks, Muse, but had gotten back full ownership just a few years later in exchange for his half-share of a joint venture that controlled rights to the Copa Libertadores, a popular annual South American professional tournament. Then in 2008, the French media conglomerate Lagardère had come calling, offering $280 million for Traffic and the production studio, only to pull out when the global financial crisis hit.

Now Hawilla was eager to be done with it, to walk away and enjoy his grandchildren. Officially, he told potential buyers the price was $200 million, but in truth he'd accept $100 million just to be done.

But no less than that. Though he was already very wealthy, he still wanted to squeeze as much as he could out of Traffic. The problem was that Traffic's value depended on the rights contracts currently in its portfolio. Every single deal he lost took away from the company's worth, which in great part was why he was willing to join forces with rival sports marketing firms such as Media World.

But even with the Central American qualifiers and the Copa do Brasil back in hand, Hawilla still had little to say to would-be buyers about Traffic losing its most valuable asset of all.

Since 1987, the Copa América had been the company's great prize—it had netted almost $30 million in profit from the 2007 edition alone. It had been nearly a year since Hawilla had sued Full Play and CONMEBOL in Miami over their blatant theft of his rights, and the dispute was showing no sign of wrapping up soon. If anything, it was getting more heated. Hawilla's New York lawyers had hired private investigators to dig into the financial affairs of South American soccer officials, pushing his relations with the confederation to a new low.

Just two years earlier, a huge party had been thrown in honor of Traffic's thirtieth anniversary at the fashionable Hotel Unique in São Paulo and Hawilla had been toasted in front of some three hundred people by no less than Pelé himself.

"The most powerful man in Brazilian soccer," Rio de Janeiro daily *O Globo* had called him on the occasion.

But now Hawilla felt trapped, held hostage to what he privately called "a band of thieves." If he wanted to preserve Traffic's value so it could be sold at all, he had no choice but to continue paying bribes to crooked soccer officials. The whole of soccer seemed rotten to him, and he had begun to feel distinctly like a victim of the very industry he played a pioneering role in creating.

———

In mid-October, Hawilla flew to Punta del Este to go over some details of the wedding of his baby boy.

Rafael Hawilla and his striking fiancée, the daughter of a prominent São Paulo lawyer, were getting married on November 17, and wanted their big day to stand out. The party would stretch over several days, including gourmet meals at local eateries, a rehearsal dinner at Uruguay's top-rated restaurant, a beach ceremony for seven hundred guests beneath a custom-made canopy, a day-after poker tournament, and custom gift bags that included colorful silk scarves bearing the nicknames of the bride and groom.

There were a ton of details to coordinate, and the costs were commensurate with an event that aspired to be wedding of the year. The final bills weren't in, but when all was said and done, the whole thing would likely cost more than $1 million.

Unlike Stefano, Hawilla's older son, Rafael had steered clear of the soccer business. Concerning himself with Rafael's happiness allowed Hawilla to stop fretting over Traffic and the deplorable state of his business affairs. Traveling to Uruguay and resolving wedding problems felt like being sprung momentarily from a trap that he had unwittingly set for himself all those years back when he bought a little bus stop advertising company called Traffic.

And then, while in Punta del Este, Hawilla's phone rang.

On the line was Hugo Jinkis, the owner of Full Play. He had heard Hawilla was in town and, as it happened, so was he. They should get together, Jinkis said, to talk about the Copa América.

The soccer world is not so big. There are only so many tournaments, congresses, and championships and eventually everyone gets to know one another to a greater or lesser degree. Jinkis and Hawilla weren't by any means close, but they did have friends in common and one of them had recently put them in a room together in Rio de Janeiro to try to resolve the dispute.

In the Rio meeting, Jinkis had complained that Hawilla's lawsuit was becoming an increasingly large headache. The legal fees for a dispute litigated in U.S. courts were exorbitant, and in any case it was making it extremely difficult for Jinkis to begin selling commercial rights for the 2015 Copa América. Sponsors didn't want to touch it if there was a risk that an injunction could blow the whole tournament up. If the court fight went on much longer, Jinkis feared, it could effectively gut the value of the tournament from his perspective.

So he proposed forming a partnership to share the tournament, much as Hawilla had done with Media World and his former associate in Brazil. If Hawilla agreed to drop the lawsuit, Jinkis would cut him on the tournament all the way through 2023. But Jinkis also added an unexpected wrinkle: it would be a three-way split. The third participant, he said, would be Torneos y Competencias, an Argentine sports marketing firm that had, years earlier, been Hawilla's partner in the Copa Libertadores, and still managed the rights to that tournament.

Hawilla couldn't understand why Jinkis wanted to cut in another company, and flatly refused. From his perspective, the Copa América had been unjustly stolen from him, and it was already humiliating enough to have to negotiate with someone he privately regarded as a thief. Why should he be forced to share it with yet another rival? But as time passed and the lawsuit dragged on, it was becoming increasingly apparent that without the Copa América in Traffic's portfolio, there just wasn't much interest from prospective buyers.

So when Hugo Jinkis called him in Uruguay, Hawilla agreed to meet again. The Argentine's proposal hadn't budged. He still wanted to include Torneos y Competencias and asked if he'd please consider a third meeting, this time with the chief executive of that firm, Alejandro Burzaco, who happened to be in Uruguay as well. Hawilla reluctantly agreed.

Burzaco had made a fortune in banking and private equity before giving it up to get into the soccer business. He was extremely charismatic, and he and Jinkis, aware of Hawilla's reluctance, offered up a tantalizing sweetener when they all got together.

They'd been talking to South American soccer officials about a potentially very lucrative idea, they said, one that had bounced around for years but never gotten any traction: a special edition of the Copa América, celebrating one hundred years of the tournament, to be held in the United States in 2016.

Chuck Blazer had always blocked the notion out of concern that it would cannibalize the Gold Cup. But now that Enrique Sanz was firmly ensconced as Traffic's inside man at CONCACAF, there would finally be the opportunity to make the tournament happen.

They'd call it the Copa América Centenario, Jinkis and Buzaco said, noting that they already had buy-in from the key South American officials. Imagine: the biggest stars from South America, including Argentina's Leo Messi, Uruguay's Luis Suárez, and Brazil's Neymar, playing in Chicago, Miami, New York. Sponsors and broadcasters would be clamoring for a piece of the action. The profits could be huge. Was he interested?

Yes, Hawilla finally admitted, he was considerably more than interested.

EIGHTEEN

THE WARNER BROTHERS

WHEN FEDERAL LAW ENFORCEMENT AGENTS BECOME interested in people as targets of an investigation, there are a number of ways to keep tabs on them.

The best known is electronic surveillance, commonly known as a wiretap. With a warrant procured under Title III of the Omnibus Crime Control and Safe Streets Act of 1968, agents can bug a person's landline or cell phone, peruse her faxes and text messages, listen to her voicemail, read every single one of her emails, and scroll through her Facebook chats and Instagram direct messages, without the suspect being the wiser.

Unhappily for the feds, Title III warrants aren't easy to get. Judges make prosecutors jump through considerable hoops before issuing one. They must prove there is probable cause a crime has been committed, and describe what laws they think were broken. They have to identify whom they are targeting and, most burdensome of all, attest in extensive detail to the fact that they have already unsuccessfully tried every other possible means to gather evidence.

Wiretaps are meant as a last resort, and even when they're granted, they can be a pain. Among other things, they require huge amounts of manpower in the form of agents sitting round the clock in a dark and airless wire room, listening to every call in real time.

But there are other tools available that, while less invasive than a wire, are far easier to procure.

On September 11, 2012, a third prosecutor assigned to the soccer case, Darren LaVerne, filed a sealed application for a "pen register and trap and trace device" to be put on three South Florida mobile phones belonging to Daryan and Daryll Warner.

Pen registers provide a rolling list of all incoming and outgoing calls tied to a particular phone number, and can also be used on email. Although they don't capture the actual contents of the communications, they can help investigators gain a better sense of whom suspects talks to and how often, a particularly useful thing when trying to understand elaborate criminal organizations. Pen registers are also easy to get, as federal judges generally sign them without substantial review.

In the case of the Warners, the pen register application made no mention of soccer or the larger themes of the investigation, only that the Eastern District was "conducting an ongoing criminal investigation into possible violations of federal criminal laws." A magistrate in Brooklyn granted it for sixty days without comment.

With the pen register in place, the investigators would receive constant updates on every call the Warner brothers made, which, with any luck, would help them zero in on the real target: their father.

Bringing in Chuck Blazer had been a terrific coup. But short of Sepp Blatter himself, Jack Warner seemed just about the most important person the feds could possibly bring in. He had been the president of CONCACAF for twenty-one years, a member of FIFA's ExCo for almost twenty-nine, and an official of the Caribbean Football Union for even longer. There was almost no one in world soccer who hadn't crossed Warner's path, and given his apparent proclivity for graft, bribery, and outright theft, he doubtless had enough dirt stored in his brain and filing cabinets to bring a roaring RICO indictment home in no time.

Blazer had regaled the prosecutors in extensive detail about Warner's corrupt acts, including the bribes he took for his World Cup votes, and he'd also provided documentary evidence. But getting to Warner wouldn't be so easy as simply proving he had committed a crime.

Five months earlier, Warner had been named Trinidad and Tobago's Minister of National Security, an extremely powerful cabinet position putting him in charge of the nation's police and fire service, army, air force, coast guard, prisons, and immigration department. Even if the prosecutors wanted to request information about Warner from Trinidad or formally petition for his arrest at the U.S. government's behest, the entreaty would, bizarrely, probably have to cross Warner's own desk first.

Travel records showed that Warner came to the United States from time to time, but he was a high-level official from a foreign government and traveled on a diplomatic passport, which conferred immunity. He could not be arrested, detained, subpoenaed, searched, or prosecuted.

Jack Warner, in other words, was untouchable. But his sons were not.

———

By the time Warner's first son, Daryan, was born in 1968, Jack Warner had already committed to a life in soccer.

Five years earlier, he had been elected general secretary of the Central Football Association, a regional soccer organization in Trinidad's complex network of amateur leagues, and was a delegate to the country's national federation. Daryll, his second son, was born in 1974, as Warner was mounting a successful campaign for the federation's secretary, a position he would hold for sixteen years until taking over CONCACAF.

As his soccer career flourished, Warner traveled incessantly, seeing little of his sons and leaving the job of raising them to his wife, Maureen. She abided his absences and kept the family together, while her husband played almost no role in the upbringing of Daryan and Daryll. The boys, in turn, rarely complained.

Daryan was the bright one. He earned an undergraduate business degree at the University of the West Indies in Trinidad, a master's at Howard University in Washington, D.C., and did postgraduate work in Australia and South Korea. He spoke Korean and some Spanish, had his hands in a number of businesses, and enjoyed day trading stocks. His kid brother more strongly resembled their father, with the same wide-set eyes, broad smile, and gap between his two front teeth. But Daryll was something of a mother's boy, less academically inclined, and seemingly devoid of the entrepreneurship that drove Daryan.

Despite their differences, one thing united them: doing Dad's bidding. Daryan was the registered owner of a professional soccer club his father founded in Trinidad, and a manager of the travel agency his father ran. Daryll had for several years been a FIFA development officer in the Caribbean. And both sons were listed as directors of numerous companies started by their father.

It was Daryan who in 2006 sold World Cup tickets acquired by his father through FIFA for a huge markup, and, when FIFA hired the auditor Ernst & Young to investigate the matter, he was entrusted to cover up the evidence, take the fall, and ensure that his father wasn't implicated. Four years later, Daryll chipped in to help his father get more World Cup tickets for Daryan to scalp, ignoring warnings from FIFA that the practice was forbidden.

That was the deal in the Warner clan. Soccer was the family business and everyone was expected to participate. Dad was the boss, providing the brains and political influence, while Daryan and Daryll were the soldiers, doing the odd jobs, and, when problems arose, standing in front of the bullets so that their father remained unscathed.

———

Not long after formally joining the case, Steve Berryman checked to see if there were Suspicious Activity Reports on any suspects.

Known in law enforcement as a SAR, the reports are filed by employees of banks and other financial service providers to alert regulators to behavior that could indicate any of a number of economic crimes, particularly money laundering.

It was routine, something Berryman did on every case, and it was often a gold mine. This time was no different. In July 2011, a teller at a JPMorgan Chase branch in Midtown Manhattan filed a SAR after processing a cash deposit from Daryan Warner.

He had come to the window with 7,500 euros in cash, intending to deposit it at his account at the bank. But after being informed that under that day's exchange rate, the deposit was equivalent to $10,636.50, Warner did something odd. He asked for 500 of the euros back, bringing the total to $9,336.60.

To a trained teller, that looked highly suspicious. Under federal law, banks are required to file a currency transaction report to regulators for all cash deposits over $10,000. People who wish to avoid such government scrutiny often purposely make deposits just below that amount, breaking large sums of money into dozens of small transactions.

The practice is known as structuring or, more colorfully, smurfing—a term allegedly inspired by the image of an army of little blue men making hundreds of small deposits all at once. It is illegal, and by deliberately reducing his deposit to come in below that threshold, Warner had inadvertently given the teller the impression he was trying to hide structuring. The SAR detailing the teller's concerns was a very exciting find for Berryman.

Soon, the IRS agent had gotten a lock on many of the U.S. bank accounts belonging to Daryan Warner and other members of his family, and had begun subpoenaing for the underlying account information. He'd also figured out that the Warners flew almost exclusively on American Airlines, which had several nonstop flights a day between Miami and Port of Spain, and so he pulled the carrier's flight records as well.

With all those documents spread before him, Berryman could begin to see a crystal-clear, and highly unlawful, narrative emerge. Spotting structuring was an IRS agent's bread and butter, as easy and routine as writing a speeding ticket for a highway patrolman. Berryman had a good idea of what the Warners had been doing; now it was just a matter of proving it down to the last detail.

So, throughout much of 2012, Berryman undertook the laborious task of gathering evidence, tracking down deposit tickets and bank surveillance camera video, interviewing tellers, and getting handwriting analysis to verify that the signatures he found did indeed belong to Daryan and Daryll Warner.

It was meticulous, grindingly slow work, and Berryman loved it. It was exactly the kind of thing he relished for its completeness, for its elegance, for the fact that it didn't rely on anything except rock-solid documentary evidence. He determined to the minute when the deposits were made; he had photos of the Warners making them courtesy of the cameras on ATMs; and, thanks to an interview with the teller at the Chase branch in New York, he had evidence proving intent: by intentionally reducing the size of his deposit to come in below $10,000, Warner displayed clear knowledge of the law he was shirking.

The Warners had clearly been structuring for years, but Berryman decided to zero in on a five-month window starting soon after Warner resigned from all his positions in world soccer.

In that stretch of time, Berryman found, Daryan and Daryll traveled to New York, Frankfurt, Aruba, Las Vegas, Colombia, Jamaica, London, Prague, St. Petersburg, Guadalajara, and Dallas. Sometimes they traveled together; sometimes alone; in almost every case they'd stop for a few days in Miami before heading back to Port of Spain.

Nearly every time they set foot in the U.S., the Warner brothers would make a beeline to a bank branch or ATM to deposit cash. Mostly it was dollars, but also euros, rubles, and pounds. Berryman isolated 112 discrete cash deposits of less than $10,000 into ten different accounts at American banks made in the course of all those trips, amounting to a grand total of $619,563.70.

On August 29, 2011, for example, the two Warners got off an American Airlines flight from Aruba to Miami and, within a few hours, made deposits of $8,954.82 and $8,210.77 into accounts held by Daryll at Bank of America and Citibank. Daryll returned to Trinidad the next day, while his older brother flew a few days later to Las Vegas, where he made three separate deposits of $9,900 apiece into accounts at Chase and Citibank, before returning to Miami, depositing $9,950 into a Chase account, $9,900 into a Bank of America account, and $9,800 and $9,900 into a Wells Fargo account. Finally, on September 7, he deposited $9,950 at Chase, $9,800 at Citibank, $9,920 at Bank of America, and $9,960 at Wells Fargo, all in Miami and Coral Gables.

In the space of ten days, the brothers had deposited just over $126,000 in cash into seven different accounts at four different American banks.

Looking at all the deposit records he'd gathered, Berryman reminded himself that Warner's soccer days were over when all of this happened. He was a government minister earning a public employee's salary in Trinidad. It was hard not to wonder where all that cash was coming from.

———

Miami's waterfront is lined with soaring residential skyscrapers, glittering generic monuments to newly acquired international wealth jutting straight up from sea level. Over the past fifteen years, billions of dollars have streamed into these buildings, which seemed to sprout like saw grass as foreign investors used the real estate market to convert foreign currency into dollars and safely park them in the U.S.

The Skyline Condominium, in the Brickell neighborhood about a mile and a half south of downtown Miami, is as good an example as any of what might be called the South Florida foreign exchange school of architecture, which prizes speed of construction over any pretensions of artistic expression. The white and blue tower, completed in 2004, is thirty-five stories high and commands sweeping views of Biscayne Bay. It has a doorman, private marina, swimming pool, beach volleyball court, gym, and valet parking, features that make the edifice almost indistinguishable from the towers to either side of it.

In late 2005, Daryll Warner bought a three-bedroom penthouse in the Skyline for $990,000, financing the purchase with a mortgage that he applied for using false information about his employment, residence, income, and assets. He affirmed to the lender that he'd pay the $300,000 down payment from his own accounts, thus establishing that he was the sole purchaser, but in fact two-thirds of the money came from a cashier's check drawn on the account of a company belonging to his older brother, with the remaining $100,000 from an account in the name of the "CONCACAF Centre of Excellence."

Late on the night of Tuesday, November 20, 2012, Steve Berryman sat in a car parked outside the Skyline, staring up at Warner's unit and watching to see if all the lights had finally gone out.

———

Several weeks earlier, Jared Randall had received an automated alert from a Customs and Border Protection database that tracks the entry of every person coming into the country by air or sea. Law enforcement agents can submit names to watch out for, and as soon as one of those people so much as books an airline ticket, it alerts the system, triggering an automatic email.

As the team expanded the scope of its investigation, its border watch list had grown large, and alerts arrived with increasing frequency as global soccer officials came in and out of the country. Pending arrivals represented possible opportunities, provoking long discussions between Norris and Berryman about the benefits of serving a subpoena at the airport, for example, or trying to corner someone else and get them to flip. But because of their overriding concerns about preserving the case's secrecy, most alerts came and went with no action taken at all.

This one was different. Jack Warner was flying into Miami for

Thanksgiving, and his wife and both sons were going to be there as well. It was the opportunity the investigators had been waiting for.

Heart surgery had put Berryman out of commission for almost three weeks. Since returning to work, his heart had gone into atrial fibrillation several times, terrifying episodes that made him think he might have a stroke at any moment. When he flew to New York from California early that week, he was still so weak that he couldn't lift his suitcase off the luggage carousel without asking a stranger for help.

But early on November 20, Berryman put on a suit and tie and appeared before a United States magistrate judge in Brooklyn federal court to swear to a sealed criminal complaint against Daryan and Daryll Warner, then hopped on a flight to Miami and staked out the condo until he was sure everyone was asleep, what agents called "putting a target to bed."

About an hour before sunrise the next morning, Berryman met up with Randall, two local FBI agents, and two Miami-based IRS agents in a church parking lot. Mike Gaeta, as the C-24 squad supervisor, had largely been absent from day-to-day work on the case, occupied instead with overseeing the numerous different investigations his agents were working simultaneously, but he'd made the trip down as well. This was important. All of the agents wore bulletproof vests and nylon wind-breakers, with "FBI" or "IRS-CID POLICE" printed in oversized letters on the back.

They drove to the Warners' building together, parked in the under-ground garage, and rode the elevator up to the lobby, where a security guard accompanied them to a second, high-speed elevator, turning a key in the control panel to prevent the lift from making any unwanted stops.

The seven federal agents paused at the penthouse's black door to unholster their sidearms, letting the weapons hang at their side. Then Gaeta, arrest warrants in hand, knocked. It was barely six in the morning on Thanksgiving eve and the building was completely quiet. As they waited, the agents stood in the carpeted hallway bathed in the silence, eyes wide.

Finally Daryan, short like his father, but more muscular, with bulging biceps, a boyish face, and hints of gray in his hair, swung open the door, groggy from sleep.

"FBI," Gaeta barked. "You're under arrest."

Daryan let the agents in and they spread around the apartment, going from room to room to ensure there were no weapons, before returning and putting their pistols back in their holsters. By then, the entire Warner family was in the living room, stunned looks on their faces. The brothers needed to dress and fetch their passports, Gaeta said, and while they did, perhaps Dad would be amenable to a nice little chat.

As the other agents accompanied Daryan and Daryll to their bedrooms, Randall, Berryman, and Gaeta took a seat at the dining room table along with Jack Warner.

If they couldn't arrest the man, then maybe they could bust his kids in front of him and shock him into flipping. That was the big plan, and it was why Gaeta had made the trip to Miami. He was the talker, the one who had made a career out of converting hardened Genovese wiseguys into stool pigeons. He had started this case two years earlier and now, with any luck, he was going to take a huge step toward closing it.

"We would like to talk to you about helping us," Gaeta began, his New York diction seeming to thicken in the tense atmosphere. "This is your chance to come clean and fix things."

He wanted to know it all, he said. About the bribes. About Russia and Qatar winning the World Cup. About the tickets, the offshore companies, and about Sepp Blatter.

"You promised a tsunami," Gaeta said, referencing Warner's oft-quoted statements prior to his resignation from FIFA. "We want to know all about the tsunami."

"Where," Warner responded, "are you taking my sons?"

It was as if the two men were talking past one another, making eye contact but not really listening. As Gaeta grew more animated, laying his New York accent on stronger, Warner seemed to stiffen, and his high-pitched Trinidad drawl grew more pronounced. His initial jumpy nervousness faded, and his narrow features progressively hardened. Warner was much tougher than anyone had guessed.

"This is your chance," Gaeta repeated, "to come clean."

By then, Warner had his cell phone in his hand and seemed increasingly eager to use it.

"I'll think about it," Warner said, his eyes focusing now and filling with cold fury. "I'll get an attorney."

It was over. The conversation had lasted less than ten minutes. Warner wasn't biting.

By then, Daryan and Daryll were ready to go. The agents stood, disappointed looks on their faces. They read the brothers their Miranda rights, placed handcuffs on their wrists, then escorted them out of their penthouse, down to the garage, and drove to the FBI's drab, two-story field office in North Miami Beach.

By the time they got there, Jack Warner had retained lawyers for his sons. Hours later, Daryan and Daryll flew to New York, accompanied by Randall and several other agents, while Berryman stayed behind in Miami to interview a few more bank tellers about deposits the Warners had made.

The case he had made against them was strong. By structuring more than $100,000 in under a year's time, each brother faced up to ten years in prison on top of significant fines. They had little choice but to cooperate, and before the month was out they, like Blazer, would be proffering to the prosecutors in Brooklyn in hopes of winning a lighter sentence.

Norris and the others had viewed Warner as a key to the entire case, and had spent months strategizing about how best to reel him in before coming up with what seemed like a winning plan. But the wily Trinidadian had looked his antagonists straight in the eye, and he had not blinked.

The day after his devoted sons were arrested right in front of him, Warner flew back to the safe confines of his native Trinidad, far out of reach.

NINETEEN

"A SAD AND SORRY TALE"

EARLY IN 2008, A FEDERAL GRAND JURY IN BROOKLYN handed down a massive indictment targeting sixty-two members of the Gambino, Genovese, and Bonanno crime families, and in a series of takedowns in New York, New Jersey, and Sicily, federal agents made dozens of arrests. The Gambinos were particularly targeted, with fifty-four members of the family arrested, and eventually, an entire generation of Gambino leadership went to prison.

The operation had been a resounding success, splashed across the front pages of the tabloids, which prosecutors proudly cut out, framed, and hung on the walls of their offices. But the arrests and subsequent convictions did not fully dismantle the Gambino family business. Instead, with the old bosses out of commission, new leadership quickly stepped forward to take over, forming a three-man panel to secretly oversee the syndicate's criminal activities.

In January 2011, agents unleashed an even bigger takedown, arresting some 125 people based on sixteen different indictments. All three members of the Gambino crime family's new ruling panel were picked up, and in March of 2013, Norris temporarily left the soccer case to try one of them, a longtime mobster named Bartolomeo Vernace, handing the reins to Amanda Hector and Darren LaVerne.

On April 17, after an exhausting five-week trial, Norris won convictions on RICO, narcotics, gambling, loan sharking, robbery, firearms, and murder charges, and Vernace was eventually sentenced to life without parole. But once again, the arrests and convictions did not fully dismantle the family business. Long before Vernace's reckoning, another wiseguy, Domenico Céfalu, had stepped up as the new Gambino boss.

That was how it worked, fighting organized crime. No sooner did you bust one generation of crooks than you were chasing after the ones that came up behind them.

———

On April 19, 2013, Sir David Simmons, former chief justice of Barbados, faced the CONCACAF congress in the Westin Playa Bonita in Panama to announce the results of the lengthy internal investigation of the administration of Jack Warner and Chuck Blazer.

Working for the confederation's Integrity Committee, Sidley Austin's lawyers and a team of accountants had interviewed thirty-eight witnesses, reviewed four terabytes of data, and pored over reams of bank records, emails, and other correspondence. Their conclusion, Simmons said, was that CONCACAF's prior leadership had "misappropriated funds" and "committed fraud." Warner and Blazer had run the confederation entirely at their convenience, for their illicit profit, and should be condemned.

The 144-page final report, which had not previously been public, laid out as a breathtaking narrative of self-interest, incomplete disclosure, and outright theft. Between his 10 percent contract, other fees, and liberal use of the confederation's expense accounts to pay for his lifestyle, including rent, Blazer had skimmed an astonishing $20.6 million from the confederation between 1996 and 2011, the investigation found. He had put the soccer body at risk by failing to file its tax returns, and had caused it to buy numerous properties that were for his benefit alone.

Warner, meanwhile, had abused his presidency to secretly take ownership of the Centre of Excellence, thus appropriating for himself roughly $26 million in funds that belonged to CONCACAF, including $462,200 sent from Australia's soccer federation in connection with its 2022 World Cup bid. Warner had even set up secret bank accounts that only he controlled, in the name of the CONCACAF Centre of Excellence, that received deposits directly from FIFA that went to his benefit alone.

"I have recounted a sad and sorry tale in the life of CONCACAF,"

Simmons said. "A tale of abuse of position and power, by persons who assisted in bringing the organization to profitability but who enriched themselves at the expense of their very own organizations."

After the presentation, Jeffrey Webb, flanked by Sepp Blatter and Enrique Sanz, summoned reporters so he could loudly pronounce his disapproval. "Members are obviously very disappointed, some of them deeply disappointed," Webb said. "They have a right to be."

———

Webb had been the confederation's president for only ten months but he was already a star in the soccer world.

In late February, Webb had been named the Cayman Islands' "Person of the Year," and in early March, Sepp Blatter appointed him chairman of FIFA's new antiracism and discrimination task force.

Still just forty-eight years old, Webb was one of seven FIFA vice presidents and an increasingly in-demand public speaker and ambassador of the sport; rumors began to spread that he might someday replace Blatter as president of the entire organization.

He'd talked repeatedly with the leadership of South America's confederation about their idea for a Copa América Centenario, and he'd spent several days prior to the Panama congress escorting Blatter and FIFA general secretary Jérôme Valcke on a tour of the Dominican Republic, Haiti, and finally Cuba, where they had a face-to-face meeting with Raúl Castro himself. Everywhere he went, he touted the reforms he was making.

Indeed, Webb had made changes, considerable ones, but rather than cleaning up the sport, they seemed directed at surrounding himself with people who were loyal only to him and would protect his growing book of illicit activities.

Right off the bat, Webb brought in Sanz, his nexus with Traffic and the rich bribes that relationship promised. It was a remarkably brazen choice, one that put Webb's personal interests ahead of the confederation's, and a clear indication of how he viewed the role of president: an opportunity to grab as much gold as he could.

Sanz's opportune placement was mutually beneficial, of course, giving Traffic a massive edge over competitors since Sanz, working with

Webb, could shut out all other sports marketing firms. The arrangement eerily echoed the one forged more than thirty-five years earlier, at the dawn of modern sports marketing, when Coca-Cola and Adidas inserted young Sepp Blatter into FIFA as a development officer, ensuring their monopolization of soccer for years to come.

Next, Webb created the Integrity Committee to air out the stench of the prior administration, sending $2 million of the confederation's cash to Sidley Austin to produce its damning report, an expenditure that came on top of the law firm's generous monthly billings. In October, he formed an Audit and Compliance Committee, ostensibly charged with the critical task of reviewing the confederation's books to ensure that no more financial abuses took place, but he made sure natives of the Caribbean outnumbered all others on the panel, among them a close friend from Cayman.

In December, Webb formed a nine-man finance committee, chaired by a Jamaican power broker and a staunch supporter of Webb. That panel, too, had a Caribbean majority, including another of his friends from home.

Webb also created an integrity office, charged with monitoring corruption and particularly with rooting out what was rumored to be rampant match fixing in CONCACAF, particularly in the confederation's Central American countries, which had been targeted by gambling syndicates. Yet the office's director soon discovered that Webb had no intention of actually implementing any of her reforms, and eventually he stopped speaking to her altogether.

In January 2012, Webb pushed a Panamanian official off the confederation's Executive Committee and replaced him with Eduardo Li, a Costa Rican who had headed his country's soccer federation since 2007. Unlike the Panamanian, Li was loyal to Traffic and had a tight relationship with Enrique Sanz. In 2009, he had rejected an offer from Media World to purchase Costa Rica's World Cup qualifier rights, instead accepting one from Traffic; during negotiations, Sanz, still with the sports marketing firm at the time, had agreed to pay him a six-figure bribe.

Chuck Blazer had long ago announced that he would not seek another term on the FIFA ExCo after his current term expired, and

Webb made it clear he wanted Sunil Gulati, the U.S. Soccer Federation president, to win that coveted open seat. Gulati had been one of Webb's more vocal supporters, and had set him up with the lawyers at Sidley Austin.

There was considerable opposition within the membership to Gulati's candidacy, however, since many saw him as tainted by his well-known and long-running friendship with Blazer. Such attitudes would be "unfair," Webb told the confederation's delegates. "I would hope and I would think, that our membership is much more mature and beyond that."

Thanks to a decisive vote from the tiny Caribbean nation of Anguilla, Gulati was narrowly elected. And in the final agenda item of the congress, Webb convinced the membership to let five new full members into the confederation: French Guiana, Guadeloupe, Martinique, Saint Martin, and Sint Maarten. Yet more Caribbean members would only further solidify Webb's grip on CONCACAF.

Webb still drew no salary, and made a public show of that fact as some kind of testament to his purity. But his lifestyle was increasingly extravagant, thanks, in large part, to the bribes and kickbacks that kept flowing in.

On December 14, for example, the last half-million-dollar chunk of the money Traffic had secretly agreed to pay Webb for the CFU deal hit Costas Takkas's bank account in Cayman. Takkas turned around and sent part of the bribe to one of his own Miami accounts. Some of that cash was then transferred to the account of a local contractor who was preparing to install a swimming pool in an eight-bedroom mansion Webb had bought outside Atlanta, and when a bank official inquired about the purpose of the wire, Takkas said it was a wedding present for Webb. Another dollop was transferred to an account at SunTrust Bank in Georgia, which Webb used to expand his real estate holdings in the area.

On January 13, Webb closed on a three-bedroom, 1,500-square-foot place in Conyers, Georgia, for $64,000. Then on February 15, he bought another piece of Georgia real estate, paying $140,000 for a four-bedroom brick structure in the town of Stone Mountain that had been in foreclosure.

Chuck Blazer was still talking to the prosecutors, and Daryan and

Daryll Warner were deep into their proffers as well. But those cooperators could only tell stories about the past. They knew nothing about what
came after them.

CONCACAF was Webb's organization now, and it was just as
crooked—if not more so—as it had ever been. The growing parallels to
the Cosa Nostra cases that Norris and the other prosecutors on his team
were used to handling would have been striking—if anybody had bothered to take a look.

———

Jack Warner had been safely ensconced in Trinidad since his sons were
arrested. He hadn't breathed a word of the incident to anyone in the five
months that had elapsed, and he radiated confidence in public, mocking
the idea that he had ever done anything less than sparkling clean. But, in
truth, the walls were closing in.

On April 20, the day after CONCACAF released its integrity report
detailing decades of Warner's corruption, Trinidad and Tobago's prime
minister, Kamla Persad-Bissessar, cut short a visit to Washington. She
raced home to her private residence outside Port of Spain and convened
an emergency Saturday afternoon cabinet meeting.

Warner arrived in a pink and white guayabera, and waited on the
front porch, chatting with other ministers. A little after four, he was
received by Persad-Bissessar. The two met in private for an hour, then
Warner drove away without answering questions from reporters who
were waiting outside.

The seemingly endless string of scandals that dogged Warner had
made him a highly controversial figure ever since his first cabinet appointment three years earlier. But he was chairman of the United National Congress, the country's most powerful political party, which
controlled the ruling coalition that had put Persad-Bissessar into power.
He also sat on the country's National Security Council, which runs Trinidad's domestic and international intelligence operations. Although
Warner was despised by some, he was enormously popular among his
base, and feared by other politicians, who worried about his vast capacity for blackmail and revenge.

As a result, Warner was able to weather the global outcry over the

Port of Spain bribery scandal, as well as his subsequent resignation from FIFA, CONCACAF, and the CFU. In fact, Warner's power at home seemed only to grow.

Starting in February 2013, rumors began to swirl that Warner's sons, who had not been seen in Trinidad for months, were under house arrest in Miami. Warner, ever the cagey politician, refused to confirm or deny anything, stating he would "not say anything until somebody is bold enough to print something or to say something."

Then on March 27, Reuters reporter Mark Hosenball did just that, publishing an article claiming that Daryan Warner had become a cooperating witness in "an FBI probe into alleged corruption in international soccer." The article, which quoted an anonymous government official saying that "it's shaping up like a major case," curiously did not mention Daryll Warner, but made clear that Jack Warner was a focal point of the investigation.

It had been more than a year since anything about the case had been mentioned in the global press. Clearly sourced from directly within law enforcement, the new leak was exactly the kind of indiscretion that Norris, as lead prosecutor, had tried so hard to prevent.

Public reaction in Trinidad was immediate and fierce, and cries for Warner's resignation rose from rival political parties and trade unions. But the prime minister said in a statement that she was reserving judgment, and was awaiting corroboration of the information in the article from U.S. authorities "before making any determination or pronouncement."

The drumbeat grew louder when the *Trinidad Express* began to publish, on April 14, a massive, multipart investigation into Warner's financial affairs, revealing decades of missing, possibly stolen money, diverted soccer player salaries, scalped World Cup tickets, and public deception. Yet on April 18, the prime minister's spokesman insisted Warner "enjoys the full support of every single member of the Cabinet," noting that "he is one of the most hardworking ministers in our Cabinet and we wish more people had that work ethic."

The CONCACAF report, with all its specificity and detail, proved, finally, to be the last straw. Warner had become a public embarrassment and distraction for the administration, and was dominating conversation on the island. For his part, Warner said that the matter was "of no concern to me and as far as I am aware it is baseless and malicious."

The sun had long set on that spring Saturday when the prime minister finally stepped outside her residence to the glare of television lights and flashbulbs. Looking fatigued in a stylish red dress, she greeted the press with a tight smile.

"I have accepted the offer of resignation from Jack Warner as Minister of National Security," Persad-Bissessar said.

Three months later, Warner received a phone call from Trinidad's chief immigration officer, Keith Sampson, who asked for the return of the diplomatic passports he and his wife held. The island's Foreign Ministry, it turned out, had expected Warner to return the travel documents, along with his government-issued cell phone, keys, and computer, when he resigned. But he had not done so, and, according to local reports, pressure from the U.S. government had prompted a more urgent official request.

On the phone, Warner asked for an extra week so he could transfer his American visas, issued the previous December, to a regular passport. Seven days passed, but Warner still had not handed over the documents. He did, however, publish in a political newspaper he funded a virulent screed against the government for daring to ask for the documents in the first place.

Finally on July 26, Trinidad's immigration department canceled the two passports. Warner's diplomatic immunity was stripped, and he could now be charged with a crime in the United States of America.

Warner, defiant, told reporters he didn't care about the passport. He had no intentions of traveling overseas anytime soon.

———

On April 29, 2013, just ten days after CONCACAF aired its dirty laundry, FIFA's Ethics Committee published the long-anticipated results of its internal review of the ISL matter. Like the Swiss prosecutors before them, FIFA's ethics investigators found that the sports marketing firm had bribed officials at least since the early 1990s in exchange for soccer rights, including the World Cup. ISL had kept paying bribes up until its bankruptcy in 2001.

Other than the ISL officials who actually paid the bribes, it wasn't clear that anyone knew how many FIFA officials had been on the company's dole. But in the end it was corruption that killed it: the firm greased so many palms that it couldn't afford its aboveboard payments to FIFA and other sports organizations. ISL, for years one of the most powerful sports marketing firms in the world, had literally bribed itself into insolvency.

A week before FIFA published its findings, the ninety-six-year-old Havelange—whom Blatter had made honorary president of FIFA for life when he stepped down in 1998—quietly resigned. Teixeira, for his part, had given up all his soccer positions in early 2012. Swiss prosecutors had found that the two men had taken at least $15 million from ISL over the years, but let them off after they paid back scarcely a third of that. FIFA said Leoz, meanwhile, had taken $130,000 from ISL in 2000, and may have gotten an additional $600,000 over the years. On April 24, just five days before FIFA published its findings, he resigned as well.

With all three men formally out of the game, FIFA closed its investigation, on grounds that "any further steps or suggestions are superfluous."

TWENTY

"LEAVE US OUT OF THIS"

SOON AFTER THE TURN OF THE TWENTIETH CENTURY, the Miami River was dredged, and the huge quantities of silt, sand, and limestone pulled from its bed were dumped into Biscayne Bay, creating two unsightly waste islands just offshore, reeking and crawling with rats.

The islands were eventually consolidated into one landmass and named Brickell Key. Starting in the late 1970s, developers built a bridge connecting it to the mainland, and began erecting a series of soaring condominium towers that were mostly sold to wealthy buyers from Latin America. Most didn't live there full-time, creating an eerily quiet enclave just across a narrow canal from one of Miami's busiest districts.

Brickell Key is largely hidden behind locked gates and patrolled by security guards. One of its only public spaces is the five-star, 295-room Mandarin Oriental, a grand hotel that is among Miami's finest.

Early on the morning of May 3, 2013, Jared Randall, accompanied by another FBI agent and a translator, approached the front desk at the Mandarin Oriental. He identified himself, showed his badge, and asked the clerk to call José Hawilla's room and request that he come down.

Hawilla, bald with a soft chin, wire-rim glasses, and big dark eyes, had been sound asleep with his wife; it was not yet 6:30 in the morning. But he quickly got dressed and went to the lobby to see what this was all about. It was natural to feel nervous, especially as a foreigner, when the FBI showed up unannounced.

Choosing his words with care, Randall told the surprised Brazilian that the government was investigating corruption in soccer. Then Randall made a point of formally admonishing Hawilla: telling him deliberately that before they went any further, he needed to understand that any lies or misrepresentations could be considered criminal acts.

Hawilla, speaking in Portuguese, identified himself and acknowledged that he owned Traffic, which had its Miami offices on the fourth floor of a building on Brickell Key, not a hundred yards away from the hotel.

Then Randall cut to the chase. Had Hawilla ever bribed Ricardo Teixeira, Nicolás Leoz, or Julio Grondona, the Argentine soccer association president?

No, Hawilla responded, Traffic was a clean company that did things the right way. It didn't engage in that sort of conduct, he emphasized, and never had.

What about Chuck Blazer, Randall asked. Had Traffic or its intermediaries ever bribed Chuck Blazer or offered to do so?

No, Hawilla replied.

Did he know about any companies that had been used to send money to Blazer?

No, Hawilla repeated.

Could he recall if any money had ever been sent to Blazer on Traffic's behalf through a company in Panama?

No.

What about a company in Uruguay?

No, Hawilla insisted, he had no memory of any of that.

Calmly, Randall repeated the questions several times, accompanying Hawilla to the hotel's restaurant, where the Brazilian ordered coffee and breakfast. The agent did not partake.

And then, after no more than fifteen minutes, the brief interview concluded. Randall thanked Hawilla for his time and departed, leaving the South American executive puzzled and shaken.

————

It had been a stressful few months.

In early 2013, Hawilla had finally put most of his newspapers up for sale. His many attempts to turn the small dailies around had done little to slow the precipitous decline in circulation, and even after laying off eighty employees, the bleeding just wouldn't stop. He'd finally admitted defeat, preparing to write them off as a near total loss.

Then Hawilla had flown to Buenos Aires to firm up plans for the Copa América deal with his former rivals. They'd gotten together on March 13 in Full Play's offices on the thirteenth floor of a shiny office tower just blocks from the Estadio Monumental, Argentina's largest and most storied soccer venue, where the country's national team beat Holland to win its first World Cup title thirty-five years earlier.

About fifteen people were in the meeting, and the executives and their lawyers went over the three-way shareholders agreement, as well as technical aspects of the partnership, allocating responsibilities for each company. Torneos would be in charge of production of the Copa América, Traffic would sell sponsorships, and Full Play would sell broadcast rights and also administer this new, three-headed company they were forming, which they called Datisa.

The Jinkises of Full Play and Alejandro Burzaco of Torneos said they had negotiated to pay CONMEBOL $80 million for each edition of the tournament, including the Centenario edition in 2016. That was a substantial premium over the old price, but considering how much soccer rights had appreciated in recent years—and how many editions of the Copa América the contract covered—everyone agreed it was a bargain.

The meeting happened to fall on the same day that Jorge Bergoglio, the archbishop of Buenos Aires, was elected the first South American pope, and the Vatican's announcement interrupted the meeting. Jubilant Argentines had taken to the streets to celebrate Pope Francis, and Hawilla and Burzaco used the opportunity to take a walk together. The two men had known each other for some time, and got along well.

As they strolled, Burzaco confided to Hawilla that all three South American members of FIFA's ExCo had solicited bribes in exchange for their votes on where to hold the 2022 World Cup, and had agreed to split $5 million to endorse Qatar. But it later came out, Burzaco said, that Ricardo Teixeira from Brazil had actually negotiated a $50 million bribe for the votes and kept nearly all of it for himself, infuriating the other two officials—Julio Grondona and Nicolás Leoz—when they learned the truth.

It was a terrible revelation, Hawilla thought, a profound corruption of the sport's most important event. But it somehow felt dismally predictable. He recalled Teixeira once showing him a very expensive watch he'd gotten from Mohamed bin Hammam, and it all began to make sense. He wasn't the only one who couldn't escape the bribes; it was impossible to be involved in the soccer business without them.

When the two men returned to Full Play's offices, Mariano Jinkis said he wanted to meet with them privately. Hawilla knew right away what the topic would be. Sure enough, Jinkis and Burzaco told him that they had paid large bribes to a dozen South American officials, including the entire Group of Six, to secure the Copa América, and had pledged to keep paying them for each successive edition of the tournament. So far the tally was $40 million, Jinkis said, and as an equal partner in Datisa, Traffic owed a third of that. He also would be expected, Jinkis reminded him, to withdraw the lawsuit he filed against Full Play and CONMEBOL as soon as possible.

Hawilla felt sickened. He had foolishly hoped this deal was different. But he put up no resistance; he had a flight back to Brazil in an hour, and felt desperate to escape the conversation. Mariano Jinkis followed him on the way out, explaining that Hawilla would never have to make the bribe payments directly. He preferred, he insisted, to handle them himself.

"You can be calm," Jinkis said, smiling broadly. "Because I already took care of everything."

———

Hawilla had come to Miami at the outset of May for a brief visit mainly to close on a property he was purchasing on Fisher Island. Studded with luxury condos arrayed around one of America's highest-rated golf courses, Fisher Island's zip code was the wealthiest in the whole country.

For $6.5 million, half of it cash, Hawilla was buying a 4,400-square-foot, three-bedroom unit on the island's Atlantic-facing side, just above a man-made beach that featured fine white sand imported from the Bahamas. The unexpected interruption from the FBI had come on a Friday, and Hawilla was set to meet his lawyer for the formal closing on the condo the following Tuesday. He'd be back in Brazil in less than a week.

Over the weekend, however, it was hard for him not to dwell on what had happened. How much did the FBI know? Where was this young agent getting so much information about old business affairs? It was puzzling. And then, on Monday Hawilla's phone rang. It was, of all people, Chuck Blazer.

Speaking Spanish, Blazer shocked Hawilla, saying that FBI agents had come to his apartment that very morning asking probing questions about his Cayman Islands bank account and about "two companies, one from Uruguay, another from Panama." Did Hawilla have any idea, he wondered, what was going on and how much the FBI knew?

"Please, I'm asking you as a friend to . . . to . . . to . . . leave us out of this because of the investigation," Hawilla replied, becoming upset.

"They went to visit me, too," he continued. "Two people from the FBI, they also visited me."

"You?" Blazer asked, a seeming note of surprise in his husky baritone.

Hawilla explained that the agents had asked repeatedly about transfers of money to Blazer from accounts in Uruguay and Panama, and that he'd replied that he didn't know anything.

"They asked me if there were payments outside the contract," the Brazilian continued. "I don't know. The truth is I don't know. I only ask that you not mention us because otherwise it will involve us in a . . . a . . . a . . . a very serious problem, you know?"

————

Blazer had started covertly recording phone calls with Hawilla nearly a year earlier.

After telling Norris and the rest of the team about Traffic's decades of bribery, he had combed through his old archives in search of documentary evidence.

He recalled receiving six-figure payments related to the Gold Cup contracts he'd signed with Hawilla's companies, and eventually found a handful of documents from 1999 and 2000 showing wires to his bank account in the Cayman Islands. The wires—for $200,000, $100,000, and $99,985—came from accounts for companies based in Uruguay and Panama.

The firms, Tansy S.A., and Metrobank S.A., didn't have any obvious connection to Traffic, but Blazer clarified that was because Hawilla was careful and almost always used intermediaries to make wires on his behalf so the payments to the officials wouldn't be on his books. There were, in fact, a host of shell companies that Hawilla's trusted bagmen used to make payments.

Digging further, Blazer also found the phony contract he and Hawilla had created to explain the $600,000 wire he'd received in 2003, as well as the emails he'd sent to the Brazilian about the money at the time.

The prosecutors were increasingly convinced that Hawilla, if they could get him to flip, would be an incredible asset to the case. Snaring someone who for decades had been the one paying the bribes could blow the case wide open. A man like Hawilla could prove just as valuable—if not more so—than a Jack Warner.

Hawilla was the one paying the bribes. That meant he could lead them to who knows how many corrupt officials, and provide the paperwork to prove it.

Blazer, based on memory and the documents he'd dug up, had provided a strong lead, but it wasn't quite enough. They needed to prove that Hawilla had knowledge of the payments despite the fact that his fingerprints weren't directly on them. Wires from Traffic to Tansy or Metrobank at roughly the same time those shell companies sent money to Blazer, and for the same amount of money, for example, would definitely help close the loop.

The easy solution, Berryman suggested, was to subpoena Delta National Bank & Trust Co. in Miami, which he'd identified through correspondent bank transfers as one of Traffic's two main U.S. banks and the one it appeared to use for bribe payments. If any bribes had originated from Delta, the IRS agent reasoned, they would pop up immediately.

But Norris refused. Delta wasn't some giant like Wells Fargo or Chase; it was a tiny private bank with just three branches in the whole world. It had been doing business with Traffic for so long it was possible, if not likely, that its bankers would tip off Hawilla or some other Traffic employee about the subpoena. The risk was just too great.

Instead they decided to make Blazer pick up the phone. Unlike a lot of cooperators, he seemed to have no compunctions about making covert recordings. In fact, at times Blazer seemed to relish it. If he could trick Hawilla into admitting he'd made the payments, that could be enough.

Blazer first called early the previous June, trying to get Hawilla to send him documents showing he'd made the bribes. But Hawilla didn't quite remember the exact payment, and denied having any of the paperwork, so Blazer tried to guide him to discuss the older ones, from Panama and Uruguay. Hawilla resisted, explaining that "we're not directly involved, because we do this with other companies, you see?"

Blazer called again at the end of June 2012, and this time got both Hawilla and his elder son, Stefano, who spoke English, on the line. He managed to get Stefano to admit to knowing about Tansy, the Uruguayan company used to funnel bribes, but it still seemed thin, and so the prosecutors came up with the idea of recording Hawilla at the London Olympics. That, too, had come up empty.

Proof of intent aside, Hawilla presented another major obstacle. Brazil did not extradite its citizens. Even if the prosecutors built a perfect case, they couldn't touch Hawilla so long as he was at home.

So they dreamed up a new plan. Hawilla, they knew, came to Miami from time to time to check in on Traffic's local office. If they sat back and waited, perhaps they could make an approach the next time he came into the country and catch him lying, or telling others to lie, then collar him and lean on him hard to cooperate.

Lying to a federal agent was a crime in and of itself, and attempting to get others to lie or intentionally fail to cooperate was clear-cut obstruction of justice. The trick was for an agent to come in looking innocent and just get the person talking; soon enough they'd dig their own ditch. It was straight out of the FBI playbook. Approach someone you already have dirt on and try to catch them in a lie.

When the opportunity finally arose in early May, the prosecutors sent Randall in the role of the young and ingenuous agent on a fishing expedition. They were banking on the fact that Hawilla wasn't an American and was probably even more unprepared than most to deal with an FBI agent asking questions. The smart thing to do in that situation was to say nothing and get a lawyer. Happily for the investigators, Hawilla did no such thing.

IRS Special Agent Steve Berryman, who joined the soccer investigation in late 2011, walking into federal court in Brooklyn to testify on December 7, 2017.

Ken Bensinger

Jared Randall (in tie, holding box) was the FBI's lead agent in the United States' investigation of international soccer corruption. He is pictured in a joint FBI-IRS raid on May 27, 2015. *Reuters/Javier Galeano*

The Department of Justice's soccer probe was led by Evan M. Norris, a Harvard-educated assistant United States attorney in New York's Eastern District.

© *C-Span*

FIFA CORRUPTION INVESTIGATION
EVAN NORRIS
Assistant U.S. Attorney Eastern District of New York

Over time, the FIFA Case grew to be one of the largest and most complicated in Justice Department history. By the time the second indictment was unsealed, nearly a dozen prosecutors were on the case, including (from left) Sam Nitze; Amanda Hector; Darren LaVerne; Kristin Mace; and Evan Norris. *U.S. Department of Justice*

Joseph "Sepp" Blatter, FIFA president, with Vladimir Putin in St. Petersburg on July 25, 2015, during the preliminary draw for the 2018 World Cup, to be held in Russia. *Reuters*

Blatter (left) served under president João Havelange at FIFA, who hired him in 1975 and promoted him to general secretary in 1981. Blatter was elected president in 1998, when Havelange retired. *ASL/Nationaal Archief/Fotocollectie Anefo/CC0*

Austin "Jack" Warner (left) and Chuck Blazer (right) with Sepp Blatter at a soccer event. Warner, from Trinidad and Tobago, was elected CONCACAF president in 1990 and named Blazer, a New Yorker, the confederation's general secretary. In 2011, Blazer began secretly cooperating with American prosecutors. *Pressefoto Ulmer/ullstein bild via Getty Images*

Jeffrey Webb (left) was elected CONCACAF president in May 2012, a year after Jack Warner resigned amid corruption allegations. Webb, who made sports marketing executive Enrique Sanz (right) his general secretary, was indicted for corruption in May 2015. *Ricky Fitchett/ZUMA Press, Inc./Alamy Stock Photo*

A former sports journalist in Brazil, José Hawilla was a pioneer in commercializing soccer, becoming extremely wealthy and powerful. In 2013, he was arrested by federal agents and began secretly cooperating with the U.S. investigation. *Zanone Fraissat/ FOLHA IMAGEM*

Nicolás Leoz (left) of Paraguay was president of the South American soccer confederation from 1986 to 2013. His successor was the Uruguayan Eugenio Figueredo (right). Both men were indicted on corruption charges by the Department of Justice in May 2015. *Reuters*

Alejandro Burzaco (standing) became a major player in the sports marketing business after making a fortune as a banker in Argentina. Here, he is pictured with soccer officials (left to right) Sergio Jadue of Chile; Luis Bedoya of Colombia; and Juan Angel Napout of Paraguay. All four were eventually convicted on corruption charges. *U.S. Department of Justice, trial exhibit*

Julio Grondona (left), longtime president of Argentina's soccer association, was one of the sport's most feared and powerful men and close with Alejandro Burzaco (right), who for years controlled broadcast rights to Argentina's professional leagues. *Collection of the author*

Son Mariano (left) and father Hugo Jinkis (right) began scooping up rights to major soccer tournaments starting in 2010. Both were indicted, but have eluded extradition. Here they are seen with Juan Angel Napout (center), convicted of wire fraud and racketeering in December 2017. *U.S. Department of Justice, trial exhibit*

Muckraking British journalist Andrew Jennings has been writing about corruption in FIFA for nearly twenty years. His articles played a role in advancing the criminal investigation of American soccer official Chuck Blazer for tax crimes. *José Cruz/Agência Senado/Creative Commons*

Mohamed bin Hamman of Qatar (front row, left) with Blazer and Leoz at the press conference announcing that Russia and Qatar would host the 2018 and 2022 World Cups, respectively. Seated behind them are Bill Clinton and U.S. Soccer President Sunil Gulati. *Michael Regan/Getty Images*

Julio Grondona with Pope Francis, a soccer fan. Grondona, who controlled Argentine soccer for thirty-five years, was a primary target of the U.S. criminal investigation, but died in July 2014 before he could be indicted. *Collection of the author*

Jack Warner (right) with his elder son, Daryan, at an event in their native Trinidad and Tobago. Daryan and his brother, Daryll, were quietly arrested by federal agents in November 2012, and began cooperating with the U.S. criminal investigation. Jack Warner was indicted in May 2015. *Robert Taylor/Trinidad Express*

The FIFA executive boardroom, where voting on where to hold the 2018 and 2022 World Cups took place in 2010. It's located three floors below ground in the soccer body's $200 million headquarters on a hill high above Zurich. *albinfo/Creative Commons*

The luxurious Baur au Lac hotel in Zurich. In May and December 2015, Swiss police conducted early morning raids at the hotel and elsewhere in town, arresting a total of nine soccer officials at the request of U.S. prosecutors. *Adrian Michael/Creative Commons*

After his first encounter with Hawilla in the lobby, Randall returned to the Mandarin Oriental on May 9, this time accompanied by Berryman. He asked the front desk clerk to call Hawilla's room and tell him to come down. The FBI agent had sworn out a criminal complaint for obstruction of justice the previous day in Brooklyn, then come back to Miami to make the arrest.

Hawilla's flight back to São Paulo was scheduled for later that day, and he and his wife had packed their bags the night before. Now, instead of the airport, the sixty-nine-year-old was marched back up to his hotel room by the two agents, instructed to get dressed, and then escorted to the local FBI field office.

Handcuffed to the wall in a bleak interview room, he was given a stark choice. He could, as was his legal right, insist on a court appearance to make an initial plea. It was already fairly late on Thursday, so he likely wouldn't get before a magistrate until the next day, in which case Hawilla would have to trade his street clothes for a prison jumpsuit and spend the night with hardened criminals in the Miami Federal Detention Center.

Then he'd be transferred to Brooklyn, where the complaint had been filed, and he'd fly "Con Air," the government's prisoner transport system, to get there, which meant a crazy itinerary around the country in a series of rickety old planes stuffed with scary inmates rather than a direct flight. Once in New York, he'd face potentially more time in jail before even the possibility of bail arose. To top it off, the whole thing would be public, and he'd face the humiliation of people finding out he'd been arrested. It could even make the news in Brazil.

Alternatively, Hawilla could waive his right to an appearance and agree to cooperate with the ongoing investigation of international soccer corruption. In that case, the agents explained to him, he'd fly commercial to New York that same day, be put up in a nice hotel, and not have to spend a single second in jail. Everything would be hush-hush, a big secret, and nobody would have to know.

Hawilla had been wealthy for a long time. He flew first-class when he wasn't on a private jet, ate at Michelin-starred restaurants, and stayed in $1,000-a-night hotels. He socialized with famous athletes and powerful businessmen. He spoke little English and was almost completely unfamiliar with the U.S. system of justice. But he'd seen enough movies to have strong opinions of American jails, overflowing with vicious gang members who preyed on the weak.

Fighting the charge would certainly mean some time behind bars, at least until he made bail, and Hawilla wanted no part of that, not even for a minute. If cooperating meant getting out of the handcuffs and avoiding jail, then it really didn't feel like much of a choice at all. Hawilla signed the waiver and agreed to help. He would discover the true ramifications of that decision later.

————

After the feds had taken her husband away from her, warning her not to tell anyone about what had happened, the first person Eliani Hawilla thought to call was Aaron Davidson. So far from home, Eliani had no idea who else to turn to. Davidson, the president of Traffic Sports USA, was the obvious choice. He was American, spoke Portuguese, and lived in a condo just across Brickell Key, a five-minute walk from the hotel. Most importantly, she was sure he would be discreet, ensuring the arrest didn't end up in the gossip pages back home. Over the phone, near hysterical, she told Davidson that his boss had just been arrested and needed help.

A forty-two-year-old lawyer who grew up in Dallas, Davidson had been at Traffic for a decade. He'd first met Hawilla when working as an attorney for Hicks, Muse, the Texas-based private equity fund that briefly took a stake in the Brazilian firm in the late 1990s. In 2003, when Davidson was promoting a regional golf tour in Mexico, Hawilla recruited him to come to Miami and work for Traffic.

Over time, Hawilla came to rely on Davidson to be his eyes and ears in the U.S. Davidson, meanwhile, grew deeply loyal to his boss; he looked up to him and considered him both a visionary marketing genius and a warm and encouraging father figure.

Davidson raced to Eliani's side. He stayed with her until, hours later, Hawilla was finally permitted by the agents to call his wife and explain what was going on. Then Davidson drove to the Miami airport with a bag full of Hawilla's medication, handing it off to Randall and Berryman curbside.

That evening, Davidson went out to eat with Eliani and Enrique Sanz. Over dinner, it was hard to talk about anything but the arrest. The news was shocking for everyone. Eliani was petrified, anguished for her spouse of thirty-six years, and didn't want to be alone. Davidson and Sanz, meanwhile, couldn't help but be worried. They'd been deeply wrapped up in Traffic's dirty doings for years.

None of them knew why Hawilla had been arrested, and the federal agents certainly hadn't been willing to share any information about the case.

What exactly were the feds looking into?

TWENTY-ONE

I AM NOT YOUR FRIEND

HAWILLA BEGAN TO PROFFER THE MORNING AFTER HE was arrested. He initially stayed at the Plaza Athénée, a fancy hotel on New York's Upper East Side. But as it became clear the case would drag on for some time, he relocated to an apartment a friend loaned him in a building on 64th and Park, directly upstairs from Daniel, an elaborate Michelin three-star restaurant where the Brazilian frequently dined.

Despite the considerable comforts of his lifestyle. Hawilla was constantly reminded of his newfound status as a presumptive criminal. For starters, he hated New York, where by his standards, too few people spoke Spanish or Portuguese. He was subject to a nighttime curfew and location monitoring, and obliged to wear an ankle bracelet with a built-in GPS location monitor. Anytime he wanted to go anywhere outside of a carefully circumscribed orbit, he had to call Jared Randall to get permission.

Right up front Norris had quizzed Hawilla extensively about his assets, and finally settled on a bond of $20 million, guaranteed by $5 million in cash, the deed to his brand-new condo on Fisher Island, and title to all of Hawilla's U.S. assets, including Traffic Sports USA, his Gold Cup and World Cup qualifier contracts, his stake in the North American Soccer League, and all his U.S. bank accounts. Hawilla also, of course, had to surrender his passport.

Because of his work in soccer, Hawilla had traveled frequently for decades, but he was also very much a homebody. Other than the two years he spent in Boca Raton in the early 1990s, he had never lived outside Brazil, and he rarely left home for more than a week or two at a time. His family was in Brazil, as were his friends. Homesickness quickly began to define his life.

The matter came to an uncomfortable head when Hawilla brought up his wife's birthday.

Eliani was turning sixty on June 3, 2013, and Hawilla had planned an elaborate party for her in São Paulo. Between friends, family, and colleagues, the couple were expecting as many as 150 people to show up. Then on June 11, Hawilla was turning seventy, and he felt certain his three children were planning a surprise party in honor of the milestone.

Missing those events, he told the prosecutors, would "*termine minha vida*"—end my life. Not only that, he said, but it would raise suspicions back home. He was a public figure. People would notice his absence; they might even write about it in the sports or gossip pages. And that, he pleaded, could be bad for the case.

Norris was unswayed. The answer was no. Brazil didn't extradite its citizens, and the risk that Hawilla would never return was far too great. But Norris didn't say that. Instead, he gingerly hinted that a return to Brazil could eventually be a reward for being helpful and truthful to the investigation.

For the time being, the prosecutor suggested, Hawilla could throw Eliani's party in Miami and invite people to come up. Alternatively, he could send his wife back to Brazil for the party along with his regrets, or simply cancel the whole thing. But for now, there was no way he was going home.

But Hawilla was right about one thing: his extended absence did raise some issues. What he needed was a good cover story. The prosecutors suggested that he could tell people he was in the U.S. on business, trying to sell Traffic; the due diligence process would give him a plausible excuse for requesting so much paperwork. Another idea was for Hawilla to tell people he was meeting with architects and supervising a major remodel of his new condo on Fisher Island.

A third option, suggested by Hector, was blaming some kind of physical ailment. Hawilla considered blaming prostate cancer, but São Paulo was crawling with top-notch doctors so the story seemed flimsy. He could blame ear issues, perhaps, or heart problems. Finally, the prosecutors settled on Hawilla telling people he was suffering panic attacks that prevented him from flying and was seeking treatment, but until then couldn't travel. It was thin, and some folks in Brazil seemed suspicious, but it would have to do.

The whole distasteful situation was a source of continual frustration for Hawilla. He was a man accustomed to enormous comforts and even greater liberties, an admired and powerful public figure, and now everything about his daily existence reminded him how all that had been taken away.

Stuck in New York, Hawilla had little social life to speak of other than dining at expensive restaurants with his wife. All his phone calls, his interactions with Traffic employees in Brazil and Miami, were wrapped in lies and deception. As he began to undertake covert operations for the prosecution, wearing a wire, he found himself spending increasing amounts of time with Jared Randall. As the only Spanish speaker on the soccer case, Randall was delighted to be able to put his language skills to use while watching over Hawilla.

The care and feeding of sources is, arguably, the thing the FBI does best. Agents are tasked with working directly with cooperators, keeping track of them, planning the details of their covert operations, and, when nothing in particular is going on in a case, simply being there for them. They attend proffers and take notes, keep an eye on them when they're in the field, and, when the day comes for them to testify at trial, help them prepare. A good agent must be a shrink, babysitter, and life coach, working tirelessly to keep cooperators motivated.

In a sense, Randall had been by Hawilla's side the whole time, escorting him from the Mandarin Oriental to the Miami FBI office, sitting next to him in the last row of the American Airlines flight to New York, then guarding him during the tense few days before he was given bond and had to be watched around the clock. Among this new circle of people who controlled Hawilla's life, who asked him endless questions, demanded his records, and pushed him to confess every indiscretion, Randall stood out as someone he could talk to without feeling pressured; someone he trusted.

But as an FBI agent, it was also Randall's duty to remind Hawilla of the true nature of their relationship.

"*José*," Randall said, "*no soy tu amigo.*"

I am not your friend.

———

"It would be a mistake," Norris had told Hawilla in a conference room in the U.S. Attorney's Office in Brooklyn, "to try and guess what this investigation is about."

It was the standard warning he gave every cooperator, reminding them that the only path forward was total honesty. Norris was good at keeping secrets, and shared almost nothing about the case with cooperators, including whom else he'd talked to. He made an effort to keep them in the dark about how the case developed and where it was going; at times he even allowed them to believe things about the investigation that were not true if he felt it could advance the work being done. Yet at the same time, Norris expected complete candor from cooperators.

Hawilla was eager to earn his cooperation agreement. If Norris and the other prosecutors wanted him to help them gather evidence on more people, to expand the case, to provide their vaunted "substantial assistance," then he was happy to give them what they seemed to be asking for. Corruption in soccer was rampant, Hawilla said, and the people in the business were very dirty. It was about time, he said—in a refrain that was beginning to sound awfully familiar to Norris and the others—that somebody cleaned it up.

Hawilla had started paying bribes in the late 1980s, he said, and began ticking off names of people who had taken money. They were the same people that Berryman and Norris had been talking about in their late night conversations, the heavyweights of South America: Julio Grondona, the head of Argentina's soccer association; Nicolás Leoz, the former president of CONMEBOL; and Ricardo Teixeira, the ex-president of the Confederação Brasileira de Futebol, or CBF. Chuck Blazer, also, had taken money, as had Jack Warner.

It was like a long, gripping history lecture, told not by some stodgy academic but by one of the real live actors in the drama, a general who had been on the front lines with the troops.

Hawilla told the prosecutors about his early days at Traffic, about brokering sponsorship deals with Brazil's soccer association when Teixeira took over and it had no money, first bringing in Pepsi, then Coca-Cola, and Nike. He explained how many of those high-profile deals had involved multimillion-dollar payments to Teixeira. The Nike contract, for $160 million over ten years, was by itself worth more than $2 million in annual marketing commisions from the American sportswear brand to Traffic, and Hawilla would secretly wire half that to Teixeira as a kickback. Hawilla had the original contracts for those deals, signed by the top executives of the companies, although there was no conclusive evidence that the sponsors were themselves aware that their legitimate marketing payments were being quietly used to bribe the CBF. Hawilla told the prosecutors about his even more profitable rights deals, and how he learned to pay bribes to soccer officials to push out competitors and keep prices low.

And in particular, Hawilla talked about the Copa América. He recounted its origins, how he approached Nicolás Leoz with his ideas for turning the forgotten tournament into a moneymaker, and how Leoz, and later Teixeira and Grondona, too, began demanding bribes with each new contract. The tournament had been a big moneymaker, Hawilla said, until the Argentine firm Full Play took it away from him following the 2011 edition.

Without the Copa América, and with his business in general disarray, he was now completely out of the bribe-paying business, Hawilla said, and just wanted to sell Traffic and be done with it. He hadn't made any corrupt payments in two years, he insisted, but nonetheless patiently walked the prosecutors through the many complicated ways he had devised to send bribes in the past. His preferred method, he said, was using intermediaries with offshore companies that supplied him with bogus contracts he'd use to justify making payments; those payments would then be forwarded to the intended bribe recipients in an arm's length transaction originating in a neutral location like Panama. One of his trusted bagmen charged $150,000 a year for the service, not including commissions on every wire.

What the investigators were hearing felt profoundly affirming. Berryman had already gone deep on all these big names, subpoenaing

CHIPS and Fedwire, finding bank accounts and subpoenaing those, too, until he had built a fat file on each potential suspect, uncovering a web of interconnected companies and payments that could only be explained as bribes. But to hear all that work validated by the man who was on the other end of those bribes was nothing short of thrilling. There was a palpable, electrifying feeling that they were very close to something big.

The fire hose of information hardly stopped there. Hawilla supplied them new names to subpoena, and less than two weeks after his arrest, the prosecutors flew Hawilla down to Miami to start making recordings. Hawilla, unlike Blazer, found the idea of wearing a wire distasteful and dishonest. Affronted, he pushed back, but the prosecutors were clear: he had no choice.

At their behest he reached out to Ricardo Teixeira. The two men hadn't talked in years, but Teixeira had been living in a spectacular water-front Miami mansion since early 2012, and the opportunity seemed ripe. According to Hawilla, the former soccer official had taken tens of mil-lions of dollars in bribes; he'd left Brazil only because he was being in-vestigated by police there for his involvement in a massive fraud scheme related to a friendly match. Teixeira seemed happy to hear from his old colleague, but he denied involvement in anything untoward, and the ini-tial recordings, at least, didn't prove too fruitful.

Hawilla had also been asked to go to lunch with Enrique Sanz wear-ing a wire. That meeting's main objective was to see if Sanz would con-fess to having made bribe payments to Jack Warner in the late 1990s and early 2000s, when he was still at Traffic. But Sanz seemed to dance around the issue, changing the subject and saying nothing.

The prosecutors also wanted Hawilla to try to figure out whether Sanz suspected anything about the investigation, given the risk that word of his arrest might have leaked out. According to Hawilla, Sanz had no clue, and a story Hawilla told about the feds focusing only on Blazer and Warner and possible tax issues seemed to have convinced Sanz that his former boss wasn't involved.

For Norris and the others, those initial recordings hadn't produced a smoking gun or some admission of guilt, but they nevertheless marked an auspicious starting point. Hawilla was promising to provide detailed breakdowns of each of the many corrupt schemes he'd been involved in over the years, dating back to the late 1980s and early 1990s, and pledged to provide copies of all the relevant documents.

It was going fantastically, the investigators all agreed; the rich old Brazilian might be a bit stuffy and sensitive, but he was proving to be one hell of a cooperator.

None of them suspected that Hawilla might not be telling them the whole story.

———

Soon after the March meeting in Buenos Aires to discuss the Copa América, Alejandro Burzaco of Torneos flew to Zurich, where the FIFA ExCo was holding its quarterly meetings. Burzaco used the opportunity to sit down for lunch with Enrique Sanz, Aaron Davidson of Traffic, and Mariano Jinkis from Full Play to negotiate the final missing component of the deal: CONCACAF's participation in the Centenario edition of the tournament.

The offer on the table from the new partnership, Datisa, had been $40 million to the confederation for its broadcast and commercial rights, and a $7 million to bribe Jeffrey Webb to sign the contract. But Sanz said Webb wanted more. The CONCACAF president had heard rumors about a much larger total pot of payments for South American officials, and, infuriated at what he perceived to be an insultingly low offer, demanded an incredible $15 million just for himself. Finally, Burzaco was able to negotiate the bribe down to $10 million—still a massive payment by any measure—with the confederation's above-the-board share dropping to $35 million.

With that last hurdle cleared, the contract could be completed, and in late May—about the same time that Hawilla was making his first clandestine recordings for the Justice Department—Burzaco flew around the world gathering the necessary signatures from the key soccer officials. As a kind of signing bonus, the heads of nine South American national associations would be getting bribes, as would the new president of CONMEBOL, Eugenio Figueredo, and its general secretary. By the time the 2023 Copa América took place, the sum of bribes paid for the tournament would surpass $100 million; it was the largest scheme any of the participants had ever been involved in.

Everything was in place, and now it was Hawilla's turn to chip in his share of the first rounds of bribes.

On June 3, less than a month after he was arrested, Hawilla personally authorized a wire of $5 million from Traffic's account at Delta National Bank in Miami to an account in Switzerland controlled by Burzaco. Three days later, he signed a second wire instruction, sending another $5 million to a different Swiss account, controlled by Hugo and Mariano Jinkis. The balance of two payments of $1.67 million owed to each of his partners, bringing Hawilla's total contribution to $13.33 million, would be sent three months later.

Both wires, as is to be expected for international transactions originating in the U.S., passed through American correspondent banks and would have been easily traceable. But only if someone had been looking for them.

TWENTY-TWO

ONE IS SILVER, THE OTHER GOLD

STEVE BERRYMAN CLIMBED SLOWLY UP THE FOUR flights of stairs to Zorana Danis's office on Tuesday, September 24, 2013, wondering if he was in the right place. He had been meticulously researching Danis for months, ever since Hawilla brought up her name in connection to South American soccer corruption.

The IRS agent, still struggling to get in shape a year after his heart surgery, was heading for the top floor of an old brick warehouse across the street from an industrial supply shop and an overgrown empty lot in a down-in-the-heels section near downtown Jersey City. A few glints of gentrification had begun to crop up in the neighborhood, but for the most part it looked rough, just about the last place Berryman would expect an important player in world soccer to be based.

Yet there it was, the headquarters of International Soccer Marketing, the company Danis owned and operated.

Berryman made a point of looking up financial records for every suspect in the case, but Danis had stood out, and not just because she was the rare woman involved in such a male-dominated industry. She wasn't a citizen, but she was based in the U.S., and, he soon discovered, she had an account at Citibank, which meant he could aggressively subpoena her accounts with no fear she'd catch wind of what he was up to.

What Berryman found was encouraging. There were dozens of payments, big, juicy, six-figure ones, to bank accounts in Switzerland, Paraguay, and Uruguay, over a period of many years. Over one thirty-month period, for example, Berryman traced just over $2 million in payments that his gut told him had to be bribes of some kind. Many of the recipient accounts looked as though they could be related to Nicolás Leoz, the former CONMEBOL president, who Hawilla had said was close to Danis.

He'd pulled her taxes, too, and combing through them found she'd made a suspicious deduction a few years earlier that looked an awful lot like trying to write off a bribe as a legitimate business expense.

Even more intriguing was Danis's background. Berryman, who spent most of his time reading soccer history when he wasn't working through his voluminous subpoenas, discovered that Danis had soccer in her blood.

Her father had been a goalie who played eight games for the Yugoslavian national team in the late 1950s, winning a gold medal at the 1960 Olympics. A flamboyant and charismatic Macedonian, Blagoje Vidinić was a chain-smoker known for singing opera during matches to keep his teammates on their toes and was, briefly, considered one of Europe's most promising young goalkeepers.

His prospects never fully panned out, and after bouncing around clubs in Europe, he ended his career playing for a series of low-rent teams in Los Angeles, San Diego, and St. Louis during the early days of American pro soccer. Vidinić went on to become an international coach, taking Morocco's national team to the 1970 World Cup, and Zaire's to the 1974 tournament. En route he fell in with Horst Dassler, the Adidas boss credited with inventing modern sports marketing who would go on to found the hugely successful and highly corrupt firm ISL.

Dassler had outfitted Vidinić's teams with free Adidas gear, and Vidinić repaid the favor on the eve of FIFA's landmark presidential elections in June 1974. Sharing a drink in the lobby bar of a Frankfurt hotel on the eve of the vote, Vidinić informed Dassler that he had been backing the wrong horse. Sir Stanley Rous, the English incumbent, was going to lose, Vidinić informed him, because his Brazilian rival, João Havelange, had won over Africa's large voting bloc. Scrambling, Dassler rushed to Havelange's room to offer the future FIFA president his support, launching what became one of the most influential relationships in the history of sports. The incident also cemented an enduring friendship between Dassler and Vidinić, who would work for Adidas for many years.

Danis was born while her father played for a club in Belgrade, and she followed him around the world on his soccer adventures. When she was a teenager, her father coached the national team in Colombia, where she picked up Spanish. In 1989, not long after graduating from Georgetown, she and her father founded International Soccer Marketing in order to buy and sell soccer sponsorship rights.

By the late 1990s, she landed what would be her meal ticket: the Copa Libertadores, South America's annual international club championship. Although CONMEBOL handled the tournament's TV rights separately, Danis was in charge of the sponsorship end, and had sold the rights to the likes of Toyota, Santander, and Bridgestone. The millions of dollars in suspect payments flowing out of her accounts, Berryman decided, looked a lot like bribes to Leoz and other officials to ensure she'd continue to receive those rights. It was the exact kind of thing he'd seen with Traffic.

In mid-July, Norris put a pen register on Danis to try to get a sense of whom she talked to. Meanwhile, the team strategized about the best way to make an approach. With a husband and two kids in the U.S., Danis didn't seem like a flight risk, so an arrest seemed a bit heavy-handed. But given what Berryman had gathered, they certainly could put a good scare into her.

Berryman opted for a softer approach. He figured Danis would assume American law enforcement, particularly a numbers-focused IRS agent, wouldn't know anything about soccer. So he'd play it dumb to see if she let anything slip. As he did before all his interviews, Berryman wrote out a detailed outline of how he wanted things to go, much the same way some athletes visualize scoring a goal or winning a race.

"I'm based out in California," Berryman said, sitting in her office. "I'm looking into something and ran across some foreign payments from your company involving something called . . . FIFA . . . ? "

He deliberately mangled that last word, pronouncing it "Fie-Fa," and letting it hang in the air as he put a blank expression on his face. He was there with a rookie IRS agent out of Orange County named J. J. Kacic, who had recently been assigned to help Berryman. With a boyish face, Kacic looked very young, and unlike the older agent truly did know nothing about soccer, so his presence only made the act more believable.

It was no big deal, Berryman hastily added, just a boring tax case. He'd pulled some bank records and seen some money moving overseas, and was just wondering what they were all about, that's all. Then he read off a list of wires originating from her account that he'd carefully selected beforehand. They were ones he felt certain weren't bribes, but instead legitimate payments to vendors. That way, Berryman figured, she'd assume he had no clue what she was up to.

Again, he repeated, it was no big deal, but would she mind pulling a few records to show what those payments were for? Danis, tall and slender, looked puzzled, but also relieved. She agreed, and Berryman, keeping up the Inspector Clouseau act, gathered his papers, thanked her, and left, Kacic trailing after him.

On October 18, Norris and the other prosecutors gave Daryan Warner the cooperation agreement he'd been craving since his arrest, allowing him to plead guilty to just three criminal counts in a cleared federal courtroom in Brooklyn.

Although he'd been pinched for structuring, the prosecutors had, over months of questioning, determined that Jack Warner's eldest child had in fact taken part in a number of other corrupt schemes, many involving soccer.

For starters, he'd moved a great deal more cash around, for far longer, than Berryman had detailed in his complaint. Moreover, working with a string of partners, Warner had been scalping World Cup tickets for nearly two decades, dating back at least to the 1994 World Cup in the U.S. Most importantly, he'd helped his father take the $10 million bribe from the South African bid committee for the 2010 World Cup, the same payment that had eventually exacerbated tensions between Blazer and Warner in the months before they went at each other's throat.

There was little question that Daryan, and to some degree his kid brother, Daryll, were in deep. But there were also limits to what the two could be asked to do against their own father.

When it became clear that Daryll Warner had limited knowledge of other conspiracies, the prosecutors moved on, giving him a cooperation agreement and letting him plead guilty to two non-soccer-related counts in mid-July. It was the case's first conviction, but the younger Warner brother had proven a somewhat disappointing cooperator.

His older brother had seemed to hold more promise, given his more enterprising spirit when it came to the family soccer business. He'd been willing to provide evidence against others, and to make consensual recordings or wear a wire if necessary. But the people he could inform on proved less interesting than hoped. In the end, Daryan Warner simply couldn't deliver, especially when compared to Hawilla, who seemed to have bribed every big-name official in the hemisphere.

By letting him plead guilty, Norris was giving Daryan Warner what every cooperator wants: a promise that the prosecution will ask for leniency from the judge when it comes to sentencing. Once the plea was official, the formal proffers ended. Warner's movements were still restricted, he still was out on $5 million bond, guaranteed by $600,000 in cash and eight properties, and he was still subject to GPS location monitoring with tight travel restrictions. But mainly all he had to do was await sentencing.

Warner had pleaded guilty to two criminal conspiracy charges related to scalping, as well as the original structuring charge he'd been arrested on. Moving money around, or even hiding it, isn't a crime by itself. It's only money laundering if the funds are in some way "dirty," meaning that they are the proceeds of a separate crime, like fraud or embezzlement, and someone is trying to "wash" them. As a result, money laundering charges come coupled with at least one prior, or "predicate," offense.

In the case of Daryan Warner, the predicate was wire fraud: he had conspired with others to lie to FIFA about his plans for the tickets it had allocated, telling the organization he wouldn't be scalping them, and he used email—a kind of electronic communications wire—to help commit the deception. The money laundering piece came after he had scalped the tickets and then used international bank transfers to distribute, and thus hide, the profits of the conspiracy.

By statute, those crimes carried a combined prison sentence of up to forty years, but nobody expected Warner to serve anywhere near that, given his clean prior record and willingness to cooperate. Much more painful, in some ways, was the $1,177,843.95 that he'd agree to forfeit to the U.S. government, representing "a portion of the monies that the defendant received from ticket sales in connection with the 2006 FIFA World Cup."

It was considerably more than FIFA's own auditors had determined were the profits from the scheme in the first place, but just a drop in the bucket compared to what the American investigation would soon begin to bring in.

––––––––

The second time Berryman went to see Danis, he rode out from Manhattan with John Penza of the FBI. Penza was a former New Jersey cop who had made the jump to the Bureau and worked for years alongside Mike Gaeta on Italian mafia cases.

Gaeta loved Penza, and when the opportunity arose, convinced him to come over to C-24, the Eurasian Organized Crime Squad, as his second-in-command. Then word came that Gaeta had won a coveted assignment to work full-time as an assistant legal attaché in the U.S. embassy in Rome. It was a plum posting, usually reserved for guys late in their careers, and impossible to turn down. Gaeta would be leaving New York early in 2014 and he'd be gone for at least two years, if not longer, which meant Penza would be taking over the squad.

The soccer case had become one of C-24's biggest, and worth learning more about, so Penza, who had a thick pompadour of shiny black hair cut by a single streak of gray and was fond of expensive, showy suits, was eager to ride along. On the drive out, Berryman congratulated him on his impending promotion.

Danis had found the documents Berryman had requested, but they were a red herring and he didn't care what they said. He just needed a pretext to meet her in person again, which he did in the second week of November.

"This is Special Agent Penza," Berryman said to Danis, intentionally avoiding mentioning that he was from the FBI, because he wanted to keep up the illusion that this was just a boring tax case. He had come back to New Jersey, he went on, to talk about the wire transfers in more detail.

But Berryman soon began describing a different set of wires than he had before, the ones he was confident were in fact bribes. He asked Danis about them innocently, not letting on that he knew what they were.

This $250,000 wire, he inquired, a perplexed look on his face, made on October 21, 2008, from your Citibank account to a Banco do Brasil account in Paraguay . . . now what was that for? How about this wire, for the same amount and to the same account, on December 15? And what about the $800,000, spread out over six wires sent in a two-year span to a Merrill Lynch account in Uruguay? What was that all about?

As he went through the long series of transfers, Berryman carefully observed Danis's face. He began to detect a slow but palpable change. Without ever saying where he was going, he was laying out almost his entire case against her.

Then, after nearly an hour, Berryman suddenly changed his tone.

"Zorana," he said, leaning away from the papers piled on his lap and staring at her intently in the face. "Should we knock this off and talk about why I'm really here?"

There was a long and uncomfortable pause. It must have been five full seconds.

"I know why you're here," Danis said quietly. "The payments."

"What payments?" Berryman asked, his dark eyes narrowing. "You mean the bribes?"

"Yes, the payments," she replied, a note of resignation in her voice. "In South America."

Like her father, Danis was a smoker, and she suddenly felt the urgent need for a smoke.

"Do you mind if I step out for a cigarette break?" she added.

"Sure," Berryman said. "But don't call anyone."

Danis left the men sitting in her office while she escaped momentarily, clutching a pack of Marlboro Reds. While they waited, Penza, who had been quietly taking notes, looked up, a small grin on his face.

When Danis returned a few minutes later, she looked calmer, and seemed resolved to tell her story. She wasn't smiling, but she looked relieved—almost thankful—that the truth was coming out at last, and she sat at her desk ready to talk.

The two agents ended up staying all day.

Chuck Blazer's health had been in steady decline.

Weighing upward of 450 pounds, Blazer found it increasingly difficult to walk for anything longer than short distances. He did no exercise, exacerbating his other conditions, which included type 2 diabetes and coronary heart disease, and was on a steady regimen of pills to keep the symptoms in check. The undercover work he had done at the Olympics was exhausting, and in November 2012 Blazer collapsed, ending up in the hospital with an acute bout of pneumonia. When he finally returned home, he did so with an oxygen tank strapped to his mobility scooter.

Then, in the spring of 2013, he was diagnosed with rectal cancer, requiring twenty weeks of chemotherapy, followed by radiation treatment. Depending on how effective that proved, he'd likely have to undergo surgery that would leave him, at least temporarily, with a colostomy bag.

As Blazer's health declined, so did his usefulness as a cooperator. He no longer had any official position within soccer at any level, and after CONCACAF released its report on him and Warner the previous April, he was a pariah in the sport. There was little chance he could get anyone to admit to anything serious, so pushing Blazer to make more recordings not only seemed cruel, given his health problems, but pointless.

At 10:10 in the morning on November 25, 2013, Blazer wheeled into Judge Raymond J. Dearie's courtroom in Cadman Plaza, flanked by his lawyers, ready to confess to what amounted to a very limited sampling of his decades of criminal activity in soccer.

He wouldn't face punishment for helping Warner get a bribe from the Moroccan World Cup bid committee in 1992, or for scalping tickets in the 1994, 1998, and 2002 World Cups, which he'd admitted to, or for the hundreds of thousands of dollars in bribes he'd taken from Hawilla in exchange for the Gold Cup rights. There were to be no charges for willingly failing to file CONCACAF's tax returns, or for the many other fiduciary indiscretions he'd perpetuated as the confederation's general secretary.

Instead, Blazer was being allowed to plead to the tax counts that Berryman had dug up, as well as a single wire fraud conspiracy charge and a related money laundering conspiracy charge for his role in taking bribes to vote for South Africa to host the 2010 World Cup. He'd have to forfeit nearly $2 million to the government.

There was one additional, incredibly significant, crime he would have to plead to as well.

Blazer had been an invaluable cooperator, opening the prosecutors' eyes to the pervasive rot that ran through seemingly every level of soccer and the sports marketing companies that lubricated the system with bribes. He had delivered them Hawilla, and handed over a river of evidence on dozens of other suspects, chief among them Jack Warner. Perhaps most importantly, Blazer had helped the prosecutors grasp the premise that FIFA and all the many confederations and associations that radiated out from it operated as a single cohesive, corrupted enterprise.

Thus it was fitting that Blazer would be the first defendant in the case to confess to a RICO violation.

"The principal purpose of the enterprise," Blazer's charging document read, "was to regulate and promote the sport of soccer worldwide." Yet he and other soccer officials had "corrupted the enterprise by engaging in various criminal activities, including fraud, bribery and money laundering, in pursuit of personal gain," and by "abusing positions of trust, engaging in undisclosed self-dealing, misappropriating funds and violating their fiduciary duties."

Looking down at Blazer, a sick and broken man, Judge Dearie, who was known among lawyers for his often humorous touch from the bench, took on a somber tone as he asked how Blazer pleaded.

"Guilty," he replied.

Almost two years to the day after he had been confronted in the glass atrium adjoining Trump Tower, it was, at last, time to let Chuck Blazer rest.

TWENTY-THREE

TRUST AND BETRAYAL

FOR THE FIRST DOZEN YEARS OF HIS CAREER, ENRIQUE Sanz was on the hustle side of the soccer business, attending to the needs of the self-important presidents, vice presidents, and treasurers of even the puniest soccer associations scattered around the Caribbean and Central America so they would sign the rights contracts Traffic needed.

That all changed when Sanz was made CONCACAF's general secretary in mid-2012. Suddenly he was the one in demand, the one to whom everybody came bearing gifts. He had attended soccer conferences and other events for years, joining the crowd of hungry sports marketing guys standing at the back of the room, praying for an opportunity to buttonhole some official after listening to him give some tiresome speech. Now Sanz was the one taking the podium at congresses, and when he looked out across the room, he could spot the eager young salesmen salivating in his direction.

It was hard not to enjoy the fresh aura of importance that came with the job—the sporting press sometimes even referred to him as a "dignitary," particularly when he appeared alongside FIFA president Sepp Blatter. The money wasn't bad, either. Sanz's salary as general secretary was $800,000 a year, a massive bump from what he got at Traffic, and among the many perks of the job were a seemingly unlimited expense account and a shiny new BMW X5 sport utility vehicle, which proved useful for making frequent trips between the CONCACAF and Traffic offices to negotiate new rights deals.

On November 15, 2013, for example, Sanz sat down with his close friend Aaron Davidson, Traffic Sports USA's president, to hammer out final details on a renewed Gold Cup contract that would hand the sports marketing firm rights to the tournament all the way through 2021.

For years, the two contemporaries had worked as a team, with Sanz acquiring rights from soccer officials and Davidson turning around and reselling those rights to TV stations and sponsors. When Sanz left Traffic, it felt odd, at first, to be sitting across the table from his old pal, but the two men understood what was really going on, and their close relationship, and common goals, made deal-making a snap. With little debate they got to a $60 million price for the rights to the Gold Cup and CONCACAF Champions League games through 2022. As for president Jeffrey Webb's private cut, $2 million seemed like a pretty good number.

Life was good. In early November, Sanz had rewarded himself for all his luck with a $1.4 million dream home in a desirable corner of Miami's Coconut Grove. Tucked behind protective walls, thick foliage, and tall palms, the property featured a lush tropical garden, swimming pool, and a guesthouse.

On the wall, he hung a painting that Costas Takkas had bought from a New York gallery at Sanz's request, paying with a check drawn from funds from the first round of bribes paid to Webb. From the same pool of money, Takkas also paid for a remodel of Sanz's new kitchen.

Then, one day in early January 2014, FBI special agent John Penza walked up the short path to Sanz's entrance gate and rang the doorbell.

As the primary case agent, Jared Randall would have ordinarily made the trip to Miami, but he was out of the country on a temporary duty assignment at the U.S. embassy in Colombia. Mike Gaeta was out of the picture, too, having just moved to one of those coveted foreign spots in Rome, so the task fell to Penza.

The flashily dressed supervisor was still new to the case, which, with its massive quantity of bank records and multiple languages, had become mind-bendingly complex. If the prosecutors wanted someone to approach a man in Miami named Enrique Sanz, then that was what Penza would do, but he wasn't going to try to flip him on the spot.

He didn't bother to do any surveillance or anything fancy. Penza simply flew down that same day, drove to the house, and when Sanz's wife came to the door, asked her to call her husband, who was at work, and tell him to come home. She did. When Sanz arrived, Penza asked to speak privately. He gave him his card, said there was a grand jury investigation of corruption in soccer under way in Brooklyn, that he was being looked at by the prosecutors, and he should probably get a lawyer.

Before leaving, Penza told Sanz one more thing: he wasn't to tell anyone.

————

In August 2013, Brazil passed its first law conferring benefits on defendants who help an ongoing criminal investigation. In exchange for identifying criminals involved in organized crime, preventing further illegal acts, or locating victims, cooperators could get their sentences reduced by as much as two-thirds, or in some cases even have their convictions completely wiped. The controversial law has since been used to power several massive investigations of the country's rampant corruption, and led to criminal charges being filed against two former presidents.

Previously, though, Brazil had no formalized system for cooperation, and defendants saw little upside to aiding law enforcement. On the contrary, the country's judicial system was viewed as itself hopelessly corrupt, with punishment dispensed only to the poor and unfortunate. Wealthy Brazilians like José Hawilla, meanwhile, were accustomed to erasing their legal woes with the help of pricey lawyers, and viewed justice as just one more thing that could be bought and sold.

As serious as his legal predicament was, Hawilla had never seemed to fully grasp the concept of cooperation, or, for that matter, that he had actually done anything wrong. The bribes he'd paid over the years were certainly an unpleasant part of the business, but as far as he was concerned, they were just what Brazilians referred to as *propinas*—literally, tips—and part of the day-to-day cost of doing business.

Norris and other prosecutors had tried to open his eyes to his situation. They were sure that forcing him to put up all his assets, to live in New York during its long, cold winter, wear an ankle bracelet, and constantly check in with the FBI would convince him of the gravity of his situation.

But no sooner had the handcuffs come off than Hawilla refocused on protecting Traffic, so it could be sold for the highest possible price. It was critical, as far as he was concerned, that the prosecutors never learn that his company had not only continued to pay bribes, but was at that very moment smack in the middle of a gargantuan corruption scheme entailing tens of millions of dollars in bribes to officials at two confederations simultaneously. If that piece of information got out, the prosecutors might find a way to pull the plug on the Copa América deal, and Hawilla would lose a lot of money.

More than once, Hawilla had considered abandoning the proffers altogether, halting his cooperation, and fighting the charges against him, just so he wouldn't have to keep talking to the prosecutors. But that was a highly risky move, and probably would land him in prison, so instead Hawilla worked hard to tell the investigators what he thought they wanted to hear, while assiduously keeping the rest of the story quiet.

Accordingly, Hawilla played the role of the repentant sinner, telling Norris and the others that he was ashamed of his past corruptions, apologizing for what he called "mistakes" in his past, and insisting he had moved on from that kind of thing.

Hawilla backed up his stories with reams of old contracts, bank payment instructions, and correspondence. He helped connect the dots in some of the incredibly complicated payments that Berryman had tracked down with his exhaustive searches.

He was meeting suspects while wearing a wire and popping into Traffic's Miami offices once a week for appearances' sake, taking advantage of the visits to pick up documents Norris had asked him to retrieve. The old Brazilian could be a handful, no doubt, but everyone on the case agreed that he was a far better cooperator than they could have hoped for.

And then, unbeknownst to Hawilla, Enrique Sanz began cooperating as well.

After his visit from the FBI, the CONCACAF general secretary had hired a lawyer and, after considering his options, decided to help the investigation. He flew to New York to attend the Super Bowl on February 2, and the next day went to Brooklyn to make his first proffer.

The investigators had targeted him largely because of the years he'd spent at Traffic and its predecessor company in Miami negotiating bribe payments to Jack Warner, and at first that was a primary focus of their conversations with the young soccer official. But as Sanz continued to talk, a distinctly different, and very much ongoing, tale of corruption began to emerge. Unlike his former boss, he told them everything.

As it happened, Norris and the other prosecutors had been meeting separately with Hawilla at the same time, quizzing him in one session about decades-old sponsorship deals Hawilla had brokered between Coca-Cola and Brazil's soccer confederation, among other relatively dusty topics. It seemed like just another proffer session, and Hawilla behaved as he always did. So when, just a day or two later, Sanz made it clear to the prosecutors that the Traffic boss had been lying to their faces for months, they were beyond furious.

A cooperator who lied was useless to the prosecution. Less than useless. If Hawilla were caught in a lie by a defense attorney on the witness stand, it could make it impossible to secure a conviction and taint the whole case. The entire investigation was at risk.

Norris summoned Hawilla to Brooklyn the following Monday, March 3, and made himself as clear as he could. Hawilla could be arrested a second time. Right that instant. They could slap him with new obstruction charges and put him behind bars. He had no idea how miserable they could make him.

"We are here because I believe you have some things to tell us," Norris said, masking his seething fury in a cold and quiet monotone. Without mentioning Sanz, or even hinting at what he knew or where he got the information, Norris told Hawilla he needed to understand that they were watching him, spying on him, listening to his calls. There was nothing they didn't already know and everything he said now, and from that point on, would be a test of his honesty. This was his last chance, and his retinue of $1,000-an-hour lawyers, embarrassed as they were at their client's behavior, couldn't protect him.

The message, finally, sank in.

Hawilla confessed to the prosecutors that even though he knew he wasn't supposed to, he had privately told Davidson and Sanz about the criminal investigation. He had also warned Sanz that he specifically could be targeted for recordings. Hawilla had done that, he said, in hopes that they would be careful, and avoid saying anything that could further implicate Traffic or reveal his big secret. That, he made clear, was why Sanz had been evasive when Hawilla recorded him.

But that was not all. Far from it.

There had been multiple meetings, he said, with executives of Full Play and Torneos to resolve the Copa América lawsuit and join forces. There was the secret agreement with Media World to split the Caribbean World Cup qualifiers. And there were many, many bribes—to the South Americans, sure, but particularly to Jeffrey Webb. There was the $3 million promised to him for the CFU World Cup Qualifiers deal, and another $1 million for the 2013 Gold Cup, plus an agreement to pay $2 million more for the next several Gold Cups, and probably others as well. It was hard to keep track of so many payments.

Just a few weeks earlier, Hawilla added, he had discussed all of this over lunch in Miami with Davidson. The younger man had filled him in on the latest with the Copa América Centenario. The contracts were just about ready for signing, Davidson said, and Webb's take was going to be huge—$10 million, if they could just come up with a discreet way to channel that much money to him.

It was stunning. Sanz had given the prosecutors a strong suggestion something was amiss, but what Hawilla was telling them was far worse than they had ever imagined—and highly embarrassing. Traffic had continued spraying bribes everywhere; the man brought in to clean up CONCACAF, Jeffrey Webb, was even dirtier than his predecessors; they had no idea a Copa América to be hosted in the U.S. in 2016 was even in the works; and it was all happening right under their noses.

When Hawilla finally finished, Norris told him to go home and decide if he was 100 percent committed to cooperating. If he wanted to stay out of jail, he'd better be.

———

Late in the morning of March 16, Aaron Davidson got off a flight at LaGuardia and took a shuttle to a nearby airport hotel, where Hawilla was waiting for him in the bar.

Davidson had been in Los Angeles the previous week to attend a match in CONCACAF's annual club tournament, and, soon after returning to Miami, his boss had called to ask if they could meet. It was fairly urgent, Hawilla said, and the conversation had to be in person. Could he fly up to New York the next day?

The lawyer knew his boss had been arrested, but he wasn't worried he would personally be implicated. Hawilla had repeatedly assured Davidson it was strictly a tax case and nobody from the government had even considered looking at him.

For nearly a year, that last part had been true. As president of Traffic USA, Davidson ran the Miami office, looked after the NASL, the failing little pro soccer league Traffic owned, and sold a few sponsorships. He had stayed clear of soccer's seamy side, and for a long time Norris and the other prosecutors had told Hawilla not to even bother recording him. But now it had become clear that once Sanz left Traffic, Davidson had stepped directly into the same filth.

A bar and grill at the Courtyard by Marriott hotel deep in Queens struck Davidson as an odd meeting place, particularly given Hawilla's predilection for gourmet meals and five-star hotels. But he was a loyal employee; if Hawilla asked him to do something, he did it.

The two men ordered lunch, and after a few minutes of conversation in Portuguese and Spanish, Hawilla lifted his pants leg, revealing the GPS monitor he wore on his ankle.

"Can you see this?" he asked Davidson. "I'm wearing this bracelet here in order not to go to jail."

The feds, he said, were all over him, and were planning to meet him the next day. In order to "protect the company, to protect myself, to protect you, and Enrique," Hawilla said he needed to supply the agents with information about the various bribes Traffic had been involved with, particularly to Jeffrey Webb.

"You do not think that he is . . ." Davidson replied in a hushed voice.

"No, no, no," Hawilla said, "There is no such risk."

The young lawyer looked up to the scrawny old Brazilian, regarding him as a pioneer who tapped soccer's financial potential, lifted the parochial sport out of obscurity, and had given him a great career. He trusted his boss implicitly.

Webb wasn't being investigated, Hawilla assured him. But it was critical for Davidson to update him on the status of their rights deals, including the bribes, so he could fill in the feds the very next day. If he was caught lying to the government, he said, he'd be in serious trouble.

So for the next hour and a half, Davidson answered all his mentor's questions.

He described how Webb had originally wanted a $15 million payment for the Copa América Centenario, and how Sanz and Burzaco had walked it down to $10 million, plus the $2 million for a long-term Gold Cup contract. He told Hawilla that Mariano Jinkis of Full Play had called him the previous week asking for suggestions on how best to pay Webb that $10 million bribe, but that Davidson had told him they could discuss it face-to-face.

Media World, Traffic's partner for CONCACAF's World Cup Qualifiers, was also having problems paying Webb, Davidson added. It still owed the confederation president $1.5 million—its half of the $3 million payment Sanz had negotiated two years earlier.

As the conversation progressed, Hawilla kept circling back, asking Davidson to repeat information about payments, to confirm and clarify what he had already said. And he also wanted Davidson, as a lawyer and an American, to address something for him. Was making all these payments, strictly speaking, illegal?

"Is it illegal?" Davidson replied, somewhat incredulously. "It is illegal. Within the big picture of things, a company that has worked in this industry for thirty years, is it bad? It is bad."

After the meeting was over, Davidson returned to the airport and flew back to Miami, contemplating all that had to be done in the coming weeks. Hawilla, meanwhile, left the hotel and met Jared Randall, who had been waiting nearby. He grimly handed the agent the hidden recording devices he had been carrying during lunch.

Hawilla was now 100 percent committed.

––––––

One day in the middle of March, Joe DeMaria, a fast-talking, high-energy defense attorney in Miami, called up Amanda Hector with some bad news.

His client, Enrique Sanz, had leukemia. He was just thirty-nine, so the prognosis wasn't terrible, but it was a very serious disease and needed to be treated immediately. Sanz couldn't keep proffering or doing undercover work, at least not for the time being, and by month's end would be announcing a leave of absence from CONCACAF.

DeMaria had quickly developed a good rapport with Hector, who had taken the lead on handling Sanz's cooperation. He had chatted with her about the case, and told her he thought the RICO theory in the case was too aggressive: more far-reaching than anything he'd ever seen. DeMaria was skeptical that so many crimes in so many places could be tied together with one central argument, and told her as much. Hector listened without comment. She knew, after all, much more than he did.

"Thank you," Hector said to DeMaria when he told her about Sanz's cancer. "Keep us posted."

The diagnosis presented a dilemma. In a very short time, Sanz had become a vital piece of the investigation.

He had been in the room for nearly every deal Traffic had signed in Central America and the Caribbean since the late 1990s, which meant he could personally walk the investigators through vast new avenues of corruption they had never even considered. He could also continue to serve as a kind of backstop to Hawilla, helping fact-check the information the reluctant Brazilian provided.

Perhaps most promisingly, as the general secretary of CONCACAF, Sanz was well situated to help keep the case moving forward. It was as if Chuck Blazer had been wearing a wire for them back in 2010, when everything was happening, rather than after he'd been discredited and largely pushed out of the sport.

Already, Sanz had shown flashes of greatness as a cooperator. He understood what he had to do, and unlike Hawilla, kept his cooperation absolutely secret; he hadn't even told his wife. And just a few weeks in, his undercover work was already paying off.

On February 25, 2014, for example, Sanz had worn a wire to a meeting in Miami with Julio Rocha, the former president of Nicaragua's soccer association. Three years earlier, Sanz told the prosecutors, he had negotiated a contract for Traffic to buy Nicaragua's 2018 World Cup qualifier rights, and to close the deal had sent a $150,000 bribe that Rocha said he would split with a colleague.

Rocha was no longer running soccer in Nicaragua, but he wondered if Sanz could put in a good word with him at Traffic, which would soon be negotiating for the rights to the 2022 World Cup qualifiers. Did Sanz think, Rocha wondered aloud on tape, he could get a taste on that deal, too?

It was clearly only the beginning. But now that Sanz was sick, the question was what to do with him. He had been involved in extensive illegal acts over a period of years and was by any definition a criminal; cutting him completely loose was out of the question.

But at the same time it seemed a bit sadistic, and maybe even unethical, to continue to prosecute Sanz, obliging him to keep cooperating. During chemo, his hair would fall out, he'd suffer terrible nausea and diarrhea, and he'd be incredibly weak and susceptible to infection, which meant he had to avoid contact with other people.

Hector was a serious prosecutor. She and her twin sister had both graduated from Yale Law and gone on to be assistant U.S. attorneys, one in Brooklyn and the other across the river in Manhattan. She was competitive and known for a hard-charging demeanor that sometimes came across as harsh. But Hector advocated for mercy. Sanz, she said, was the father of a young child and he could die—surely that was more important than any bribery case.

Berryman took a more strident position; he had reviewed the bank records and traced all the bribes; he wanted to be sure that Sanz didn't get away with his crimes. But it ultimately was Norris's call, and he came down on Hector's side. For now, Norris said, they were going to give Sanz a break.

Hector called DeMaria back to tell him that although they reserved the right to charge him down the road, for the time being he should focus on getting his treatment. Still, she added, Sanz wasn't off the hook.

When they called, he'd better answer.

TWENTY-FOUR

"ALL OF US GO TO PRISON"

ON THE MORNING OF MAY 1, 2014, MOST OF THE WESTern Hemisphere's top soccer bosses descended on the luxurious St. Regis Bal Harbour Resort just north of Miami to watch Jeffrey Webb, along with CONMEBOL's president, Eugenio Figueredo, formally announce the Copa América Centenario.

After a typically effervescent presentation from the two officials, the media was given the chance to ask questions. Reporters from the mostly Spanish-language outlets in attendance wondered whether the tournament, jammed awkwardly into an already busy 2016 summer calendar, might be a dud.

It was scheduled at nearly the exact same time as the ultra-popular European Championship, and just before the Olympics in Rio de Janeiro, which also had a soccer tournament. Not only that, but this wholly manufactured event wasn't yet on FIFA's official schedule, which meant it was possible professional clubs wouldn't release big stars to play in the tournament.

Figueredo, a slight man in his early eighties who was dwarfed by the far younger and more robust-looking Webb, brushed off the concerns, cracked a few jokes, and took a moment to mention his "very good friend" Enrique Sanz. "We are praying for his recovery," he said. Webb, for his part, called the tournament, still more than two years away, a "once in a lifetime celebration."

For the investigators working the soccer case, the day's events felt no less important.

They'd only learned of the existence of the Centenario tournament less than two months earlier, but once they did, they realized it presented them a golden opportunity to catch people on tape. A joint CONCACAF/CONMEBOL press conference would draw any number of the targets of their probe, and, unlike the London Olympics where Blazer had made his recordings, this event was taking place within the friendly confines of the U.S.

So, racing against the clock, the prosecutors and special agents worked to prepare their key cooperator, José Hawilla, for action. At their direction, he set up a series of meetings for the days around the press event.

It wasn't hard to do. Because Hawilla hadn't left the country in almost a year, people throughout Latin America were eager to see him, particularly his new partners at Full Play and Torneos y Competencias.

The Copa América enterprise was proving a resounding success. The Jinkises had been able to sell the U.S. Spanish-language rights to the Centenario edition to broadcaster Univision for $71 million, more than double the value of the equivalent rights to the 2015 tournament, to be held in Chile.

They figured they could get another $30 million from Fox for the English-language rights in the U.S. That meant all other rights sales, including broadcast in the rest of the world, plus sponsorships, would be pure profit. By their calculations, the joint venture, Datisa, was going to net between $80 million and $100 million in profit for each edition of the Copa América.

But there were also reasons to be concerned. Hawilla's partners had learned that Jeffrey Webb still hadn't been paid his $10 million bribe, and wanted to understand what the holdup might be. They also knew that Hawilla had been trying to sell his company, and worried that a new owner of Traffic wouldn't understand how their business really worked.

"My fear," Mariano Jinkis said during a private meeting with his father and Hawilla at their beachfront hotel the night before the press conference, "is to have a partner who says 'I can't pay payoffs. We don't make payoffs here.' "

Hawilla refused entreaties to sell his share of Datisa back to his partners, saying he felt it would "make Traffic very weak." At the same time, he expressed discomfort with how aggressively the owners of Full Play handed out bribes—almost as if they enjoyed it. As they talked, Hugo Jinkis appeared to almost relish explaining the complicated chain of shell companies he used to pay them out, bouncing wires from country to country to evade scrutiny.

"This will not change," Mariano Jinkis added. "There will always be payoffs. There will be payoffs forever."

Although Hawilla had originally balked at wearing a wire, and never truly became comfortable recording his friends and associates, he had grown more adept at steering conversations toward where Randall or other agents on the case instructed him to take them.

Immediately following the press conference the next morning, Hawilla, with Davidson in tow, approached Webb. The three posed for a photo alongside the imposing Copa América trophy, and then Hawilla, using Davidson as a translator, insistently attempted to get the CON-CACAF president to talk about the $10 million bribe. When that went nowhere, Hawilla retired to the bar in the St. Regis lobby, where he met up with Burzaco and Hugo and Mariano Jinkis.

That meeting proved much more successful. Over snacks, Hawilla managed to get his Argentine partners to go over, repeatedly and in detail, the mechanics of the Copa América bribes, who received them, and what steps were taken to cover their tracks and make everything look legitimate. Satisfied he'd checked that box, Hawilla opened another line of questioning he'd been coached to ask, similar to the questions he'd posed to Davidson a few weeks earlier.

"Think about this," Hawilla asked. "Who could get hurt by this thing?"

"You mean, with this contract, with this issue?" Burzaco replied with a laugh. "All of us."

A potential buyer of Traffic would examine the Datisa deals, and the phony contracts they'd drummed up to justify bribe payments and see right through them. It would be far worse, the Torneos y Competencias executive said, if law enforcement got involved.

"Tomorrow the money laundering agency from Buenos Aires could come to investigate, for example. Or from Brazil. Or the DEA, or anyone. And they will say 'what are all these payments?' " Burzaco said.

"All of us go to prison," he added. "All of us."

Hawilla had made a host of recordings over the previous few days, sitting down with numerous people including the president of Brazil's soccer federation, who was tied up in at least three different bribery schemes at once. Despite his awkward demeanor and reticent behavior, the cooperator had convinced people to admit to all sorts of complicity.

But this last tape was the cherry on top.

Reviewing the translated transcript of the meeting, the prosecutors in Brooklyn could hardly feel happier. It was exactly the kind of evidence they were hoping for. The net was getting tighter.

———

As he did every morning, Berryman picked up his phone and scanned through his inbox before getting out of bed. Amid the junk mail, personal messages, and a string of Google Alerts was an email from Evan Norris, which the IRS agent opened immediately.

Norris kept written communications brief and to the point. Julio Grondona, he wrote, was dead.

Wide awake now, Berryman looked at a few of the alerts. There were dozens of stories with the same news. Grondona, a FIFA vice president and chairman of its powerful Finance Committee, who had been president of the Argentine soccer association since 1979 and was one of the most powerful men in all of soccer, had died suddenly of a ruptured abdominal aorta at eighty-two. It had happened in Buenos Aires the previous day, July 30, 2014.

Berryman sighed. He had put a ton of work into Grondona.

Known as Don Julio, Grondona was the soccer world's closest equivalent to a movie mobster. Tall and sleek, with slicked-back hair, drooping jowls, and cruel hangdog eyes, he spoke Spanish in a grunting mumble and steadfastly refused to learn any other language. He lambasted critics, ridiculed his rivals, and was known for disparaging comments about Jews and, in particular, the English.

Grondona had proudly admitted to voting for Russia and Qatar to host the World Cup, saying "a vote for the United States is like giving it to England," and, throughout his career, managed to escape numerous criminal probes within Argentina.

Notorious for his gold pinky ring that said *Todo Pasa*, or "All Things Pass," Grondona projected a humble image, holding court in a hardware store he owned in a hardscrabble neighborhood on the outskirts of Buenos Aires, or in the cramped back office of an out-of-the-way gas station. But in truth, decades of kickbacks and bribes had made him immensely wealthy, with properties scattered around the Argentine capital, including his residence in a luxury condominium in Buenos Aires's fashionable Puerto Madero district.

At first, Berryman had been stymied in his attempts to root out the Argentine's bribes. Grondona was unusually careful, never using his own accounts to send or receive money, and seemed to assiduously avoid transactions within the U.S.

But the determined IRS agent eventually discovered a way in: Alejandro Burzaco. Hawilla, in proffers, had described him as "the same person" as Grondona and, indeed, it was hard to tell where one man's financial affairs ended and the other's began. Other than Grondona's children, in fact, Burzaco was the only person at Don Julio's bedside in the Buenos Aires hospital as he died.

For the past several months, Berryman had focused his attentions on Burzaco and his company, Torneos, using subpoenas to Fedwire and CHIPS as the initial can-opener and soon discovering numbered bank accounts in Switzerland that looked particularly suspect. Berryman wasn't sure yet, but it seemed as if Burzaco maintained special accounts that Grondona could access without having to actually put his name on them. He also seemed to do a lot of business in cash.

Unwinding all this was a complicated project, and just as he was really getting into it, Berryman received word that he'd been offered a temporary duty assignment to work in the London embassy. Berryman loved England and for years had wanted to live there again; he made no secret of the fact that he aspired to a permanent assignment there to finish his career.

At the same time, Berryman didn't want to lose a step on the soccer case, and so after consulting with Norris, he decided he could go to London for a few months and simply work more hours in order to get everything done.

He had also found some help. J. J. Kacic, the IRS agent in Orange

County, who had accompanied him on his first approach of Zorana Davis, was now on the case full-time. To free himself up to focus on Burzaco and Grondona, Berryman handed off tracing Full Play's money to the young agent. Every morning, Berryman would report to duty at the U.S. embassy in London, helping coordinate tax and money laundering investigations between American and British law enforcement. Then, every night, he'd take advantage of the eight-hour time difference to California, getting on the phone with Kacic to read through spreadsheets, line by line, and suggest new subpoenas to file.

The soccer case had been open for almost four years, and Berryman had been working on it full-time for three of them. They'd made tremendous progress, but they couldn't wait forever. The men who ruled soccer weren't getting any younger and, for that matter, neither was Steve Berryman. A few months earlier, he'd learned that the Brazilian soccer boss Ricardo Teixeira had returned to Brazil, where he was safe from extradition, and it was frustrating to think of all the hard work he'd put in on the former CBF president that might now be for nothing.

Because of the five-hour time difference, the IRS agent was forced to wait for hours before he could call Norris to discuss the news. Norris was more than a dozen years younger than Berryman, and sometimes jokingly referred to him as "Dad." But now it was Berryman who looked to the prosecutor for fatherly guidance; only Norris could soothe the feelings and frustrations that inevitably emerged on a case that meant so much to him.

Losing Grondona and Teixeira was without a doubt frustrating, but there was not a thing they could do. They had to stay focused. They would move when they were ready to move, the prosecutor insisted, and not a moment earlier.

"Oh, well," Norris added. "Let's move on."

———

In the waning days of August, officers of the Royal Cayman Islands Police Service arrested a man named Canover Watson on suspicion of perpetrating a massive, multimillion-dollar scheme to defraud the British territory's health care system.

Watson had been on Berryman's radar, albeit distantly. He was treasurer of the Cayman Islands Football Association, one of eight members of FIFA's Audit and Compliance Committee, and one of Jeffrey Webb's best friends and closest confidants. He even owned the mansion right next door to Webb's outside Atlanta.

Whatever Watson was mixed up in back home had nothing to do with soccer, although the arrest did prompt FIFA to temporarily suspend him. It seemed to Berryman like yet another potential target might be falling out of his grasp, but the arrest did not come as a surprise.

Some three months earlier, investigators with the Caymanian police force's Anti-Corruption Unit had reached out to both the FBI and the IRS through legal attachés stationed in the Caribbean. They were looking for information about Watson, and also about Webb, and because of that, their requests were soon filtered up to Jared Randall and Berryman. The RCIPS officers were asking questions about the properties both men had purchased in Georgia, and were hoping to get information from the banks involved in those transactions.

The first instinct of Norris and the other prosecutors was to ignore the queries. They weren't going to risk the integrity of the whole investigation to help some minor corruption case in a tiny tourist resort with sixty thousand residents.

But Webb had become a central target, and it was hard not to wonder what these island cops might be poking around on. The arrest of Watson brought the issue, nearly forgotten, back to the fore. After considerable debate, the team decided to invite the RCIPS officers to New York to hear them out.

As time passed, it had become ever more frustrating not to be able to ask other countries for help. Thanks to the Berryman's money tracing, the team had been able to uncover a considerable amount about suspects, but there were vast stores of financial information tucked away abroad that they simply could not touch, most notably in Switzerland, with its strong protections for banking privacy. The alpine country had a policy of notifying account holders whenever it provided foreign governments with financial records, which made such inquiries worthless in a clandestine investigation.

But this situation was different. The Caymanians had come to the U.S. seeking information, not the other way around, and meeting the foreign officers seemed like a good opportunity to learn a thing or two without having to reveal anything about their own case.

Coordinating a visit took some doing, and it was freezing cold when the Caymanians finally arrived in New York. After some whining about the weather, they explained Canover Watson's fraud. He'd been a rising star in the business community, the winner of the Young Caymanian Leadership Award, and in 2009 was named chairman of a government board overseeing its national health care system. A year later, the board awarded a multimillion-dollar contract for a new health care payment system called CarePay.

But the system didn't work well and was never fully implemented, and soon local authorities began poking around. They discovered that Watson and a partner secretly controlled the company being paid for the system, which was a clear conflict of interest and had never been disclosed. The partner was Watson's dear friend Jeffrey Webb.

A few months after the CarePay contract was awarded, the visitors continued, a series of suspicious transactions began to emerge. Webb bought his 9,800-square-foot house in Loganville, Georgia, on June 24, 2011, and, exactly seven days later, Watson closed on the 7,600-square-foot house right next door.

Around the same time, Fidelity Bank, where Webb still worked at the time, approved a $240,000 loan to J&D International, a company controlled by Jack Warner. The proceeds of that loan were wired to the account used to receive the CarePay funds, and from there to a Wells Fargo account in Georgia. A few months later, when the first CarePay money came through, the J&D International loan was paid off in full. Among other things, the foreign investigators were hoping to learn what had happened to the money in the Wells Fargo account.

Norris and Berryman glanced at each other. Webb was clearly involved in a great deal more than crooked Gold Cup contracts. Considering his importance to the investigation, not to mention his connections to Warner, it was tantalizing to think about accessing Cayman Islands bank records.

But it seemed too risky. Foreign police, they had learned, simply could not be trusted. The Americans didn't think they could be of any help, the prosecutors were sorry to say, but would be happy to buy their visitors dinner that evening and congratulate them on their good work.

As a British territory, by law the commissioner of the RCIPS must be from the United Kingdom. A large share of the 360-member police force is also British—drawn by the chance to live for a few years on a tropical paradise with some of the lowest crime rates in the entire Caribbean.

It so happened that the investigators looking into Canover Watson were all expatriate Brits, and Berryman, an anglophile to the core, hit it off with them.

"I can guess from what part of England you're from," Berryman said. Drawing on his childhood years in England, as well as his recent stint in the embassy in London, he listened to their accents, a grin spreading over his face. "You're from the north of London," he said. "And you're from Leeds, or Manchester."

"And you," he said, looking at the third cop, "support either Sunderland or Newcastle."

A few hours of socializing had convinced Berryman that these men could be trusted, and though it took some persuasion, Norris and the other prosecutors eventually came around as well. They would help the Caymanian investigation after all, and in exchange they would get invaluable information on Webb's financial doings that could help tie up the case they were building against him.

America's soccer investigation, shaping up to be one of the largest international corruption probes in history, touching on dozens of countries spread over multiple continents, finally had a foreign partner.

The irony of the fact that it happened to be one of the world's most notorious havens for tax evasion and money laundering was lost on no one.

TWENTY-FIVE

PAYBACK

"ROTTEN" SCREAMED THE HUGE HEADLINE ON THE NEW York *Daily News* on Sunday, November 2, 2014: "Secret Life of Soccer's Mr. Big."

The front page carried a picture of Chuck Blazer standing next to Sepp Blatter, with the World Cup trophy superimposed over the image. Inside, a four-page spread broke the news that Blazer had been busted for failing to file taxes, became a cooperator for the FBI, and wore a wire at the London Olympics.

The story, in classic New York tabloid style, pulled no punches, calling Blazer "corrupt and corpulent" and recounting, breathlessly, his over-the-top lifestyle, personal peccadilloes, and how he used a key-chain containing a recording device to secretly tape conversations. A "Falstaffian figure," Blazer "came to inhabit a world of private jets, famous friends, secret island getaways, offshore bank accounts and so much fine food and drink that he eventually needed a fleet of mobility scooters to move from feast to feast."

It was lurid, certainly, but the article's authors were also delivering a big scoop, revealing to the world for the first time that Blazer had been secretly helping a criminal investigation. The story noted that both the IRS and the FBI were involved, that the prosecutors were in Brooklyn, and that the investigation was looking at both fraud and money laundering.

It was, at first blush, a rather troubling thing for Norris to read early on a Sunday morning. There was little mystery about the source: Blazer's former girlfriend, Mary Lynn Blanks, the former soap opera actress who had been living with him at the time he flipped. She hadn't been present when Berryman and Randall first approached Blazer, nor had she attended any of the proffers or covert operations, but it was obvious that the former soccer official had told her what was going on.

The two lived together, after all, and had been constant companions for years. Not long after the Olympics, however, they had split up acrimoniously. Blanks and her children moved out, leaving Blazer alone in his cavernous Trump Tower apartment.

That the leak came from Blanks rather than someone inside the investigation tempered Norris's dismay. He was also relieved to see that the *Daily News* had made no mention of Blazer's guilty plea, any of the other cooperators, or that the investigation was being built around RICO, with defendants around the world.

Blazer was burned as a cooperator, but frankly, he was seriously ill and of little use to the investigation anymore. If nothing else, the *Daily News* story reminded Norris that a case this large couldn't remain a secret forever. Wait too long, and the next leak could be truly damaging.

The sheer amount of evidence the investigators had gathered by that point, including countless bank and business subpoenas, thousands of documents handed over by cooperators, and hundreds of hours of covert recordings in multiple languages, bordered on overwhelming.

There was incriminating evidence, to a greater or lesser degree, on current or former soccer officials in nearly every country in the Western Hemisphere. After struggling with a case that initially seemed to be going nowhere, Norris's biggest problem now was not finding targets but deciding when to cut off the investigation so they could move to indict.

For some time, Norris and the growing team of prosecutors, now numbering four in all, had been thinking about when and where to finally bring the case into the light. The goal, as it was in mafia cases, was a big takedown, nabbing as many defendants as possible at once.

Clearly, the best opportunity to act was going to be at some FIFA event. The organization's meetings and tournaments attracted not only top officials, but also the sports marketing executives that kept the whole enterprise running.

The biggest FIFA event of all was, of course, the World Cup. But the 2014 edition, in Brazil, had wrapped up months earlier and, given the country's constitutional prohibition on extraditing its citizens, a Copacabana takedown had never been under serious consideration.

The coming year, 2015, held a number of regional tournaments and congresses, such as the Copa América in Chile and the CONCACAF congress in the Bahamas, but it was no sure bet that any one of them would draw enough targets from other regions to be worth the effort. The most obvious choice was a big FIFA meeting in Zurich. In the third week of March, the FIFA Executive Committee would meet, and then, in late May, FIFA would hold its annual congress, concluding with the presidential elections, in which Sepp Blatter was running for his fifth consecutive term.

Each had its pros and cons. The elections were certainly higher profile, but some on the team worried that a takedown then would send the wrong message about what the U.S. was attempting to do; it could, they feared, be read as a frontal attack on soccer itself. The March meetings, on the other hand, were coming up quickly and, since they were not as high-profile, ran the risk of drawing fewer suspects. Either way, it seemed clear that the big event was going to happen in Zurich, which meant coordinating with Switzerland's notoriously prickly law enforcement agencies.

For the past decade, American prosecutors had been aggressively pursuing Swiss banks for abetting tax evasion, extracting $780 million from UBS in 2009 and $2.6 billion from Credit Suisse earlier in 2014, while forcing scores of other financial institutions to pay smaller fines and change their practices in order to avoid prosecution. Among other things, the nation's famous wall of silence had been partially breached: for the first time, Swiss banks had been obliged to provide account information on U.S. taxpayers to American law enforcement.

The Justice Department's campaign had been roundly criticized by both the Swiss press and public, who viewed it as American imperialism, a kind of legal bullying that had buckled the knees of the country's most revered institutions and forced them to alter a deep-seated culture of secrecy that was a matter of national pride. Convincing the Swiss to conduct a huge and very public takedown of yet another of the country's most prominent organizations, FIFA, was going to require some delicate negotiations.

Then, less than a week after the *Daily News* story was published, President Obama announced he was nominating Loretta Lynch to succeed Eric Holder as attorney general.

Lynch was the sitting U.S. attorney for the Eastern District of New York and, as such, the soccer investigation was her case. Although she was numerous rungs up the ladder from Norris and the other prosecutors, she had been read in on the investigation since its early stages, and Norris had briefed her regularly on its progress. With a big office to oversee, she had plenty of other cases to worry about, and was known for trusting her prosecutors; for the most part, she just let Norris follow his instincts.

As attorney general, however, she could potentially be invaluable. Since she knew the case well, she could almost certainly be counted on to help smooth the way with top officials in the Swiss attorney general's office and help get them on board.

One of the arguments that would be critical was that this case wasn't, in fact, directed against soccer. At heart, it was an international money laundering case; the vehicle used for the bribery and fraud, generating all that dirty money, just so happened to be soccer. Rather than an attack on FIFA, the prosecutors would argue the case was in fact an attempt to rid the sport of the officials that had corrupted it. America, the sales pitch went, was looking out for the sport's best interests.

Besides, the Swiss public had little love for FIFA. After years of negative press and endless accusations of corruption, it had become something of a national shame, an institution increasingly defined by its inability to police itself.

Michael Garcia's Ethics Committee investigation was a perfect case in point.

After more than a year and a half of interviews around the world, reviews of hundreds of thousands of pages of documents, and billings reported to approach $10 million, the former U.S. attorney had finally submitted his hotly anticipated report on the bidding process for the 2018 and 2022 World Cups to FIFA in early September.

A month later, however, FIFA announced that it would not publish the 434-page document because it had to "respect the personal rights of the people mentioned in the report" and instead would release only a summary. Then, when the forty-two-page synopsis was released on November 13, 2014, Garcia publicly condemned it, saying it contained "numerous materially incomplete and erroneous representations of the facts." And when FIFA rejected an appeal by Garcia to release the full report, the American resigned in protest, producing yet another very public embarrassment for the organization.

Without subpoena power, Garcia had been able to dig up little interesting new information. None of the people the feds were interested in—Ricardo Teixeira, Mohamed bin Hammam, Nicolás Leoz, or Jack Warner—had agreed to sit for an interview with Garcia. The former prosecutor had been unable to even conduct the Russian portion of the investigation himself because he had been, ironically enough, added to a list of Americans barred from setting foot in the country as retribution for Magnitsky Act sanctions imposed by the U.S. In any event, the Russians almost completely avoided scrutiny by claiming that the computers they used for the bid had been leased and that their owner had destroyed all of them.

As an investigative document, then, the Garcia report seemed disappointing at best. If anything, it stood out to the prosecutors in Brooklyn as symbolic of the cancerous impunity plaguing FIFA. If the report contained any important evidence of corruption, FIFA was clearly not going to do anything with it. As far as the small team of investigators working on the soccer case were concerned, there was nobody on the entire planet making any serious attempt to clean up the sport except for them.

As winter approached, and the days grew short, they began to talk more concretely about the moment they would finally make their big move and the whole world would find out what they had been up to.

It was going to be a great and important day. To celebrate the years of hard work, Norris promised to take Randall and Berryman to dinner at Peter Luger, a famous Brooklyn steakhouse, where gruff old waiters throw down $80 platters of sizzling porterhouse. It seemed a fitting tribute because Luger's happened to be Chuck Blazer's favorite restaurant.

Blazer had been a terrific cooperator. There never could have been a case without him. When the *Daily News* article appeared, Randall tore off the front page and pinned it to the wall of his cubicle on the twenty-third floor of 26 Federal Plaza, next to the receipt from the first lunch he'd had with Blazer more than three years earlier.

As a joke, somebody had marked up the newspaper.

"I don't carry keychains," a speech balloon out of Blazer's mouth read.

"You do now," a second bubble said. "You work for me."

———

Since the moment they flipped Hawilla eighteen months earlier, the prosecutors had been intensely interested in figuring out exactly what he owned and how much it was worth.

He was very rich, of course, but the government attorneys wanted him to catalogue, in detail, all his assets and also provide a sense of what they could be sold for. So, even as he recounted the specifics of the bribes he paid, the intermediaries he used, and the phony contracts he concocted, the Brazilian was obliged, many times, to expose the inside of his figurative wallet.

The prosecutors listened with rapt attention as Hawilla told them about Traffic and its various divisions, about the North American Soccer League, about his TV stations, the multiple farms he owned in rural São Paulo state, his four houses in Brazil and the condo on Fisher Island, his many cars, his various bank accounts, and even his collection of Brazilian art, which included one painting worth, by Hawilla's estimate, $200,000.

They also kept tabs on his efforts to sell Traffic. Despite some interest from European buyers, the company still lingered frustratingly on the market. Meanwhile, Hawilla had, in September 2013, unloaded his newspapers, including *Diário de S. Paulo*, for just 30 million reales, or about $13 million—a huge loss on what had turned out to be a terrible investment. Most recently, Hawilla had convinced Chinese investors to buy the soccer training grounds he'd built in Porto Feliz, along with Desportivo Brasil, the local team he owned, for a total of 38 million reales, or roughly $17 million.

Hawilla's gross dishonesty over the first nine months of cooperation was to a large degree an attempt to protect the value of the companies he had built from nothing. But his infuriating behavior betrayed a grave misreading of the rules underlying cooperating with a federal investigation, of human nature, and most importantly, of the Racketeer Influenced and Corrupt Organizations Act.

When RICO was passed into law in October 1970, it marked the first time in 180 years that the federal government had been empowered to seize assets from individuals as a direct consequence of their crimes. Until then, the government could seize assets used to *commit* crimes—such as the boat a drug runner used to smuggle cocaine—but it could not remove property from criminals simply because they committed a crime.

RICO codified efforts to bind criminals to the enterprises they corrupted and the ill-gotten gains of their corruptions. Violators faced fines and up to twenty years in prison, but perhaps the most innovative and powerful punitive tool was asset forfeiture. Those convicted under RICO could be obliged to forfeit any assets tied directly or indirectly to the criminal enterprise they were involved in. Forfeiture serves as both penalty and deterrent, designed to send a powerful message to other would-be criminals: the government can take every penny.

On December 12, 2014, José Hawilla finally was permitted to sign his cooperation agreement with the prosecutors from the Eastern District of New York.

It said the Brazilian would agree to plead guilty to RICO conspiracy, wire fraud conspiracy, money laundering conspiracy, and obstruction of justice—a charge that had been expanded to include not just the interactions with Blazer that provoked his arrest, but his months of lying to prosecutors while cooperating. Hawilla's prolonged deception had set the investigation back, but more important, it had put it at terrible risk. Altogether, his crimes carried a maximum sentence of eighty years, and although prosecutors could make recommendations, the judge would have final word on how much prison time would be dispensed.

But it is the prosecutors in a RICO case who make the final determination of how much money will be criminally forfeited. Under terms of his cooperation agreement, negotiated and countersigned by Norris, Hawilla was consenting to forfeit to the United States of America a total of $151,713,807.43.

It was a shocking sum, more than seventy-five times larger than

Chuck Blazer's forfeiture and triple the gross domestic product of Montserrat, one of the CFU members whose World Cup qualifier rights Hawilla had acquired thanks to a $3 million bribe to Jeffrey Webb. To pay the forfeiture, Hawilla would have little choice but to liquidate much of what he owned at whatever price he could get, including—and especially—Traffic.

The first installment, of $25 million, was due that very same day, when Hawilla, a humbled man of seventy-one, faced Judge Raymond Dearie shortly after 10:15 in the morning in his courtroom in Cadman Plaza.

Hawilla had come to the U.S. in May 2013 for just a week and had never left.

For the past nineteen months, he'd been trapped in a country that was not his own, separated from his friends and family, and subject to the whims of a handful of government lawyers who didn't speak his language and knew next to nothing about the sport to which he had dedicated his life. Hawilla had watched his companies come under assault from aggressive competitors and his business empire shrink, and when he was cornered, he'd been forced to break confidences and betray people he'd known and loved for decades.

With an indictment still far on the horizon, and a trial where he might be called upon to testify long after that—not to mention a likely prison term—it could be years before Hawilla was allowed to go home. Quite apart from his concocted cover stories of plausible ailments, Hawilla had in fact been diagnosed with cancer in his mouth while cooperating and had gone through a brief round of chemotherapy and radiation. A pre-existing lung condition, meanwhile, had been exacerbated by all the stress.

It had been depressing, frightening, and profoundly isolating. Because the investigation was still secret, Judge Dearie's courtroom had been cleared, and Hawilla was forced to confess to his crimes alone, without even his faithful wife, Eliani, by his side.

TWENTY-SIX

THINGS FALL APART

A MORE FISCALLY RESTRAINED PERSON WOULD PERHAPS have organized a different CONCACAF congress than the one put on at the Atlantis Paradise Island Resort in the Bahamas on April 16, 2015.

It might not have been strictly necessary to put up dozens of staffers in luxury rooms, to arrive on a private jet, to host multiple late night parties with open bars, or to rent out multiple suites for oneself, one's friends, and one's family, also flown in on the confederation's dime. The event, which cost CONCACAF roughly $3 million, could, quite possibly, have been carried off with a slightly more modest touch.

But that wouldn't have been Jeffrey Webb's style.

The confederation president had been traveling nonstop, as was his habit, and bringing a growing retinue of friends and advisors along with him. He'd swept into the Bahamas, in fact, right after returning from a trip to Cairo, where he had attended the congress of the Confederation of African Football, along with Enrique Sanz and both of their wives.

That event had been nice, but CONCACAF's was going to be a blowout. It was a chance to show the world and, particularly, Sepp Blatter, who would be in attendance, how far the confederation had progressed in the three years since Webb had replaced Jack Warner. The Atlantis, a well-appointed yet thoroughly glitzy establishment, was overrun by uniformed confederation staffers, and a huge video screen looping highlights of Webb's accomplishments loomed over the event.

Blatter arrived at the Atlantis on the 15th, stepping out of a chauffeured Mercedes sedan in a light sport coat and white shirt looking a bit tired. The seventy-nine-year-old was in full campaign mode and had dropped in on nearly every FIFA event on the schedule over the previous few months, but the Caribbean was special.

The region had been his political base since Jack Warner supported his first presidential campaign in 1998, and in Webb, Blatter had found a loyal successor. In fact, the two men had been scratching each other's backs for more than a dozen years.

In 2002, when he was just thirty-seven and all but unknown in soccer circles, Webb had risen to defend Blatter, then facing corruption accusations, from his own general secretary and multiple members of the FIFA Executive Committee.

At the FIFA congress in the Grand Hilton Seoul, Blatter had denied requests from fifteen different member associations to speak, among them Somalia, the Netherlands, and England. But Webb was given the floor, and he responded by suggesting, as a banker, that the soccer body's finances were just fine and that he didn't know what all the fuss was about.

"FIFA is family," Webb had said, "and family must stay together."

He was rewarded with his first FIFA appointment, as deputy director of the Internal Audit Committee, and two years after that, FIFA pledged $2.2 million toward building a "Centre of Excellence" in the Cayman Islands. In 2009, Blatter, flanked by Warner, visited Webb at home to celebrate the inauguration of a small office built with some of the funds—the majority of which were sent to the local soccer association and never fully accounted for. Webb, calling Blatter the "father of our football family," hosted a black-tie gala in his honor.

In 2013, Blatter named Webb chairman of a new Task Force Against Racism and Discrimination, and that October proclaimed that FIFA could have a new president "in the near future" and that person "could be Jeffrey Webb," a coy prediction that vastly elevated the confederation president's status.

Now in the Bahamas, it was once again Webb's turn to be helpful. He complied by barring what he termed "political" speeches at the congress, thus preventing Blatter's rivals for the presidency—Prince Ali bin Al Hussein of Jordan, Michael van Praag of Holland, and former star midfielder Luís Figo of Portugal, all of whom were in attendance—from even addressing the congress. It was the same trick Warner had pulled all the way back in 2002.

Webb, Blatter told the delegates, is "my colleague, my friend, my brother," and once again suggested that he saw in the Caymanian a likely heir to his throne. "He is a winner," Blatter said, "so let's see where he's going."

As far as Webb was concerned, however, the day's main event came when he was elected by the confederation's membership associations to serve a second term as its president. It was a formality, as Webb again ran unopposed, but he noneless treated the vote as if it were a glorious victory.

"CONCACAF," Webb said in a statement, "is more than ever united by one vision."

That vision, of course, was his. Indeed, the entire congress seemed carefully planned to impart to Webb a still greater air of importance.

Attendees, including a large press contingent, were barraged with a series of cheerful reports about the confederation's activities, its successful reforms, and its ambitious plans for the future. Enrique Sanz, looking drawn and pale, his once thick locks reduced to a thin buzz cut after all the cancer treatments, announced that the confederation would report a $1.1 million budget surplus for the fiscal year, to the nodding approval of the audience.

But that figure, like so much of what was really happening in the confederation, was a lie.

When CONCACAF's finance department crunched the numbers a few weeks earlier, they projected a $6.5 million loss for the year, due in large part to ballooning marketing and travel expenses, yet Webb had rejected that data in favor of rosier numbers. After publicly refusing compensation following his initial election, Webb had begun quietly taking a $2 million salary, and dropped as much as $100,000 apiece on international junkets, trotting around the world with his friends aboard private jets chartered by a travel agency that had offered him kickbacks in exchange for the confederation's book of business.

The congress itself had originally been planned for the Cayman Islands, but had been relocated to the Bahamas, at significant cost, and with little explanation. The unmentioned reason was that Webb had not set foot in his native land since Canover Watson's arrest the previous August, and had no intention of going back.

Watson had been formally charged in November 2014 with corruption, money laundering, and fraud and was awaiting trial. At one point, Webb had sent his wife to George Town to take care of a few affairs, but the local police had picked her up for questioning. Since then, Webb had lived in constant terror that the investigation of Watson, his best friend, would catch up with him. He'd warned Costas Takkas, his bagman, to avoid Cayman as well.

Everywhere Webb went at the Bahamas congress, he was surrounded by three enormous and intimidating bodyguards who prevented anyone from approaching him. Normally eager for press, he denied interview requests and avoided journalists.

Isolated and paranoid, Webb gamely presented an optimistic face, projecting himself as a future president of FIFA. But it was, increasingly, a shell game.

He'd worked out under-the-table deals with more than a dozen vendors that benefited him at the confederation's expense, and as a result the confederation's cash reserves were dwindling. The Copa América Centenario represented a huge influx, to be sure, but it was a one-time event that would have been worth at least $5 million more if not for Webb's greed. Bean counters in the finance office had bleakly started to warn that the confederation would soon be insolvent.

Yet none of that prevented Webb from throwing one more party in his own honor. After the congress at the Atlantis concluded, revelers stayed up all night, a DJ played, and alcohol flowed. The party alone, confederation employees whispered to one another, cost $70,000.

———

Among the hundreds of soccer officials, sports marketing executives, staffers, caterers, vendors, athletes, wives, girlfriends, and other soccer creatures who had convened at the Atlantis resort, one attendee in particular stood out: FBI agent Jared Randall.

The CONCACAF congress was the last chance to make clandestine recordings of large numbers of soccer officials before the takedown in Zurich, which was now a little more than a month away. Once the whole world knew what the feds had been up to, it was going to be far tougher to get people to chat openly about corrupt acts.

With that in mind, Randall had pulled together an operation in the Bahamas. Unlike previous undertakings, such as the 2012 visit to London, the schedule was less scripted and more open to improvisation this time. Also unlike prior trips, Randall went alone.

Once he checked into the Atlantis, he'd meet with Enrique Sanz, wire him up, and put the cooperator to work. The young general secretary was so well placed within CONCACAF, and such a rising star in the soccer world, that he could doubtless get in a room with anybody; even, perhaps, Sepp Blatter himself. Despite his serious health problems, Sanz had proven a very enterprising and discreet cooperator.

With any luck, they'd develop some damning new evidence. And in any case, it was a great opportunity for Randall to personally take in the kind of lavish FIFA-related event he'd been hearing about for nearly five years.

That was the plan. Get in, watch some soccer officials, and go home. But Randall didn't figure that people would be watching him, too.

In addition to the beefy security guards, Jeffrey Webb had brought a small detail of private detectives from Miami to the Bahamas. Paranoid about the criminal case in the Cayman Islands, and petrified there might be leaks, the CONCACAF president had become convinced that there was a mole inside the confederation, and could think of little else.

One of those private eyes made Randall within hours of his arrival, sitting in shorts on a sofa in a public area, playing with his cell phone and carrying a backpack. Something about him just didn't look right. He wasn't talking to anyone, he wasn't taking part in any of the CONCACAF events, and, oddly, he kept lugging the backpack everywhere he went.

On a hunch, the investigator followed him as Randall walked through the sprawling hotel and then stepped outside through a glass door for what turned out to be a face-to-face meeting with Enrique Sanz. He snapped a photo of the encounter on his cell phone, and forwarded it to his boss.

Why the hell was the general secretary of CONCACAF secretly meeting with this outsider?

The uneasy feeling grew even stronger that evening, when Randall was spotted lurking outside a barbecue for CONCACAF's guests, still in shorts when everyone else was dressed up for the evening, and still with the backpack.

After conferring, the private eyes decided to take action. They confronted Randall, asking him who he was and what he was doing there.

The FBI agent was suddenly put in an impossible position. If he told the truth, it risked the whole investigation. Word of an American soccer corruption probe would spread through the hotel like a virus, and the Zurich takedown could be completely blown up. But if he were caught in a lie, on the other hand, things could get very sour for Randall in a hurry.

When he didn't respond, the private eyes said they were going to call the police. All color drained from his face, the agent returned to his room, packed his bags, headed straight to the airport, and flew home.

Randall's operation was over.

———

One morning early in May, Roberta Sanz returned home from dropping her son at school to find her husband, Enrique, collapsed and unresponsive on the floor.

Their house in Coral Gables happened to be directly across the street from Mercy Miami Hospital and Sanz was rushed to the emergency room. He was unresponsive, as if in a coma, and nobody knew for sure what had happened to him. It was critical, the doctors said, to find out.

Since being diagnosed with a particularly nasty form of leukemia, the CONCACAF general secretary had spent considerable time in therapy battling the disease. He had officially returned to work on January 1, but relapses were common with his condition, and he had expressed increasing exasperation at the treatment options. Stem cell transplants, his best hope, often had even worse side effects than chemo.

Sanz, frustrated and tired, had been trying alternative therapies, including blue scorpion venom, an allegedly miraculous cancer cure that originated in Cuba and had never been approved by the FDA. Could Sanz have taken too much and poisoned himself, or had some sort of allergic reaction?

Desperate, Roberta Sanz took her husband's cell phone from his hospital room. Maybe it contained some hint at what he'd been doing that could help the doctors caring for him. The phone had been issued by CONCACAF, and figuring someone at the confederation could unlock it, she made sure it got to Webb, who had been deeply shaken by news of Sanz's collapse. He, in turn, handed it to Eladio Paez, a private investigator he had hired to watch his back.

Paez, a former Miami police detective, had been working for Webb for more than two years. In that time, he had performed countless odd jobs, researching the backgrounds of Central American soccer officials, for example, or organizing a security detail for a trip to El Salvador.

Bald and stocky, with glasses and a salt-and-pepper beard, Paez had struck a close relationship with Webb, who spent more and more time brooding over the ongoing criminal investigation of Canover Watson. In February, Watson's personal assistant had been charged in the probe; in early April, prosecutors in Cayman said they had located new evidence, including emails, suggesting that more people could be implicated in the case, and that an unnamed "third party" was helping fund Watson's defense.

Paez had warned Webb repeatedly that there could be additional criminal investigations in other jurisdictions, including and especially the United States. He pointed to the reports of Chuck Blazer wearing a wire, and of Daryan Warner cooperating as well, but Webb brushed off those matters as legacies of the past administration, and of no concern to him.

The private eye unlocked the phone and copied its contents. He then began methodically reviewing its files. Among the first things he checked were the device's messages, which is where he discovered text after text from FBI agent Jared Randall, who was labeled "J-Rod" in the phone's address book. The messages, dating back months, mentioned prosecutors, an investigation, and secret recordings. They left Paez little doubt about what had been going on.

Webb had been right. There was a mole in CONCACAF.

———

Over the previous few years, Jeffrey Webb had amassed an impressive array of luxury goods, including five Rolexes and more than a half-dozen other high-end watches, as well as a jewelry case overflowing with diamonds and pearls that he'd given to his second wife. He owned five houses in the U.S., including the remodeled three-story mansion outside Atlanta where he lived, and the couple owned a Mercedes-Benz and a Range Rover. And then Webb bought himself a $263,553 Ferrari 458 Spider.

The Ferrari convertible was a growling modern chariot, proclaiming that a man had unquestionably made it and wasn't afraid—indeed very much wanted—to be caught in the act of being important.

Webb hadn't grown up wealthy; his father was an immigrant from Jamaica and the family had struggled at times when he was young. He'd gotten involved in soccer when he was young, and though the Cayman Islands Football Association had never fielded anything close to a respectable national team, he'd managed to bring it some repute and considerably more cash over the years.

The way Webb saw it, CONCACAF was just a stepping-stone; he was being groomed for greatness. Someday, maybe in just four scant years, he would be sitting atop the soccer world, the first black man to lead the most powerful sporting organization in the world. The Italian supercar, in a very noticeable way, spoke to that ambition.

On May 1, 2015, Webb registered his brand-new, fire engine red Ferrari with the Georgia Department of Revenue. The soccer official put the title in his wife's name, but there was no question about who the vehicle was for. He paid extra for vanity plates bearing his initials: "JW."

Three weeks later, Webb boarded a flight bound for Zurich to attend FIFA's annual congress.

He would never drive his new car again.

TWENTY-SEVEN

TAKEDOWN

STEVE BERRYMAN ATE A LIGHT DINNER AT A DOWN-
town Manhattan restaurant on the evening of Tuesday, May 26, 2015,
then went back to his hotel to take a nap. It was hard to slow his rapidly spinning thoughts enough to fall asleep, but somehow the IRS agent
managed to squeeze an hour and a half in before he rose, got dressed,
and headed out into the cool spring night.

He arrived at the entrance of 26 Federal Plaza shortly after eleven
that night, where he met Richard Weber, the chief of the IRS Criminal Investigation division, along with his small retinue of advisors and
a public information officer. They rode up the elevator to the FBI field
office, nervously chattering, and went into a long, wide chamber that
everyone referred to as the war room.

Inside were rows of tables, whiteboards, and, toward the back of the
room, several televisions tuned to cable news stations with the volume
muted. Evan Norris and the four other assistant United States attorneys
on the case were already there, as was John Penza, the head of the FBI's
Eurasian Organized Crime Squad, and several other FBI agents who had
helped out. Someone had brought a box of donuts.

Most big field offices have a war room. Staffed around the clock
by agents monitoring different activities of the Bureau, they are also
frequently used for important operations. What was coming in about
forty-five minutes certainly qualified. There was an almost giddy anticipation in the room as everyone greeted one another, shaking hands and
trading smiles. An enormous amount of work had led up to this moment, and it was finally show time.

Norris had begun writing the indictment around the beginning of the year, but in reality he'd been carefully crafting and refining it for far longer, ever since Chuck Blazer pleaded guilty.

He'd been making frequent trips to Washington to consult with attorneys in the Justice Department's Organized Crime and Gang Section, fine-tuning his drafts to make sure that his central argument—that RICO applied because soccer itself had become a corrupt criminal enterprise—would stick.

After many late nights and working weekends, Norris had finished a draft of the indictment in early March, in anticipation of the quarterly FIFA ExCo meetings that were scheduled for later that month. The Swiss, after multiple visits from Norris and other American officials, had agreed to assist with the case, but at the last minute put off the March takedown, saying there wasn't enough time to arrange everything.

By then, however, the prosecutors had already submitted their first Mutual Legal Assistance Treaty (MLAT) request to Switzerland. An MLAT was the equivalent of an international subpoena, explaining the nature of the investigation, and identifying nearly two dozen possible targets. It formally requested information on fifty-five different bank accounts, a copy of the Garcia report filed to FIFA the previous autumn, and files from the long-concluded ISL investigation.

The nearly sixty-page MLAT, which was translated into German, was filed on March 17, and a second one, requesting information on additional bank accounts, was filed with Switzerland's Federal Office of Justice on April 21.

Berryman had arrived in New York in early May, working around the clock with a young prosecutor named Keith Edelman who had been added to the case to help bring it home. The two meticulously prepared additional MLATs they would be sending out to other countries once the indictment was public.

When the MLATs were completed, they had to draft scores of seizure warrants. Berryman had a list of all the bank accounts, spread all over the world, that he'd identified as belonging to each defendant. A key part of the strategy was to squeeze the defendants financially: even as the Swiss police were dragging people off to jail, their accounts would be frozen, making them more vulnerable and, it was hoped, favorably inclined to cut a deal with the prosecutors.

Finally there was grand jury preparation. Berryman and Randall had spent hours with the prosecutors going over the testimony they'd be giving, carefully rehearsing exactly what they'd say in order to help convince at least twelve citizens that they should return the indictment as a true bill, giving the investigators the green light.

The key was Norris's finished indictment. Nobody on the case had ever seen anything like it.

It was what is known as a "speaking indictment," which meant that rather than just reciting the forty-seven different crimes it charged, the document recounted in detail the narrative behind the allegations. At 161 pages, it read like a carefully researched work of nonfiction, telling the complicated tale of several generations of soccer officials and sports marketing executives who took and received bribes "to further their corrupt ends."

The argument could have been ripped nearly verbatim from one of Norris's mafia cases. FIFA and its myriad regional confederations and national associations, he wrote, were in fact part of a single enterprise that over the past twenty-five years had been corrupted by its own officials, "engaging in various criminal activities, including fraud, bribery, and money laundering, in pursuit of personal and commercial gain."

A critical lever in the case was the concept of honest services fraud, which is most often used against crooked public officials. Under the codes of ethics of FIFA and of the regional confederations, soccer officials were bound not to take bribes and kickbacks. By taking bribes and kickbacks, therefore, these officials had deprived the soccer organizations they worked for of their "rights to their honest and faithful services." Because the officials used email, telephones, text messages, and bank transfers to negotiate and accept the bribes, they were being charged with wire fraud and wire fraud conspiracy.

Since the officials also attempted "to conceal the location and ownership of proceeds of these activities" through elaborate layers of shell companies, overseas bank accounts, and phony contracts, they were being charged with money laundering and money laundering conspiracy.

And finally, because the officials secretly plotted with one another to corrupt and twist the soccer bodies for their own personal gain, and had defrauded the "organizations they were chosen to serve," they were being charged with RICO conspiracy.

To counter potential criticisms that the case involved judicial overreach and was an example of America applying its laws on other countries, the indictment was carefully crafted to charge crimes that, at some point, took place on U.S. soil—money passing through domestic correspondent banks, for example, or bribery schemes hatched on phone calls made to Florida.

The indictment also sidestepped another possible broadside: that commercial bribery wasn't even illegal in some of the defendants' countries. That was irrelevant; the officials were being charged with using American wires to defraud their soccer organizations of their honest services, not of breaking bribery laws.

It was immensely complicated, but in essence, Norris's theory boiled down to this: if Traffic paid Jeffrey Webb $1 million under the table to sign a Gold Cup rights contract, CONCACAF had not only been cheated out of the value of the bribe, which was money that could have been paid directly to the confederation, but also whatever higher price it would have received for the rights had a fair and competitive bidding process been allowed to take place.

And because all these soccer organizations were created to "develop and promote the game of soccer globally," Norris wrote, the ultimate victims of the rampant corruption were all of the sport's hundreds of millions of stakeholders. Picture, in other words, the impoverished, soccer-loving child of the developing world, with no pitch to play on, no cleats to wear, and no ball to kick.

That hypothetical child, tears streaming down his grimy little face, was the one who ultimately suffered from the towering greed of Chuck Blazer, José Hawilla, Jeffrey Webb, and all the other rotten soccer officials around the world.

On Wednesday, May 20, the prosecutors, as well as Berryman and Jared Randall, went into the grand jury room in the Brooklyn federal courthouse and asked for permission to indict Jeffrey Webb, Jack Warner, Nicolás Leoz, Aaron Davidson, Alejandro Burzaco, Hugo and Mariano Jinkis, Costas Takkas, and six other soccer officials.

The grand jury returned the indictment and it was placed under seal. The following day, May 21, formal arrest requests were transmitted to the Swiss authorities, along with a third MLAT requesting yet more bank records.

Everything was ready.

Since the regional soccer confederations were holding their meetings in Zurich on the 26th, and FIFA's congress began on the 28th, the plan was to strike on May 27.

To avoid attention, the Swiss had asked that no American law enforcement be on hand. Plainclothes Swiss police would start at the Baur au Lac hotel, where the ExCo members were staying. There would be no guns, no dark blue windbreakers, no bulletproof vests, and no handcuffs. The police would be gone before anyone else in the hotel had even gotten out of bed. If everything went according to plan, nobody would even know what happened until the indictment was unsealed at a press conference in Brooklyn hours later.

At ten minutes before midnight, the team in the New York field office raised an FBI agent posted in Switzerland on an international line. He was waiting near the Baur au Lac and would pass along information as it came in.

Things got very quiet in the war room. It was time.

At precisely six in the morning on May 27, 2015, a beautiful, cloudless spring day in Zurich, roughly a half-dozen policemen, dressed in jeans, tennis shoes, and light jackets, walked through the revolving doors of the Baur au Lac and approached the front desk. The small lobby, surprisingly austere for a hotel that charged more than $600 a night for its cheapest room, was nearly vacant.

The police quietly explained why they were there, asking for room numbers and keys, which the clerk gave them before calling the rooms to alert the guests to what was coming.

Then, just a few minutes later, something unexpected happened.

The scroll across the bottom of the CNN feed on one of the televisions in the FBI war room, which had been carrying reports of the National Basketball Association Finals and a heat wave in India, suddenly displayed a new message: "U.S. to announce corruption charges against senior officials at FIFA, world soccer's governing body, officials say."

The takedown had been treated with the utmost secrecy. Some people on the team hadn't even told their spouses. Paranoia ran so high that the IRS commissioner, John Koskinen, had been informed of the investigation only that very day because he had once been president of the U.S. Soccer Foundation and there were concerns he might inadvertently let slip about the case to a friend involved in the sport.

Yet somehow, despite the best efforts of the prosecutors, someone had leaked.

More than an hour before the Swiss police arrived at the Baur au Lac, two *New York Times* reporters and a photographer had arrived at the hotel. At 5:52 a.m. Zurich time, the newspaper posted a carefully edited story on its website under the headline "FIFA Officials Face Corruption Charges in U.S."

The story quoted an anonymous law enforcement official: "We're struck by just how long this went on for and how it touched nearly every part of what FIFA did."

The journalists—a criminal justice reporter who had flown in from the U.S., and a European sports correspondent—sat quietly in the lobby, discreetly snapping pictures with their mobile phones as the police arrived. Twenty-six minutes after posting the first story, the newspaper updated it to confirm that arrests were taking place in Zurich.

"Swiss authorities began an extraordinary early-morning operation here Wednesday to arrest several top soccer officials and extradite them to the United States on federal corruption charges," the article said, noting that the case was out of the Eastern District of New York and that the still sealed indictment alleged wire fraud, money laundering, and racketeering. This time the quote from the unnamed law enforcement official, who clearly knew the case well, had been removed.

The *New York Times* reporters had begun tweeting out photos of the raid, almost in real time, and their story was quickly picked up by other outlets, including CNN, rocketing around the world, far too fast to keep up with.

Norris turned to Berryman, who was standing next to him in the big room. He leaned close so they couldn't be overheard. The normally controlled prosecutor was apoplectic, as angry as he had ever been.

"Those motherfuckers," he said. "Those motherfuckers."

Jeffrey Webb had arrived in Zurich in time to attend FIFA's ExCo meeting, which was scheduled for Monday afternoon and Tuesday morning. It would be a relatively long stay, as a second, extraordinary, meeting of the ExCo was scheduled for Saturday, the day after the presidential election. From there, he'd fly directly to New Zealand for the Under-20 World Cup.

Tuesday, May 26, had been busy. Webb and his wife were staying at the Baur au Lac. But most of CONCACAF's delegates, as well as those from CONMEBOL, were staying at the Renaissance Zurich Tower, a slightly less luxurious, business-oriented hotel fifteen minutes away.

Webb's schedule on what had been a gray, overcast Tuesday included a ceremony with Juan Ángel Napout, the latest president of CONMEBOL, to announce the signing of a "strategic alliance" between the two confederations. After that, CONCACAF's delegates gathered to hear final campaign appeals from Sepp Blatter and Jordan's Prince Ali, the only rival candidate still in contention for the FIFA presidency. All the others had dropped out. That evening, Webb hosted a cocktail party for his confederation's delegates at the Sheraton.

It was late when Webb finally walked through the Baur au Lac's revolving doors, arm draped around his wife's shoulder. They went upstairs to bed, and were still sound asleep when the Swiss police knocked, politely told Webb to get dressed and pack a bag, then escorted him outside to an unmarked car.

By the time the officers had escorted his colleague Eduardo Li, a Costa Rican member of the ExCo, downstairs, droves of reporters were descending on the Baur au Lac. Panicked hotel employees, desperate to protect guests' privacy, scurried ahead, ushering Li out a side entrance. One particularly diligent staffer draped a bedsheet between the hotel door and the unmarked Opel hatchback waiting for Li by the curb, preventing a photographer from taking his picture. Within minutes, that iconic image—of freshly laundered linen hiding the identity of a soccer official arrested for being dirty—would spread around the world.

Upstairs in one of the hotel's suites, Neusa Marin, the wife of former Brazilian soccer confederation president José Maria Marin, desperately

dialed the room of Marco Polo Del Nero, who had succeeded her husband atop the CBF in March. The police had come knocking a few minutes earlier, and while her husband packed a bag of clothes to take to jail,
she begged Del Nero to help. He told her to remain calm and said he'd
be there shortly.

"He's coming," Neusa assured her eighty-three-year-old husband.

But Del Nero didn't come. Instead, he went downstairs, had breakfast, attended an emergency meeting for Brazilian soccer officials in another hotel, then went to the Zurich airport and flew back to Brazil.

Among those also breakfasting in the hotel's restaurant that morning was Alejandro Burzaco. He had arrived in Zurich the day before, but
was staying a few blocks away at the Park Hyatt.

The head of Torneos y Competencias had previously made plans to
meet the new president of CONMEBOL at the Baur au Lac at nine to
discuss bribe payments for the Copa Libertadores, and had left his hotel
half an hour early.

On his walk over, Burzaco received two text messages telling him to
look at *The New York Times.* There was an American criminal investigation into soccer corruption, there were arrests, and he was somehow
mixed up in it. Alarmed, but also curious, he continued to the hotel, to
see what it was all about.

When he arrived, the Baur au Lac was ringed by throngs of reporters, and security guards had closed the main entrance, but Burzaco was
allowed into the restaurant through a side door. Inside the breakfast
room he found a chaotic scene. Crying wives whose husbands had been
dragged away. Frantic soccer officials trying to hire criminal lawyers for
their arrested colleagues. The raid had happened hours earlier, the police
were no longer around, and nobody knew exactly what was going on.

Burzaco ordered food, staying for nearly an hour and a half as he
gravely discussed the situation with friends and colleagues. People wondered who had been arrested, and whether the investigation would af-
fect FIFA's presidential election on Friday.

After breakfast, the Argentine went upstairs to visit another soccer
official in his room, then left the hotel and walked to a nearby café where
he met a lawyer to discuss his situation. In the café, he called the son-in-
law of his deceased friend, Julio Grondona, who also was in Zurich, and

asked if he could drive him to Italy right away. Within hours, Burzaco was in Milan, far from the Swiss police.

The authorities did manage to track down Rafael Esquivel, who had been president of Venezuela's soccer federation for twenty-eight years and stood accused of taking bribes from Hawilla, Burzaco, and the Jinkises for both the Copa América and the Copa Libertadores. He was staying at the Renaissance, and breakfasting with Luis Segura, who had taken over Argentina's soccer association after Grondona had died.

As they ate, the two men excitedly discussed the arrests, wondering whether they might somehow be implicated.

"Hey look," Segura suddenly blurted out as he scrolled through his phone, "your name is on the list."

Esquivel was escorted out of the hotel by Swiss police a few minutes later, dragging a wheeled suitcase behind him.

Barraged by calls from reporters, the Swiss authorities soon acknowledged the arrests, breaking with the day's carefully scripted plan. Swiss privacy laws prohibit the publication of a defendant's name or image until the person is convicted. But May 27 had quickly turned into an anarchic free-for-all.

"We were under orders to conduct the arrests in secret, avoiding photographs," one of the officers arresting Esquivel confessed to a reporter who witnessed the scene firsthand.

The FBI agent in Zurich, in constant contact with Swiss authorities, relayed news of each successive arrest to his colleagues in New York. The defendants' names had been written on a whiteboard, and agents crossed them off one by one as arrests were confirmed for Webb, Li, Julio Rocha, Costas Takkas, Eugenio Figueredo, Marin, and, finally, Esquivel. And that was it. The raid, he said, was finished.

It was only half their list. The prosecutors knew that Warner was in Trinidad, and a provisional arrest request was already on its way to Port of Spain, with another one heading to Paraguay for Nicolás Leoz. But they had hoped to sweep up Burzaco, as well as Hugo and Mariano Jinkis, in the Zurich raids. Was it possible they had been alerted by the press and escaped?

Berryman finally left the New York field office around 2:30 in the morning. He still had a long day ahead, but for the moment there wasn't much to do except try to get a few hours' sleep.

As he walked, Berryman noticed how empty the streets of Manhattan were at that hour. He had just taken part in the biggest, most difficult, and exciting piece of law enforcement work of his entire life. News of the raids would throw Europe into chaotic turmoil, shutting out everything else. Yet here in the financial capital of the world, where so much of the bribe money had flowed through over the years and where the criminal case had been made, it seemed as if nothing had happened at all.

"Holy shit," Berryman thought to himself as he walked. "Holy shit."

———

The knock on Aaron Davidson's door came well before sunrise.

He'd bought the three-bedroom condo, on the twelfth floor of a tower on Brickell Key, in late 2012, right around the time Sanz had bought his house in Coconut Grove. Traffic's office was just a short stroll across the island, and Davidson's unit, which had cost $1.2 million, had a spacious balcony overlooking Biscayne Bay and a nice gym.

He had gone to bed Tuesday night before the news broke and was oblivious to the tumult sweeping the soccer world when Jared Randall and several other federal agents arrived bearing an arrest warrant. Davidson was surprised, but he could feel a light coming on in his head. So many of the strange things that had happened over the past few years suddenly began to make sense now, and he felt a slow swelling of hurt and anger at Hawilla welling up.

It was Hawilla, he now realized, who had betrayed him, urging him to take that sudden and peculiar trip to the hotel bar near LaGuardia the previous year; it was Hawilla who had assured him endlessly that the investigation had nothing to do with him, that he was safe, that he wasn't being investigated. It had all been a lie. How could he have been so stupid?

Davidson was struck by how friendly Randall was, and didn't resist. As had Hawilla, Daryan and Daryll Warner, he went along with the agents to the FBI field office, hired a lawyer, waived his right to a first appearance in Miami, and flew to New York in custody. He was the eighth person arrested that day.

Randall had flown to Miami the previous day, insisting on being there rather than in the war room with the other core members of the team. After arresting Davidson, Randall rushed to South Beach to join a group of FBI and IRS agents serving a search warrant on CONCACAF's headquarters.

Those agents had arrived before six a.m. in an unmarked minivan with dozens of cardboard boxes and showed the warrant to the building's security. Like everything else in the carefully orchestrated takedown, the raid was supposed to be conducted in secret, so that it could be announced when the indictment was unsealed later that day. But somehow a television camera crew was already waiting for them when they arrived, and filmed the whole operation.

At 10:30 a.m., Norris, in a conservative gray suit, white shirt, and blue tie, stood attentively with his hands clasped before a packed room of reporters and cameramen in the U.S. Attorney's Office in Brooklyn, listening to other people describe his case to the world.

The big guns were all there. Loretta Lynch, who had begun serving as attorney general only a month before, after one of the most drawn-out confirmation fights in history, spoke first. Then it was her replacement in Brooklyn, Acting U.S. Attorney Kelly Currie, followed by FBI director James Comey, who at six foot eight towered over the diminutive new attorney general. Richard Weber, the shiny-headed IRS Criminal Investigation chief came next, proudly delivering a showstopper he had rehearsed leading up to the press conference.

"This really is the World Cup of fraud," he said, "and today we are issuing FIFA a red card."

Norris had helped draft all the talking points, prepared charts explaining how the bribery schemes worked, and put together the press release and information packet handed out to reporters. He'd won admiration from his peers in the Justice Department at how long he'd kept things quiet, and even other prosecutors in Brooklyn marveled at how tight-lipped he'd been about the case that had dominated his life for nearly five years.

After nearly forty minutes, a reporter asked a detailed question about the Copa América, and Currie, who had zero involvement with the case until he joined the Eastern District of New York late the previous year, beckoned Norris to the microphone.

Finally Norris had a chance to claim credit for all his hard work. His moment in the spotlight, however, lasted no more than thirty seconds.

"The indictment is very detailed and there's a table of contents on the second page," he said, looking even more serious than usual. "I'd just refer you to the Copa América scheme." That was all Norris said.

The press conference was supposed to have been the first time the world heard about the takedown, about the indictment, and about the guilty pleas from Blazer, Hawilla, and the Warner brothers, all of which were being unsealed at the same time. That was the plan.

Soon thereafter, the Swiss attorney general would announce its own criminal investigation, focused on the bidding for the 2018 and 2022 World Cups, and inform the public that, in addition to the arrests, it had raided FIFA headquarters that morning.

But it hadn't worked out that way.

The Swiss authorities were furious because the leak had compromised the privacy of the defendants, and drawn journalists to FIFA's headquarters to witness what was supposed to be a clandestine raid by the police. Even more embarrassing, the presence of *New York Times* reporters in the hotel had given the public the impression that Switzerland's police force acted at the beck and call of American law enforcement. It was, to put it mildly, an awkward situation.

Still, if the goal was to attract publicity, it worked.

The news was big in the U.S., but elsewhere it was as if a nuclear bomb had been detonated. There was no other topic of discussion. America had taken on soccer corruption, something nobody thought would ever happen anywhere, and Loretta Lynch had crowned herself with glory on her first major case as attorney general.

Amid the frenzy, FIFA had already held its own impromptu press conference. A spokesman, Walter De Gregorio, bizarrely claimed credit for the investigation and assured the press multiple times that the presidential elections would still take place two days hence. Sepp Blatter, a testy De Gregorio said, "is quite relaxed because he knows and he knew it before and he has confirmed once again today that he is not involved."

Mohamed bin Hammam and Vitaly Mutko, Russia's sports minister, both weighed in on the news hours before the indictment was unsealed. Even Jack Warner, ensconced in Trinidad, managed to get a word in before the people who actually put together the most important criminal case in the history of soccer had a chance to speak.

"If U.S. Justice Department wants me, they know where to find me," Warner told a reporter. "I sleep very soundly in the night."

Less than three hours later, Warner surrendered to police in Port of Spain. Although a magistrate agreed to bail of 2.5 million Trinidad dollars, or roughly $400,000, Warner wasn't able to present the proper paperwork in time and he was forced to spend the night in jail.

A provisional arrest warrant was sent to Paraguay as well, but before it could be served, Nicolás Leoz checked himself into a hospital, claiming he'd suffered a coronary crisis. Sources close to his lawyers coyly noted that Paraguay's criminal code prohibits imprisonment of anyone suffering from a serious illness.

Argentina, too, had received provisional warrants, but so far nobody had been arrested, meaning there were at least three defendants unaccounted for—Burzaco and the two Jinkises. Randall, finished serving the warrant in Miami, flew back to New York and began preparing so-called red notices to submit to Interpol, which would alert every country in the world to detain the remaining defendants if they attempted to cross their borders.

Next came the extradition requests. There were seven men sitting in jail in Zurich, plus Warner in Trinidad, and Leoz in Paraguay, and the United States had to formally request extradition for each.

There was, in other words, a tremendous amount of work still to be done. As night approached, people on the case began trickling out of the U.S. Attorney's Office in Brooklyn and heading home. A few had managed to catch some sleep in the hours between the midnight takedown and the press conference, but everyone was exhausted.

Norris, still fuming about the leak, eventually left as well. He didn't say a word about Peter Luger, the steakhouse where he'd been planning to take Randall and Berryman to celebrate.

TWENTY-EIGHT

"A GREAT DAY FOR FOOTBALL"

THIRTEEN HOURS BEFORE THE TAKEDOWN, ZORANA Danis walked into a federal courtroom in Brooklyn, flanked by her lawyers. With so much happening that day, the prosecution could spare just a single assistant U.S. attorney, Sam Nitze, who had joined the case about a year earlier, to witness Danis's moment of truth.

Charming and personable, the owner of International Soccer Marketing had grown popular with the investigators since she flipped in late 2013. She had helped them understand some of the complexities of South American soccer, and had been instrumental in building the case against Nicolás Leoz.

Danis was being allowed to plead to just two counts, neither of them involving racketeering. One was wire fraud conspiracy, for some of the bribes she paid in exchange for Copa Libertadores sponsorship rights, and the other was for making a false statement on her tax returns, because she had tried to write off a $1.25 million bribe as a deductible expense.

"I knew that my conduct in paying these bribes and kickbacks was wrong," Danis, who also agreed to forfeit $2 million, told the judge. "It shouldn't have happened."

The following morning, when the big indictment was unsealed in Brooklyn, so, too, were the charging documents against Blazer, Hawilla, and the two Warner brothers. But Danis's was not.

In fact, the prosecutors had made absolutely sure that not a single word about her was uttered to anyone at all.

In RICO cases, prosecutors rarely consider the investigation to be finished when the indictment is handed down. In fact, that's often just the beginning. Long before they ever face the grand jury, prosecutors are planning a second charging document, called a superseding indictment, that expands the number of defendants. The first indictment itself can be a critical tool in getting there.

In writing that document, Norris made sure to describe each criminal conspiracy in detail, identifying the role played by every defendant, while liberally salting in clues about bank accounts, shell companies, and other potential evidence. He also filled the indictment with mentions of unnamed co-conspirators, twenty-five in all, leaving strong hints about who each was.

Co-conspirator #10, for example, was described as "a high-ranking official of FIFA, CONMEBOL and the Asociación del Fútbol Argentino," which identified him as Julio Grondona. Co-conspirator #7 was clearly Mohamed bin Hammam, mentioned as "a high-ranking official at FIFA and AFC, the regional confederation representing much of Asia" who ran for the FIFA presidency in 2011.

Co-conspirator #5 was "the controlling principal" of a Jersey City company that controlled "sponsorship and title sponsorship rights associated with the Copa Libertadores" and who paid "bribes and kickbacks to the defendant Nicolás Leoz" and others to keep those rights. The only person who could possibly fit that description was Zorana Danis.

When the indictment was unsealed, Norris knew that it would spread like wildfire among crooked soccer officials the world over. They would scrutinize every line, trying to decipher how the case developed, where it was going, and whether they might also be under investigation.

The description of Co-conspirator #5 would identify Zorana Danis to those who knew her. Norris had done that quite deliberately. And by keeping her guilty plea a secret, the prosecution was signaling that she must be a target as well.

Someone would almost certainly call Danis to discuss bribes, to ask her what she knew, or to tell her to keep her mouth shut, never suspecting that she was cooperating with the feds and would be recording all her calls.

That was the beauty of a richly detailed speaking indictment: as soon as it drops, phones start ringing off the hook.

———————

The morning after the arrests, CONCACAF convened an emergency meeting in Zurich to install a new president. Alfredo Hawit of Honduras was the confederation's most senior vice president and thus by statute automatically assumed the post, just as—ironically—Lisle Austin had unsuccessfully tried to do exactly four years earlier.

Samir Gandhi, the Sidley Austin attorney, had flown into town overnight from New York, and the scene he witnessed at the Renaissance hotel resembled a funeral home. The Caribbean delegates, in particular, were stunned. Some were openly weeping, while others furiously protested it was a big conspiracy. Nobody could believe that Jeffrey Webb, the great reformer, the Caribbean hope, had in fact been a crook.

Amid all the gnashing of teeth, Gandhi presented an action plan. The confederation needed to immediately launch an internal investigation, both to figure out how much Webb had stolen, and to determine how large its criminal exposure might be. "Will you retain us?" he asked the delegates. For the second time in three years, CONCACAF was investigating itself for corruption.

The following day, May 29, Sepp Blatter stood for reelection, ignoring growing legions of angry protesters gathering outside Zurich's Hallenstadion, where the vote would be held. Taking the podium before the association's 209 members, he derisively cast aside arguments that seventeen years atop FIFA was, finally, enough.

"What is this notion of time? Time is infinite and we slice it up. I find the time I've spent at FIFA is very short and it will remain short," Blatter defiantly said. "I would quite simply just like to stay with you."

The feeling appeared mutual. Just two days after the world learned there was a huge and ongoing criminal investigation that blatantly compared the organization over which he presided to the mafia, Blatter was elected to a fifth term. He easily outdistanced Prince Ali, 133 votes to 73, in the first round of voting, leading his rival to withdraw.

The following day, Blatter told a radio reporter that the arrests had been carefully planned to undermine his mandate. "With all the respect to the judicial system of the U.S.," he said, "if they have a financial crime that regards American citizens then they must arrest these people there and not in Zurich when we have a congress."

On Sunday, Jack Warner, out of jail on bond, released two video-taped interviews he'd conducted, dressed in the lime green colors of his political party. He, too, accused the United States of conspiring against soccer, claiming that "no one gives them the right to do what they are doing."

As proof of the plot, Warner held up a printout of a news article from an American publication: "FIFA Frantically Announces 2015 Summer World Cup in United States," the headline read.

"If FIFA is so bad, why is it the U.S. wants to keep the World Cup?" Warner asked, an incredulous look on his face. "Take your losses, like a man, and go." But Warner's allegations soon turned him into a punch line when it was revealed that the article he cited had come from *The Onion*, a satirical publication.

Then on Monday, came another leak. *The New York Times*, once again quoting unnamed sources close to the American criminal investigation, reported that Jérôme Valcke, Blatter's general secretary, had personally approved transfer of the $10 million bribe paid to Jack Warner by South Africa as part of its scheme to win the 2010 World Cup.

The next day, June 2, FIFA summoned reporters to its hilltop headquarters for an unscheduled press conference. Given short notice, only a few dozen journalists arrived in time to watch Blatter, in a blue suit and striped tie, take the podium.

"FIFA needs a profound overhaul," Blatter said, speaking in French. "While I have a mandate from the membership of FIFA, I do not feel that I have a mandate from the entire world of football—the fans, the players, the clubs, the people who live, breathe and love football as much as we all do at FIFA. Therefore, I have decided to lay down my mandate at an extraordinary elective Congress. I will continue to exercise my functions as FIFA President until that election."

It was extraordinary; something soccer fans could not have imagined only a week earlier. Sepp Blatter, just reelected as overlord of world soccer three days earlier, was going to resign. "A Great Day for Football" read the headline in the British tabloid the *Daily Mirror*. "Blatt's All Folks," crowed the *Daily Express*.

―――――

By a somewhat stark coincidence, *United Passions*, a $27 million film ordered up by Blatter and almost entirely paid for by FIFA, had its American premiere just three days after the Swiss soccer boss announced his resignation.

Only two people showed up at the Laemmle theater in Los Angeles's North Hollywood neighborhood for the first screening on the afternoon of June 5. One, an older Mexican immigrant, said he was there because he liked the World Cup. The other, after watching the film, said it was "very strange" and it seemed to him to be less than honest in its portrayal of history.

The film, starring Tim Roth as Blatter, presented itself as a biopic with FIFA as the main character. But in truth, it was a story about how seemingly everyone within FIFA, for over a century, was irredeemably tainted, bigoted, corrupt, or incompetent—except for Blatter, who emerges from the film as a kind of hardworking, earnest saint, dedicated only to the sport, and to the millions of impoverished children who play it around the globe.

João Havelange, his predecessor, is depicted as a cold-hearted, vote-buying schemer, who shocks Blatter by telling him to keep a black book on his rivals to use against him, while the English, whose press corps tormented Blatter throughout his presidency, are portrayed as racist, sexist, self-important buffoons. Tellingly, the only character in the film other than Blatter who escapes such rough treatment is Horst Dassler, the intellectual father of the sports marketing industry that was now at the heart of FIFA's worst ever crisis.

By the time it was screened for a final time, on June 11, the film's entire U.S. box office amounted to $918. *United Passions*, a film conceived to lionize Sepp Blatter had earned the distinction of being the lowest-grossing commercial release in American history.

―――――

Late on the morning of June 9, Alejandro Burzaco, accompanied by a lawyer, walked out of the upscale Hotel Greif in the medieval mountainside town of Bolzano in northern Italy. Dressed in a blue oxford shirt and jeans, he crossed the town's market square, passed its distinctive eight-hundred-year-old Romanesque cathedral, and finally reached the police station, where he surrendered.

He'd been keeping a low profile since arriving in Milan on May 27, moving around Italy in the company of an Argentine lawyer who was a close friend and had cut short a vacation to meet him. To avoid being tracked, the two men shared hotel rooms booked under the attorney's name, and soon moved to a nondescript condo near the beach on Italy's west coast.

Burzaco retained a New York defense attorney, who flew to Italy twice to discuss his situation. Burzaco had dual Italian-Argentine citizenship, and thus could stay in Italy, try to lie low, and take his chances that if he were ever picked up, he might not be extradited. He could try to return to Argentina, but ran the risk of getting arrested at the airport. Or he could call up the prosecutors in Brooklyn and offer up his cooperation in hopes of leniency.

Burzaco was from a prominent family in Argentina. His brother had been a congressman and chief of the Buenos Aires police and was closely linked to the front-runner to be the country's next president. Most of his assets had been frozen at the request of the U.S. government in coordination with the raids, and on the same day, his employees in Buenos Aires had destroyed countless sensitive company documents, as well as a secret computer server in Uruguay where years' worth of bribes had been painstakingly accounted for.

After some thought, Burzaco elected to waive extradition and try his luck with the Department of Justice. He chose to surrender in Bolzano because it was out of the way, and hoped it would draw little attention. But the publicity-starved local police decided to hold a press conference, and reporters soon swarmed the city's small jail.

Two days later, Burzaco received a call from his brother telling him that he was in danger. An order had apparently been given within the Buenos Aires provincial police ranks to prevent him from speaking to the U.S. prosecutors at any cost, even if it meant killing him.

Burzaco was still in Italy, now under house arrest at a bed-and-breakfast outside Bolzano as he anxiously waited for the extradition formalities to conclude. His family and some friends came to visit him during that time, and he become convinced he was making the right decision.

Finally, on July 29, Burzaco flew from Italy to Kennedy airport in New York, where Jared Randall met him at the gate and put him under arrest. He would start meeting with prosecutors the next day, but it so happened that his favorite team, River Plate, was playing in the first leg of the Copa Libertadores final that evening. Randall, who had to watch over him until he made bond, tracked down a portable radio so he could listen to the match.

Burzaco was arraigned two days later, with his sister, mother, brother, ex-wife, and several friends watching from the gallery.

According to a 2009 study of criminal courts around the country, the average bail for all types of felonies was $55,400, with murder, the most serious crime, tipping the scale at just over $1 million. The fifty-one-year-old chief executive of Torneos y Competencias was not accused of any violent crimes, much less murder. The charges he faced were wire fraud, money laundering, and racketeering. But he was no typical defendant, and this was no typical case.

Burzaco's bond would be $20 million, secured by $3.3 million in cash, three pieces of real estate, and his stake in Torneos, which the prosecutors estimated was worth at least $15 million. He'd be placed under house arrest in New York, unable to go outside without permission from the FBI, and would have to pay for round-the-clock private security, as well as GPS monitoring.

The investigation had reeled in another cooperator, as important in some ways as Hawilla or Blazer. Burzaco told prosecutors he had paid more than $150 million in bribes to dozens of soccer officials over the course of many years. He was highly intelligent, knowledgeable, loved soccer, and spoke flawless English. Almost four months later, Burzaco won his cooperation agreement, too, consenting to plead guilty to three felony counts and to forfeit the tidy sum of $21,694,408.49.

On July 26, Mexico handily defeated Jamaica, 3–1, before 69,000 fans at Lincoln Financial Field in Philadelphia to win its tenth Gold Cup title. Immediately afterward, CONCACAF's new Honduran president, Alfredo Hawit, stood at midfield and handed the oversized trophy to Mexican midfielder Andrés Guardado, who had scored the match's first goal with a spectacular volley.

That same day, Hawit met privately with Fabio Tordin, a consultant based in Miami, to discuss sports marketing firm Full Play's failed attempt, more than three years earlier, to win rights to the Gold Cup and other CONCACAF tournaments. Tordin had played middleman in the scheme, first putting Hugo and Mariano Jinkis in touch with Hawit and the two other Central Americans, and then helping coordinate the bribe payments.

Now that the American criminal investigation was public and the Jinkises had been indicted, Tordin told Hawit, he worried that the bribes would come to light. Hawit alone had received $250,000, and Tordin was terrified. The confederation president responded calmly. There was no cause for concern, he said, as he'd come up with a clever way to cover his tracks using a fake contract. Nobody would ever know.

Unfortunately for Hawit, Tordin was wearing a wire. Shortly after the indictment was unsealed, the prosecutors in Brooklyn had sent him what's known as a target letter, advising him he was under investigation. So Tordin hired an attorney and in short order he was cooperating, too.

Hawit's tenure as CONCACAF president would prove exceedingly short.

TWENTY-NINE

A ZEALOUS ADVOCATE

DAVID TORRES-SIEGRIST WAS DRIVING HOME IN HIS minivan after singing in choir at midweek mass in Arcadia, California, when his assistant soccer coach called him on his cell phone.

"It's my uncle," the man said. "He's been arrested and needs help. His name is Eugenio Figueredo."

Torres-Siegrist had five children. In addition to his church commitments, he volunteered as the youth soccer team's head coach, as an assistant scoutmaster for the Boy Scouts, and was involved in the PTA at his kids' school. He was also an attorney who had handled a wide variety of civil litigation over the past dozen years, largely involving suing or defending small municipalities in contract disputes.

The name Figueredo didn't ring a bell, but Torres-Siegrist figured the problem was something minor, maybe a DUI, and said he'd be glad to help. Great, his friend replied, how soon can you leave for Zurich?

Torres-Siegrist, who had curly brown hair, a short-cropped beard, and an informal manner, was born and raised in Southern California; he favored shorts and flip-flops and had never before felt the need to own a passport. The next morning he drove to a government passport agency in West Los Angeles and waited in line for hours to get one on an expedited basis.

He left for Zurich the next day, May 29, taking advantage of the eleven-hour flight to catch up on the torrent of FIFA news that had erupted since word of the arrests had broken two days earlier. He didn't follow international soccer at all, and until then had no clue that his friend's Uruguayan uncle was one of the sport's global elite, much less that he had been one of the officials arrested at the Baur au Lac.

Once in Switzerland, he went directly from the airport to meet Figueredo's wife, Carmen Burgos, who was staying with a friend. Figueredo's bank accounts had been frozen and Burgos, already overwrought, discovered she couldn't withdraw a single Swiss franc from a cash machine.

The indictment was from the U.S., so she knew her husband needed an American lawyer, but the few she'd already talked to mentioned gigantic fees, and Burgos found the whole process intimidating.

Torres-Siegrist was American, and he spoke Spanish. Perhaps, Burgos suggested, he could help negotiate a better price. But after spending a few days in Zurich meeting with lawyers from several big law firms, the California attorney felt disgusted.

Rather than discuss the facts of the case, they wanted only to talk fees. One firm's blended hourly rate was $1,400; another's was $1,800; a third refused even to come to Zurich unless Burgos put several hundred thousand dollars in escrow. Torres-Siegrist suggested a more affordable alternative: hire him instead. It was true he'd never handled a criminal case, much less one as massive as this, but something deep inside him told him he could handle it.

What did they have to lose? The Swiss lawyer Figueredo had already retained was urging them to waive extradition and cut a deal as fast as possible; an Uruguayan lawyer who had flown in from Montevideo offered the same advice. The United States, they said, was just too powerful. Figueredo would lose the initial extradition proceeding, they said, and even with appeals all the way up to Switzerland's supreme court, he would end up dragged to Brooklyn in no more than six or seven months.

Torres-Siegrist thought he could do better than that. When he wasn't with Burgos, interviewing lawyers, or visiting Figueredo in his immaculate little Swiss jail cell, he was thinking relentlessly about the criminal case and the issues it touched.

This was not a typical RICO case. This was something much bigger. It was about sports, sure, but also global politics, and huge and complicated issues involving national identity, not to mention countless billions of dollars spent on television, sponsorship, and infrastructure revolving around each World Cup. FIFA was powerful, and despite the wild jubilation of fans around the world in the wake of the arrests, it was hard to believe everyone on earth was so delighted at the state of affairs. Surely, Torres-Siegrist thought, there must be somebody out there who was unhappy with the investigation and had some useful advice to share.

After a week in Zurich, he had to get home to his family. The day before departing, however, he took the train to the Swiss capital, Bern, and hailed a taxi. It was a gloomy day and a heavy rain fell as Torres-Siegrist rang the bell at the gate outside the Russian embassy.

The inspiration, he would later claim, had come to him in a flash. Russia was hosting the next World Cup, in 2018. If there was anybody who would be critical of a massive U.S. investigation calling into question the integrity of FIFA and the sport of soccer as a whole, and who also had the resources to do something about it, surely it was Russia.

After some time, a guard appeared. It was Saturday, so nobody from the embassy's legal department was there, he explained. Torres-Siegrist, dripping wet, handed the Russian guard his business card and climbed back into the waiting taxi.

"A lawyer," Torres-Siegrist often repeated to himself, quoting the American Bar Association's rules of professional conduct from memory, "can be a zealous advocate on behalf of a client."

———

Figueredo, short and slender with hangdog eyes, had started his life in soccer as a right winger for Huracán Buceo, a club in Montevideo, and slowly ground his way up the sport's hierarchy, eventually becoming president of CONMEBOL in 2013. Outside of soccer, the only job Figueredo ever had for any length of time was as a used car salesman. He had worked briefly, as a young man, at a Volkswagen dealership, but quit to open his own tiny used car lot. He closed the dealership when he was sixty, claiming it was his only source of income. But he'd grown very wealthy along the way thanks to the decades of bribes he'd been taking from sports marketing firms in his capacity as a soccer official, first in Uruguay and particularly at CONMEBOL.

He'd poured most of the money into real estate, largely in Uruguay, but also into a well-to-do enclave east of Los Angeles called Arcadia, where his wife's favorite nephew lived. Among the properties was an ornate six-bedroom house with a pool just two miles from the Santa Anita race track, which Figueredo had purchased for $475,000 and was now worth at least three times that.

He was careful, and used an archipelago of shell companies, as well as numerous variations of the names of his wife and children, to hide the true ownership of all that property. He had also, in 2005, applied for U.S. citizenship, falsely claiming he suffered from "severe dementia" to get out of the English proficiency requirement.

Steve Berryman had tracked down that little detail, as well as a series of fraudulent tax returns, allowing the prosecutors to slap Figueredo with a host of slam-dunk additional charges that could add twenty-five years to his maximum sentence and make it that much more likely he'd volunteer to cooperate.

Figueredo had been entrenched in CONMEBOL for two decades, and was closely tied to some of the most powerful men in the sport. There was no telling what leads he'd hand over once the Swiss authorities rubber-stamped his extradition and he began cooperating like all the others.

————

Sitting across a conference room table from Evan Norris in Brooklyn, Torres-Siegrist found himself plunging into a truly foul mood.

It was toward the second half of July, and his client, Figueredo, was still in a jail cell in Switzerland. The Swiss and Uruguayan attorneys also on the case were still urging Figueredo to cut a deal, arguing that the faster he got in the door, the better the prosecutors would treat him.

That seemed to have been Jeffrey Webb's strategy. Advised by his American attorney, a partner at a big multinational firm who had been a federal prosecutor in New York for almost a decade, Webb waived extradition as soon as the formal petitions were submitted by the U.S. on July 1.

The former CONCACAF president arrived at Kennedy airport on July 15, and he was arraigned and released three days later on $10 million bond. To secure his liberty, Webb had to put up the deeds to ten properties owned by himself, his wife, and numerous family members; his wife's retirement account; her stake in a medical practice; a dozen high-end watches; much of his wife's jewelry; and three automobiles—including his brand-new Ferrari.

Webb even had to hand over his wife's wedding ring. That was Berryman's suggestion. He'd traced a suspect $36,000 payment to a jewelry wholesaler and then, after spending time looking at photos posted online of the couple's gala 2013 wedding, realized where that money had gone.

Torres-Siegrist was eager to talk with the prosecutors about what cooperation would look like. But Norris was only interested in discussing bond. He wanted $15 million, he said, with a large chunk of that in cash, and it was not negotiable. Cooperation was something they could talk about once Figueredo was in Brooklyn.

Torres-Siegrist had heard about how the prosecutors had put the screws to Webb, who had bent over backward to accommodate them. He'd been speaking with attorneys for some of the other defendants, sharing bits of information about the case, and they, too, had been complaining about giant bond requirements. Even Aaron Davidson, small fry compared to some of the officials in the case, had to post $5 million.

The California lawyer looked around the conference room. It was a bit shabby with years of use, utilitarian, and certainly not impressive. So this, he thought to himself, was what the belly of the beast looks like.

The two lawyers were about the same age, but in some ways they couldn't be more different. Norris had gone to Harvard Law, and everything about him rubbed Torres-Siegrist the wrong way, particularly his cold, superior demeanor. Torres-Siegrist had gone to Southwestern in Los Angeles, known for its part-time law programs for people holding down jobs while studying, and he'd spent years paying dues on penny-ante cases in small courtrooms around Los Angeles County. Norris, he thought, was acting like an elitist prick.

En route to Brooklyn, Torres-Siegrist had made a brief stop in Washington, where he'd gone to the Russian embassy to meet with a lawyer who had gotten in contact with him soon after he'd dropped his card off in Switzerland. The Russian attorney said research was being done on the case; he also suggested returning to the embassy in Switzerland again the next time he was over there.

Figueredo, eighty-three years old, had been crystal clear: he did not want to be extradited. Accepting every one of the prosecutor's intractable demands didn't feel like zealous advocacy for his client, it felt like surrender. For Torres-Siegrist, that wasn't an option.

On July 24, Torres-Siegrist sat down with a political liaison at the Russian embassy in Bern, who provided him with a stack of cases in which the U.S. had lost extradition fights in Switzerland. One, from 2005, involved a Russian nuclear scientist whom the Swiss had arrested at the behest of American prosecutors accusing him of stealing $9 million in Department of Energy funds. Before he could be extradited, however, Russia filed its own extradition request, also alleging financial crimes. Russia won out, and the U.S. was never able to lay a finger on the man.

The key to keeping someone out of the U.S. was, for some other country, preferably one where he was a citizen, to file a competing extradition petition. Torres-Siegrist, the liaison hinted suggestively, should try to figure out if Uruguay could make its own criminal case against Figueredo.

The liaison also emphatically suggested he go to St. Petersburg, where FIFA would be holding the preliminary draw for the 2018 World Cup at the Konstantin Palace the following day. As the first official event leading up to the tournament, all of FIFA's top officials would be in attendance, and there was someone important who wanted to meet him there.

In less than three hours, the liaison arranged for a seven-day visa, and Torres-Siegrist booked a flight while he waited. He spent the afternoon of July 25 mingling with soccer officials at the Konstantin Palace, where he was given red-carpet treatment and admitted to the VIP area. Finally, a call came in telling the lawyer to be at Levashovo airport the next morning, and that someone would come by his hotel that night to collect all his electronics—cell phone and laptop—prior to the meeting.

Levashovo turned out to be a military air base, completely different from the commercial airport Torres-Siegrist had arrived at. It was sometimes used for private aviation, and as he waited, a steady stream of FIFA officials in chauffeured Bentleys arrived to catch planes home, among them Sepp Blatter.

Finally, Torres-Siegrist was summoned to a meeting room, where he was warmly greeted by Vitaly Mutko.

Mutko, with a round, expressive face and dark slicked-back hair, was president of the Russian Football Union, a member of FIFA's Executive Committee, and chairman of the local organizing committee for the 2018 World Cup. Since 2009, he had also been Russia's minister of sport, and was a close advisor to Vladimir Putin, whom he had first met in the early 1990s when both worked in the St. Petersburg city government.

Speaking in thickly accented English, Mutko told Torres-Siegrist that he was familiar with the Figueredo case and was eager to help. "As you can see," the minister said, "we've spent billions of dollars on infrastructure for the World Cup." It would be highly undesirable, he added, for the U.S. to blemish FIFA and, by extension, Russian's World Cup.

The meeting lasted twenty minutes, during which time Mutko talked generally about the case, but also mentioned specific strategies that could be used to beat the American extradition request. Some things, he said, Torres-Siegrist would be informed about and take an active role in; others would, by necessity, be done without his knowledge.

"All available resources will be given to this," Mutko assured him before saying goodbye.

Torres-Siegrist headed back to his hotel, collected his cell phone and laptop, and flew back to Switzerland, his head spinning. He wasn't entirely sure how his mundane life as an attorney litigating municipal contract disputes had taken such a dramatic turn. But at least he had a pretty clear picture of where his client's case was now heading.

––––––––

On September 14, Loretta Lynch held a joint press conference in Zurich with Michael Lauber, Switzerland's attorney general. Ostensibly, she had traveled there to attend an annual meeting of federal prosecutors, but normally America's highest-ranking law enforcement official skipped such events.

In truth, her presence was part of an effort to smooth things over with Swiss authorities, still upset about the leaks during the May 27 raids. The fact that the prosecutors' conference happened to be in Switzerland that year provided a perfect excuse for Lynch to get onstage with Lauber, shake his hand for the cameras, and praise the work of her counterparts.

"I want to thank the Swiss government for its assistance in the extradition process," Lynch said. "We could not ask for a better partner than Attorney General Lauber."

Three days later, Switzerland's Federal Office of Justice ruled in favor of the petition to bring Figueredo to the United States, making him the first soccer official arrested in the case to face forced extradition. By law, Figueredo had a month to appeal.

On October 13, just days before the deadline, Uruguay's Court for Organized Crime formally submitted to Switzerland a petition for the extradition of Eugenio Figueredo, accusing him of fraud and money laundering.

Prosecutors in Montevideo had resurrected a nearly two-year-old criminal referral that had been filed against Figueredo accusing him of corruption.

The referral, filed by private citizens, alleged he and other CONMEBOL officials had conspired to reject competitive offers for rights to soccer tournaments because they were taking bribes. It offered no concrete proof, just the suggestion that authorities "follow the money to determine who was unduly benefitting." The Uruguayan prosecutors had largely ignored it when it was filed—questioning, among other things, if it should have instead been filed in Paraguay, since that's where CONMEBOL is headquartered—and it fell into a kind of legal limbo, moribund.

Then suddenly, and with uncanny timing, the unsubstantiated referral was converted into an active investigation. In its extradition petition, the court said that Figueredo had indicated he was disposed to "cooperate with the Uruguayan judicial system," which would seek a prison term of between two and fifteen years against him.

Few gave Uruguay's petition much chance of success. It was, after all, a tiny country, comparable in both size and population to the state of Oklahoma. While it was, relative to other South American countries, a fairly stable democracy, its reputation for law and order was nowhere near that of the United States.

The biggest difference, however, was the tenor of the accusations. The charges leveled by the U.S. against Figueredo were backed by a thorough, detailed investigation that unequivocally laid out the prosecution's argument for criminality, based on multiple witnesses and reams of documents.

Uruguay's case seemed paper-thin by comparison. It was based largely on the unproven accusations of the two-year-old referral, and the only evidence it supplied were records of a dozen years' worth of real estate transactions handed over by Figueredo himself that Uruguay argued "bear no relation to his economic capacity, nor the legitimate income derived from work as a sports official."

Furthermore, the petition made no substantive argument about the nature of the frauds that allegedly generated all Figueredo's money, other than to say vaguely that so much money could only be "the fruit of conspiracies and artificial schemes" designed to injure various soccer institutions.

Despite the striking contrast between the two petitions, the Swiss Federal Office of Justice on November 9 shockingly ruled in favor of Uruguay. In a terse ruling, it said that because Figueredo was willing to waive extradition to Uruguay but not the U.S., it would send him home—provided the U.S. didn't object.

But the U.S. did object. Justice Department attorneys argued that since the U.S. had first requested the arrest of the South American soccer official back in May, "well before Uruguay had charged or sought the extradition of Mr. Figueredo," it ought to have first priority.

With the U.S. appeal pending, Torres-Siegrist made plans to fly to New York in early December and meet with Norris a second time to discuss bond for Figueredo. Everyone expected Uruguay to lose; it was time, the prosecutors had said, for him to get serious. Yet something in the lawyer's gut told him not to go just yet, and he postponed the meeting.

On December 18, the Swiss court once again came down in Uruguay's favor, stating that the criminal charges described in its petition covered "all the facts contained in the U.S. extradition request" and pointing to Figueredo's age and health as deciding factors. "The better prospect of social rehabilitation seems to be in Uruguay," the ruling said, noting that the decision did not preclude the U.S. from petitioning

Uruguay for Figueredo's extradition to the U.S. for the immigration fraud charge at a later date.

Torres-Siegrist was sound asleep when the call came in with the good news. It was three in the morning in Arcadia, but he didn't mind. It had been the most exciting, difficult case of his life, and he danced around his bedroom, whooping and overcome with joy.

Later that day, after he had triple-confirmed that Figueredo was indeed going to Uruguay and the decision was truly final, Torres-Siegrist drove to the Arcadia post office and mailed a gaily decorated holiday card to Norris.

"Merry Christmas!" it said.

THIRTY

PLUS ÇA CHANGE . . .

IN PREDAWN DARKNESS, PLAINCLOTHES SWISS POLICE once again walked into the lobby of the Baur au Lac at precisely six o'clock on the morning of Thursday, December 3, 2015.

As they had six months earlier, the officers arrived with no fanfare and as inconspicuously as possible. This time, however, they were determined to keep the secret operation under wraps, and instructed hotel staff to clear the lobby. Then they went upstairs to the guest rooms of CONCACAF president Alfredo Hawit and Juan Ángel Napout, the Paraguayan president of CONMEBOL.

Both men were FIFA vice presidents and were in town to attend two days of meetings of the ExCo, which had commenced the previous afternoon. The two Latin Americans had attended a dinner for top soccer officials at the exclusive Sonnenberg Restaurant the night before, and on this day were expected back in the underground boardroom of FIFA house at nine a.m. for the second meeting, where the committee would vote on a series of reforms aimed at improving FIFA's integrity.

Hawit, who had traveled to Zurich with his wife, opened the door almost immediately after the police knocked, and one of the officers read him the arrest warrant, which was translated into German, English, and Spanish. He told the official he had the right to contact the Honduran consulate.

He and Napout were each given time to dress and pack a bag, then were led out of the hotel into the frosty winter air and hustled across a bridge to a parking garage where several unmarked vehicles awaited. In little more than half an hour, they were gone, and Baur au Lac staffers hurriedly finished preparations for the breakfast service.

The arrests, which so closely mirrored those of the past May, marked the culmination of the second phase of the soccer investigation.

Eight days earlier, a federal grand jury in Brooklyn handed down a superseding indictment, which somehow managed to make the first version of the document look puny. Weighing in at 236 pages, the new charging document was among the longest and most detailed in the history of America's federal courts.

The indictment was written by Norris with input from eight other assistant U.S. attorneys now on the case. Its table of contents alone ran a page and a half, and it leveled ninety-two criminal counts against twenty-seven defendants. Sixteen of those defendants were new, although many were in fact officials that Norris and the other prosecutors had been targeting for years, but hadn't quite been able to charge the first time around, such as Ricardo Teixeira and Marco Polo Del Nero of Brazil.

Those men were joined by a host of other soccer officials tied up in various corrupt schemes. The prosecutors had been able to expand the case substantially thanks in large part to the flood of cooperators who had rushed to Brooklyn in hopes of leniency over the past few months.

Indeed, no fewer than seven people had pleaded guilty that November, among them Alejandro Burzaco, Jeffrey Webb, and José Margulies, a Brazilian-Argentine bagman who had helped Hawilla, among others, pay countless bribes over multiple decades. All were secretly helping the investigation, and collectively they had agreed to forfeit more than $41 million in exchange for their cooperation agreements.

All the additional help allowed the prosecution to significantly deepen and solidify the allegations first unveiled in May, fortifying the existing case against men like Leoz, Warner, and both Jinkises, who were still fighting extradition in their home countries.

Yet a close reading of the new charges showed that the bulk of the new ground broken in the previous six months came in Central America. Seven of the new names atop the indictment were from the region, among them Hawit.

Just as Jeffrey Webb had come into the CONCACAF presidency in the wake of a scandal that toppled the prior leadership and immediately cast himself as a reformer, so, too, had Hawit assumed power amid chaos and promised positive change.

"CONCACAF has been the victim of fraud," Hawit said just one day after the May 27 arrests. "We are at an important moment for the game, a moment that we must not squander. CONCACAF stands ready to assist in the process of rebuilding FIFA in a way that strengthens the game for many years to come."

Among the first acts he oversaw as president was the decision to formally dismiss Webb, and, a few days later, CONCACAF also suspended Enrique Sanz, motivated by the revelation that he had been secretly cooperating with the Department of Justice. In August, Hawit fired the cancer-stricken general secretary, paying him an undisclosed sum as a termination settlement.

Just as Webb began his term announcing an internal investigation of the confederation's prior leadership conducted by Sidley Austin, so, too, did Hawit launch an internal probe conducted by Sidley Austin.

And just as Webb had been the very first name atop the original indictment, and had, long before sunrise, been yanked from the luxurious embrace of the Baur au Lac and cast into ignominy and public shame—so, too, was Hawit just six months later.

Three successive presidents of CONCACAF—Warner, Webb, and Hawit—and three successive presidents of CONMEBOL—Leoz, Figueredo, Napout—corrupted, indicted, and disgraced. As the saying goes, it was déjà vu all over again.

"The corruption of the enterprise became endemic," Norris wrote in the indictment. "Certain defendants and their co-conspirators rose to power, unlawfully amassed significant personal fortunes by defrauding the organizations they were chosen to serve, and were exposed and then either expelled from those organizations or forced to resign. Other defendants and their co-conspirators came to power in the wake of scandal, promising reform. Rather than repair the harm done to the sport and its institutions, however, these defendants and their co-conspirators quickly engaged in the same unlawful practices that had enriched their predecessors."

There was one additional way that the second round of arrests in the Baur au Lac proved hauntingly similar to those that had taken place in May.

Fifteen minutes before the Swiss police walked into the luxury hotel in the heart of Zurich on the morning of December 3, a reporter from *The New York Times* pushed through the revolving doors and took a seat with a good view of the lobby. As the cops arrived in their cars, a photographer waiting outside texted the reporter, who relayed the information to editors in Manhattan.

The reporter sent out a tweet from his phone breaking the news of the arrests at 6:01 a.m., and twenty minutes later the newspaper posted an article on its website, more than twelve hours before Loretta Lynch was scheduled to announce the indictments in a press conference in Washington.

Once again the prosecution had been scooped by the *Times*.

———

As he did every day, Sepp Blatter woke up early on February 26, 2016, and started to dance. It was how the seventy-nine-year-old stretched his compact frame and his principal form of exercise. With the radio tuned to a local pop music station, Blatter shimmied and bopped around his large, spare apartment, located in the city's wealthiest district, high on a hill overlooking Lake Zurich's eastern shore.

It was by no means a typical morning, however, for within hours Blatter—and the world—would be witnessing the election of FIFA's first new president in nearly eighteen years.

The election was the centerpiece of a FIFA congress starting that morning at the Hallenstadion, the cavernous arena on the other side of town that was home to Zurich's formidable hockey team, the ZSC Lions. Although thousands of people, including delegates, press, and observers, would jam into the stadium for the election, Blatter would not be among them. He had been banned by FIFA's Ethics Committee from all soccer activities, which meant he would be forced to watch the election from home, streaming on his tablet.

The Swiss administrator had never imagined his life in soccer would end this way. FIFA had occupied the center of his entire life over the previous four decades; he ate most of his meals, and received most visitors, at the Sonnenberg, the restaurant directly adjacent to the old FIFA House; his home was located directly between the two headquarters buildings; even the drink coasters in his kitchen bore the FIFA logo.

His decision to resign in the wake of the humiliating arrests the previous May had not been an easy one, but at least it would provide him with a way to gracefully transition out of the powerful office while playing a role in blessing a chosen successor—as João Havelange had done for him when Blatter first was elected in 1998. After all, Blatter had not been named in the U.S. indictment, and given that investigation's focus on North and South America, it seemed unlikely he would be.

His plan was to have been in the Hallenstadion on this special day, so he could personally, and very graciously, hand the crown to FIFA's next leader, who hopefully would reward him with the same honorary lifetime presidency that he had given Havelange in 1998. It was to be the capstone of Blatter's legacy, which now mattered to him more than anything else.

But it hadn't worked out as planned. During ExCo meetings in late September, the Swiss attorney general raided FIFA headquarters, searching Blatter's office and seizing numerous boxes of documents, as well as his computer. The Swiss federal prosecutor then announced that it had opened a criminal investigation of Blatter.

The probe revolved around a 2 million franc payment Blatter had made to another soccer official in early 2011, while he was campaigning for reelection against Mohamed bin Hammam. Coming so soon before the vote, it looked worryingly as if Blatter had been trying to buy political support with FIFA's money. Prosecutors, then, wanted to know whether the money was in fact a "disloyal payment" made "at the expense of FIFA," which under Swiss law would be a crime.

Two weeks later, FIFA's Ethics Committee provisionally banned Blatter for ninety days pending its own probe of the payment. The stress of the situation was beginning to take a serious toll on Blatter. He appealed the ban, but as he awaited a ruling, Blatter suffered a nervous collapse in early November, and was admitted to the hospital.

"I was really between the angels who sing and the devil who lights the fire," Blatter said after being discharged from the hospital.

FIFA eventually rejected his appeal, and subsequently banned

Blatter from the sport for eight years, a penalty that was reduced to six years. For Blatter, who would be eighty-five by the time the punishment expired, FIFA's ban was as good as a lifetime expulsion.

Over the previous nine months, Blatter had been publicly humiliated, shamed, mocked, and scolded, targeted by prosecutors in two countries, and cast out of the organization that had defined most of his adult life. And yet, as the February congress began with a video promising "a new way forward," the sprightly former public relations man seemed in surprisingly good spirits.

Dressed in jeans and a tailored gray sport coat over a dark blue shirt with his initials monogrammed on the cuff, Blatter sat on a stool at his kitchen counter and watched the event on his iPad, pulling faces at the long-winded speeches and dropping sarcastic comments about the five candidates for the presidency.

"Why do you wear this silly green tie, Jérôme?" he asked, pointing at the screen as the former French diplomat Jérôme Champagne, an old friend of Blatter's, began his speech.

Champagne, like Jordan's Prince Ali and the South African candidate, Tokyo Sexwale, was a long shot. The frontrunners were Sheikh Salman bin Ibrahim Al Khalifa of Bahrain—the successor to Mohamed bin Hammam as president of the Asian Football Confederation—and Gianni Infantino, another Swiss who was general secretary of the European soccer confederation, UEFA.

FIFA's elections are extremely long events, and this one was no different, clocking in at more than five and a half hours. As Blatter watched, Corinne, his only child, periodically came into the kitchen to check on him. In another room, two of his advisors chatted quietly about his public relations strategy.

The apartment was typically Swiss, immaculately unadorned in a way that betrayed an extreme degree of attention to every detail. There were almost none of the trophies one might expect from a man who, for forty-one years, had stood at the summit of world soccer. In the living room, beside a blue vase of dried flowers was a certificate from Real Madrid naming Blatter an honorary member. On a shelf above it stood a framed memento from Pope Benedict XVI, and beside that an empty silver picture frame. That was all.

On the day of the May arrests at the Baur au Lac, Blatter had called Switzerland's minister of defense, whom he knew personally. That man informed him that the justice ministry had warned nobody in government what was coming; it had been an absolute and total secret. That, Blatter said, convinced him that the entire criminal investigation was an elaborate form of revenge by the U.S., which he believed was bitter it had not been selected to host the 2022 World Cup. The soccer corruption investigation, in other words, was just an extreme case of sour grapes.

"If they had won," Blatter said, ruefully, "they would not have started this."

In the Hallenstadion, the second-to-last candidate to speak, Gianni Infantino, had taken the podium. With a bald, bulging head, and thick black brows, he began by showing off his linguistic dexterity, speaking first in English, then Italian, German, Swiss German, French, Spanish, and finally Portuguese.

"Five months ago, I was not thinking to be a candidate," Infantino said, returning to English. "But many things have happened in the last few months.

"FIFA is in a crisis," he continued. "I'm not afraid of taking my responsibilities and go ahead and do what is right for football and to do what is right for FIFA."

Infantino had campaigned widely throughout Africa and Latin America preaching transparency and reform. But the centerpiece of his platform was money. He pledged repeatedly to boost the funds distributed to each of FIFA's 209 member associations every four years to $5 million, more than two and a half times above what was currently handed out. In addition, Infantino promised an additional $1 million to poorer national associations to cover travel costs, $40 million to each confederation that could be dispensed for development projects within member countries, and $4 million for youth tournaments. Finally, he said, he would expand the World Cup to forty teams from the current thirty-two, which meant eight more countries stood to receive huge cash influxes every four years.

Sheikh Salman was critical of Infantino's plan, saying it would "bankrupt" FIFA. In the wake of the arrests, a string of sponsors, including Sony, Johnson & Johnson, and Emirates Air, had torn up their contracts with FIFA. Meanwhile, its legal costs exploded. The Swiss nonprofit would soon announce a $122 million loss for 2015, a year in which, it would later be revealed, it had paid Blatter $3.76 million.

Salman, too, had made financial promises, but they were far more modest and, he said, realistic. But the Bahraini was clearly missing the point.

Infantino's platform was unvarnished, naked patronage. Regardless of which language he spoke in, he was simply offering to buy votes using the incredible cash-generating powers of the world's most popular sport to fund the expenditure, just as Blatter had done before him, and Havelange before that. Lucre needed no translation; despite all the scandal and promises of reform, soccer's governing body was still organized around financial opportunism.

"The money of FIFA is your money," Infantino boomed, prompting a sustained round of applause and approving cheers from the audience.

The actual voting was an agonizingly slow process, as each delegate approached the voting booths in turn, crossing the arena's large floor and stopping to socialize and glad-hand along the way. With no absolute majority conferred in the first round, the process was repeated. The full democratic exercise took nearly four hours, and to occupy part of that time, Blatter and his daughter stepped outside his home, climbed into the chauffeured Mercedes S-Class sedan that FIFA still provided him free of charge, and retired to the Sonnenberg for lunch.

In the end, Infantino and his promise of great buckets of money cascading down from the mountains of Switzerland won out, 115 votes to 88.

At forty-five, Infantino was a far younger man than his predecessor. He immediately pledged profound change and cast himself as a new kind of leader, memorably playing in an exhibition match starring numerous retired soccer stars that he organized for the Monday after his election—in miserable, wet snowy weather. But it was hard to overlook the remarkable similarities between him and Blatter.

Both were multilingual Swiss who lived for their jobs, micromanaging every aspect of the organizations they oversaw. Both had served as general secretaries in their previous positions. And both had grown up in the remote mountainous region of Switzerland known as the Valais, in

the small towns of Visp and, in Infantino's case, Brig, perched on the
banks of the headwaters of the Rhône River, just six miles removed from
each other.

Before departing for lunch, Blatter glanced back at the screen on his
tablet and watched the slow voting procession, then shook his balding
head.

"I cannot be the conscience of all these people," he said, pausing for
a moment. "I am happy my presidency is over."

———————

The first time Steve Berryman met with Evan Norris and Amanda Hector
back in September of 2011, he'd come prepared with a long list of names
of soccer officials he believed were corrupt and should be brought to justice. Since then, the prosecutors had nabbed a few of them and indicted
several others, but many more remained untouched.

The fallout from the two indictments and all the publicity they had
generated had been tremendous. People were popping up in the most
unexpected places offering to provide helpful information, such as former employees of Torneos y Competencias and Full Play who had for
years maintained secret lists of bribes to soccer officials and were all now
eager to talk.

Others—including the money-laundering son of a South American
soccer official whom two of Berryman's colleagues at the IRS confronted
getting off an airplane in Los Angeles and immediately caught in a lie—
needed a bit of encouragement.

Those new cooperators helped tie up loose ends, making it increasingly clear that the theory of the case Norris had developed was true
and, even more importantly, would stick in court. This was not going to
turn out like the ill-fated Salt Lake City case.

But tracking down every last possible witness in order to ensure
convictions for every defendant in the trial, or busting Central American
soccer officials who had taken a few bucks for a friendly match wasn't
what motivated Berryman and kept him at it day after day; it felt a bit
like housekeeping.

More than four years of ceaseless digging had added a considerable
number of new names to Berryman's original wish list, and it was his

desire to hunt them all down that drove him forward. They were the men who had debauched and cheapened the beautiful game for their own selfish ends. If the ultimate victims of all the corruption were the fans themselves, then Berryman, as a fan, also felt like a victim.

For that reason, he had suggested early on that Norris include language in the criminal forfeiture agreements making it clear that the money was intended for the victims of corruption rather than going to the U.S. Treasury, as usually happens. The idea was for soccer organizations, once they cleaned up their act, to request the money and reinvest it in the sport, underscoring the idea that it was the individuals, not the institutions, that were corrupt.

Norris loved the idea, feeling it would help send the message that the case wasn't a huge money grab by Uncle Sam. Starting with Hawilla, every forfeiture agreement in the case noted that the funds would be "subject to a restitution hold" and that "any individuals or entities that qualify as victims" could apply for it. In March 2016, FIFA, now led by Infantino, did just that, formally requesting that the Justice Department hand over some of the more than $200 million the defendants in the case had so far consented to forfeit.

It had also been Berryman who had pushed Norris when he filed his first MLAT to Switzerland, to include a request to see the documents underlying the country's International Sport and Leisure investigation.

Switzerland's initial response ran only two pages, thanks to Switzerland's restrictive privacy laws, but in late 2015, the lead prosecutor on the case, Thomas Hildbrand, agreed to let Berryman look over everything on the condition that he not take pictures or notes. So Berryman flew to Switzerland and sat in a police facility for a week, reading seventy-two boxes' worth of documents before going home.

It was incredible stuff, so beautifully thorough, and it inspired Berryman to keep going, showing him that many of his suspicions about FIFA's highest officials had been warranted. The work the investigators had done over the past five years was groundbreaking, but he was convinced that much more could still be done. With two indictments completed, Berryman redoubled his efforts.

In early 2016, Berryman flew to Brooklyn to make another sales pitch. Facing a much larger group of prosecutors than he had in 2011, he delivered a three-hour PowerPoint in a bid to convince Norris and the others to let him train his attentions on a new region of the world.

The Asian Football Confederation has forty-seven member associations, stretching from Palestine and Jordan in the Middle East, to Japan and South Korea in East Asia, as well as Australia. No AFC country has ever won the World Cup, but the quality of the region's play, and particularly the influence of its members on soccer's world stage, has been steadily progressing.

What most interested Berryman about the confederation was the fact that, until mid-2011, its president had been Mohamed bin Hammam, the billionaire Qatari whose cash-stuffed envelopes in Port of Spain had set everything in motion, and who had been accused many times of paying bribes to help his country win the right to host the 2022 World Cup.

Bin Hammam was one of the names near the very top of Berryman's original list. Although the Qatari was referred to in both indictments as an unnamed co-conspirator, the prosecutors had never been convinced they had enough evidence to actually indict him.

Asia was a tough nut to crack. With huge financial centers in Hong Kong, Shanghai, and Singapore, its banking system didn't depend as heavily on American correspondent banks for wire transfers as the West, which made it harder for Berryman to hunt for leads without leaving fingerprints. Still, he well knew, all it took was a well-placed cooperator and everything could open right up.

So while the rest of the team focused on milking their new South American cooperators for evidence, leaning on reticent defendants to take pleas, and reviewing old subpoenas to make sure no stones had been left unturned, Berryman busied himself researching dozens of AFC officials in search of a weak link. And when he finally found what he was looking for, he got the same charge of excitement he'd felt when he first peered into Chuck Blazer's file all those years earlier.

Right around the time that FIFA elected Infantino as its new president, Berryman sent two of his colleagues across the Pacific Ocean to visit the offices of an obscure national association in a country hardly known for the quality of its soccer. The agents asked if they could see some innocuous documents, and left behind Berryman's business card.

When the association president nervously reached out a few days later to see what it was all about, Berryman downplayed the significance. He had already traced the man's accounts, and knew he had been taking bribes for years, including a highly suspicious $100,000 payment from Bin Hammam himself. But, just as he had with Zorana Danis, the IRS agent played dumb, suggesting they meet face-to-face.

It was nothing to worry about, Berryman assured the soccer official, "just a boring tax case."

THE TRIAL

SOON AFTER SEVEN ON THE EVENING OF NOVEMBER 14, 2017, Jorge Delhón, wearing a suit and carrying a leather briefcase, found a small gap in the barbed wire that fenced off the train tracks of the commuter line running through the Buenos Aires suburb of Lanús and squeezed through. The fifty-two-year-old lawyer stopped on the other side of the wall and waited.

At 7:26 p.m., train 3251 of the Roca line struck Delhón as it barreled south, killing him instantly. The engineer later said he saw the man dash onto the tracks, and pulled the emergency brake, but far too late to stop the train. Police investigating the scene found various papers and legal documents inside Delhón's briefcase, as well as a hastily scrawled note, apparently for his wife and four children.

"I love you," the scrap of paper said. "I can't believe it."

Several hours earlier, Delhón had been the subject of testimony during a trial in a federal courtroom in Brooklyn. Alejandro Burzaco, the former chief executive of Torneos y Competencias, and, after his own guilty plea, a government cooperator, told the jury that over a three-year period he had paid more than $4 million in bribes to Delhón and an associate.

The bribes, Burzaco explained, were given at a time that Delhón was working as a contract attorney for a government initiative called Fútbol Para Todos, which in 2009 had acquired broadcast rights to Argentina's top professional soccer leagues. For many years, Torneos had controlled those rights, and the loss of the business had been a terrible blow.

The payments, which allowed Torneos to keep a hand in the Argentine league, represented only a tiny sliver of all the bribes that Burzaco had confessed to paying during his roughly fifteen years in the sports marketing business. By his own estimate, he'd paid at least $160 million in bribes to some thirty individuals over the years before he was indicted in May 2015.

The revelation was shocking, marking the first time the sordid web of secret payments outlined in the Justice Department's case had been linked directly to public officials. Delhón's gruesome death came less than ninety minutes after word of Burzaco's testimony had broken in Argentina, where news outlets were following the case avidly. The lawyer's final phone calls were to the other alleged bribe recipient, who later said Delhón seemed so agitated that he invited Delhón to come over. He never made it.

The following morning, Burzaco, looking tired and drawn, broke down in tears in the witness box before the jury had been seated and had to be escorted out in order to regain his composure. The courtroom gallery, packed with lawyers and journalists, buzzed with speculation over what had just happened. Was he upset about the apparent suicide? Was the pressure too much?

But outside the courtroom, Burzaco told an FBI agent that one of the defendants had made a threatening gesture at him, moving his hand as if he were cutting his throat, and had made the same slicing motion across his neck while glaring at him the previous day.

The defendant, Manuel Burga, had been president of the Peruvian Soccer Federation for a dozen years until the end of 2014, and was charged in the second indictment in the soccer case a year later. He was eventually extradited to the United States and now stood charged of one count of RICO conspiracy, which carried a maximum sentence of twenty years. The two other defendants, José Maria Marin, who had been president of Brazil's soccer confederation, and Juan Ángel Napout, the Paraguayan former president of CONMEBOL, were also charged with RICO conspiracy, as well as a host of wire fraud and money laundering counts.

After an hour, Burzaco returned to court and swiftly made international headlines again with his account of how Torneos, along with Mexican media giant Televisa and Brazilian broadcaster TV Globo, had paid $15 million in bribes to a high-ranking FIFA official in exchange for television rights to the 2026 and 2030 World Cup.

Burzaco walked the jury, in detail, through the mechanics of years' worth of crooked Copa Libertadores and Copa América deals, and explained how he employed phony contracts and overseas shell companies he called "vehicles" to skim bribes from seemingly legitimate payments.

Burzaco was a fantastic witness. Exhaustively prepared by his attorney, a former federal prosecutor named Sean Casey who had been with him in Italy when he decided to flip, the charismatic Argentine was deadly serious at times and riotously funny at others. As he told the story of his decision to help the prosecution, Burzaco was somber and sympathetic, breaking out, once again, in tears and leaving the courtroom in total silence.

When he was done for the day, and the jury marched out of the court, Judge Pamela Chen returned to Manuel Burga's gesture from that morning. The judge, herself a former prosecutor, said she'd viewed a security tape of one of the incidents, and thought there was "probable cause to believe" that Burga had attempted to tamper with a witness, a serious federal crime.

Over the vehement protest of Burga's lawyer, who said he might call for a mistrial, Judge Chen placed the defendant on what she called "extreme house arrest," severely limiting whom he could call and cutting off his Internet access and email for the remainder of the case.

If there had been any concerns that the long-awaited trial in America's soccer investigation would be a dreary and tedious bore, dragging jurors through painfully dull technicalities, they had been forgotten. Twice, a government cooperator had wept in the witness box; one of the defendants had, apparently, made death threats in the courtroom; and a lawyer more than five thousand miles away had taken his own life after his name was mentioned in court.

And it was only the third day.

Evan Norris walked into courtroom 4F North of the Brooklyn federal courthouse the following morning wearing a dark blue overcoat. He sat down in the gallery among the reporters, families of the defendants, and other onlookers, a slightly wistful expression on his face.

After more than five years leading the case, from its first spark of an idea through two massive indictments, he had walked away in early 2017 and left the Justice Department altogether that August. As happened with most federal prosecutors in New York, the financial pressures of life in an expensive city on a government salary had finally caught up with Norris.

He joined the international investigations group at white-shoe firm Cravath, Swaine & Moore, working closely with one of his former supervisors from the Eastern District. In June, he won an award recognizing him as the top Assistant United States Attorney in the country, and at his farewell party in Brooklyn, Norris pledged to use some of his new corporate salary to buy his first television, which, he said, he'd researched exhaustively.

Amanda Hector, who had joined the case early on and worked directly with a number of the most important cooperators, had left the Justice Department the prior December, taking a job as general counsel at a hedge fund.

Jared Randall, the young FBI agent who was the first to meet with Blazer, was also gone; months earlier he'd been reassigned to the Bureau's Los Angeles field office to work on international corruption investigations. He followed the trial, as best he could, through news reports.

Mike Gaeta, the seasoned FBI supervisor who first learned about a potential case against FIFA from Christopher Steele back in 2010, had kept in contact with the former British spy. As a result, he'd been the first in American law enforcement to receive Steele's controversial dossier of allegations about attempts by Russia to influence the 2016 U.S. presidential election and the candidacy of Donald Trump.

In the summer of 2017, Gaeta returned to New York after more than three years posted in Rome, but C-24, the Eurasian Crime Squad, was no longer his. Approaching retirement, he was given a new squad to supervise instead and didn't catch the FIFA trial in person.

The only remaining prosecutor with considerable time on the case prior to the first indictment, Sam Nitze, was now leading the three-attorney trial team, which also included Keith Edelman and Kristin

Mace. A rangy former newspaper reporter who had given up journalism for law, Nitze had been ramping up for the trial since July, and by early autumn he and the other prosecutors were working seven days a week to prepare.

It was a gargantuan job. All trials are hard work, but none of the prosecutors had ever dealt with a case even half as complicated as this one. The sheer volume of evidence, running into millions of pages, and the long list of potential witnesses from around the world requiring exhaustive preparation, was nearly overwhelming. The run-up to trial put a strain on all of their personal lives and left them exhausted even before jury selection began.

Of the more than forty people charged in the case, twenty-four had pleaded guilty and agreed to cooperate, including, most recently, an Argentine banker who in June confessed to helping Burzaco maintain Swiss accounts where millions of dollars' worth of bribes to Julio Grondona were secretly deposited.

Fifteen other defendants had eluded prosecution. Jack Warner and Nicolás Leoz, two primary targets of the investigation, had staved off extradition with a series of appeals.

Hugo and Mariano Jinkis, meanwhile, had managed to beat extradition altogether when, in late 2016, an Argentine judge denied the request on grounds that the Jinkises, owners of Full Play, were being investigated for similar crimes in their home country. That criminal probe, which some whispered had been based on evidence supplied by the Jinkises themselves, seemed to be going nowhere: Just two months later, Mariano Jinkis came in second in a national golf tournament, and his smiling picture was printed in the local newspaper.

But with just three exceptions, every single defendant who had been successfully brought to America had eventually copped a plea. It was those three men, each of whom had been extradited against his will and insisted on his innocence, who faced trial starting November 13.

As part of various schemes involving bribes offered by sports marketing firms in exchange for soccer rights, prosecutors claimed Manuel Burga had conspired to take $4.4 million; José Maria Marin, $6.5 million; and Juan Ángel Napout, some $10.5 million.

Proving their guilt to a jury of citizens unfamiliar with soccer and even less so with complex racketeering and fraud statutes would test the theories Norris had first developed years earlier: that because of corruption, FIFA and international soccer operated like organized crime syndicates; that the corruption was endemic; that the men running the sport had abused their positions of trust for their own interests; and that they had relied heavily on American institutions to perpetrate their crimes.

But it would not be Norris making those arguments. All he could do, sitting in the gallery among the onlookers, was watch.

———

In the petition FIFA filed in federal court seeking restitution of tens of millions of dollars forfeited by defendants convicted in the case, the Swiss nonprofit claimed it was a victim of its own corrupt officials who "grossly abused their trust to enrich themselves, while causing significant direct and proximate harm to FIFA."

"The damage done by the Defendants' greed," the petition continued, "cannot be overstated."

Thanks to fleeing sponsors eager to distance themselves from a tarnished organization, as well as titanic legal expenses, FIFA reported net financial losses of $122 million in 2015 and $369 million in 2016, and it projected even wider losses going forward.

In March 2017, a seemingly chastened FIFA turned over a 1,300-page internal corruption investigation it had commissioned in the wake of the first takedown to the Swiss attorney general. Three months later, it finally published the long-secret Garcia Report into the 2018 and 2022 World Cup bidding, but only after a German news outlet threatened to leak the document.

The Swiss attorney general, meanwhile, had given no sign of being close to resolving its ongoing investigation of Sepp Blatter. It did announce, in June 2017, its first conviction related to soccer: the same Argentine banker who pleaded guilty in Brooklyn in June. He agreed to pay a $650,000 fine as punishment for the crimes of document forgery and failure to report suspected money laundering and would face no jail time.

France, too, opened its own criminal investigation into possible corruption in the bids for the 2018 and 2022 World Cups. And in May and July of 2017, Spanish police arrested the former president of the ultra-popular club Barcelona, as well as the sitting president of Spain's national federation, as part of separate investigations involving allegations of money being skimmed from friendly matches played by the Brazilian and Spanish national teams.

Torneos—Burzaco's former firm—signed a deferred prosecution agreement with the Justice Department, having replaced its entire management structure and instituted American-style governance. It agreed to forfeit almost $113 million. CONMEBOL broke its contract with Datisa in the wake of the indictments, freeing it to find other commercial partners to put on the Copa América Centenario. The tournament was by every measure the most successful in Copa América history, with attendance reaching almost 1.5 million, and matches televised in more than 160 countries.

The 2018 World Cup, meanwhile, which Russia had fought so hard to win in 2010, drawing the unwanted attentions of former British spies and active FBI agents in the process, would proceed as planned.

Eight years of one of the most intensive, ambitious, and thorough international investigations in U.S. history had profoundly shaken FIFA and its confederations, but Russia still had its World Cup.

Starting in June 2018, hundreds of millions of fans would, once again, turn their attention to the field of play, where the world's thirty-two best teams would compete for soccer's greatest prize.

It would be the first World Cup held since American law enforcement had revealed to the world the true extent of the corruption underpinning the sport and, as such, a major test of the relationship between FIFA and the sporting public. Would the soccer investigation leave a lasting impact on the sport, or would all be swiftly forgotten amid the surge of nationalistic fervor surrounding the massively popular event?

Whatever the case, one thing was clear: when it came to actually playing the game of soccer, the United States had a lot to learn. On October 10, scarcely a month before the trial began, America's national team faced Trinidad and Tobago in its final World Cup qualifier. After heavy rains, the pitch in the stadium outside of Port of Spain was completely waterlogged, and with the visiting team heavily favored, only fifteen hundred people showed up to watch.

But an own-goal by American defender Omar Gonzalez, followed by a clean strike by a Trinidad forward, proved decisive. The U.S. lost, 2–1, and was eliminated from the 2018 World Cup.

It was a shocking, humiliating result: the first time that the U.S. had been eliminated from the tournament since 1985, when a young Chuck Blazer was the executive vice president of the United States Soccer Federation. Tasked with international competitions and managing the national team, he witnessed the team's elimination in person, continuing what was then a thirty-five-year stretch without qualifying for the sport's biggest event.

Blazer had been on hand again four years later when the U.S. team, in Trinidad, finally cracked through and qualified for the 1990 World Cup in historic fashion. No longer at the USSF, he had the very next day gone to Jack Warner's house to launch his career as an international soccer official, and for the next twenty-five years, America qualified for every single World Cup.

Over that time, Blazer played a key role in developing a modestly popular hobby into a legitimate, thriving cultural and economic power in America. Whether it was vision, or luck, or some statistician's insight into the fast-changing demographics of the country, the former salesman had tied himself to a rocket.

Yet Blazer also proved to be one of the most tainted sports officials in American history, a pioneer not only in soccer's growth, but in its corruption. If he hadn't been taking bribes all the way back to the late 1990s, it's nearly impossible to imagine the U.S. criminal investigation ever achieving what it did.

On July 12, 2017, Chuck Blazer's criminal lawyers announced that he had succumbed to the various illnesses he suffered during the final years of his life. He died still awaiting his sentence.

"His misconduct, for which he accepted full responsibility, should not obscure Chuck's positive impact on international soccer," Blazer's attorney, Mary Mulligan, wrote in a press release announcing his death.

Jack Warner, Blazer's former friend and longtime partner atop

CONCACAF, had not left Trinidad since returning there after his show-down with the FBI in late 2012. Three months after he was indicted, Warner lost a parliamentary election and remained a private citizen since, fighting against his extradition.

True to form, Warner greeted news of America's elimination from the World Cup with jubilation, calling it "the happiest day of my life."

————

Steve Berryman arrived in New York six weeks before the trial was to begin and checked into a hotel downtown. Displaying the exhaustive, detail-oriented habits that defined his work, the IRS agent assisted Nitze and the other prosecutors prepare potential witnesses, many of whom never ended up testifying. He spent countless hours reviewing evidence in the case, rereading thousands of his own emails, and running through Excel spreadsheets until he felt he could remember every cell.

Compared to the immense amount of work the prosecutors had to deal with—including dozens of motions and endless disputes with de-fense attorneys over evidence—Berryman's share didn't seem like too much, but he was committed to being as helpful as possible.

Once the trial began, he sat alongside the prosecutors at their long table in the courtroom, cannily studying the defense attorneys and scru-tinizing each witness, serving as an extra pair of eyes on the team.

From the first moment he'd met him in July 2015, Berryman felt cer-tain Alejandro Burzaco would make a great trial witness if it ever got to that point. He was smart, passionate about soccer, and spoke excellent English. Most of all, Burzaco was precise, which made him credible. He thought before he talked, and he was devastating to defense attorneys on cross-examination, never giving them a millimeter to work with, while somehow managing to appear sympathetic to the jury. There were only a few times in his career that Berryman had ever met a better natural witness.

José Hawilla was another matter.

Four years, six months, and twenty-five days after he was arrested in Miami, José Hawilla took the stand. It was the thirteenth day of the trial, December 4. He wore a scraggly beard and his lung condition had progressed substantially, forcing him to carry an oxygen tank with him to the stand.

Although he had seemed sharp and ready in prep sessions leading up to trial, his demeanor changed in the witness box. His testimony was critical because he had made many of the recordings that would help incriminate the defendants and reinforce the narrative that FIFA and its confederations had been co-opted by criminals who ran them for illicit personal profit.

Standing at a lectern near the jury, Nitze asked Hawilla to tell his life story, and then played tapes of him chatting with soccer officials and business partners over leisurely meals, calling old friends on the phone, and confiding with employees about the business. Where did this meeting take place? Nitze would ask. Who is this person talking?

But as the morning progressed, Hawilla's pauses grew longer, and his answers more vague. When Nitze asked him about the total value of the bribes he and his partners had agreed to pay for the Copa América, he paused.

"I am not sure. I'm confused. I don't know what you're referring to," Hawilla said through his translator.

It was worse on cross-examination. The defense attorneys had reviewed Hawilla's case file and knew about his obstruction, how a lie had gotten him busted in the first place, and how he had continued to lie even while cooperating. They portrayed him as deceptive and untrustworthy, someone who had secretly recorded and betrayed his closest friends. He had even, they noted, been dishonest to the FBI.

"You sat across the table from them and you lied to them?" a lawyer defending José Maria Marin indignantly asked Hawilla.

"Yes," Hawilla quietly responded.

Despite his obvious problems, Hawilla had been an essential part of the case—the man who had doled out more bribes, for longer, than anyone else in all of North or South America, and whose extensive book of business in both regions reinforced the jurisdiction the case needed. From the prosecution's point of view, he and Burzaco were nearly identical: professional bribe payers who became cooperators only after their backs were up against the wall.

But to a jury, the two men couldn't appear more different. Burzaco emerged from his four days of testimony bathed in virtue, a selfless man who voluntarily turned himself in because he wanted to clean up the sport he loved. Hawilla, meanwhile, was out only for himself, a person who would say or do anything to save his own neck. Even his apologies, which he repeated numerous times during two days on the stand, rang hollow.

"It was a mistake," he said. "We shouldn't have paid. I regret it very much."

Jurors heard from a long list of witnesses, but as the case progressed, Nitze, confident things were moving along smoothly, began culling names. It was a calculated risk. Too few witnesses and the case seems thin and unconvincing. But hammering a point too forcefully can make a prosecutor seem like a bully.

After almost four weeks of testimony, and with Christmas fast approaching, the jury was showing signs of fatigue. One juror, in fact, had been sound asleep so often that the judge struck him from the case, bringing in an alternate. There was, however, one final witness Nitze had no plans on crossing off his list.

Steve Berryman took the stand a few minutes after noon on December 7, beginning three days of testimony that went to the very heart of the entire case. As Nitze manned an overhead projector, Berryman marched through a series of wire transfer receipts, spreadsheets, statements from banks in a dozen different countries, deposit slips, payment orders, emails, photographs, Fedwire and CHIPS correspondent bank records, hotel receipts, and airline records, meticulously tracing the trail of money and, often, the parallel movements of defendants to pick up bribes paid in cash.

In a dramatic crescendo, Berryman showed how Hawilla wired $5 million of his share of the Copa América bribes from a bank in Miami to a Swiss account controlled by Burzaco in June 2013; how just a few weeks later, $3 million was sent from that same Swiss account to an account in Andorra, where it was transferred to a second account at the same bank; and, beginning just a week later, how half of the $3 million was sent from the Andorran account, in three equal installments, to an account at Morgan Stanley in the United States.

That last account, Nitze proved by displaying to the jury a copy of the signed signature card from Morgan Stanley, belonging to José Maria

Marin, who had been promised half of the $3 million going to Brazil's soccer leadership for Copa América bribes. Putting a cherry on top, Berryman and Nitze, working as a tag team, then revealed how Marin had spent $118,220.49 from that same account on luxury items at high-end stores in New York, Las Vegas, and Paris in a single month.

It was devastating testimony, virtually impossible to rebut. Marin's lawyers fumed that the prosecution had embarrassed their client by revealing his spending habits, including the fact that he had spent $50,000 in just one transaction at upscale retailer BVLGARI. But privately they marveled at how effective the IRS agent had been on the stand. The entire case could never have come together without his diligent work, they all agreed.

When Berryman finally stepped down on December 12, the prosecution rested. Later that day, one of the defense attorneys tracked the agent down and, breaking with protocol, gave him a hug.

"You did a great job, Steve," the attorney said. "I just wanted you to know that."

———

On December 15, deliberations began. The jurors' instructions, read by Judge Chen, ran fifty-four pages long. She cautioned them about the complicated RICO, wire fraud, and money laundering statutes they had to consider.

The defense, throughout the trial and in its closing arguments, had never argued soccer wasn't corrupt; in fact they had frequently complimented the prosecution for the work it had done to scour the sport of decades of self-dealing. Their argument, instead, was that although other officials had clearly taken bribes, their clients had not. The investigation, they said, had overreached and accused innocent men.

In his closing argument, prosecutor Sam Nitze scoffed at the idea that "everyone except them" accepted bribes. The decision facing the jurors, he said, was an easy one. "There are mysteries to be solved, there are whodunits," said Nitze, visibly exhausted after the strain of six weeks of trial and the months of preparation leading up to it. "This isn't one of them."

"Some things," he added, "are just the way they appear."

A week later, José Maria Marin and Juan Ángel Napout were convicted on nine of twelve counts against them, including the critical RICO charges. Napout faced a maximum sentence of sixty years in prison; Marin, one hundred and twenty.

Nitze asked the judge to send them directly to jail rather than await their sentences under house arrest, as is common in white-collar cases. Given their wealth and foreign citizenship, he argued, "the risk of flight is at its zenith."

Judge Chen, noting she would likely impose "very significant" sentences, agreed. Napout, whose entire family had sat in the courtroom throughout the trial, turned to his wife and grimly handed her his watch, wedding ring, a chain from around his neck, and his belt before marshals took him and Marin into custody.

The two South American soccer officials would spend Christmas in the Metropolitan Detention Center in Brooklyn.

Then on December 26, the jury returned one last verdict, pronouncing Manuel Burga not guilty of RICO conspiracy, the lone count against him.

Burga, tall and laconic, had spent his free hours during the lengthy trial and deliberation reading historical fiction novels and doing puzzles in a magazine called *Super Mata Tiempo*—"Super Time Killer." While Napout and Marin had large trial teams, with multiple lawyers arguing their case; Burga had just one attorney, a harried former prosecutor from Fort Lauderdale, who complained repeatedly to the judge that he didn't have enough time to do everything.

Burga had been extradited from Peru a year earlier on condition that the U.S. prosecute him only for the RICO conspiracy count. Peru was conducting its own investigation of Burga for fraud and money laundering and didn't want to see the man charged twice for the same crimes.

Perhaps, the prosecutors theorized after the verdict, it was because he had only one count against him that the jury ruled as it did. Compared to Napout and Marin, with all their complicated charges, perhaps Burga seemed small-time. It could have been, alternatively, because the theory of his corruption was more complicated—that because he knew of the Peruvian investigation, he chose not to actually receive the bribes he negotiated, planning to take them later. Maybe the jurors, after seven weeks, were just exhausted and wanted to go home.

Whatever the reason, the acquittal stung, and Nitze, Mace, and Edelman found it hard not to wonder what had gone wrong. The guilty verdicts against Napout and Marin had been a huge relief, upholding the premise of the entire investigation—that soccer itself had been tarnished, and that its officials knowingly defrauded the institutions they were supposed to serve. Burga, they were certain, was no different.

But he had walked nonetheless.

————

Berryman heard about the verdicts at home in Southern California. He'd flown back on December 21, eager to be with his family after three grueling months in New York. Over the course of his career, Berryman had sat through eight other trials, and had never once missed a verdict. But the holidays were approaching and he desperately needed a rest.

Among the prosecutors, used to winning nearly 100 percent of the time, there was second-guessing. But Berryman refused to speculate; after sitting through so many trials in his career, he knew juries were impossible to predict. He was satisfied he'd done his job.

December 26, the day Burga's verdict was read, is Boxing Day, traditionally a huge day for soccer in England. There were eight different Premiership matches played, all of them televised in the United States.

For Steve Berryman, it turned out to be a good day: his beloved Liverpool spanked Swansea City, 5–0.

ACKNOWLEDGMENTS

As with any large project, this book would have been impossible without the contributions of others, who generously provided the information, resources, occasional flogging, and inspiration I needed along the way. A list of everyone who helped in some way would run into the hundreds. To all of them I am enormously grateful. Although some of my most valuable supporters prefer to be anonymous, I want to single out a few people who were especially essential to making this book a reality.

Thanks are due to my wonderful and patient colleagues at Buzz-Feed, who set me on the path to finding this story and then granted me the time to report and write it. In particular, I am indebted to my editor, Mark Schoofs, who hired me and, despite his general disdain for sports, allowed me to launch my BuzzFeed career with a lengthy profile of Chuck Blazer. Gratitude, too, goes to Ben Smith, who supported the idea of this project as well as me taking considerable time away from the news to make it a reality; to Nabiha Syed, who schooled me on battling the courts for public information and how to write an effective letter to a judge; to Ariel Kaminer, who called first dibs on throwing me a book party; to Katie Rayford, who helped me figure out how to get out the good word and sit for a headshot; to Heidi Blake, who blazed the path on FIFA corruption coverage and provided key pointers; and to Jonah Peretti, who championed BuzzFeed's investigative team from the outset, encouraged us to take risks, and zealously defended our work.

I was bowled over by the support of the many international journalists who were patient enough to teach me a thing or two about the world's most popular sport. In particular, I was aided by Martyn Ziegler, Richard Conway, Simon Evans, Andrew Jennings, and Tariq Panja in Britain; Jamil Chade in Switzerland; Martín Fernandez, Allan de Abreu, Sergio Rangel, and Juca Kfouri in Brazil; Diego Muñoz in Uruguay;

Alejandro Casar González, Ezequiel Fernández Moores, Gustavo Veiga, and Marcela Mora y Araujo in Argentina; and Tim Elfrink, Kartik Krishnaiyer, Paul Kennedy, Brian Quarstad, and Clive Toye in the U.S.

Many non-journalists also pitched in, sharing knowledge, insights, and hospitality on my numerous reporting trips throughout Europe and North and South America. Patrick Nally was an extraordinary resource on the development of sports marketing, while Scott Parks LeTellier taught me more than I ever thought could be known about the 1994 World Cup. Ariel Neuman helped me understand the minds of prosecutors, while Judy Mahon and Jill Fracisco brought to life, in vivid detail, the inner workings of CONCACAF. Over tea and biscuits in his West End theater office, Greg Dyke provocatively asked me, "But who are the *good guys* in this story?" while David Dein, over tea and biscuits at the Wolseley, graciously suggested where I might look to actually find them.

The wonderful Baranzellis of Basel not only welcomed me into their home, but also nursed me out of one of the nastiest colds I've ever had. Likewise, my aunt, Jane Kanter, and uncle, Byron Cooper, offered me a place to stay in Manhattan and, boy, did I take them up on that. Florence Urling-Clark and Sophie Davidson opened their doors to me in London and environs, while Martin Plot and Anabel Wichmacki housed me in Buenos Aires and stuffed me with amazing asado.

Credit goes to my manager, Justin Manask, for having a vision of how far the seed of an idea could go and being one hundred percent correct. And to my agent, David Patterson, who shepherded that idea to Simon & Schuster and fielded many anxious phone calls. Within S&S, I want to thank Johanna Li for her patience and clarity, Jonathan Evans for his eagle eye, Lisa Rivlin for her sharp legal review, and Jonathan Karp for agreeing to bid on my proposal while my editor was on vacation. Bob Bender, my imperturbable editor, returned from that vacation with his trademark calm and good cheer to show me how mountains can be moved with a feather, and that too many characters is never, ever, a good thing.

I am indebted to Peter Nichols and David Jelenko at Lichter Grossman Nichols Adler & Feldman for holding my hand through several lengthy contract negotiations, and to Chantal Nong at Warner Brothers, Jennifer Todd at Pearl Street Films, and Guymon Cassidy and Darin

Friedman at Management 360 for believing there might be a movie in all this soccer business. Thanks also to Gavin O'Connor and Anthony Tambakis for adding their creative vision to that project.

It would have been much more difficult for me to finish this book without the nurturing of friends and loved ones. Jason Felch stands out as a true friend with a great head for a story, while Jon Weinbach's passion for obscure soccer trivia kept me inspired. Steve Kandell provided critical reads and several genius ideas late in the game, as did James Ellsworth and Harriet Ryan, while Laura Geiser rescued me from learning how to be a photo editor while on a screaming deadline.

The great newspaperman Shelby Grad was my own personal cheerleader throughout this process, and over countless bowls of steaming pho he gradually convinced me that writing a book might not be impossible after all. And there aren't enough words to adequately thank my colleague and friend Jessica Garrison for all she did to get me through to the end.

My brother, Greg, has always been my best friend and was there whenever I needed to just talk. My father, Richard, has been a rock and a hero for my entire life and is a darn good writer to boot. And my mother, the best editor I've ever met, set me on this writing path long ago and never stopped inspiring me with her fire, passion, and creativity.

More than anyone, I want to thank my amazing family. My children, Mateo and Sofia, endured my many long absences, while always welcoming me home with boundless enthusiasm and hugs. And my loving, patient wife, Patricia, supported my decision to take this on, held the fort on my innumerable trips in search of just one more scrap of information, and soothed my nerves when nobody else could. She listened to me read my mangled prose, untangled me when I was stuck, and was simply always there. She is the best partner and friend I could ever desire. Now I'm glad to be home with her again.

NOTES

A Note on Sources

The long-running probe of corruption in soccer that burst into public view with the sensational arrests of May 27, 2015, quickly became one of the most widely publicized and closely watched sports scandals in history.

Three years, dozens of indictments, and one public trial later, the criminal case remains open. It is still being pursued as an active investigation, with American law enforcement agents continuing to dig. Criminal probes in other countries, including and especially Switzerland, are also ongoing.

Because the investigations are not closed, individuals with direct knowledge of their workings have proven extremely reluctant—and in many cases legally barred—to discuss them at any level of detail. As a result, gleaning information about the origins and development of the U.S. probe, which has informally come to be known as the FIFA Case and is the subject of this book, has proven a daunting and elusive task.

In order to produce this narrative, I was obliged to turn to numerous sources who agreed to talk only on condition that they be granted anonymity and that the information they supplied would not be attributed to them. A substantial portion of the story contained in this book is reliant on the generous contributions of these protected sources.

In almost all cases, I used the information they shared to develop second and third sources that could verify and amplify particular interactions, strategies, conversations, or aspects of the case; that in turn allowed me to return to my original sources to further refine their recollections. This process of comparing and reverifying allowed me to home in on the truth, identifying key dates, events, and locations. To the degree it was possible, I have attempted to protect the identity of my sources by getting others to fill in details about their thinking and backgrounds. Quotations that are unattributed in the Notes come from direct interviews and are not identified in order to honor my commitment to protect sources' identities.

The five-week criminal trial of Juan Ángel Napout, José Maria Marin, and Manuel Burga that began in Brooklyn federal court on November 13, 2017, nearly all of which I observed in person, proved an invaluable resource for checking and confirming information contained in this book, as well as for expanding and sharpening my understanding of numerous aspects of the case. Close to fifteen hundred exhibits were admitted into evidence during the trial, ranging from photographs to email correspondence to clandestine recordings, and many of those items were extremely helpful tools as well.

In addition, I also made use of thousands of pages of court filings, including the three highly detailed indictments and other charging documents from the FIFA Case, as well as files from dozens of other criminal and civil cases, arbitrations, corporate records, personal emails, handwritten notes, and other memoranda of meetings. Some of those documents are in the public domain; many others are not. Finally, I relied heavily on contemporaneous media accounts of many of the events described herein; without the daily contributions of the sporting press, this project would have been impossible.

Since it was secretly opened almost eight years ago, this investigation has involved what one defense attorney dubbed "Herculean" contributions from some two dozen federal prosecutors and investigators directly assigned to the case, as well as from hundreds of other American law enforcement officials who played smaller but vital roles, not to mention the part played by countless soccer officials and marketing executives entrenched in the murky and clubby world of international soccer. Capturing all the detail and nuance of a case so sprawling and complex would be an impossible endeavor at any length. Nonetheless, I believe this is the most complete and accurate accounting of the FIFA Case to date. I am deeply grateful for the generosity of those individuals who agreed to provide me so much invaluable assistance.

CHAPTER 1: BERRYMAN

1 *the huge federal office building:* The Chet Holifield Federal Building in Laguna Niguel houses local offices of numerous federal agencies, including the Social Security Administration, the National Archives and Records Administration, and the Internal Revenue Service. A brief history of this unusual architectural monument appears in *Chet Holifield Federal Building: GSA's Decision to Renovate and Retain Appears Appropriate* (Washington: U.S. General Accounting Office, 1987).

1 *an article by the Reuters news service:* Hosenball, Mark. "FBI examines U.S. Soccer Boss's Financial Records," Reuters, August 16, 2011.

3 *landed the county's well-known sheriff:* Berryman was one of a number of IRS and FBI agents involved in an investigation of Orange County sheriff Michael S. Carona that led to his indictment on corruption charges in late 2007. He was convicted of witness tampering in January 2009 and sentenced to sixty-eight months in prison.

8 *critics accused the prosecution:* There has been extensive legal, journalistic, and academic review of the U.S. criminal case, which was for months the most prominent criminal case in the world. See, for example, Cecily Rose, "The FIFA Corruption Scandal from the Perspective of Public International Law," *ASIL Insights*, October 23, 2015.

8 *represented its own kind of conspiracy:* Beyond what has been recorded in the press, numerous soccer officials expressed this sentiment to me personally in the course of reporting; among them Sepp Blatter, the former president of FIFA, who believes the case was personally ordered up by President Barack Obama. Several white-collar lawyers representing defendants in the case evinced similar views, alleging that former attorney general Eric Holder opened the case at former president Bill Clinton's behest.

CHAPTER 2: TICKLING THE WIRE

14 *"The last time I did it in 12 minutes":* Charles Sale, "England 2018 Chairman Geoff Thompson's Wife Ann Sees Her Woes Pile Up After a FIFA Crash," *Daily Mail*, June 8, 2010.

14 *South Africa spent more than $3 billion:* Gerald Imray, "South Africa spent $3 billion on 2010 World Cup," Associated Press, November 23, 2012. For a full accounting of South Africa's expenditures, see "2010 FIFA World Cup Country Report," November 23, 2012.

15 *A handful of artificial turf soccer fields:* Andrew Harding, "South Africa's World Cup Advice to Brazil," BBC, June 9, 2014. See also: Andrew Guest, "What's the legacy of the 2010 World Cup?" Pacific Standard, June 10, 2014.

17 *"We shall work for the next generation":* Graham Dunbar, "FIFA President Declares Re-election Bid," Associated Press, June 10, 2010.

17 *Steele had spent several years undercover:* Steele became the subject of extensive media coverage beginning in January 2017 due to his authorship of memoranda alleging ties between President Donald J. Trump and the Russian government. Additional details about Steele's background and business come, in part, from interviews with numerous associates, past and present, many of whom were granted anonymity due to the sensitivity of Steele's activities and sources.

18 *Steele had been retained:* Information on Steele's work for the England 2018 World Cup bid, as well as his suspicions about Russia's activities, detailed on this and subsequent pages, comes in part from an eighteen-page submission in November 2014 by *The Times* of London to a British parliamentary committee investigating FIFA's World Cup bidding process. That information was corroborated and substantiated by interviews and press accounts, including Mark Hosenball, "Former MI6 Spy Known to U.S. Agencies Is Author of Reports on Trump in Russia," Reuters, January 11, 2017.

19 *to a London tabloid:* The exposé on Triesman was first published in an article by Ian Gallagher in *The Mail on Sunday* on May 16, 2010.

20 *Special Agent Mike Gaeta:* Descriptions of Gaeta come from numerous interviews with current and former law enforcement officials, including but not limited to John Buretta, a former federal prosecutor from the Eastern District of New York; Richard Frankel, a former FBI special agent in charge; and Dave Shafer, a former assistant special agent in charge in the FBI's New York field office.

20 *godfathers such as Vyacheslav Ivankov:* Ivankov, a native of Georgia also known as "Yaponchik," has been the subject of considerable literature and has been called "the father of extortion." See, among others, James O. Finckenauer and Elin J. Waring, *Russian Mafia in America: Immigration, Culture, and Crime* (Boston: Northeastern University Press, 1998).

22 *the most intriguing figure was Alimzhan Tokhtakhounov:* There is considerable information available about the alleged Russian organized crime figure known as Taiwanchik in the two criminal cases filed against him and others in New York's Southern District. In addition, he has been the subject of extensive media coverage, including a 2013 interview conducted in a Moscow restaurant in which he proclaimed "I am not bad, like you think." Andrew E. Kramer and James Glanz, "In Russia Living the High Life; in America, a Wanted Man," *New York Times,* June 1, 2013.

CHAPTER 3: "HAVE YOU EVER TAKEN A BRIBE?"

24 *"Have you ever taken a bribe?"*: Michael E. Miller, "How a curmudgeonly old reporter exposed the FIFA scandal that toppled Sepp Blatter," *Washington Post*, June 3, 2015.

26 *At last, he thought:* Jennings has recounted aspects of this first encounter with the FBI numerous times throughout the years, as, for example, in a first-person article published in *The Mail on Sunday* on May 31, 2015. Additional details were filled in by Jennings in the course of several interviews.

27 *"the General Secretary, his wife"*: This and some other quotes from Havelange come from the former FIFA president's memoirs, some of which were published by FIFA on April 24, 1998, in preparation for his retirement.

28 *had revenue of about $25 million:* David Yallop, pp. 154–55.

28 *Their vision was to bring in:* Patrick Nally, in a series of interviews, provided an in-depth understanding of the project he and Dassler first brought to FIFA in the mid-1970s. That history has been widely recounted, but nowhere better than in Barbara Smit's excellent and thoroughly researched *Sneaker Wars.*

30 *Ethiopia on November 17, 1976:* From *A Guide to the FIFA/Coca Cola World Football Programmes*, published by West Nally.

31 *"that is what hotels are for"*: Interview with Sepp Blatter, February 26, 2016.

32 *"18 African voters accepted bribes"*: Andrew Jennings, "Scandal at Fifa. Top African Official in Cash-for-Votes Claim Against President," *Daily Mail*, February 28, 2002.

32 *FIFA filed a criminal complaint:* From "Swiss Prosecutors Close Investigations Against Blatter," *Deutsche Press-Agentur*, December 4, 2002.

33 *Hildbrand's probe uncovered evidence:* On May 11, 2010, the prosecutor's office of the Canton of Zug dismissed its criminal proceedings against Havelange and Teixeira and released a 42-page order detailing the findings of its criminal investigation of "disloyal management to the detriment of Fédération Internationale de Football Association." It found that both men had secretly accepted "commissions" from ISL, but that Swiss law allowed both men to avoid prosecution.

34 *"The company would not have existed"*: Andrew Jennings, "Fifa 'Misled' Detectives on Trail of Missing Pounds 45m," *Daily Telegraph*, July 30, 2008.

CHAPTER 4: A GUY FROM QUEENS

36 *"very special occasion"*: Blazer detailed his travels, including the trip to Russia, in the travel blog he maintained, which originally was called

"Travels with Chuck Blazer" and was later renamed "Travels with Chuck Blazer and His Friends."

38 *Born in 1945:* Biographical information about Blazer here and in subsequent pages comes, in part, from Pappenfuss and Thompson, as well as several depositions from a 1984 civil lawsuit in New York Supreme Court against Blazer, *Fred Singer Direct Marketing Inc. v. Charles Blazer, Susan Blazer and Windmill Promotions Inc.* Additional information was gathered from my own reporting on Blazer in "Mr. Ten Percent: The Man Who Built—And Bilked—American Soccer," BuzzFeed News, June 6, 2014.

38 *Southern New York Youth Soccer Association:* The SNYYSA was founded in 1972, but as it spread geographically to incorporate a larger swath of the state, the name no longer fit. In 1984 it was renamed the Eastern New York Youth Soccer Association, or ENYYSA, the name it carries to this day.

39 *"There's no magic":* Bill Varner, "Soccer Official Rises Through the Ranks," *Yonkers Herald Statesman*, September 25, 1984.

39 *paid himself a $48,000 salary:* Information on Blazer's income at the American Soccer League, as well as other details of his time working there, are drawn from a July 24, 1989, deposition of Blazer taken as part of a civil suit, *Fred Singer Direct Marketing Inc. v. Charles Blazer, et al.,* before the New York Supreme Court, County of Westchester.

39 *"the suburban soccer family":* Bruce Pascoe, "Soccer Club Tops Canada in Debut, 2–1; 2,716 Attend at Mason," *Washington Post*, July 27, 1987.

40 *"some spiritual force looking after us":* Singh, Valentino p. 173. These books provided extensive additional information about Warner's background and early years at CONCACAF with Blazer.

40 *died of a sudden heart attack:* Guillermo Cañedo died early on January 21, 1997. Blazer was elected by a 5–2 vote on Friday, January 24.

41 *$35 million in 2009:* Revenue information for CONCACAF here and elsewhere in this volume drawn from the confederation's 990 tax forms for the years 2008–2011. Although Blazer failed to file, CONCACAF filed the returns retroactively in 2012.

41 *he had a $900,000 beachside condo:* Details of Blazer's financial activities come in substantial part from CONCACAF's *Integrity Committee Report of Investigation*, published on April 18, 2013.

42 *The August email from Warner:* The email and aspects of Blazer's and Warner's involvement in the 2010 World Cup bribery scheme, as well as various other criminal schemes, are described in detail in various court documents filed in the Eastern District of New York, including p. 23 of

the criminal information against him that was filed under seal on November 25, 2013.

42 *"support the African Diaspora":* FIFA press release, June 2, 2015.

43 *"I'm proud of my vote for South Africa":* Jack Bell, "Soccer Report; Gre-
nada Has Hopes of Upset," *New York Times,* May 25, 2004.

43 *"For deposit only":* From a scanned image of the check in the author's
archive.

CHAPTER 5: THE VOTE

44 *known in soccer circles as FIFA House:* Technical information about
the building drawn from FIFA press materials as well as materials from
its Zurich-based architect, Tilla Theus. Additional descriptions drawn
from an unofficial, firsthand tour of the building, including the Executive Committee boardroom, in August 2016.

45 *"places where people make decisions":* Michael Marek and Sven Beck-
mann, "Underground Skyscraper Serves as FIFA's Headquarters," *Deutsche Welle,* May 16, 2010.

46 *"cannot see the advantages of such a federation":* The English Football
Association, known as The EFA, maintains records of this correspondence, which is widely cited in literature on soccer and its history.

47 *"These arguments":* From FIFA's own, official history of the World Cup,
found on its website.

47 *booked a record profit:* FIFA's financial books are maintained and organized on a four-year cycle coinciding with the World Cup, which is far
and away its largest moneymaker. Annual results, as well as four-year
round-ups, are published for public consumption and available from
FIFA dating back to 2002. Earlier financial results are compiled from
FIFA documents available elsewhere, as well as from contemporaneous
press reports.

48 *"a sad day for football":* Martyn Ziegler, "We Will Rid Game of Its Devils:
Blatter," Press Association Sport, October 20, 2010.

48 *"unpatriotic":* Owen Gibson, "FIFA Officials Accused of Taking Bribes
in $100m Scandal: Panorama Claims Could Affect England 2018 Bid,"
The Guardian, November 30, 2010.

49 *"make their decision in peace":* Martyn Ziegler, "England Chances Improve in World Cup Race," Press Association Sport, December 1, 2010.

49 *"How are our chances?":* Details of this phone call are from two extended
in-person interviews with Sepp Blatter, in February and August 2016.

49 *"I am a happy president":* The entire dual World Cup announcement,
with footage of both the stage and audience, was video-recorded and is
available online.

50 *"wallowing in money":* A complete transcript of Putin's press conference in Zurich was published by the Russian Information Agency, ORE-ANDA, on December 3, 2010.

51 *a heavily guarded federal office tower:* Descriptions of the FBI's New York field office come from multiple interviews with current and former FBI agents, as well as firsthand observation of the building and offices.

51 *"Russia and Qatar Expand":* Jeré Longman, "Russia and Qatar Expand Soccer's Global Footprint," *New York Times,* December 2, 2010.

CHAPTER 6: JACK VS. CHUCK

54 *"I hope this is an April Fool's Joke":* Details of this and other communications between Warner, Blazer, and Bin Hammam in this chapter come courtesy of the archive of British journalist Martyn Ziegler.

54 *"What's in it for us?":* From a June 2, 2011, document entitled *Affirmation of Chuck Blazer.*

56 *a $3 million television studio:* Information on this and the Centre of Excellence in Trinidad drawn from CONCACAF's *Integrity Committee Report of Investigation.*

57 *"thinks that he can go through anything":* From *Affirmation of Chuck Blazer.*

57 *the bell rang at Warner's house:* The account of Blazer's visit with Warner in Trinidad comes largely from Valentino Singh, pp. 162–64, as well as Jack Warner with Valentino Singh, pp. 71–73.

58 *multiple mortgages and car notes:* Information on Blazer's finances at the time comes from the July 24, 1989, deposition of Blazer.

59 *born in January 1943:* Warner's biographical history is drawn heavily from his two biographies.

59 *soldiers came to the house of André Kamperveen:* A total of fifteen people, including trade unionists, lawyers, and journalists, were kidnapped, tortured, and killed by government forces in what became known as the December Murders, which led to widespread protest and the severing of relations and direct aid to Suriname from the Netherlands. Of particular interest is the Inter-American Commission on Human Rights' *Report on the Human Rights Situation in Suriname,* published December 3, 1983.

61 *The scheme involved a company:* Simpaul Travel. This episode is described in detail in Andrew Jennings, *Foul!,* pp. 329–52.

61 *"It cannot be proven that Jack Warner knew":* Comment from Marcel Mathier, as quoted in "FIFA Vice-President Escapes Sanction over World Cup Tickets," Agence France Presse, December 6, 2006.

CHAPTER 7: PORT OF SPAIN

65 *the CFU conference was finally finished:* Many aspects of the events of May 10 and 11, 2011, described throughout this chapter are recorded in two separate reports on the alleged bribery incident: *Report of Evidence of Violations of the FIFA Code of Ethics,* prepared by John P. Collins, May 22, 2011; and *Report to the FIFA Ethics Committee on Allegations Related to the Meeting of the CFU on May 10–11, 2011 in Trinidad and Tobago,* prepared by FGI Europe AG on June 29, 2011. Additional details are drawn from affidavits, memoranda, cell phone text message screen shots, and affirmations of Blazer, Anton Sealey, and Fred Lunn, copies of all of which are courtesy of Martyn Ziegler. Still more information is available in copies of the decisions by the May 29, 2011, FIFA Ethics Committee ruling on Jack Warner, and the Court of Arbitration for Sport arbitral award for Bin Hammam handed down July 19, 2012.

65 *"more say, more support, and more pay":* Paul Kelso, "Revealed: Fifa's Secret Bribery Files on Warner and Bin Hammam," *Sunday Telegraph,* May 29, 2011.

69 *"birthday present":* Arny Belfor, *"New Evidence of $40K Cash Gifts in FIFA Scandal,"* Associated Press, June 10, 2011.

69 *"Bin Hammam asked to come to the Caribbean":* Warner's full speech was secretly recorded, and a copy of that video was first published by *The Telegraph* on October 12, 2011.

71 *Two days later, Blazer called Jérôme Valcke:* Affidavit of Chuck Blazer, May 23, 2011, courtesy of Martyn Ziegler.

72 *"clear evidence of violations":* Copy of Collins & Collins "Report of Evidence of Violations of the FIFA Code of Ethics," May 22, 2011, in the author's archive.

72 *"bribery allegations":* Martyn Ziegler, "FIFA Duo Face Corruption Charges," Press Association Sport, May 25, 2011.

72 *Early on May 29:* An excellent, blow-by-blow account of the FIFA ethics hearings of that day, including direct quotations from transcripts, as well as the subsequent press conference, can be found in Heidi Blake and Jonathan Calvert, pp. 358–78.

73 *"I am in FIFA for 29 consecutive years":* A full transcript of Warner's remarks outside Trinidad and Tobago's parliament was published by the *Trinidad Express* on May 27, 2011.

CHAPTER 8: A MADE MAN

75 *"all sponsorships and TV rights fees":* A copy of the contract is in the author's archives.

77 a "witty, gregarious" man: Nancy Armour, "Chuck Blazer Is Witty, Gregarious and a Whistleblower," Associated Press, June 4, 2011.

79 reach out to FIFA's head of security, Chris Eaton directly: Randall wrote Eaton a brief email on the evening of June 13, 2011, noting that "if you have any plans to travel back through the US, or specifically New York, I would love to speak with you."

80 Bin Hammam wired the money: The complex wire transfers were first detailed in Heidi Blake and Jonathan Calvert, pp. 390–91. They were subsequently verified in Department of Justice documents sent to Trinidad and Tobago. See Camini Maraji, "US $1.2M Bribe for Jack," Trinidad Express, June 9, 2015.

80 Warner resigned from all positions: The timing of the letter is detailed in Report to the FIFA Ethics Committee on Allegations Related to the Meeting of the CFU on May 10–11, 2011 in Trinidad and Tobago, p. 4.

80 "I'm not going to back a complaint": Warner was interviewed by Bloomberg TV on June 20, 2011.

82 "we don't tolerate the type of behavior": Martyn Ziegler, "Blazer: I Had to Act on Bribery Claims," Press Association Sport, May 29, 2011.

82 the last time it was brought up was in 2002: CONCACAF's Integrity Committee Report of Investigation, pp. 55–56.

83 He wrote a book on communist guerrillas in Peru: Strong's two books are Shining Path: Terror and Revolution in Peru (New York: Crown, 1993); and Whitewash: Pablo Escobar and the Cocaine Wars (London: Pan, 1995).

84 "Find another villain": Jennings published much of his correspondence with Blazer, including messages detailed in this chapter, on his website, transparencyinsport.org.

84 story on the exorbitant lifestyles of FIFA officials: Doreen Carvajal, "For FIFA Executives, Luxury and Favors," New York Times, July 18, 2011.

86 "were not income items nor subject to tax": email from Blazer to Jennings, August 12, 2011, published on transparencyinsport.org.

86 "A New York–based FBI squad assigned to investigate": Mark Hosenball, "FBI Examining U.S. Soccer Boss's Financial Records," Reuters, August 16, 2011.

CHAPTER 9: RICO

87 The true hero behind Capone's fall: Wilson, a hero among a certain group of forensic accountants, wrote an autobiography, Special Agent: A Quarter Century with the Treasury Department and the Secret Service, which was published in 1965 and is no longer in print.

88 "fears nothing that walks": Elmer L. Irey, Tax Dodgers: The Inside Story of the T-Men's War with America's Political and Underworld Hoodlum

(New York: Greenberg, 1948). Irey was chief of the Treasury's Intelligence Unit throughout the Capone investigation.

88 *kickbacks to officials in Thailand:* Gerald and Patricia Green were convicted by a Los Angeles federal jury in 2009 for paying $1.8 million in bribes in order to get nearly $14 million in contracts from the Bangkok Film Festival. See Ben Fritz, "Hollywood Producers Are Guilty of Bribing Thai Official," *Los Angeles Times*, September 15, 2009.

88 *bribed officials at the U.K. Ministry of Defence:* Two officials at defense contractor Pacific Consolidated Industries pleaded guilty, in 2008 and 2009, to paying some $70,000 in bribes to win contracts with the Ministry of Defence.

94 *"the lack of selflessness and compassion":* Letter to the editor, *Columbia Daily Spectator*, October 7, 1998. Norris was reacting to an op-ed extolling the virtues of sweatshop labor.

94 *"the best thing I've done at the law school":* Sarah McGonigle, "Legal Aid Sees Rise in 3L Retention," *Harvard Law Record*, December 10, 2002.

94 *a particularly nasty assassin:* The six-week trial of Charles Carneglia began in January 2009, with Norris delivering a five-hour-long closing argument. "Ladies and gentlemen, Charles Carneglia was no choir boy as a young man, and he's no choir boy today," Norris said to the jury, which convicted the former Gambino hit man on four murder counts, as well as racketeering, robbery, extortion, kidnapping, and conspiracy to distribute marijuana.

CHAPTER 10: BLAZER'S MONEY

96 *the case offended his "sense of justice":* After Welch and Johnson were acquitted on December 5, 2003, federal judge David Sam remarked that he had never seen a case so devoid of "criminal intent or evil purpose." Paul Foy, "Judge Throws Out Salt Lake City Case," *Washington Post*, December 6, 2003.

99 *He'd first met Blazer on the sidelines:* There are numerous accounts of the friendship between Gulati and Blazer. See, for example, Nathaniel Vinton, Christian Red, and Michael O'Keeffe, "From Fifa Storm to Reform: U.S. Soccer Prez Gulati Wades Through Shock of Corruption Scandal to Pave New Road for World's Game," New York *Daily News*, December 13, 2015.

99 *without having to be elected:* Gulati was unanimously appointed to the seat at a meeting of the CONCACAF Executive Committee in Curaçao on March 28, 2007.

100 *"never had occasion to borrow money from Blazer":* Gail Alexander, "Jack Clears Air on $$ Paid to Blazer," *Trinidad Guardian*, September 3, 2011.

101 *asked only that Blazer refrain:* CONCACAF's *Integrity Committee Report of Investigation*, p. 53.

101 *"pursue other career opportunities":* CONCACAF issued a press release announcing Blazer's planned resignation on October 6, 2011.

102 *the confederation had $60 million in revenue:* From CONCACAF's federal tax return form 990, for tax year 2011, which was filed with the IRS on December 28, 2012. Total revenue was $60,044,279, while total expenses were $30,986,338, yielding a net return for the nonprofit organization of over $29 million.

102 *his corporate American Express card:* CONCACAF's *Integrity Committee Report of Investigation*, pp. 63–65.

102 *did the same thing with his rent:* Ibid., pp. 59–60.

103 *already allocated himself $4.2 million:* Ibid., p. 50.

104 *wire $1.4 million to his Sportvertising account:* Ibid., p. 53.

CHAPTER 11: THE FLIP

108 *"happy, if self-satisfied, affluence":* Paul Goldberger, "Atrium of Trump Tower Is a Pleasant Surprise," *New York Times*, April 4, 1983.

109 *illegal under the Bank Secrecy Act:* U.S. citizens and permanent residents are required by law to file a Report of Foreign Bank and Financial Accounts, or FBAR, along with their tax returns. The maximum penalty for criminal failure to file an FBAR, considered a money laundering violation, is five years in prison.

109 *Title 31 subpoenas:* At least five different circuit courts of appeal have sustained the argument that the Fifth Amendment privilege against self-incrimination does not apply to subpoenas for foreign bank records. See Lynley Browning, *"New U.S. Tactic for Suspected Swiss Bank Tax Cheats,"* Reuters, December 28, 2011.

112 *"substantial assistance":* A series of legislative reforms of the criminal justice system in the mid-1980s led to the drafting of guideline policy statement *5K1.1, Substantial Assistance to Authorities*: "Upon motion of the government stating that the defendant has provided substantial assistance in the investigation or prosecution of another person who has committed an offense, the court may depart from the guideline" for sentencing purposes. Cooperators seek what is now known as a 5K letter, requesting a downward departure at sentencing.

CHAPTER 12: THE CROWN JEWEL

114 *first met Hawilla in 1987:* Certain aspects of the history of the relationship between Blazer and Hawilla are drawn from Blazer's personal blog,

"Travels with Chuck Blazer and His Friends," including a May 9, 2008, post touching on that topic.

115 *cofounded the sports marketing firm Inter/Forever Sports:* Hawilla incorporated the company, along with Colombian immigrant Jorge Martinez, on May 11, 1990. Hawilla eventually bought out Martinez's share and the company's name was changed to Traffic Sports USA Inc. on September 2, 2003. After a long illness, Martinez died in 2017.

115 *signing a contract in October 1994: USA v. Hawit, et al.,* superseding indictment, November 25, 2015, p. 70.

115 *CONCACAF's rights in-house:* CONCACAF's *Integrity Committee Report of Investigation,* p. 6.

116 *an eager young sports reporter:* A number of profiles of Hawilla from the Brazilian press were particularly helpful in sketching his biography. Among them: Allen de Abreu and Carlos Petrocilo, "J. Hawilla, do cachorro-quente ao império," *Diário da Região,* May 31, 2015; Adriana Negreiros, "O dono da bola (e do time, do jogador, do campeonato, do jornal, da TV, da publicidade)," *Playboy Brazil,* March 2009; Joyce Pascowitch, "Bola na rede," *Poder,* December 2010; José Roberto Caetano, "O dono da bola é J. Hawilla, dono da Traffic," *Exame,* November 8, 2013.

118 *sold Traffic the rights to the 1987 edition: USA v. José Hawilla,* criminal information, filed December 12, 2014, p. 21. Substantial information about Hawilla's business activities in this chapter is drawn from this and other charging documents in the several criminal cases filed in the Eastern District of New York. In addition, Hawilla was deposed a great length in December 2000 and April 2001 by the Brazilian Senate and House of Representatives, respectively, and transcripts of those interviews, running in the hundreds of pages, are filled with important details about his business activities. Finally, a September 5, 2002, deposition of Hawilla taken in the action *T&T Sports Marketing v. Dream Sports International v. Torneos y Competencias,* before the Southern District of Texas, was useful to clarify certain aspects of his business holdings, including the brief investment of Hicks, Muse.

119 *"you have to know how to take risks":* Joyce Pascowitch, "Bola na rede."

119 *every Copa América deal included side payments: USA v. Hawilla,* criminal information, p. 24.

120 *Blazer and Warner, too, began demanding money: USA v. Charles Blazer,* criminal information, filed November 25, 2013, p. 18.

120 *Hawilla's empire was under attack:* The Honduras soccer federation sued Traffic in U.S. federal court in Miami in September 2006; Traffic

countersued; the dispute was eventually forced into arbitration. Details on the matter are drawn from those court records.

121 *Pay CONMEBOL $46 million for the deal:* Copies of Traffic's Copa América contracts were filed with the Miami-Dade County Court in *Traffic Sports v. CONMEBOL and Full Play.*

124 *The civil complaint: Traffic Sports v. CONMEBOL and Full Play* in Miami-Dade County Court on November 21, 2011.

124 *On December 1, Mariano Jinkis wired:* Ibid., p. 127; some additional details about the bribe payment drawn from several other court documents, including the criminal information and guilty plea transcript of Miguel Trujillo on March 8, 2016; the criminal information and guilty plea transcript of Fabio Tordin on November 9, 2015; and the guilty plea transcript of Alfredo Hawit on April 11, 2016.

CHAPTER 13: QUEEN FOR A DAY

126 *"FBI launches investigation":* The *Telegraph* article was written by Claire Newell and Paul Kelso.

126 *published a second article:* Paul Kelso, "FBI's Investigation in Alleged Fifa Corruption Heads for the Caribbean," *The Telegraph*, December 14, 2011.

128 *It was December 29:* Dates of Blazer's proffers are detailed in his cooperation agreement, signed November 25, 2013.

131 *had originated 127 million wire transfers:* Monthly, quarterly, and annual statistics on Fedwire transactions are posted by the Federal Reserve on its website.

134 *Blazer confessed he had agreed:* Details of the corrupt acts Blazer confessed to are contained in *USA v. Blazer*, criminal information, as well as his plea agreement, both filed on November 25, 2013.

135 *FIFA . . . booked $2.4 billion:* Figures come from FIFA's final accounting of the 2007–2010 World Cup cycle.

136 *ESPN had paid a respectable $100 million:* Brian Trusdell, "ABC and ESPN Get U.S. Rights to 2010, 2014 World Cups for $100 Million," Associated Press, November 2, 2005.

136 *CONCACAF took in $31.1 million:* Drawn from the confederation's 990 tax filing.

136 *a measly $18 million:* From January 2001 contract between Traffic and CONMEBOL, exhibit to November 21, 2011, complaint in *Traffic v. CONMEBOL and Full Play.*

CHAPTER 14: THE KING IS DEAD, LONG LIVE THE KING

139 *split all costs and revenue, including bribes: USA v. Hawit, et al.,* superseding indictment, p. 131.

140 *he incorporated one such company, J&D International:* Michael Klein, "Webb Was Director of Jack Warner's Cayman Company," *Cayman Compass,* July 8, 2015.

141 *expect to receive "side payments":* Transcript of guilty plea of Jeffrey Webb, November 23, 2015, p. 26.

141 *"I am humbled":* "Webb Accepts Nomination for CONCACAF President," Cayman News Service, March 26, 2012.

142 *"It is difficult to predict":* Graham Dunbar, "CONCACAF Tries to Oust Chuck Blazer from FIFA," Associated Press, May 23, 2012.

143 *"we must move the clouds":* Ibid.

144 *"a professional with competence and integrity":* Michelle Kaufman, "New CONCACAF Chief Could Enhance South Florida's Soccer Appeal," *Miami Herald,* July 27, 2012.

145 *"They could have conducted a worldwide search":* Michelle Kaufman, "New CONCACAF Chief Could Enhance South Florida's Soccer Appeal."

145 *Finally, they settled on a plan:* Details of the complicated series of transactions are derived from numerous sources, but principally from *USA v. Hawit, et al.,* superseding indictment, pp. 133–35.

CHAPTER 15: FASTER, HIGHER, STRONGER

146 *had attempted to bribe him and Warner: USA v. Blazer,* information, pp. 16–17.

149 *secretly recorded a handful of Russians:* Mary Papenfuss and Teri Thompson, pp. 145–46.

149 *"targeted lobbying within the body of FIFA":* Michael J. Garcia and Cornel Borbély, *Report on the Inquiry into the 2018/2022 FIFA World Cup Bidding Process,* p. 66.

151 *The plan was to focus on a peculiar payment:* Many details of Blazer's recorded interactions with Hawilla, leading to his eventual arrest, come from a copy of the sealed criminal complaint and FBI affidavit against Hawilla, which was filed on May 8, 2013, and signed by Jared Randall.

152 *"the source of these funds":* from a February 18, 2003, fax sent from First-Caribbean International Bank to Sportvertising.

152 *"render consulting services to CLIENT":* Copy of the four-page contract reviewed by the author.

153 *Hawilla had invited Blazer to the wedding:* "Travels with Chuck Blazer and His Friends," May 9, 2008.

CHAPTER 16: MY WAY

154 *"ensuring accountability, transparency"*: CONCACAF press release.

155 *he noticed documents being shredded*: CONCACAF's *Integrity Committee Report of Investigation*, p. 16.

155 *"We decline to comply with your request"*: Ibid., Appendix B.

155 *"the reform efforts initiated by Webb"*: Ibid., p. 12.

156 *a gala dinner was held in his own honor*: Ron Shillingford, "Webb Spun His Charm Superbly," *Cayman Compass*, July 18, 2012.

158 *Traffic wired $1 million of the bribe*: USA v. Hawit, et al., superseding indictment, p. 133.

CHAPTER 17: THE PACT

159 *"Internacional's fans are devastated"*: Paulo Maia, "A morte do Papa e o jogo de futebol," *Jornal do Brasil*, August 8, 1978.

160 *obliged to sign another collaboration agreement*: Hawilla's old friend and associate, Kleber Leite, bought the rights to the Copa do Brasil, the country's top-level professional league, through 2022. The deal, struck in December 2011, wasn't revealed until the following May. Traffic and Klefer, Leite's company, signed a cost- and revenue-sharing agreement on August 15, 2012. Details of the arrangement found in *USA v. Hawit, et al.*, pp. 80–82.

161 *unloaded 49 percent of Traffic*: Jill Goldsmith, "Hicks Muse Nabs 49% of Brazil's Traffic SA," *Variety*, July 28, 1999.

162 *"The most powerful man in Brazilian soccer"*: Gilberto Scofield, Jr., "J. Hawilla, a dono do nosso futebol," *O Globo*, June 4, 2010.

162 *wedding of his baby boy*: Rafael Hawilla was married to Adriana Helú on November 17, 2012 on Manantiales Beach. The wedding and honeymoon was the event of the season in Punta del Este and received considerable press attention in Brazilian style and society blogs.

162 *cost more than $1 million*: Denise Mota, "50% dos casamentos de luxo no Uruguai tem brasileiros no altar," *Folha de S. Paulo*, January 31, 2013. An owner of the beach club where the wedding was held estimated its cost at $1.5 million.

CHAPTER 18: THE WARNER BROTHERS

166 *Warner had been named Trinidad and Tobago's Minister of National Security*: Warner was first elected to Trinidad and Tobago's parliament in 2007 as chairman of the United National Congress (UNC) party. In May 2010, the UNC, forming an alliance with several other parties, won the national elections by a huge margin, and Warner, who received more votes than any other candidate nationwide, was awarded with

the Ministry of Works & Transport. Opposition leader Keith Rowley said his subsequent appointment "should be a matter of concern for all right-thinking citizens of Trinidad and Tobago."

167 *Daryan was the bright one:* Details on Daryan Warner's education from *USA v. Daryan Warner*, transcript of guilty plea, October 18, 2013.

168 *ignoring warnings from FIFA:* In a statement, FIFA said, "Jack A. Warner should, in particular, ensure that his son, Daryan Warner, does not abuse the position held by his father." Rob Hughes, "FIFA Clears Warner in Ticket Scam," *New York Times*, December 6, 2006.

168 *He had come to the window with 7,500 euros:* Details of the Warner brothers' structuring transactions are taken from a sealed criminal complaint in *USA v. Daryan Warner and Daryll Warner*, filed on November 20, 2012. Steve Berryman swore to the complaint.

168 *an army of little blue men:* There is some debate about the author of the term "smurfing," as understood to mean criminal structuring. Gregory Baldwin, a former Justice Department trial attorney based in Miami, is often credited with having coined the term in the late 1980s. However, congressional testimony from July 1985 indicates use of the term in a House Judiciary Committee hearing on money laundering.

171 *Daryll Warner bought a three-bedroom penthouse:* The younger Warner brother's mortgage scam is detailed in *USA v. Daryll Warner*, criminal information, filed July 15, 2013, pp. 1–3.

CHAPTER 19: "A SAD AND SORRY TALE"

175 *a massive indictment targeting sixty-two members: USA vs. Agate, et al.,* is commonly known by its code name, Operation Old Bridge. The takedown led to sixty guilty pleas, with most defendants facing long prison terms.

175 *an even bigger takedown:* Called "the largest mob roundup in FBI history" by government officials, the operation was based on four separate indictments and the takedown involved some eight hundred law enforcement agents. Attorney General Eric Holder announced the news at a press conference in the Eastern District of New York on January 20, 2011.

176 *"I have recounted a sad and sorry tale":* Juan Zamorano, "Regional Ex-Soccer Executives Accused of Fraud," Associated Press, April 20, 2013.

177 *"They have a right to be":* Graham Dunbar, "CONCACAF Financial Scandal Could Hurt US," Associated Press, March 20, 2013.

177 *"Person of the Year":* Sean Williams, "Football Propels Webb to Cayman's Person of the Year," *Jamaica Observer*, February 28, 2013. "One's work in football is not just restrictive to football, but on the broader scope, it's in

service of all other positive aspects of life and the human reality," Webb said upon hearing of the honor.

178 *sending $2 million of the confederation's cash:* Letter from Samir Gandhi of Sidley Austin to Fabrice Baly, president of the St. Martin Football Association, dated January 5, 2016. The letter was circulated to all CONCACAF member associations.

178 *Sanz . . . had agreed to pay him a six-figure bribe:* USA v. Hawit, et al., pp. 100–101.

179 *"I would hope and I would think":* Graham Dunbar, "CONCACAF Financial Scandal Could Hurt US," *Associated Press,* March 20, 2013.

179 *Some of that cash was then transferred:* An accounting of the movements of the bribe money is in *USA v. Hawit, et al.,* superseding indictment, pp. 133–34.

180 *convened an emergency Saturday cabinet meeting:* Mark Fraser, "Warner Resigns; Jack Hits the Road," *Trinidad Express, New York Times,* April 21, 2013.

181 *"until somebody is bold enough to print something":* Mark Bassant, " 'I'm Not Under House Arrest'; Daryan Warner Bares His Ankles in Miami," *Trinidad Express,* March 19, 2013.

181 *"an FBI probe into alleged corruption":* Mark Hosenball, "Exclusive, FBI His Cooperating Witness for Soccer Fraud Probe: Sources," Reuters, March 27, 2013.

181 *"before making any determination or pronouncement":* Mark Bassant, "Jack's Son A Witness," *Trinidad Express,* March 27, 2013.

181 *a massive, multipart investigation:* The series, by *Trinidad Express* investigative reporter Camini Marajh, began on April 14, 2013, with "Over $100m Withdrawn from TTFF Accounts." It continued throughout 2013 with over a dozen exposés and sidebars, taking deep looks at much of Warner's financial doings.

181 *"one of the most hardworking ministers in our Cabinet":* Statement by Communications Minister Jamal Mohammed, quoted in "Govt Backs Jack," *Trinidad Newsday,* April 19, 2013.

182 *"it is baseless and malicious":* Linda Hutchinson-Jafar, "Trinidad's National Security Minister, Ex-FIFA Official Warner Quits—Official," Reuters, April 21, 2013.

182 *"I have accepted the offer of resignation":* Mark Fraser, "Warner Resigns," *Trinidad Express,* April 21, 2013.

182 *Warner received a phone call:* Shastri Boodan, "Warner Must Return Diplomatic Passport," *Trinidad Guardian,* July 19, 2013.

182 *the long-anticipated results of its internal review:* FIFA published its eight-page *Statement of the chairman of the FIFA adjudicatory chamber,*

Hans-Joachim Eckert, on the examination of the ISL case on April 29, 2013.

183 *let them off after they paid back scarcely a third:* Havelange and Teixeira stood accused of "embezzlement possibly disloyal management," but Article 53 of the Swiss penal code allows for "the exemption from punishment in the event of reparation being made. If the offender has paid for the damage or undertakes all reasonable endeavors to compensate for the injustice he caused, then the competent authority will refrain from prosecuting him, bringing him to court or punishing him." This statute generally applies only to crimes with sentences of less than two years. By making partial reparations, prosecutor Thomas Hildbrand determined, the two Brazilians had satisfied Article 53. This is described in exhaustive detail in order on the dismissal of the criminal proceedings of May 11, 2010, published by the Canton of Zug prosecutor's office.

183 *"any further steps or suggestions are superfluous":* Ibid.

CHAPTER 20: "LEAVE US OUT OF THIS"

184 *May 3, 2013:* Some information on Randall's first interaction with Hawilla, as well as his prior and subsequent phone calls with Blazer detailed throughout this chapter, are drawn from the sealed criminal complaint in *USA v. Hawilla*, dated May 8, 2013. Additional details come from Hawilla's trial testimony in December 2017.

186 *Hawilla had flown to Buenos Aires:* Some details of this meeting, as well as of the Copa América contract, from *USA v. Hawit, et al.*, superseding indictment, pp. 141–43, as well as from Hawilla's trial testimony.

190 *Blazer first called early the previous June:* The first recorded call from Blazer to Hawilla was on June 1, 2012. A second call, on June 26, also involved Stefano Hawilla, the executive's oldest son. From the May 8 criminal complaint in *USA v. Hawilla*.

190 *Lying to a federal agent was a crime:* Often called "making false statements," 18 USC 1001 is a favorite statute of federal agents attempting to make a case against someone. It carries a maximum five-year sentence, and has been used with success against Martha Stewart, Bernie Madoff, Jeffrey Skilling, and, more recently, George Papadopoulos, the former Trump foreign advisor. The best way to avoid a 1001 charge is to ask for the agent's card, say nothing more, and get a lawyer.

190 *say nothing and get a lawyer:* If an FBI agent ever approaches wanting to ask you questions, seriously, don't say anything and get a lawyer.

192 *A forty-two-year-old lawyer who grew up in Dallas:* Some biographical details for Aaron Davidson are drawn in part from the transcript of his October 20, 2016 guilty plea in *USA v. Hawit, et al.*, as well as

from several profiles in the press, notably Tim Elfrink, "Aaron David-son's Stunning Soccer Bribery Case Could Clean Up FIFA's Corruption," *Miami New Times*, September 1, 2015.

CHAPTER 21: I AM NOT YOUR FRIEND

194 *finally settled on a bond of $20 million:* Details of the terms of Hawilla's conditional release come from copies of a May 2013 escrow agreement executed between Hawilla and the U.S. Attorney's Office for the Eastern District of New York, represented by Assistant U.S. Attorney Amanda Hector.

198 *more than $2 million in annual marketing commissions:* The $160 mil-lion CBF-Nike deal was negotiated starting in 1994 and signed in New York on July 11, 1996. It is described in some detail in *USA v. Hawit, et al.,* superseding indictment, pp. 83–86. Nike agreed to pay Traffic $40 million, in regular installments, over and above the contract price as an agency fee. Hawilla secretly agreed on July 14, 1996, to split that fee with Teixeira, amounting to a kickback. The deal with Nike was the subject of an eight-month parliamentary inquiry in Brazil that began work on October 17, 2000. The commission ultimately recommended charges against a number of soccer officials, including Teixeira, but not against Hawilla. Due to the political power of those individuals, how-ever, no charges were ever filed. A complete accounting can be found in Sílvio Torres, *Comissão parlamentar de inquérito destinada a apurar a regularidade do contrato celebrado entre a CBF e a Nike,* published in June 2001.

199 *Teixeira had been living in a spectacular waterfront Miami mansion:* In the face of a criminal investigation in Brasilia, Teixeira left Brazil on February 17, 2012, on a private jet belonging to Wagner Abrahão, owner of Grupo Águia, a travel agency that had, with Traffic, rights to sell VIP World Cup ticket packages in Brazil. Just weeks earlier, Teixeira had closed escrow on a 6,630-square-foot, $7.45 million mansion on Sun-set Island in Miami that had previously belonged to Russian tennis star Anna Kournikova. He resigned as president of the CBF on March 12, 2012, when he was already installed in Miami. Teixeira's story, in excel-lently reported detail, can be found in Jamil Chade; and in Ribeiro Jr., et al., which covers the soccer official's flight on pp. 233–34.

200 *On June 3, less than a month after he was arrested:* Details of Hawilla's payments to Torneos and Full Play for his share of the Copa América bribes come from testimony in the November and December 2017 trial of Juan Ángel Napout, José Maria Marin, and Manuel Burga, as well as from *USA v. Hawit, et al.,* superseding indictment, pp. 144–45.

CHAPTER 22: ONE IS SILVER, THE OTHER GOLD

202 *dozens of payments:* An accounting of Danis's bribe payments, as well as her tax issues, is contained in *USA v. Zorana Danis*, criminal information, filed May 26, 2015, pp. 15–16, 18.

203 *Blagoje Vidinić:* There are numerous accounts of Vidinić's life as a player, coach, and Adidas employee, and the story of his conversation with Horst Dassler on the eve of the historic 1974 FIFA elections in Frankfurt has been told by several notable sports journalists, including Andrew Jennings, Keir Radnedge, and Pal Odegard, among others. Perhaps the best account comes from Barbara Smit, *Sneaker Wars*, pp. 139–40.

204 *after graduating from Georgetown:* Aspects of Danis's biography and business come from her criminal case, *USA v. Danis*, including the transcript of her guilty plea on May 26, 2015, as well as from affidavits and other documents in a civil suit filed by CONMEBOL against Danis and International Soccer Marketing in New York Supreme Court on October 21, 2016.

204 *Norris put a pen register on Danis:* The prosecutor filed the application under seal on July 19, 2013, requesting surveillance of email accounts belonging to Danis, Ricardo Teixeira, Jorge Martínez, and Horace Burrell. A further application, to monitor Danis's phone, was entered on July 25. Both applications, good for sixty days, were extended twice, through to the beginning of 2014.

205 *a number of other corrupt schemes:* A litany of criminal acts perpetrated by Daryan Warner is included in his cooperation agreement, which was read into the transcript of his guilty plea, taken on October 18, 2013.

207 *"a portion of the monies":* *USA v. Daryan Warner*, order of forfeiture, filed October 23, 2013, p. 1.

209 *Blazer collapsed:* Mary Papenfuss and Teri Thompson, p. 152.

209 *He wouldn't face punishment:* A list of corrupt acts that Blazer admitted to but for which he was not charged is contained in the cooperation agreement he signed on November 25, 2013, pp. 8–9.

210 *forfeit nearly $2 million to the government:* The exact amount is $1,958,092.72, "which represents a portion of the monies that the defendant received from bribes, kickbacks and unauthorized World Cup ticket sales." *USA v. Blazer*, order of forfeiture, November 25, 2013. Terms of his forfeiture called for the full $1.9 million to be paid by the time of his guilty plea; a second, unspecified amount was to be paid at the time of his sentencing, but Blazer died in July 2017, before he could be sentenced.

210 *"The principal purpose of the enterprise":* *USA v. Blazer*, criminal information, p. 2.

CHAPTER 23: TRUST AND BETRAYAL

211 *a shiny new BMW X5:* Some details on Sanz's perks at CONCACAF
from Tariq Panja and David Voreacos, "Can One of the Dirtiest Corners of Global Soccer Clean Up Its Own Act?," *Bloomberg*, February 23,
2016.

211 *Sanz sat down with his close friend: USA v. Hawit, et al.*, superseding
indictment, p. 139.

213 *Brazil passed its first law:* Brazilian law 12,850 was passed on August 2,
2013. It was designed to combat organized crime by providing benefits
to those who collaborate with criminal investigations. The law has been
highly controversial, and critics say it gives collaborators incentives to
falsely accuse others in order to receive lighter sentences.

216 *Late in the morning of March 16:* Some aspects of the meeting between
Hawilla and Davidson are drawn from transcripts of a clandestine audio
recording entered into evidence in the 2017 trial of Juan Ángel Napout,
José Maria Marin, and Manuel Burga.

218 *"Is it illegal?": USA v. Hawit, et al.*, superseding indictment, pp. 147–48.

219 *On February 25, 2014, for example:* Ibid., p. 105.

CHAPTER 24: "ALL OF US GO TO PRISON"

221 *On the morning of May 1: USA v. Hawit, et al.*, superseding indictment,
pp. 58 and 146. Many details of the events surrounding the press conference are drawn from testimony as well as transcripts entered into evidence in the 2017 trial of Napout, Marin, and Burga.

221 *"We are praying for his recovery":* The press conference was recorded
and a full video of the event is available online.

224 *"All of us go to prison":* This and other quotes came from transcripts of
Hawilla's clandestine recordings.

226 *arrested a man named Canover Watson:* Brent Fuller, "Canover Watson
Released on Bail," *Cayman Compass*, August 29, 2014.

228 *a $240,000 loan to J&D International:* Brent Fuller, "CarePay Trial: Bank
Chief Confirms 'Loan' to Webb," *Cayman Compass*, January 8, 2016. The
Cayman Compass provided extensive and top-quality coverage of the
investigation and subsequent trial of Canover Watson, which ended on
February 4 with his conviction for fraud, conflict of interest, breach of
public trust, and conspiracy to defraud. He was sentenced to seven years
in prison, and in July 2017 was named a target of a separate investigation into fraud at the Cayman Islands Football Association. Jeffrey Webb
was charged by Cayman Islands authorities in July 2015 for conspiracy
to commit fraud, breach of trust, and "conspiracy to convert criminal
property."

CHAPTER 25: PAYBACK

230 *Mary Lynn Blanks, the former soap opera actress:* Blanks was, indeed, later proven to be the source of the *Daily News* article, and became the principal source for the book on Chuck Blazer written by Mary Papenfuss and Teri Thomson, *American Huckster.* In fact, they dedicated the book to her.

232 *Swiss banks had been obliged:* Of the 20,000 clients of UBS who were U.S. taxpayers, some 17,000 concealed their identities and the existence of those accounts. Credit Suisse, for its part, initially turned over the names of just 238 account holders who were U.S. taxpayers, out of a total of more than 22,000 such accounts. See James Vicini, "UBS to Identify Clients, Pay $780 Million in Tax Case," Reuters, February 18, 2009; and Eric Tucker and Marcy Gordon, "Credit Suisse Pleads Guilty, Pays $2.6 Billion in U.S. Tax Evasion Case," Associated Press, May 19, 2014.

233 *"respect the personal rights of the people":* Owen Gibson, "FIFA Set to Publish Summary of Inquiry," *The Guardian,* October 18, 2014.

234 *"erroneous representations of the facts":* Graham Dunbar, "FIFA Under Fire After Report on Qatar, Russia," Associated Press, November 13, 2014.

234 *barred from setting foot in the country:* In response to the Magnitsky Act sanctions passed in late 2012, Russia on April 13, 2013, banned eighteen Americans from entering the country, including Garcia, who as the U.S. attorney for the Southern District of New York had been involved in the prosecution of a Russian arms dealer, Viktor Bout.

235 *Hawilla had, in September 2013, unloaded his newspapers:* Chico Siqueira, "Grupo Traffic vende Diário de S. Paulo," *O Estado de S. Paulo,* September 6, 2013.

235 *convinced Chinese investors:* Marcio Porto, "Chinese compram CT e São Paulo é quem deve administrá-lo," *Lance!,* April 17, 2014.

236 *When RICO was passed into law:* The history of criminal forfeiture, including the concept of "corruption of blood," which was used by the First Congress of the United States to ban the practice in 1790, is a fascinating topic, excellently and clearly explored in Karla L. Spaulding, *Hit Them Where It Hurts. Journal of Criminal Law and Criminology,* Vol. 80, Spring 1989, pp. 197–292.

237 *The first installment, of $25 million:* Hawilla's original forfeiture agreement called for him to pay $25 million at the time of pleading guilty, $75 million more within a year of that date, and the remaining $51 million by the time of his sentencing, or December 2018, whichever came first. Although Hawilla has paid an additional $20 million, he has been unable to sell Traffic, blaming the criminal case and Brazil's bad economy. He

has therefore received extensions allowing him to pay the full balance of $106 million by December 2018 or the time of his sentencing.

CHAPTER 26: THINGS FALL APART

239 *"FIFA is family"*: Andrew Jennings, *Foul!*, p. 224.

239 *"father of our football family"*: Beverly Melbourne, "When FIFA Came to Cayman Islands," Cayman Net News, June 16, 2009.

239 *that person "could be Jeffrey Webb"*: Robert Christopher Woolard, "CONCACAF Chief Rules Out Bid for FIFA Job," Agence France Presse, October 22, 2013.

240 *"so let's see where he's going"*: Sean Williams, "Blatter Endorses Webb for Second Term as CONCACAF Boss," *Jamaica Observer*, April 18, 2015.

240 *they projected a $6.5 million loss for the year*: Letter from Samir Gandhi of Sidley Austin to Fabrice Baly, president of the St. Martin Football Association, dated January 5, 2016.

240 *quietly taking a $2 million salary*: Tariq Panja and David Voreacos, "Can One of the Dirtiest Corners of Global Soccer Clean Up Its Own Act?"

244 *an unnamed "third party" was helping fund Watson's defense*: Brent Fuller, "Others Implicated in CarePay Probe," *Cayman Compass*, April 2, 2015.

244 *Jeffrey Webb had amassed an impressive array*: Details of Webb's assets come, in part, from *USA v. Webb, et al.*, Order Setting Conditions of Release and Bond, filed July 18, 2015; and also from *USA v. Webb*, Amended Preliminary Order of Forfeiture, filed December 1, 2016.

CHAPTER 27: TAKEDOWN

250 *At precisely six in the morning*: This account of the events of the morning of May 27, 2015, is drawn from a series of interviews as well as social media and press accounts from the day. In particular, the rapidly evolving *New York Times* story, first published a few minutes before the raid, and which underwent nearly three dozen revisions and seven different headlines over the next twenty-four hours, is a critically important document. Tweets by seven different reporters involved in writing and reporting the story, as well as by other media outlets involved in coverage, including CNN's breaking news account, aided with contextualizing events in real time.

251 *"FIFA Officials Face Corruption Charges in U.S."*: The first version of the *New York Times* story carried the bylines of Matt Apuzzo, Michael S. Schmidt, William K. Rashbaum, and Sam Borden, and dwelled heavily on allegations of corruption in the bidding for the 2018 and 2022 World Cup. That aspect of the story was removed in subsequent drafts.

252 *Tuesday, May 26, had been busy:* Many details of Webb's activities in Zurich prior to his arrest are drawn from Vernon Silver, Corinne Gretler, and Hugo Miller, "FIFA Busts at Baur au Lac: Inside the Five-Star Takedown," Bloomberg, May 27, 2015.

252 *Neusa Marin . . . desperately dialed:* There are several accounts of the raid and immediate aftermath from the Brazilian perspective. Some details are drawn from Silvio Barsetti, "Amigo relata abandono de Del Nero a Marin na hora de prisão," *Terra,* June 17, 2015; others from Jamil Chade, *Política, Propina e Futebol.*

253 *breakfasting in the hotel's restaurant that morning was Alejandro Burzaco:* Details of Burzaco's experiences on May 27 are drawn from his testimony in the 2017 trial of Napout, Marin, and Burga.

254 *"your name is on the list":* Ignacio Naya, " 'Tu nombre está en la lista de acusados': así fueron los arrestos en Zurich," *La Nación,* May 28, 2015.

256 *a television camera crew was already waiting for them:* reporters for the Associated Press were on hand for the early morning raid. A video of some of their footage, "FBI Raid CONCACAF Office in FIFA Probe," was posted to YouTube on May 27, 2015.

256 *"This really is the World Cup of fraud":* Weber's carefully rehearsed remarks, as well as everything else said at the press conference, were recorded in a video of the nearly forty-three-minute-long event, which is available online.

257 *"he is not involved":* A video of Walter De Gregorio's half-hour-long press conference, in which he claimed FIFA actually played a hand in calling for the Swiss investigation, is available online. "FIFA is the damaged party," he said. De Gregorio was fired on June 11, allegedly for making a joke on Swiss television: "Q: FIFA's president, general secretary, and communications director are in a car. Who is driving? A: The police."

258 *Warner told a reporter:* Tweet by Steven Goff, soccer reporter at *The Washington Post,* May 27, 2015.

CHAPTER 28: "A GREAT DAY FOR FOOTBALL"

259 *Zorana Danis walked into a federal courtroom: USA v. Danis,* transcript of guilty plea, May 26, 2015.

261 *For the second time in three years:* Unlike its first internal investigation of CONCACAF, Sidley Austin has never released the results of this second audit. Although CONCACAF, in December 2012, filed four years' worth of tax returns, which are available to the public, it has not made tax information about subsequent years available, and sources indicate it is unlikely to ever publish information about the confederation's finances under Jeffrey Webb and Enrique Sanz.

261 *"What is this notion of time?"*: Owen Gibson, "Sepp Blatter Re-elected as Fifa President for Fifth Term," *The Guardian*, May 29, 2015.

262 *"not in Zurich when we have a congress"* Martyn Ziegler, "Sepp Blatter Blames English Media and US Justice Authorities for Trying to Oust Him After Being Re-Elected as FIFA President," Press Association Sport, May 30, 2015.

262 *"no one gives them the right"*: Tim Reynolds, "Ex-FIFA VP Warner Hits Out at US Based on Satirical Story," Associated Press, May 31, 2015.

263 *Only two people showed up:* Daina Beth Solomon, "FIFA Film 'United Passions' Makes Muted Debut in Los Angeles," Reuters, June 5, 2015.

264 *Alejandro Burzaco, accompanied by a lawyer:* Burzaco described his travel to Italy and ultimate surrender in his trial testimony.

265 *forfeit the tidy sum of $21,694,408.49: USA v. Burzaco*, sealed preliminary order of forfeiture, filed November 16, 2015.

266 *Hawit met privately with Fabio Tordin:* Details of the secret recording of Hawit drawn from *USA v. Hawit, et al.*, superseding indictment, pp. 129–30.

CHAPTER 29: A ZEALOUS ADVOCATE

267 *David Torres-Siegrist was driving home:* Significant portions, but by no means all, of the material described in this chapter come from several interviews with Torres-Siegrist. Additional emails, legal documents, press coverage, and other records were vital in filling in and substantiating the account. Of particular use was the excellent Uruguayan work of investigative journalism, *Figueredo: a la sombra del poder*, by Diego Muñoz and Emiliano Zecca, which is cited in this book's bibliography.

269 *a right-winger for Huracán Buceo:* Ibid., pp. 33–51.

270 *formal petitions were submitted by the U.S. on July 1:* AUSA Sam Nitze signed an Affidavit in Support of Request for Extradition on June 24, 2015; it was approved and given the seal of the United States of America on June 29, and formally submitted by the U.S. embassy to Switzerland on July 1.

271 *Webb even had to hand over his wife's wedding ring:* A "diamond wedding ring owned by Kendra Gamble-Webb" is listed among other assets used to secure Webb's release in *USA v. Webb*, order setting conditions of release and bond, signed July 18, 2015.

272 *involved a Russian nuclear scientist:* The physicist, Yevgeny Adamov, had been head of the Russian atomic energy ministry, and was arrested in May 2, 2005, in Switzerland at the request of the United States, which said he had stolen some $9 million in funds intended to improve nuclear

security in Russia and charged him with money laundering, tax evasion, and fraud, among other charges. Russia also requested Adamov's extradition, and its petition prevailed in December 2005.

275 *"bear no relationship to his economic capacity"*: From Uruguay's twenty-four-page petition for Figueredo's extradition, finalized October 21, 2015.

CHAPTER 30: PLUS ÇA CHANGE . . .

277 *Swiss police once again walked into the lobby:* As with the May 27 raids the best and most complete account of events is found in *The New York Times* article on the event, as the reporters were installed in the hotel prior to the arrests. In addition, because only two defendants were taken from the Baur au Lac, the operation was completed more quickly, so few if any other journalists arrived in time to witness the raid.

279 *"CONCACAF has been the victim of fraud"*: Steven Goff, "Blatter Remains Defiant as U.S. Withdraws Its Support," *Washington Post*, May 29, 2015.

279 *fired the cancer-stricken general secretary:* Letter from Samir Gandhi of Sidley Austin to Fabrice Baly.

279 *"The corruption of the enterprise became endemic"*: *USA v. Hawit, et al.*, superseding indictment, p. 40.

280 *a reporter from* The New York Times: Sam Borden, then a European sports correspondent for the paper, memorialized the day's events in a Storify post, noting that he arrived at the Baur au Lac at 5:45 a.m.

280 *Sepp Blatter woke up early:* Details on what Blatter did on February 26 come from a lengthy interview conducted with the former FIFA president at his residence on that very day.

281 *the Swiss attorney general raided FIFA's headquarters:* Nick Gutteridge, "FIFA Boss Sepp Blatter Hauled Out of Meeting and Quizzed by Swiss Cops over Fraud Claims," *Express Online*, September 25, 2015.

281 *"between the angels who sing and the devil"*: Teddy Cutler, "Sepp Blatter 'Nearly Died' but Faces Extended Ban," *The Sunday Times*, November 24, 2015.

283 *"I was not thinking to be a candidate"*: A video of the entire six-hour-long affair, including Infantino's speech, is available online.

288 *He had already traced the man's accounts:* The target, Richard Lai, president of the Guam Football Association, agreed to cooperate with the investigation. He ultimately pleaded guilty to two counts of wire fraud conspiracy and one count of failing to report foreign bank accounts on April 27, 2017, and agreed to forfeit $870,000.

EPILOGUE

289 *On the evening of November 14:* Delhón's apparent suicide was covered extensively in the Argentine press, which, among other things, obtained a photograph of the note found in his briefcase. It read *"Los Amo No puedo creer."*

290 *had paid $15 million in bribes:* Following Burzaco's testimony, both Televisa and TV Globo released statements denying involvement in corrupt activities.

292 *he won an award recognizing him:* On June 20, Norris was named the winner of the J. Michael Bradford award by the National Association of Former U.S. Attorneys, beating out eighteen other nominees. The association called the FIFA case "one of the most significant prosecutions ever brought by the Department of Justice" and praised Norris for devising the "investigative and prosecutorial strategies for this groundbreaking cross-border case."

293 *A rangy former newspaper reporter:* Nitze worked as a reporter for the *Asbury Park Press* and the *Miami Herald*, where he worked on an investigative series about a 1959 Florida law designed to protect farmers that instead was exploited by property developers.

293 *an Argentine banker:* Jorge Arzuaga pleaded guilty to money laundering on June 15, 2017, and agreed to forfeit $1,046,000, "which represents bonuses paid to the defendant by executives of Torneos y Competencias S.A. and its subsidiaries and affiliates to compensate him for his participation in the money laundering conspiracy," according to the forfeiture agreement in the matter. The case is *USA v. Arzuaga.*

294 *In the petition FIFA filed:* The soccer organization filed a "Victim Statement and Request for Restitution" to the Eastern District of New York on March 15, 2016. It sought an unspecified sum, but noted that the money forfeited to the U.S. in the case "should be used to compensate the victims . . . particularly FIFA and its member associations and confederations."

297 *"happiest day of my life":* Susan Mohammed, "Jack Feels Like Partying," *Trinidad Express*, October 11, 2017.

301 *José Maria Marin and Juan Ángel Napout were convicted:* Marin was convicted on one count of RICO conspiracy, three counts of wire fraud conspiracy, and two counts of money laundering conspiracy, while being acquitted on one additional count of money laundering conspiracy. Napout was convicted on one count of RICO conspiracy and two counts of wire fraud conspiracy. He was acquitted on two counts of money laundering conspiracy.

BIBLIOGRAPHY

Aguilar, Luís. *Jogada Ilegal: os Negócios do Futebol, os Grandes Casos de Corrupção, uma Viagem aos Bastidores da FIFA*. Rio de Janeiro: Gryphus Editora, 2013.

Araújo Vélez, Fernando. *No era Futbol, era Fraude*. Bogota: Planeta Colombia, 2016.

Blake, Heidi and Calvert, Jonathan. *The Ugly Game: The Qatari Plot to Buy the World Cup*. London: Simon and Schuster, 2015.

Bondy, Filip. *Chasing the Game: America and the Quest for the World Cup*. Philadelphia: Da Capo Press, 2010.

Borenstein, Ariel. *Don Julio: Biografía no autorizada de Julio Humberto Grondona*. Buenos Aires: Planeta Argentina, 2014.

Casar Gonzalez, Alejandro. *Pasó de Todo: Cómo la AFA, la FIFA y los Gobiernos se Adueñaron de la Pelota*. Buenos Aires: Planeta Argentina, 2015.

Castillo, Hernán. *Todo Pasa: Fútbol, Negocios y Política de Videla a los Kirchner*. Buenos Aires: Aguilar, Altea, Taurus, Alfaguara, 2012.

Chade, Jamil. *Política, Propina e Futebol: Como o "Padrão FIFA" Ameaça o Esporte Mais Popular do Planeta*. Rio de Janeiro: Editorial Objectiva, 2015.

Conn, David. *The Fall of the House of FIFA*. New York: Nation Books, 2017.

Foer, Franklyn. *How Soccer Explains the World: An Unlikely Theory of Globalization*. New York: Harper Perennial, 2010.

Forrest, Brett. *The Big Fix: The Hunt for the Match-Fixers Bringing Down Soccer*. New York: William Morrow, 2015.

Goldblatt, David. *The Ball is Round: A Global History of Football*. London: Penguin Books, 2007.

——. *Futebol Nation: The Story of Brazil through Soccer*. New York: Nation Books, 2014.

Harding, Luke. *Collusion: Secret Meetings, Dirty Money, and How Russia Helped Donald Trump Win*. New York: Vintage Books, 2017.

Hartley, Ray. *The Big Fix: How South Africa Stole the 2010 World Cup*. Jeppestown, South Africa: Jonathan Ball Publishers, 2016.

Hill, Declan. *The Fix: Soccer and Organized Crime*. Toronto: McClelland & Stewart, 2008.

Huerta, Gustavo. *Jadue: Historia de una Farsa.* Santiago: Planeta Chile, 2016.

Jennings, Andrew. *The Dirty Game: Uncovering the Scandal at FIFA.* London: Arrow Books, 2016.

———. *Foul! The Secret World of FIFA.* London: HarperSport, 2006.

Kistner, Thomas. *Fifa Mafia.* Barcelona: Editorial Corner, 2015.

Kuper, Simon and Szymanski, Stefan. *Soccernomics: Why England Loses, Why Spain, Germany, and Brazil Win, and Why the US, Japan, Australia— and even Iraq—are Destined to Become the Kings of the World's Most Popular Sport.* Philadelphia: Nation Books, 2014.

Leoz, Nicolás. *Pido la Palabra: I Request the Floor.* Buenos Aires: Ediciones Salvucci y Asociados, 2002.

Llonto, Pablo. *La Vergüenza de Todos: el Dedo en la Llaga del Mundial 78.* Buenos Aires: Ediciones Madres de Plaza de Mayo, 2005.

Mattos, Rodrigo. *Ladrões de Bola: 25 Anos de Corrupção no Futebol.* São Paulo: Panda Books, 2016.

Muñoz, Diego and Zecca, Emiliano. *Figueredo: A la sombra del poder.* Montevideo: Penguin RandomHouse Grupo Editorial, 2016.

Papenfuss, Mary and Thompson, Teri. *American Huckster: How Chuck Blazer Got Rich From—And Sold Out—The Most Powerful Cabal in World Sports.* New York: Harper, 2016.

Pieth, Mark (ed.). *Reforming FIFA.* Zurich: Dike Verlag AG, 2014.

Ribeiro, Amaury Jr.; Cipoloni, Leandro; Azenha, Luiz Carlos; and Chastinet, Tony. *El Lado Sucio del Fútbol: La Trama de Sobornos, Negocios Turbios y Traiciones que Sacudió al Deporte más Popular del Mundo.* Mexico: Editorial Planeta, 2014.

Rosell, Sandro. *Bienvenido al Mundo Real.* Barcelona: Ediciones Destino, 2006.

Singh, Valentino. *Upwards Through the Night: The Biography of Austin Jack Warner.* San Juan, Trinidad: Lexicon Trinidad Ltd., 1998.

Smit, Barbara. *Sneaker Wars: The Enemy Brothers Who Founded Adidas and Puma and the Family Feud That Forever Changed the Business of Sports.* New York: Harper Perennial, 2008.

Toye, Clive. *A Kick in the Grass.* Haworth, NJ: St. Johann Press, 2006.

Veiga, Gustavo. *Deporte, Desaparecidos y Dictadura.* Buenos Aires: Ediciones al Arco, 2010.

Warner, Jack, with Singh, Valengino. *Jack Austin Warner: Zero to Hero.* Newtown, Trinidad and Tobago: Medianet Limited, 2006.

Yallop, David. *How They Stole the Game.* London: Constable, 2011.

INDEX